Christian Pilgrimage in Modern Western Europe

Studies in Religion

Charles H. Long, *Editor*
Syracuse University

Editorial Board

Giles B. Gunn
University of California at Santa Barbara

Van A. Harvey
Stanford University

Wendy Doniger O'Flaherty
The University of Chicago

Ninian Smart
University of California at Santa Barbara
and the University of Lancaster

Christian Pilgrimage in Modern Western Europe

Mary Lee Nolan & Sidney Nolan

The University of North Carolina Press
Chapel Hill & London

© 1989 The University of North Carolina Press

All rights reserved

Manufactured in the United States of America

The paper in this book meets the guidelines for permanence and durability of the Committee on Production Guidelines for Book Longevity of the Council on Library Resources.

93 92 91 90 89   5 4 3 2 1

Library of Congress Cataloging-in-Publication Data
Nolan, Mary Lee.
   Christian pilgrimage in modern Western Europe
     Mary Lee Nolan, Sidney Nolan.
     p. cm.—(Studies in religion)
   Bibliography: p.
   Includes index.
   ISBN 0-8078-1814-3 (alk. paper)
    1. Christian pilgrims and pilgrimages—Europe.
    2. Christian shrines—Europe. 3. Europe—
Religious life and customs. I. Nolan, Sidney. II.
Title. III. Series: Studies in religion (Chapel Hill,
N.C.)
BX2320.5.E85N65   1989   88-14364
263'.042'4—dc 19   CIP

To David and Mary

Contents

ACKNOWLEDGMENTS   xvii

one
INTRODUCTION   1

two
THE SHRINES OF WESTERN EUROPE   11
    Shrines and Religious Tourism   14
    Variations in Shrine Importance   19
    Indicators of Shrine Importance   22
    Shrine Distribution   28

three
PILGRIMAGE IN THE EUROPEAN TRADITION   36
    Types of Pilgrimages:
        Individual and Communal   36
    Pilgrimage and Religious Tourism   42
    The Sacred-Secular Mix   46
    The Annual Cycle   53
    The Continued Vitality of Minor Shrines   64
    Pilgrims' Offerings   67

four
PERIODS OF PILGRIMAGE SHRINE FORMATION   80
    Dating the Shrines   82
    The Shrine-Formative Cycle   84
    Shrine-Formative Periods   86

Regional Variations in
  Time Period Importance   105
  The Periods in Perspective   111

five

HOLY PERSONS: THE SUBJECTS OF DEVOTION   115
  Relative Importance of
    Mary, Christ, and the Saints   116
  National and Regional Variations
    in Primary Subjects   119
  The Saints   128
  Subjects of Devotion and Periods
    of Shrine Origin   152
  Shrine Rank and Devotional Focus   156
  Regional and Temporal Variations in
    Subject Focus   157

six

SACRED OBJECTS: FOCAL POINTS FOR VENERATION   160
  Origins of Object Veneration   163
  Cult Objects in Modern Times   171
  Miraculous Images   179
  Pilgrimage Iconography of
    Christ, Mary, and the Saints   187
  Image Modification and Replacement   209

seven

WONDROUS EVENTS, MIRACLES, AND LEGENDS:
  ORIGIN STORIES EXAMINED   216
  Types of Origin Stories   221
    Significant Site Shrines   221
    Votive Shrines   226
    Devotional Shrines   237
    Spontaneous Miracle Shrines   241
    Acquired Object Shrines   249
    Found Object Shrines   257
    Apparitional Shrines   266

Types of Vision-Related Stories 269
The Continuation of
 Shrine Establishment 289

eight

LOCATION AND ENVIRONMENT:
 SHRINES AS HOLY PLACES 291
 Location Relative to Communities 294
 Central versus Remote Shrines 299
 Contemporary Shrines at Pre-Christian
  Holy Sites 301
 Environmental Site Features 303
 Holy Places in a Modern Age 336

NOTES 339

BIBLIOGRAPHY 381

INDEX 403

Tables

1-1.	Number of Shrines Inventoried by Country or Region	5
1-2.	Regional Traditions	7
2-1.	Estimated Number of Shrine Visitations	26
2-2.	Levels of Shrine Importance	28
2-3.	Demographics of Inventoried Shrines	34
3-1.	Types of Contemporary Pilgrimage	40
3-2.	Religiosity of Special Events in Portugal	50
4-1.	Shrine-Formative Periods	87
4-2.	Dated Shrines in Each Time Period by Region	87
4-3.	Percentage of Dated Shrines in Each Region by Time Period	106
4-4.	Percentage of Shrine Formations by Century	106
5-1.	Subjects of Devotion	117
5-2.	Simultaneous Devotion to Holy Persons as Primary and Secondary Subjects	119
5-3.	Subjects of Devotion by Country	120
5-4.	Important Pilgrimage Saints	134
5-5.	Devotional Subjects and Shrine-Formative Periods	155
5-6.	Devotional Subjects and Rank of Shrines	158
6-1.	Object Orientations by Country	163
6-2.	Objects of Devotion	172
6-3.	Representations of Subjects at Object-Oriented Shrines	172
6-4.	Types of Relics	173
6-5.	Types of Images	184
6-6.	Estimated Emphasis on Adornment of Marian Images	214
7-1.	Types of Origin Stories	218
7-2.	Time Period Distribution of Origin Story Types	220
7-3.	Regional Distribution of Origin Story Types	220
7-4.	Origin Story Associations with Subjects of Devotion	221
7-5.	Origin Story Associations with Types of Devotional Objects	222
7-6.	Characteristics of Significant Site Shrines	224
7-7.	Characteristics of Ex-voto Shrines	228

7-8. Characteristics of Devotional Shrines	240
7-9. Characteristics of Spontaneous Miracle Shrines	242
7-10. Characteristics of Shrines with Acquired Objects	250
7-11. Characteristics of Shrines with Found Objects	260
7-12. Characteristics of Shrines with Apparition Stories	268
7-13. Characteristics of the Turners' Prototypical Medieval and Modern Visions	274
7-14. Temporal Distribution of the Sex of Seers	288
7-15. Temporal Distribution of the Social Status of Seers	288
8-1. Characteristics of Shrines with Pre-Christian Associations as Holy Places	304
8-2. Characteristics of Shrines with Sacred Environmental Site Features	307
8-3. Regional Distribution of Site Features	311
8-4. Formative Periods of Environmentally Based Shrines	313
8-5. Devotional Subject Focus of Environmentally Based Shrines	316
8-6. Origin Stories of Environmentally Based Shrines	318
8-7. Variations among Tree and Grove Cultus and Types of Trees	326

Illustrations

FIGURES

1-1.	San Sebastián de Garabandal, Spain	2
2-1.	Lourdes, France	12
2-2.	Relationships between shrines, religious tourist attractions, and festival sites	16
2-3.	Corpus Christi procession, Burgos, Spain	18
2-4.	Moorish tapestry displayed in procession, Las Huelgas, Spain	19
2-5.	Fiesta, Las Huelgas, Spain	21
2-6.	Saint Olan's Holy Well, County Cork, Ireland	23
3-1.	"Blood Ride," Weingarten, West Germany	38
3-2.	Pilgrim and family, Fátima, Portugal	42
3-3.	Carrying a cross at Altötting, West Germany	43
3-4.	Boston delegation arriving at Knock, Ireland	44
3-5.	Image of Saint Benedict, Sexias, Portugal	47
3-6.	Festive pilgrimage, São Torcato, Portugal	48
3-7.	Village pilgrims, Bavaria, West Germany	52
3-8.	Patterns of pilgrimage seasonality in various years depending on the date of Easter	57
3-9.	Penitential procession, Assisi, Italy	59
3-10.	Pilgrimage seasonality related to different subjects of devotion	63
3-11.	Candles at Lourdes, France	69
3-12.	Rag offerings, Saint Bridget's Well, Fauchart, Ireland	70
3-13.	Votive offerings, Santa Casilda, Spain	72
3-14.	Wax body parts, Nuestra Señora de Cortes, Spain	73
3-15.	Silver heart offering, Montenero, Italy	74
3-16.	Marble plaque offerings, Grammont, Belgium	76
3-17.	Painted votive offering, Pietralba, Italy	77
3-18.	Painted votive offering, Laghet, France	79

4-1.	Modern basilica and ancient bullaun stone, Knock, Ireland	81
4-2.	Cyclical patterns of pilgrimage formation	85
4-3.	Marble footprints, Quo Vadis Church, Appian Way near Rome, Italy	91
4-4.	Dancing procession, Echternach, Luxembourg	94
4-5.	Stained glass window, Canterbury, England	96
4-6.	Santa María del Cubillo near Aldeavieja, Spain	98
4-7.	Sankt Anton's, Partenkirchen, West Germany	101
4-8.	Youth Day at "The Friars," Aylesford, England	104
5-1.	Our Lady's Island, County Wexford, Ireland	118
5-2.	Image of the Trinity, eastern Austria	127
5-3.	Saint Hervé's Holy Well, Brittany, France	129
5-4.	Saint Hemma and Saint Wilhelm, Gurk, Austria	130
5-5.	A child with one of the "Magi," Barcelona, Spain	131
5-6.	Statues of Mary, the Christ Child, and Saint Anne, Annaberg, Austria	136
5-7.	Saint James's Basilica, Santiago de Compostela, Spain	138
5-8.	Sankt Georgenberg, Austria	143
5-9.	Image of Saint Benedict, Ermelo, northern Portugal	146
5-10.	Saint Leonhard chapel, Waitschach, Austria	148
5-11.	Honoring San Rocco, Gioviano, Italy	153
6-1.	São Clemente, Bom Jesus do Monte, Braga, Portugal	165
6-2.	Reliquaries, Rochechouart, France	167
6-3.	Procession with image of San Doménico Abate, Cocullo, Italy	174
6-4.	Priest's grave, Saint Gobnet's, County Cork, Ireland	176
6-5.	Statue of Christ, Erding, West Germany	178
6-6.	Painting of the Madonna and Child, Cori, Italy	185
6-7.	Crucifix, Pieve de Cadore, Italy	189
6-8.	Madonna and Child, Notre-Dame-de-la-Gorge, France	192
6-9.	Madonna and Child, Tongre-Notre-Dame, Belgium	193
6-10.	Notre-Dame de Vie, Villefranche de Conflent, France	194
6-11.	Hohenpeißenberg Madonna, West Germany	195
6-12.	Pilgrimage image of the Madonna, Agreda, Spain	196
6-13.	Touching the Virgin's hem, Agreda, Spain	197
6-14.	Pietà, Theirenbach, France	200
6-15.	Image of Mary taken to San Sebastián de Garabandal, Spain	203
7-1.	Saint Winefride's Well, Holywell, Wales	223
7-2.	Hilltop votive shrine, Archidona, Spain	230

7-3. Devotional shrine, Kaulbach, West Germany — 238
7-4. Bleeding image, Bergatreute, West Germany — 245
7-5. Display at 1978 exhibition of the Holy Shroud, Turin, Italy — 252
7-6. Stained glass window, Josselin, France — 265
7-7. Image at apparitional shrine, Savona, Italy — 270
8-1. La Sainte-Baume, France — 295
8-2. Edge-of-settlement pilgrimage church, Worms, West Germany — 297
8-3. Romería chapel near Paredes de Viadores, Portugal — 298
8-4. Photographing the sun, San Damiano, Italy — 309
8-5. Hilltop Maria Locherboden church, Austria — 319
8-6. Croagh Patrick, Ireland — 321
8-7. Holy well at Our Lady's Island, Ireland — 322
8-8. Collecting water, Collevalenza, Italy — 324
8-9. Curative water in bowl-shaped stone, Clonmacnois, Ireland — 325
8-10. Image of Saint Marguerite in a tree, Sion, France — 327
8-11. Stone resembling the Virgin, Peña de Francia, Spain — 332
8-12. Grotto at Lourdes, France — 334

MAPS

2-1. Selected Shrine Localities — 29
2-2. Distribution of Major Shrines — 31
2-3. Distribution of All Inventoried Shrines — 32
4-1. Distribution of Shrines Dating from the Early Christian Period — 88
4-2. Distribution of Shrines Dating from the Early Medieval Period — 88
4-3. Distribution of Shrines Dating from the High Medieval Period — 89
4-4. Distribution of Shrines Dating from the Renaissance Period — 89
4-5. Distribution of Shrines Dating from the Post-Reformation Period — 89
4-6. Distribution of Shrines Dating from the Modern Period — 89
5-1. Regional Variations in Percentages of Shrines Dedicated to the Virgin Mary — 121
5-2. Regional Variations in Percentages of Shrines Dedicated to Saints — 123

5-3.	Regional Variations in Percentages of Shrines Dedicated to Christ	125
6-1.	Distribution of Venerated Relics of the True Cross, Holy Blood from the Holy Land, and Remnants of Eucharistic Miracles	180
6-2.	Distribution of Dark Images	204
7-1.	Shrines with Formative Stories Describing Visions	271

Acknowledgments

Our study of Western European pilgrimage began more than 12 years ago, and, regrettably, it is impossible to mention by name all of the people who have helped us complete this work. We are particularly indebted to the many European bishops who personally answered our letters asking for information about shrines in their dioceses, or who turned our inquiries over to archivists, secretaries, or knowledgeable laymen. These people, who often worked diligently to provide us with substantial amounts of information, also deserve thanks as do the nearly 1,000 shrine administrators who answered our letters of inquiry, spoke with us when we visited their pilgrimage centers, or, in many cases, did both.

Members of the Pontifical Commission on the Pastoral Care of Migrants and Tourists were most helpful during our stay in Rome in the spring of 1981. In addition, we are especially grateful to Monsignor Charles Burns and the staff of the Vatican Library and Archives for their advice and assistance.

For access to often difficult-to-obtain secondary source materials, we are indebted to the interlibrary loan staff of the Kerr Library at Oregon State University (OSU), especially E. Doris Tilles. The hospitality and assistance extended by the staff of the Biblioteca Nacional de España during our work in Madrid is also appreciated.

We thank Gale Smith and Mary Nolan-Smith for their interest and assistance in keeping us up to date on newly published pilgrimage-related studies in West Germany during the past six years. David and Mariana Nolan have helped us maintain a worldwide perspective by keeping us advised on recent shrine-formative events in Latin America and Africa.

The basic information and details that made this study possible had to be gleaned from correspondence and other sources written or published in seven national languages and several dialects and regional languages. We could not have accomplished this task without the assistance of multilingual readers, who helped us accumulate the master data base in English by scouring large amounts of material in their native languages and extracting the information required. Many volunteered important information on pilgrimage in their native countries. More than two dozen of these readers, several of whom were foreign students at Oregon State University, assisted us over a 12-year period.

Two readers, who were not students, were of special assistance. Margarite Rice, who worked with us in her native West Germany during our 1980–81 sabbatical year, functioned more as a research associate than a reader. In addition to recording descriptive information on Germanic regional shrines from letters, booklets, and compendia, she synthesized the contents of several theological and folkloric studies in German. She also translated all German quotations in this book. Closer to home, we thank Eva Milleman of the OSU staff for her willingness to read an important Italian compendium that we obtained late in the data collection phase of our study. Her work added vital information to the data base for Italy.

Our particular thanks are also extended to Eric Bryant who, as a graduate assistant in the OSU Department of Geography, found himself immersed in the equally mystical worlds of religious pilgrimage and computer analysis. Moreover, we could not have emerged from the labyrinth of data manipulation and computer-assisted mapping without the invaluable guidance and programming assistance of Dave Fuhrer of the OSU Computer Center.

What special acquired abilities we possessed that enabled us to complete this study are largely due to training received from geographers George Carter, Clarissa Kimber, and the late Earl Cook, along with recreational travel and tourism insights provided by Clare Gunn and the critical anthropological approach instilled by Richard N. Adams.

We are grateful for the encouragement and criticism offered by Victor Turner and David Sopher in the early stages of our study. We regret that neither of these scholars lived to give us the benefit of his reactions to the results.

For assistance and constructive criticism in the preparation of the manuscript, we especially thank J. Granville Jensen, Terry Jordan, and William Christian, Jr.

The extensive travel required to complete our study would not have been possible without the income from our parallel activity of producing educational audiovisual materials for Educational Filmstrips of Huntsville, Texas, and without the continued encouragement of George, Kenneth, and Marjorie Russell.

Further, this work could not have been completed without the continuing financial and administrative support of the OSU College of Liberal Arts Research Program, the OSU Department of Geography, and the OSU Foundation. These contributors augmented major project funding contributed by the National Endowment for the Humanities.

Graphs and maps were produced by the Cartographic Service of the OSU Department of Geography. All photographs are by the authors.

We offer a final thanks to an old pilgrim whose weathered face, briefly illuminated by a shaft of sunlight filtered through stained glass and the incense smoke of the Mass in the Cathedral at Santiago de Compostela in 1965, awakened us to the realization that religious pilgrimage is a timeless aspect of human behavior.

Christian Pilgrimage in Modern Western Europe

one

Introduction

The priest stood firmly erect, his black robes blowing in the mountain breeze as he recited his prayers. At his feet knelt five young women, some with heads bowed while others stared intently toward a sacred image high in the branches of an old pine. It was one of several pines in a small grove nestled into a slight hollow on the hillside. On a rise just beyond the grove, three women knelt with arms outstretched as they prayed aloud. Leading their chorus, a fourth woman knelt beside a patch of muddy earth at the roots of the image-bearing tree. Water seeped from the ground, and among the rivulets and clumps of grass was a stone. Under the stone were soggy slips of paper and soaked pictures left by pilgrims seeking favors or giving thanks. Higher on the heather-clad hillside two women sang. Their voices mingled with the murmur of prayers rising from the grove.

The scene, with its aura of sacred interaction between place and people, could have been set in many different times and locales during the past several thousand years. This particular incident was witnessed on the heights above the village of San Sebastián de Garabandal in northern Spain on July 18, 1981 (Figure 1-1). The kneeling pilgrims were Germans. Judging from their dress and the cars parked in the village, they were reasonably affluent. The singers were French. Prayers included the liturgy of the rosary, although this site of claimed Marian apparitions in the 1960s has not been recognized by the Roman Catholic church as a proper place of pilgrimage.

Garabandal and other new, but ecclesiastically unrecognized, sites of religious pilgrimage in Western Europe represent part of a spectrum that extends from obscure, locally visited chapels and holy wells to world-famous, church-approved shrines such as Rome, Lourdes, and Fátima. At present, Western Europe's more than 6,000 pilgrimage centers generate a conservatively estimated 60 to 70 million religiously motivated visits per year. Total annual visitations at these shrines—including casual tourists, curiosity seekers, and

Figure 1-1 *Pilgrims pray in a hillside grove at San Sebastián de Garabandal, Spain, where the Virgin Mary is said to have appeared at various times between 1961 and 1965.*

persons referred to as "art history pilgrims" by West German shrine administrators—almost certainly exceed 100 million.[1]

The number of pilgrims attending traditional events is increasing at many shrines while new forms of religious travel, summarized by Vatican officials as "religious tourism," are swelling the ranks of visitors to many types of holy places.[2] A general upsurge of interest in pilgrimage is occurring in other parts of the Christian world as well. Substantial numbers of pilgrims at major European shrines come from the Americas and other areas outside Western

Europe. The late twentieth century is, therefore, the latest epoch in a dynamic pattern of rise and decline in enthusiasm for pilgrimage that has characterized the European Christian tradition for nearly 2,000 years.

Origins of Pilgrimage

Christian pilgrimage is deeply rooted in older traditions of journeying to sacred places. Upper Paleolithic cave paintings of probable religious significance suggest that prehistoric Europeans may have made pilgrimages of thanks or supplication for successful hunts. Megalithic monuments, thought to date from as early as 4000 B.C., probably were places of religious gatherings that drew people from considerable distances.[3] In historic times, various forms of pilgrimage were practiced by pagan Mediterranean, Celtic, and Germanic peoples. A few of Europe's contemporary sites of Christian pilgrimage are found at places once sacred to pagan deities.[4]

Christian pilgrimage probably began in the first century A.D. and was almost certainly occurring by the second century as veneration of saints' relics gathered momentum in the Christian communities of the Roman world.[5] Although many early influences related to the development of Christian pilgrimage came from the Eastern Mediterranean, these melded with local customs to make pilgrimage in Western Europe an indigenous aspect of culture. As such, pilgrimage has evolved with the socioeconomic changes, technological transformations, and shifting intellectual orientations of the region. There appears to be a close connection between frequencies of cult establishment and major turning points in European history.[6] Thus, pilgrimage is as much a part of the ongoing drama of European history as are wars, revolutions, the rise and fall of empires, industrialization, and urbanization. Pilgrimages have influenced and been affected by developments in the arts, sciences, literature, and philosophy.

Historians have long recognized the significance of Medieval pilgrimage in the molding of European culture.[7] Recently, more attention has been paid to the importance of cult formation and patterns of pilgrimage during the transition period between Medieval and Early Modern times, and some attention has been directed toward the upsurge of activity in nineteenth-century France.[8] Contemporary pilgrimage in Western Europe, however, has largely been neglected as a topic of systematic scholarly investigation, particularly in English-language literature.[9] Even the important anthropological work of Victor and Edith Turner on symbolism in Christian pilgrimage is primarily based on a relatively small number of cases from Ireland, England, France, and Mexico.[10] Yet, as the Turners point out, it is important to consider a "particular pilgrimage as part of a field of pilgrimages rather than as an isolate."[11]

Objectives and Procedures

Our objective in this book is to describe and interpret the dimensions of the contemporary Western European pilgrimage field with special emphasis on regional variations in types of shrines and pilgrimages. Differences between shrines that reflect ideas about mankind, divinity, and environment current when these pilgrimage centers were established are also considered as part of an effort to interpret modern pilgrimage in a time-space matrix.

In order to develop an adequately large and broadly distributed data base, we collected and analyzed information on 6,150 places of pilgrimage located in 16 Western European countries (Table 1-1). Field investigations were conducted during the summers of 1976, 1978, and 1979, the 14 months between July 1980 and September 1981, and the summers of 1982 and 1983. A brief visit to West Germany in late 1984 yielded additional information on shrines in southeastern Bavaria. During these periods in Europe we visited 852 shrines. In 68 cases, we were present at shrines during special pilgrimage celebrations, and at many other places we talked with pilgrims, tourists, and shrine personnel. We also collected information on famous churches that generally are not thought of as shrines by Europeans, and on once important shrines that are currently dormant or extinct as places of pilgrimage. By attending religious festivals that are not considered to be pilgrimages by Europeans, we sought to understand the subtle differences between pilgrimages, saints' day festivals, and high holy day processions.

In developing the shrine inventory we drew on materials sent by diocesan offices and shrine administrators in response to mail queries, festival listings provided by national and regional agencies of tourism, descriptive compendia written by folklorists and other investigators, field notes based on observations and interviews, and booklets on individual shrines obtained by mail or on site.[12] Correspondence with Vatican officials was initiated in 1976. We were informed that the Vatican does not maintain an inventory of active pilgrimage centers per se. During the spring of 1981, we inspected materials in the Vatican Library and Archives. We also conferred with officials of these institutions and with representatives of the Pontifical Commission on the Pastoral Care of Migrants and Tourists, the Vatican agency most directly con-

Table 1-1 *Number of Shrines Inventoried by Country or Region*

Country	Number Identified	Number Field-checked	Number Classified by Cult-Formative Period
Italy	1,194	120	942
France	1,034	196	722
Spain	1,014	134	476
West Germany	938	121	650
Austria	925	116	656
Portugal	332	42	73
Switzerland	283	35	221
Belgium and Luxembourg	151	17	105
Ireland	135	30	104
United Kingdom	86	34	80
Netherlands	48	4	10
Sweden	5	1	5
Denmark	3	2	3
Finland	1	0	1
Norway	1	0	1
Total	6,150	852	4,049

cerned with pastoral problems related to modern pilgrimage and religious tourism.[13]

As written materials were collected, they were read by ourselves or by bilingual assistants. Information was recorded in English on questionnaire-type sheets keyed to a coding system for computer analysis and mapping. The readers, most of whom were native speakers of the language with which they dealt, were asked to include interesting details from the literature in addition to the items specifically required on the data sheets. In this manner, a very rich body of material was consolidated into a single language. Summaries of information on each shrine were transferred to card files, and source materials such as letters, copies of archival materials, completed questionnaires, and pamphlets from shrines were filed along with copies of published compendia. Coded data were stored on computer cards and tapes. Operational definitions used for computer coding are provided in the text where appropriate for the interpretation of tables and maps.

In several sections of the book, the presentation of quantitative data has been simplified by examining seven macro-regional traditions rather than shrines in individual countries (Table 1-2). These areas consist of (1) an Italian region, composed of the modern Italian nation-state plus the Italian linguistic region of Switzerland; (2) a French region, which combines France with Walloon Belgium and French Switzerland; (3) an Iberian region, encompassing Spain, Portugal, and Andorra; (4) a South German region, including Austria, Germanic Switzerland, and the West German areas of Baden-Württemberg and Bavaria; (5) a North German region, made up of central and northern West Germany, Flemish Belgium, Luxembourg, the Netherlands, and the Scandinavian countries; (6) an Irish region, encompassing the Republic of Ireland and Northern Ireland; and (7) a British region, consisting of England, Scotland, and Wales. Data on the North and South German regions are combined in some tables in order to reduce complexity. In these cases, differences between the Germanic regions appear to be minor.

Nearly two-thirds of the identified shrines could be assigned to a general time period of cult establishment as defined by criteria explained in Chapter 4. As a general reference, shrines referred to as Early Christian appear to have been founded between the first century and 699. Early Medieval shrines were established between 700 and 1099, and High Medieval shrines date from the years between 1100 and 1399. The Renaissance period is defined as the years between 1400 and 1529, and is followed by a Post-Reformation period extending from 1530 to 1779. Modern shrines are those that came into being between 1780 and 1980.

For inventory purposes our operational definition of an active pilgrimage shrine was a place so described in available literature or mentioned as a destination point for pilgrims in response to inquiries. We included places referred to as active in the descriptive accounts of pilgrimage shrines published since 1949, places appearing on shrine lists provided by diocesan offices, and sites of activities referred to as pilgrimages in various event listings. Places we learned about from people in the area during our field surveys were also included. The word "pilgrimage" in its various translations was supplemented, when appropriate, with specialized words used in some Romance-language regions for minor communal pilgrimages, generally of a festive nature. Thus, data from Spain and Portugal include *romería* sites, and the French data encompass the destinations of *pardons* in Brittany and *apleches*, primarily in Languedoc.

We attempted to limit the study to shrines that draw pilgrims from beyond the immediate locality, but found that it is not always possible to distinguish local pilgrimage sites from vicinity or district shrines. Only a minority of compendia and diocesan lists provided a ranking of the shrines listed or

Table 1-2 Regional Traditions

Region	Shrines Inventoried	Dated Shrines	Formation Stories
Italian (Italy and Italian Switzerland)	1,210	953	878
French (France, Walloon Belgium, and French Switzerland)	1,159	801	545
Iberian (Spain, Portugal, and Andorra)	1,346	549	472
South German (Austria, Germanic Switzerland, and southern West Germany)	1,741	1,295	909
North German (Central and northern West Germany, Flemish Belgium, Luxembourg, Netherlands, and Scandinavia)	473	267	188
Irish (Republic of Ireland and Northern Ireland)	135	104	55
British (England, Scotland, and Wales)	86	80	79
Total	6,150	4,049	3,126

described; when they did, there was a wide variance in what different compilers categorized as "local." Sometimes shrines included on lists sent by diocesan offices or drawn from compendia proved to be local in visitation when we found out more about them. Other shrines described as "local" in accounts turned out to be fairly important pilgrimage centers in terms of visitation numbers and geographical drawing power. Part of the interpretive problem lies in the fact that an urban shrine visited primarily by the people of a particular city is technically local, but quite different in scale from a shrine visited only by the people of one small village. In addition, some shrines are visited by only a few devotees from several communities and thus are translocal but of minor importance. Although we excluded cases categorized or described as local in the more comprehensive compendia, our inventory contains some highly localized pilgrimage centers. On the basis of field checking, we estimate that approximately 7 percent of the inventoried shrines are "local" in the sense that they draw pilgrims almost entirely from a single rural community or urban neighborhood. Such localized pilgrimages tend to merge in type and expression with community religious festivals. William Christian's studies of folk and popular religion in Spain suggest the need for further investigation of religious expressions lying in the transition zone between pilgrimage and special saints' day celebrations.[14]

The decision to restrict our analysis to Roman Catholic shrines along with High Church Anglican and Lutheran pilgrimage centers, which are often places of ecumenical pilgrimage, was partially based on practicalities. Protestant holy places visited by religiously motivated travelers are usually not conceptualized of, or described as, pilgrimage shrines. Compilation of a suitable data base would, therefore, be difficult. It seemed better to exclude such sites as the birthplace of John Wesley or the French Protestant assembly place at Anduze-Mas-Soubeyran in the Cevennes than to add these and a few other examples on a nonsystematic basis. Furthermore, the sixteenth-century Protestant rejection of pilgrimage and features associated with it, such as the veneration of saints' relics and the cult of the Virgin Mary, suggests that an analysis of Protestant religious travel should be undertaken as a separate study. We excluded a number of ancient holy sites in the United Kingdom that can no longer be considered pilgrimage shrines even though they have retained some attractive power as wishing wells and magic rocks in the folk tradition.[15] It should be pointed out, however, that some of the shrines considered in this study are not officially sanctioned by the Roman Catholic church. Several are folk shrines at which visitation may or may not be encouraged by a local priest. Others are places where reports of recent miracles are currently drawing pilgrims, but where cultus has not received approval from the local bishop.

The attempt to inventory all active pilgrimage places of greater-than-local importance was only partly successful because European pilgrimage is a highly dynamic institution. At any time, including the present, some shrines are losing their ability to attract pilgrims while new cults are forming at other places. This rise and decline of individual shrines makes it likely that an inventory of the scope we have attempted will include some shrines that are currently dormant or extinct. Extrapolation from field checks and correspondence suggests that about 3 percent of the shrines on which this analysis is based do not attract pilgrims at present. Approximately 10 percent are currently in decline or have become very touristic in recent years, but a nearly equal proportion are either of very recent origin or are recording a major resurgence in pilgrimage visitation. Places where pilgrimage is gaining strength after a long period of dormancy, or where new cults are in the process of formation, are probably underrepresented in our inventory.[16] Undoubtedly other, more established shrines were not included in the data base, but attempting to estimate how many cases we missed in a shrine "population" of unknown dimensions would be purely speculative.

The 6,150 shrines on which our interpretations are based can be thought of as an approximate population of Western Europe's active pilgrimage centers. Large and/or well-known places of pilgrimage are probably better represented than are smaller, less famous shrines. Regional variations in the availability of detailed published literature and local ecclesiastical officials' attitudes toward pilgrimage as reflected in response to requests for lists and addresses of pilgrimage places in the diocese may constitute another bias in the data base. It is also possible that Marian shrines are somewhat overrepresented because several major national compendia deal only with pilgrimage centers primarily dedicated to the Virgin Mary. If this is the case, however, the degree of overrepresentation remained remarkably constant as additional shrines were added to the inventory from a great variety of sources including field explorations. Sixty-four percent of the 4,075 shrines on which a preliminary data analysis was undertaken in late 1979 were primarily devoted to the Virgin Mary, as compared with 65 percent of the 6,150 shrines on which the data in this book are based. Thus, a 34 percent increase in the number of shrines examined yielded only a 1 percent change in the frequency of Marian shrines. The proportion of shrines dedicated to Christ also increased one percentage point, the proportion dedicated to saints stayed the same, and the fraction with no identified devotional subject decreased from 4 percent to 2 percent.

Data on shrine origins also remained relatively constant as we added cases to the inventory after the 1979 analysis. Between 1979 and 1985 we increased the number of shrines that could be dated by decade of establishment by 1,066 cases, yet the plots showed remarkably little change in pattern, particularly in regard to high and low points in the cult-formative activities producing today's shrines. The proportion of shrines attributed to different time periods changed no more than one or two percentage points. From this observation, we concluded that individual cases could be added to or deleted from the inventory indefinitely as new information becomes available, but we have reached a point of diminishing returns in terms of identifying general patterns.[17]

Given the size of the inventory and the persistence of patterns, we think that this study represents a closer approximation of the cultural-geographical reality of Europe's current pilgrimage shrines than anything previously published. It should be of special use to cultural geographers, anthropologists, shrine administrators, and others seeking to evaluate in-depth information on particular shrines or regional pilgrimage traditions in a larger context. For students of comparative religion, it offers a foundation for examining similarities and differences between Roman Catholic pilgrimages and those of Christian Eastern Orthodox, Jewish, Hindu, Moslem, Buddhist, and other traditions. Although this work is not intended as a history per se, and is based only on active shrines, historians should find some of the temporal data useful. Important concentrations of certain types of pilgrimage-related phenomena in time and space are revealed and suggest profitable avenues for historical research.

two

The Shrines

of Western Europe

Western Europe's thousands of pilgrimage shrines range from great basilicas, such as Lourdes (Figure 2-1), that are visited by millions of people from all over the world to isolated holy wells known only to a few devotees from the immediate vicinity. Although some shrines function only as places of pilgrimage, a majority serve multiple purposes. Some are parish churches where ordinary worship services are interspersed with occasional pilgrimage events. Many are found at monasteries or convents, and others are located in great urban cathedrals. Shrines may be associated with seminaries, church schools, hospitals, or nursing homes. Along with regular Masses, prayer services, and formal pilgrimages, shrine administrators may sponsor adult retreats, conferences, youth encampments, marriage encounter sessions, concerts, and exhibitions of religious art. Weddings, baptisms, and confirmations are often celebrated at district or regional shrines in preference to the participants' parish church. Inns and other visitor facilities are frequently clustered around shrines in rural settings, thus attracting vacationers seeking a combination of recreation and religious experience.

In contrast with religious establishments generally, pilgrimage shrines may be conceptualized as especially holy places to which devotees make religiously motivated journeys. Some type of enclosed, consecrated structure is found at most shrines, but there is no universal ecclesiastical designation for a church or chapel visited by pilgrims. Churches at important shrines often hold the rank of basilica, meaning that they have special ceremonial privileges. However, only a small minority of shrine churches are basilicas, and not all basilicas are places of pilgrimage. In Ireland, and occasionally elsewhere, there may not even be a consecrated structure to mark the site. In

Figure 2-1 *Belgian pilgrims unfurl their banners at Lourdes. This famous French shrine, the scene of Marian apparitions in 1858, draws more than four million visitors per year from all parts of the world.*

continental Europe, shrines are usually places where a particular relic or image is venerated. This is less often the case in Britain, and in Ireland a natural site feature such as a holy well or sacred stone is frequently the only object of cultus.

Often, the shrine locality, or an object venerated there, is considered unusually sacred because of a past event interpreted by the faithful as a manifestation of divine power. According to anthropologists Victor and Edith Turner, pilgrimage sites "are believed to be places where miracles once happened, still happen and may happen again."[1] This generalization, however, holds true only if miracles are interpreted as any type of wonderful event. In the late twentieth century, it is often miracle enough if faith is strengthened, if the communitas of participation in a periodic pilgrimage event is felt, or if the pilgrim returns home with a sense of renewal. In the words of a European priest who ministers to pilgrims, "It is a miracle that so many come and that so many return home feeling better because they came." Ultimately, as William Christian has observed, "a shrine is defined by the devotion of its people."[2] Thus, a particular place is a center of pilgrimage if people think of it in that way and behave accordingly.

Terminology

The exact meaning accorded to the words used to describe shrines and pilgrimages varies from one part of Europe to another. In most Romance-language areas, no single term carries quite the same meaning as the English "pilgrimage shrine." *Santuario* is the closest approximation in Spanish, Portuguese, and Italian.[3] In Iberia, however, the use of the word *santuario* varies somewhat from region to region, but seldom includes country chapels, parish churches, or even all of the cathedrals and monastery churches that serve as goals for pilgrim journeys. In Spain and Portugal, the words *peregrinación* and *peregrinação* are usually restricted to long-distance journeys to major shrines. Inquiries about *lugares de peregrinación* typically yield little information about district and minor regional pilgrimage centers. Minor communal pilgrimages of a combined devotional and festive nature are called *romerías*, but the word may also be used for large regional pilgrimages as at Rocio and the shrine of the Virgen de la Cabeza, both in Andalucía. Pilgrims participating in romerías are called *romeros* in Spain and *romeiros* in Portugal.

In France and other areas where French is the principal language, the word *sanctuaire* is frequently applied to pilgrimage centers, although not all places that bear this label appear to attract pilgrims at present. Pilgrimages in Brittany are referred to as *pardons*, and the classic Iberian romería is sometimes called an *aplec* in southern France. The term *lieu de pèlerinage* seems to carry approximately the same range of meanings as the English term "pilgrimage shrine." Thus, the site of a pardon in Brittany or an aplec in Languedoc is generally viewed as a place of pilgrimage.

Santuario is the most usual reference to a place of pilgrimage in Italy where the word is applied more liberally than in Iberia. Minor pilgrimages to Italian country chapels are sometimes described only as *festas*, a term that also includes saints' day festivals, birthday parties, and Communist party fund-raising events.

The German language uses the term *Pilgerfahrt* to describe an infrequently made or once-in-a-lifetime journey to a distant and very important holy place such as Rome or Jerusalem. Technically, a *Wallfahrt* is a pilgrimage made repeatedly on special days of celebration to a district or regional shrine. The term, however, seems to be generally used for most pilgrimage activities taking place within Germanic regions where pilgrimage places of all levels of importance are called *Wallfahrtsorte*. Germans may distinguish between a *Wallfahrtskirche* and *Wallfahrtskapelle* just as English speakers may refer to a pilgrimage church or a pilgrimage chapel.

Shrines and Religious Tourism

Europe's pilgrimage shrines make up only a part of a much broader spectrum of ecclesiastical structures and sites of religious celebrations that attract visitors from beyond their immediate localities. A shrine church may be a secular tourist attraction by virtue of its artistic merits, historical associations, or the view from the terrace, but not all famous churches on the tourist circuit are considered to be places of pilgrimage. Similarly, famous and colorful pilgrimage events attract numerous onlookers, but only a minority of Europe's religious celebrations are thought of as pilgrimages. A model of the complicated relationships between pilgrimage shrines, religious tourist attractions, and festival sites is presented in Figure 2-2.

Europe's famous Medieval and Renaissance cathedrals provide examples of ecclesiastical structures that attract numerous visitors because of artistic and historical qualities. Of the 156 seats of bishops included in *The Horizon Book of Great Cathedrals* because of their special architectural or historical importance, however, only 10 are pilgrimage centers of national or international significance.[4] Twenty-eight others are important diocesan shrines and 33 are centers of local or vicinity pilgrimage. The remaining 85 are not pilgrimage goals at present, although these are well-visited tourist attractions.

Few holy day processions, Passion plays, community saints' day celebrations, or other religious events are thought of as pilgrimages. Thus, communities where such events are held are not considered shrine towns because of these celebrations. At certain times of the year, such as Christmas and Easter, most European communities have public religious festivals. In southern Europe, most villages, towns, and urban neighborhoods periodically celebrate their own special saints' days. When a festival is known to be colorful or religiously moving, it inevitably attracts people from other places. They may come only from nearby, or, in the case of Easter Week processions in Seville, from all over the world. But the drawing power of the event does not automatically make it a pilgrimage. Unless the pageantry is related to a specific place that is regarded as especially holy and the participants think of themselves as pilgrims, nothing in the fame or splendor of a festival justifies considering it a pilgrimage.

Oberammergau, West Germany, provides an example of a place famous for its Passion play, a religious pageant that draws a large international audience, both Catholic and Protestant. The event has been staged every ten years since a plague vow in the seventeenth century and, like other Passion plays, was not originally thought of as a pilgrimage event. As Christian has observed, vows to celebrate a particular feast day or to sponsor a pageant traditionally have been conceptualized as alternatives to vowing a special day of pilgrimage to an existing shrine or creating a new place of pilgrimage.[5] In other words, vowing a Passion play is something done instead of establishing a pilgrimage cultus. It rarely involves either a cult object or the recognition of a particular place as having a special kind of sanctity.

Some of the people who attend the Oberammergau Passion play, however, think of their journeys as pilgrimages. This stems partly from the fame that this particular event has gained because of the historic promotion by the monks of the nearby Benedictine monastery of Ettal, and because of recent promotion by the international tourist industry. Many tours from the United States to the regular 1980 and the special 1984 centennial performances were advertised as pilgrimages even when the Passion play was only a part of an otherwise secularly oriented package. Comments by most of the people we talked with at a performance in September 1980 indicated that they did not consider themselves to be pilgrims, or that they were not sure if witnessing the event could be thought of as an act of pilgrimage. Several American Protestants, however, did say that the town must be a pilgrimage place because they were on an "Oberammergau Pilgrimage Tour." At least one person present that day was a pilgrim. He had journeyed from his home in northern West Germany to attend the play every decade since the end of World War II in fulfillment of a vow made as a young soldier on the front lines. He affirmed that his was a vow of pilgrimage, but he pointed out that Oberammergau's huge, modern *Passionstheater* is not a holy place in quite the same sense as more conventional shrines.

Religious celebrations in Burgos, Spain, provide an example of the interrelationships between pilgrimages and other types of European religious ex-

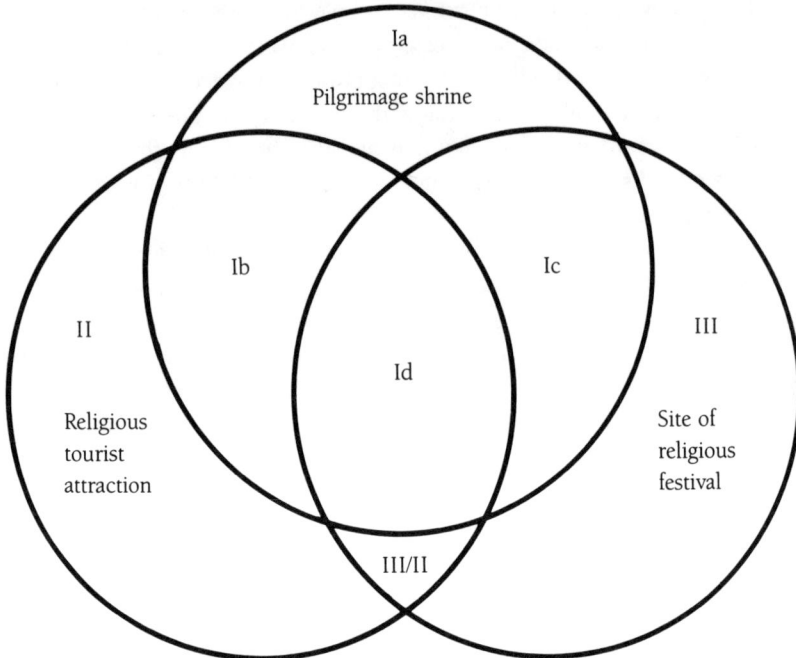

Figure 2-2   *Relationships between shrines, religious tourist attractions, and festival sites: explanations and examples.*

I. Pilgrimage shrines. *Places that serve as the goal for pilgrim journeys.*

   a. Shrines of relatively low value as tourist attractions not characterized by festivals involving pageantry or folkloric display. *The majority of visitors are either members of religious tour groups or consider themselves to be pilgrims. Most on-site activities are religious in nature.*

   b. Shrines of high value as tourist attractions. *Tourists tend to outnumber pilgrims at these places which are famous for art, architecture, features of site, or historical associations. Although there may be special days of pilgrimage, these shrines are not especially noted for great religious festivals.*

   c. Shrines primarily noted for colorful pilgrimage events. *The pilgrimage as an event is most important at these shrines. In some cases several years pass between each event, but pilgrimages are usually held on an annual or biannual basis.*

   d. Shrines combining touristic importance, pilgrimage festivals, and cultic significance. *The classic example of this type of shrine is Santiago de Compostela, Spain, visited throughout the year by large numbers of tourists and pilgrims, but* pressions in an urban setting. The Burgos Cathedral is a Medieval monument of touristic interest and a pilgrimage shrine. Among its treasures, the cathedral contains an image of Christ on the Cross venerated because "miracles and prodigies . . . attributed to it are innumerable."[6] On September 14, Burgos is the scene of a religious pilgrimage in honor of this crucifix. The city is also famous for its Corpus Christi procession, a dramatic event that is only a religious festival. The procession begins and ends at the cathedral, but the pilgrimage-inspiring crucifix plays no role in the pageantry that is confined to the central part of the city (Figure 2-3). Neither local people nor visitors think of the Corpus Christi procession as a pilgrimage.

On the day after Corpus Christi, however, citizens of Burgos and surrounding towns gather at the monastery of Las Huelgas for a celebration that falls into an intermediate zone between a pilgrimage event and a religious festival. The ancient monastery lies on the edge of the expanding city, but is several kilometers beyond the remnants of the Medieval walls. The celebration, called the *Corpillos*, centers on the exhibition of a Moorish tapestry taken as a trophy by victorious Castillian forces at the decisive Reconquest battle of the Navas de Tolosa in 1212 (Figure 2-4). After a Mass in the monastery church,

---

especially toward the end of July when the day of Saint James (July 25) is celebrated in a blaze of processions, High Masses, and folkloric displays.

II. Religious tourist attractions. *These places, usually ecclesiastical structures of some kind, are visited by secularly oriented tourists and recreationists, religious tour groups, and pilgrims en route to shrines, but they are not considered to be places of pilgrimage in their own right. Many of Europe's most famous cathedrals and monastic establishments fall into this category.*

III. Sites of religious festivals. *Innumerable religious festivals and processions in Europe are not thought of as pilgrimages per se. These include most Holy Week and Corpus Christi processions, as well as the majority of public Christmas celebrations. Most of these events are associated with churches, some of which are important as tourist attractions and historical monuments. Thus, categories II and III overlap. For example, the famous Cathedral of Granada, which contains the tombs of the Catholic monarchs, Ferdinand and Isabella, is the scene of an important civic-religious celebration each January 2 but is not generally regarded as a place of pilgrimage.*

Figure 2-3 *Giant figures parade before the Cathedral of Burgos, Spain, during the festival of Corpus Christi. Such* gigantes *feature in many Spanish religious celebrations.*

Figure 2-4 *This Moorish tapestry, taken by Christian armies at the decisive battle of Navas de Tolosa in 1212, provides a focal point for annual celebrations at the monastery of Las Huelgas near Burgos, Spain.*

officials of church, city, and nation take part in a procession. The remainder of the day is filled with eating, drinking, singing, dancing, and other amusements in a nearby park, as is the usual pattern for Iberian romerías (Figure 2-5). There is an element of symbolic journey in this event because participants leave the central city and are joined by people from nearby communities. However, neither the monastery nor the Moorish tapestry marks this place of celebration as a pilgrimage shrine in quite the same way as devotions to the Christ of Burgos distinguish the cathedral.

Variations in Shrine Importance

Numerous popular religious tourist attractions are of little or no importance as pilgrimage places, but many pilgrimage centers draw far more visitors than can be explained in terms of the historic or artistic qualities of their structures, the scenic attributes of their settings, or the splendor of their festivals. The degree of holiness that attracts pilgrims to shrines is independent of the place's appeal to casual visitors.

There is no universally recognized hierarchy of holiness, but some places are conceptualized as more sacred than others. In the Christian tradition, the holiest places are those most intimately associated with the life of Jesus. Most of these are in Jerusalem and Bethlehem and in the Galilee region. However, these shrines that mark the places of Christ's birth, ministry, and death do not occupy positions in the Christian tradition equivalent to the primacy of Mecca in Islam. In contrast with the institutionalized Islamic belief that pilgrimage should be made to Mecca if possible, Christian pilgrimage is a purely voluntary expression of religious devotion. In certain times and places pilgrimage has been encouraged, but, except for certain penitential requirements imposed on heretics and criminals during the Middle Ages, the undertaking of a religious journey has never been a Christian duty.[7]

Within Western Europe, Rome is the best candidate for the holiest of places for Roman Catholics. Holy Year pilgrimages to Rome, initiated in the year 1300, have remained major events in the church. These great celebrations are held every 25 years, and shrines throughout Europe experienced higher-than-usual visitations during the 1975 Holy Year pilgrimage. Rome, however, is sometimes viewed as marginally sacred. When asked why he did not list Rome as one of the ten most important pilgrimage centers in Western Europe, an Irish priest replied, "Well, those people who go to Rome go to sightsee and have a good time." He conceded that going to see the Holy Father might be a kind of pilgrimage, but he was adamant in his contention that the basilicas of Rome do not belong on a proper list of great pilgrimage places. He regarded Saint Patrick's Purgatory on Station Island in Lough Derg as more holy because of its reputation as the only Western European site of a purely penitential pilgrimage. If we had taken the lead of this Irish priest and tried to determine the relative sanctity of pilgrimage places based on the degree of perceived penitence rather than the number of devout visitors, the effort would have been complicated by the fact that even the Irish go in larger numbers to places with less rigorous devotional demands than the self-chastising rites of Saint Patrick's Purgatory.

Shrines subsidiary to other pilgrimage centers, such as Europe's numerous secondary Loreto, Lourdes, and Fátima shrines, are often conceptualized as less powerful than the originals. There are hundreds of Lourdes shrines in the Christian world, but only one is the geographically specific site of the 1858 apparitions. It is by far the largest and most important. Generally, how-

Figure 2-5 *Young Spaniards perform an impromptu dance during an afternoon of secular pleasures following the solemn Mass and procession at Las Huelgas.*

ever, geographer Surinder Bhardwaj's statement in his study of Hindu Indian shrines is equally true for Western Europe: "no single system defines which particular sacred place is 'the most sacred' for all times, for all regions."[8]

Although European pilgrimage places cannot be ranked from most to least sacred, there are notable differences between shrines in terms of numbers of pilgrims and distances they travel. The pilgrimage centers generally regarded as most important, such as Lourdes, Assisi, or Rome, attract pilgrims and tourists from all over the world. Crowds swell to the tens or hundreds of thousands on special days of pilgrimage. A church usually serves as the focal point of an extensive shrine complex. Parking lots, souvenir stands, and facilities for housing and feeding visitors characteristically ring the principal religious structures. Lourdes and other shrines noted for cures have special facilities for the handicapped, sick, and infirm as well as clinics and hospitals.

Purely local shrines visited only by pilgrims from a single rural village or urban neighborhood lie at the other end of the spectrum and are too numerous to inventory accurately. On the next level are district and vicinity shrines, which are usually scenes of annual or semiannual pilgrimage events. These shrines may attract individual pilgrims or small groups at various times, but the casual visitor is likely to find solitude and frequently a chapel with a locked door. In Ireland, and occasionally elsewhere, a pilgrimage site may be marked by nothing more than a hill-top cross, or a thorn tree beside a holy well and a curious stone (Figure 2-6). Shrines of regional importance display varied characteristics. Some of the more important have many of the facilities found at great pilgrimage centers, whereas others are difficult to distinguish from any other place of worship except during periodic pilgrimage events.

Indicators of Shrine Importance

Measurement of shrine importance levels can, theoretically, be based on two criteria: (1) the size of the catchment basin, or geographical area, from which the shrine draws all or most of its religiously oriented visitors; and (2) the number of annual visitations.

Range of Drawing Power

Catchment basins are usually described by such terms as local, district, regional, national, and international in reference to the extent of the political and/or ecclesiastical subdivisions from which pilgrims come. Although applied frequently by shrine administrators, compilers of descriptive accounts, and scholars, these labels are of limited use in comparing shrines on a Pan-European basis.[9] Nation-states, and politically or administratively defined regions within them, such as provinces, departments, länder, or dioceses, are of unequal sizes in Europe. In Italy, where the average diocese size is 713 square miles, the most important shrine in a diocese may draw pilgrims only from a modest-sized cathedral town and a few nearby villages. This is the case with the shrine of the Madonna del Lago, patroness of the city and diocese of Bertinoro on the southern edge of the Po Valley. In contrast, a diocesan-level shrine in West Germany, where the average diocese size is 5,047 square miles, draws from a more extensive region. Similarly, Meritxell, the national shrine of tiny Andorra, is not comparable to Mariazell, the national shrine of Austria, although in both cases the national designation is politically charged because these shrines are important religious symbols of nationhood.

The problem of different-sized regions and nations is compounded by vernacularly defined culture regions that cut across modern national boundaries.

Shrines of Western Europe 23

Figure 2-6 *A thorn tree entwines its roots in the stone cover of Saint Olan's Holy Well near Aghabulloge, County Cork, Ireland. Nearby stands an ancient menhir with crosses scratched onto its surface. A few hundred people from the immediate area make pilgrim "rounds" here each year.*

West Germany's two greatest Marian shrines at Kevelaer and Altötting draw from extensive culture regions beyond the nation's boundaries, but their catchment basins have relatively little overlap within the country and neither is viewed as a national shrine. On the other hand, these respective centers of the Lower Rhine and alpine religious culture regions are not international in the same sense as the shrines at Lourdes and Fátima, because few pilgrims come from beyond the transnational Germanic culture areas.

Some shrines draw devotees from all over the world but are of modest importance as pilgrimage goals in their home regions. The religious center of Kloster Schönstatt at Vallendar near Koblenz, West Germany, for example, is visited on an intercontinental basis. Many of its 40,000 annual pilgrims come from parts of the United States, South Africa, Australia, and South America where the Schönstatt Apostolic Movement, founded by Father Joseph Kentenich in 1914, is vigorously propagated. Subsidiary shrines in these areas inspire devotees to visit the original in West Germany. Defined by range of drawing power, Kloster Schönstatt is one of Europe's great shrines. In terms of visitor count, however, it is of modest significance because it attracts considerably fewer pilgrims than numerous other West German shrines that are visited primarily by German pilgrims from nearby areas.

A more extreme example of the lack of fit between numbers of pilgrims and the range of drawing power is the Madrid church housing an image known as the Virgen de Atocha. From a modern Spanish point of view, this parish church is not a place of pilgrimage. The local priest said that residents of Madrid prefer to make pilgrimages to countryside shrines near the city or to famous pilgrimage centers farther away, and that people from other parts of Spain rarely come to pay their respects to the Virgen de Atocha. He added, however, that Hispanic-American pilgrims occasionally show up and are disappointed to find such a modest setting for the Atocha image. In this case, a transplanted cultus centering on Nuestra Señora de Atocha has remained vigorous in the New World while the significance of the mother shrine in Madrid has faded.

Range of drawing power is also a questionable measure of importance for shrines located in areas of extensive out-migration. Some of these modest pilgrimage places have vast catchment basins because they attract emigrants and their descendants who combine family visits with a shrine journey. Small shrine chapels in rural areas of Italy, Spain, and Portugal record regular pilgrim visits from West Germany, northern France, the Low Countries, the Americas, Australia, and New Zealand.

Ideally, range of drawing power should be measured and described in terms of actual distances, perhaps excluding distances traveled by returning emigrants. However, information on the spatial dimensions of European shrine catchment basins is usually generalized and based on references to the farthest points from which pilgrims normally travel. Christian developed a detailed ranking of several hundred Spanish shrines based on intensive research in the field and on correspondence. By mapping the types of information obtainable only through contact with shrine administrators, he defined what he meant by such labels as district, province, and region with unusual precision.[10] Even this extraordinarily time-consuming approach does not adequately control for variations in settlement density. Large, well-financed urban or urban-edge shrines that draw a steady flow of pilgrims from small, but densely populated areas are obviously different from country chapels visited once a year by a relatively small number of predominantly poor pilgrims from large, but sparsely populated regions. One type of shrine is not necessarily more or less important than the other. Thus, ranking systems based only on range of drawing power, no matter how precisely determined, are of limited value for comparative analysis. The terms are useful as generalized references to the status of particular shrines in specific regional contexts.

In our inventory, 3 percent of the shrines draw nonemigrant pilgrims from national or international areas. An additional 13 percent are visited from sizable regions such as an entire province or a large diocese. The majority of shrines attract pilgrims from fairly small areas.

Number and Purpose of Visitations

Annual visitation figures provide another means of categorizing European shrines by level of importance. Many shrines, however, do not maintain precise visitation counts. Such phrases as "many thousands," "36 processions on a single day," and "all the faithful of this vast region" are common in the literature and in interview situations. Those shrines that do keep records use diverse systems. Some administrators attempt to record all nonlocal visits, while others count only the people who attend special pilgrim services or come in organized pilgrimage groups. At some shrines, the visitation estimate is broken down into categories of "pilgrims" and "tourists." These are variously defined in terms of the perceptions of local personnel and are variously publicized depending on the situation. For example, an administrator at the shrine of Sion in the French Lorraine region gave a figure of 200,000 religiously motivated visits per year when he filled out our questionnaire. An article in the shrine's 1973 centenary publication provided the same annual visitation figure, but broke it down into 50,000 pilgrims and 150,000 tourists. The anonymous author speculated that "tourists" are also seeking some kind of religious experience even though they do not appear to be interested in prayer sessions and Masses.[11]

Four hundred and twenty shrines definitely draw more than 10,000 visits each year. The actual number of shrines with that many or more visits is probably considerably higher. Available visitation figures, conservatively extrapolated and backed up by field observations of pilgrimage events, provide a useful means for estimating the number of religiously motivated visits in late twentieth-century Europe. As illustrated in Table 2-1, the 6,150 inventoried shrines receive a conservative estimate of nearly 70 million pilgrim visits per year.

Total visitation is much higher. Many of the better known shrine churches are visited by large numbers of people who do not come as pilgrims; and at

Table 2-1 *Estimated Number of Shrine Visitations*

Estimated Number of Annual Visits by Pilgrims and Religiously Motivated Travelers[a]	Number of Shrines or Shrine Complexes	Estimated Average Number of Visits per Shrine or Complex	Estimated Number of Visits
4,000,000 or more[b]	2	4,000,000	8,000,000
1,000,000 to 4,000,000	17	1,000,000	17,000,000
400,000 to 1,000,000	26	500,000	13,000,000
100,000 to 400,000[c]	90	150,000	13,500,000
10,000 to 100,000[d]	285	30,000	8,550,000
1,000 to 10,000[e]	1,586	3,000	4,758,000
Less than 1,000	225	500	112,500
No estimates[f]	3,919	500	1,959,000
Total	6,150		66,880,500

[a]Shrine visitation estimates do not take into account routine visits by persons for whom the shrine church may also be a parish church where regular services are attended. Because some shrines are visited by the same pilgrims more than once a year, and long-distance pilgrims may visit many shrines in the course of the journey and be counted at each, these visitation estimates do not represent the number of individuals who make pilgrimages to Europe's shrines annually.

[b]One of these shrines is Lourdes, France. The other is the Rome complex of the four major basilicas—Saint Peter's, Saint John Lateran, Saint Paul's Outside the Walls, and Santa Maria Maggiore. The traditional pilgrimage to the city requires a visit to each. The lower range of this category would be very conservative for Rome because Vatican officials have recorded about a million visitors to Saint Peter's alone during each Easter Week since the 1975 Holy Year.

[c]This number includes several places, such as Le Mont-Saint-Michel and Rocamadour in France, which record approximately half a million visitors annually, but where there is no attempt to distinguish between religiously motivated travelers and secular tourists who are probably more numerous.

[d]Included in this category are 22 places visited by several hundred thousand to several million persons each year, but where shrine officials consider only a small fraction of the visitors to be pilgrims.

[e]When references to visitation included such terms as "vast numbers" or "many thousands," a shrine was included in this category.

[f]The figure for these shrines was extrapolated from observations of pilgrimage events at minor shrines for which no visitation data were available.

some sites, secularly oriented tourists vastly outnumber pilgrims and religiously oriented tourists. London's Westminster Abbey, a Medieval architectural monument that has been an Anglican church since the Reformation, is an example. It is one of London's most important tourist attractions because, according to the dean of Westminster, 4.5 million people visit the abbey each year. Some visitors come on tours sponsored by their Anglican or Catholic parishes. A few hundred make an annual pilgrimage to the tomb of Saint Edward the Confessor, a pious English king who died in 1066. These two types of religiously oriented visitors, however, are far outnumbered by the millions of secularly oriented tourists who swarm through the abbey each year. Similar to the Westminster case, but on a less dramatic scale, the beautiful Romanesque church dedicated to Saint Foy at Conques, France, is visited by more than 100,000 tourists each year although the Medieval pilgrimage to this saint is virtually extinct. Conques qualifies as an active shrine site only because the famous church contains an image of the Virgin Mary that is especially venerated by people from the town and its immediate vicinity. Given the large number of tourists who include these and other shrine churches in their itineraries, it seems likely that total visitation at the shrines of modern Europe exceeds 100 million by a considerable margin.[12]

Major and Minor Shrines

There are several exceptions to the rule, but, in general, shrines that draw their devotees from extensive areas record large numbers of visitors, whereas minor regional and district shrines typically provide more modest visitation estimates. We assigned a top ranking to shrines that recorded at least 100,000 religiously motivated visits per year from nationwide or international areas. Shrines described as the most important pilgrimage place in a large diocese or province, and/or those reporting 10,000 or more pilgrim visits per year, were categorized as major shrines along with great centers of religious tourism that recorded more modest numbers of pilgrim visits. By these criteria, 830 shrines, or about 14 percent of the inventory, were ranked as major pilgrimage centers. Minor shrines were subdivided into those of considerable importance and those of little importance beyond their districts. No information was available on either range of drawing power or annual visitation in about 1,000 cases, so these shrines were assumed to be minor. The distribution of the surveyed shrines along a scale from major to minor is contained in Table 2-2.

As will be discussed in the following chapters, there appear to be relatively

Table 2-2 *Levels of Shrine Importance*

Classification	Number	Percent
Major Shrines		
Rank I[a]	139	2.3
Rank II[b]	691	11.2
Total, major shrines	830	13.5
Minor Shrines		
Rank III[c]	1,247	20.3
Rank IV[d]	4,073	66.2
Total, minor shrines	5,320	86.5
Total, all shrines	6,150	100.0

[a]International, national, or major regional drawing power with at least 100,000 pilgrims per year.

[b]Noted as one of the most important shrines in a geographically extensive region and/or with a drawing power of at least 10,000 pilgrims per year and churches of international fame drawing 100,000 or more visitors per year, but considered to be of relatively minor importance as pilgrimage centers.

[c]Shrines of importance at district or regional levels and/or with at least 1,000 pilgrims per year.

[d]This category includes 2,980 subregional, district, vicinity, and locality shrines with no mention of large numbers of pilgrims, plus 1,093 shrines for which we have too little information to warrant assignment to a higher rank.

few differences between major and minor shrines in terms of such characteristics as the holy persons of primary pilgrim devotion, shrine-formative stories, site feature associations, or other locational variables. Thus, in Europe minor shrines are, to a considerable extent, scaled-down versions of major shrines serving smaller numbers of pilgrims from less extensive areas. In this respect, Christian shrines in Western Europe appear to differ from Hindu pilgrimage centers for which Bhardwaj found numerous aggregate differences in structure.[13]

Shrine Distribution

Famous shrines, which draw large numbers of visitors from extensive regions, are found throughout most of Western Europe. Some of the most important shrine communities are indicated by name on Map 2-1. The 830 shrines identified as major pilgrimage centers are fairly evenly distributed throughout the predominantly Catholic areas of Europe and are

Shrines of Western Europe

Map 2-1 *Selected Shrine Localities*

The 72 places listed on this map have shrines that draw large numbers of pilgrims from extensive areas or are otherwise of considerable importance. At least 830 of Europe's shrines can be considered of major importance in the sense that they receive 10,000 or more pilgrim visits per year and/or are visited by religiously motivated travelers from a sizable region.

represented in Great Britain, the Netherlands, and northern West Germany (Map 2-2). South of the highly secularized and predominantly Protestant Scandinavian countries, few Europeans are very far from a pilgrimage center of considerable importance.

A different view of Western Europe's sacred topography emerges when all inventoried shrines are plotted. Map 2-3 reveals a number of high and low density shrine regions along with extensive areas of fairly even shrine distribution. A relatively even distribution pattern is characteristic of the predominantly Catholic countries of France, Italy, and Spain. The numerous shrines in and near such great urban concentrations as Madrid, Paris, Rome, and Naples show up as clusters of dots on the map. Not all such clusters indicate major cities, however, because several shrines are sometimes located close to each other in smaller towns and predominantly rural areas. This is the case with a concentration of holy places associated with Saint Francis of Assisi in the areas around Rieti and Assisi, Italy. Areas with low shrine density in Catholic countries often coincide with regions of low population density as, for example, in Austria where high alpine regions are sparsely inhabited. The high density of shrines in northwestern Portugal partly reflects population distributions, especially in terms of the lower density of shrines toward the dry, sparsely inhabited eastern margins of the country. However, the phenomenon appears to be largely cultural. Although 95 percent of the Portuguese people are at least nominally Roman Catholic, the northern part of the country is noted for a greater religiosity.

In West Germany, Switzerland, and the Netherlands, marked contrasts are evident between areas of very high shrine density and those with virtually no shrines. These patterns correspond with geographical concentrations of Catholics in some parts of these countries and the presence of strong Protestant influences in others. Similarly, the sparsity of shrines in Britain and Scandinavia reflects the minority position of Roman Catholics there.

The extremely high density of shrines in the predominantly Roman Catholic areas of Germanic Europe is particularly notable. A part of this pattern can be attributed to such factors as good diocesan records, ample funds with which to respond to mail queries, and the existence of unusually comprehensive descriptive publications such as the monumental work by Gustav Gugitz on miraculous places in Austria and a detailed book on Swiss holy places by Rudolf Henggeler.[14] Although we did not inventory the large numbers of sites ranked by these authors as local in visitation, nor the many that were described in past tense or referred to as extinct, descriptive works of this scope inspire additional studies and inform later investigators, thus affecting the

Shrines of Western Europe

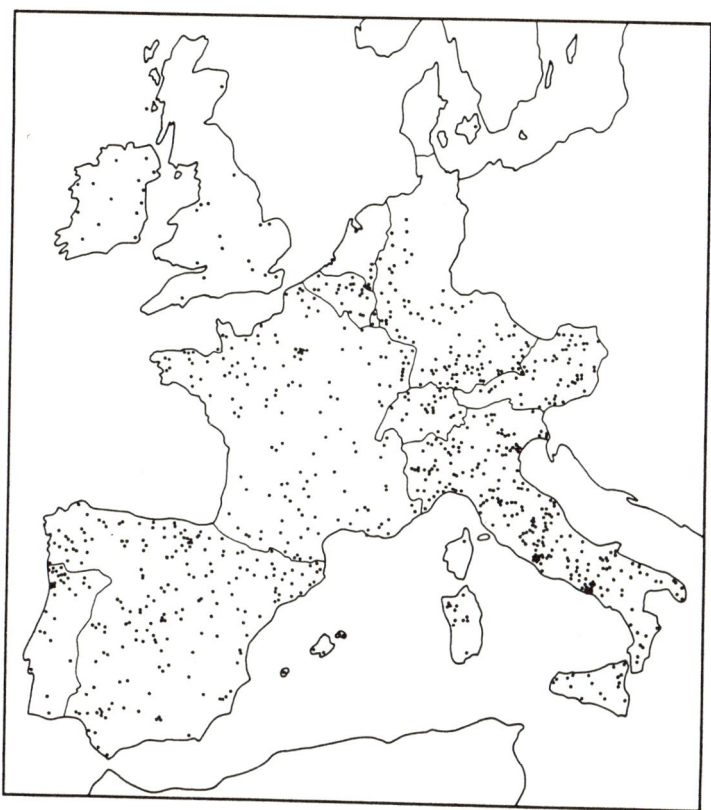

Map 2-2 *Distribution of Major Shrines*
Each dot on this map represents one major shrine. The map was generated by a computer-assisted mapping program and is based on the geographical coordinates for each shrine locality. In cases where a single community has several shrines, the dots were automatically spread over a wider area for ease of interpretation.

overall body of available materials. Such works may also stimulate contemporary pilgrimage activity. The use of the term *Wallfahrtsort* for shrines of all importance levels within Germanic regions may also have resulted in a more comprehensive count of shrines in these areas as compared with the Mediterranean peninsular regions where minor pilgrimages, and, therefore, the places to which the pilgrims go, are described in various ways that do not always translate as "pilgrimage." Certainly, however, pilgrimage is a more important part of life in Catholic Germanic regions than is suggested in most English-language literature on the subject.

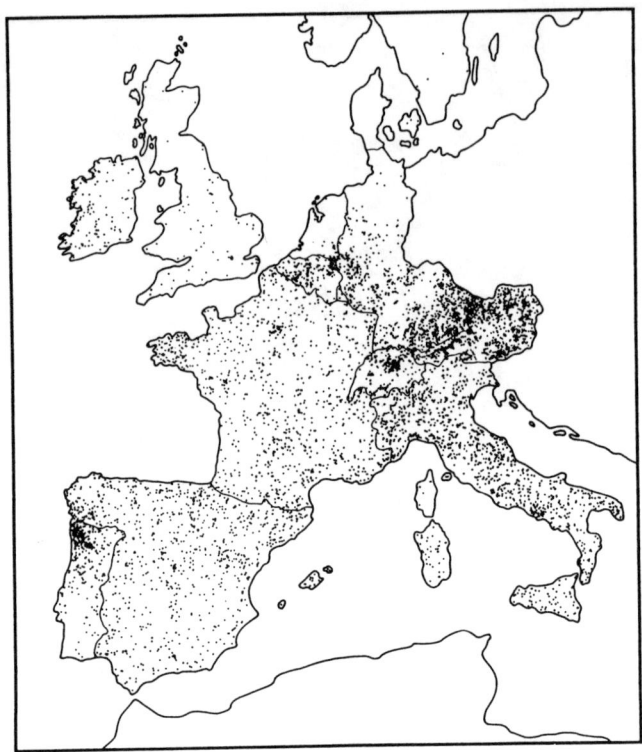

Map 2-3 *Distribution of All Inventoried Shrines*
Each dot on this map represents one shrine. Regions with very great shrine densities are readily apparent and tend to be areas with large numbers of minor shrines.

The high density of shrines in Catholic Germanic regions appears to reflect important cultural differences in orientations toward shrines and pilgrimages coinciding closely with the ancient cultural watershed between Germanic- and Romance-language areas. As is further discussed in Chapter 3, pilgrimage in Mediterranean lands is heavily interlaced with other religious expressions, and pilgrimages there more frequently coincide with secular festivities and fairs. Thus, although Mediterranean Europeans celebrate more special occasions with Masses and processions than is the case in most of the more northerly regions, there is a strong Germanic propensity toward a type of religious behavior specifically conceptualized as pilgrimage. Shrine density in

Shrines of Western Europe

Germanic lands is also related to political conditions in the seventeenth and eighteenth centuries, as will be further discussed in Chapter 4.

Major and Minor Shrine Distribution

Major shrines are proportionately more numerous in Italy, France, and Iberia than in Germanic lands, suggesting that the lack of emphasis on Germanic pilgrimage in most English-language literature may partly result from the relative sparsity of major pilgrimage centers in these lands. A small proportion of important pilgrimage shrines is especially notable in southern Germanic regions where there are many shrines, but few known or visited beyond areas of fairly limited size. Northern Germanic regions including West Germany north of Bavaria and Baden-Württemberg, along with the Netherlands, Luxembourg, and Flemish Belgium, have fewer shrines than most other areas of equal size, but a fairly high proportion of pilgrimage centers identified as major shrines. Most of these, however, draw pilgrims primarily from areas where Germanic languages are spoken and from overseas German communities and missions. In addition, the region includes portions of several countries and is very densely populated so that pilgrimage places drawing from a relatively small area may qualify as internationally visited shrines and have very large visitation counts.

Catholic-to-Shrine Ratios

The number of shrines inventoried in each country ranged from over 1,000 for Italy, France, and Spain to 1 each in Norway and Finland. Differences in numbers of shrines undoubtedly are related to variations between countries in land area and numbers of people, particularly numbers of Roman Catholics. The relationships suggested in Table 2-3 should be interpreted with caution, however, because the inventory may be more comprehensive for some countries than for others. One would not expect to find as many shrines in the relatively small country of Portugal with a population of slightly over 9 million, mostly Catholic, as in the much larger country of Spain with its approximately 37 million people, again mostly Catholic. Similarly, although Austria has only about a million more inhabitants than Switzerland, it is not surprising that more than three times as many shrines were inventoried in Austria than in Switzerland because the former country is not only larger, but also has more than twice as many citizens who are Roman Catholic.

Table 2-3 *Demographics of Inventoried Shrines*

Country	Number of Shrines Inventoried	People per Shrine (thousands)[a]	Catholics per Shrine (thousands)[a]	Square Miles per Shrine
Italy	1,194	47	46	97
France	1,034	51	44	206
Spain	1,014	36	36	192
West Germany	938	66	31	102
Austria	925	8	7	35
Portugal	332	28	26	108
Switzerland	283	23	11	56
Belgium and Luxembourg	151	68	62	84
Republic of Ireland	124	25	24	219
United Kingdom				
England and Wales	80	615	52	729
Scotland	6	867	136	4,967
Northern Ireland	11	140	46	499
Netherlands	48	290	116	262
Sweden	5	1,660	17	34,800
Denmark	3	1,715	9	5,533
Finland	1	4,758	3	130,085
Norway	1	4,082	13	125,032

[a]Based on population data in Felican A. Fay, ed., *1981 Catholic Almanac* (Huntington, Ind.: Our Sunday Visitor).

For Western Europe as a whole, we found an average of 34,000 Catholics per identified shrine. This figure dramatically illustrates the relatively great importance of pilgrimage in Catholic European life as compared with the United States where there are about 250,000 Roman Catholics per pilgrimage center.[15] Within Western Europe, West Germany and Spain are close to the average in Catholic-per-shrine ratios. France and Italy diverge to some extent from the norm in having more Catholics per shrine, while Portugal and Northern Ireland diverge to roughly equal degrees in having fewer than average Catholics per shrine. The ratios for all of these countries, however, lie within 10,000 to 12,000 potential pilgrims of the average.

Countries with relatively few identified shrines in relation to their Roman Catholic populations are Belgium, the Netherlands, and the United Kingdom except for Northern Ireland. These countries have several characteristics in common. They are, for the most part, highly urbanized and have very dense populations. Protestant influences are strong in the Netherlands and the

United Kingdom, although Anglo-Catholic pilgrimages to shrines of traditional saints and to Marian centers, such as Walsingham, have become fairly common in the twentieth century. In the rural areas of Scotland and Wales, numerous holy wells and curious stones are still visited by Catholics and Protestants for quasi-religious purposes that may be described by local people as folk traditions. These places were not included in the inventory except in cases where a formalized pilgrimage has been reestablished.

In the predominantly Protestant Scandinavian countries, where state edicts against practice of the Catholic faith remained in force until the early twentieth century, the few newly established or revitalized shrines serve very small Catholic populations. Finland, for example, has a Catholic population of about 3,200 and one shrine on the island of Koylio where Saint Henrik was murdered. Here, as at several other revitalized shrines in Scandinavia, pilgrim devotions are related to an early saint of national significance. Renewed pilgrimages to these shrines are not exclusively Catholic. High Church Lutheran pilgrimages have been taking place recently in Sweden, especially to the burial place of the Medieval Saint Bridget at Vadstena and to Saint Eric's tomb in the Lutheran Cathedral at Uppsala. Both of these places are also visited by Catholic pilgrims. At Stiklestad near Trondheim, Norway, where Saint Olaf died in battle in 1030 in his attempt to bring Christianity to the Vikings, many Norwegians of all faiths pay tribute to a national hero. An annual Catholic pilgrimage was reestablished here in the 1930s.[16]

Outside of Scandinavia, countries where the number of Catholics per shrine is substantially lower than average include Austria, Switzerland, and the Republic of Ireland. Similar Catholic-to-shrine ratios characterize much of Bavaria and northwestern Portugal. The regions with the greatest shrine density are predominantly rural. Most have extensive areas where small settlements are scattered up and down valleys that are separated from each other by hilly or mountainous terrain, and the majority of shrines are of minor importance. This fits a general model of refuge areas where old patterns have survived in a modern age. There are, however, other factors involved, and, as will be discussed in the next chapter, many minor shrines are experiencing renewed vigor.

three

Pilgrimage in the European Tradition

*A*pilgrimage shrine is defined primarily in terms of sacred qualities believed to be more concentrated there than in other places. This belief is expressed in behavior, and it is essentially the act of pilgrimage that creates a shrine and maintains it as an especially holy place through the generations. There are, however, many different behaviors that fall into the generalized category of religiously motivated journeys to holy places, and a wide variety of opinions exists among clerics and scholars on exactly what range of behavioral patterns should be considered pilgrimages.

Types of Pilgrimages: Individual and Communal

A modern European's concept of pilgrimage has been expressed by the religious scholar, Iso Baumer: "The basic structure of all pilgrimages is the same; an individual or, more often, a group, sets forth on a journey to a chosen place in order to ask God and the Saints—at that particular place—for aid in a variety of concerns. Afterwards, one returns to one's everyday world."[1] There are, however, important variations in the range of activities that fit Baumer's definition. For example, a southern Italian villager who makes a religiously motivated journey to Lourdes, whether alone, with his family, or as a member of a tour group, is doing something quite different from his neighbor who financially supports a local pilgrimage and sometimes symbolically shoulders the burden of the community by carrying the patron saint's image in procession to a holy place near his town.

In the first case, an easily defined journey takes place. The pilgrim leaves familiar surroundings, may suffer hardships, and perhaps finds transcendence in an extraordinary sequence of places and events. Through the act of travel, the pilgrim has, or may have, what anthropologists Victor and Edith Turner refer to as a "liminal," or transitional, experience. It is this kind of action that the Turners describe when they write that the point of pilgrimage "is to get out, go forth, to a far holy place approved by all," and that when the "load [of ordinary life in the home community] can no longer be borne, it is time to take to the road as a pilgrim."[2] This kind of long-distance journey can be traced back to the earliest days of Christendom when the devout, then a persecuted minority in the Roman Empire, traveled quietly and at risk to the Holy Land and to the developing shrines of the apostles and early martyrs.[3]

Deep-rooted European traditions also are expressed by community pilgrimages to regional shrines, sometimes located at nearby political or ecclesiastical centers, or to sacred places in the landscape near the towns and villages. These types of pilgrimage predate Christianity, and some contemporary sites were pagan holy places. Such pilgrimages often take the form of processions that involve the entire community delegation in the act of sacred movement (Figure 3-1). These undertakings may be sufficient in themselves, or they may represent symbolic journeys to more distant and significant Christian holy places. The word *romería*, commonly used in Iberia for festive local and district pilgrimages, implies the idea of making a journey to Rome, just as the Calvary shrines that became common in parts of Europe during the seventeenth century allowed devotees to make a symbolic journey to the Holy Land.

Pilgrims who remain within their ordinary field of circulation may be making such a token journey, but do not truly leave their community because they travel with their neighbors. If the personal motivation for pilgrimage is great, they may create hardships by making part of the journey from home to shrine on their knees or in some other difficult manner. Such actions intensify and personalize symbolic peregrinations, but these pilgrimages are essentially community rather than individual expressions. They serve to break the routine of the annual cycle, but they are as much a regular part of that cycle as planting and harvesting or, for urbanites, the annual vacation.

Numerous variations fill the range between the extremes of individual journeys to distant shrines and communal expressions of devotion represented by group journeys to nearby holy places. These variations involve such factors as shrine importance, the return of emigrants to small villages, reduced friction

Figure 3-1 *Spectacular pilgrimages on horseback take place at numerous shrines in southern West Germany and parts of Austria. One of the most famous is the Weingarten "Blood Ride" held on Ascension Friday. In 1981, 99 communities, each represented by riders and a band, took part in a procession that lasted more than four hours and included approximately 4,000 people and 2,000 horses. The ride at this shrine honors a relic of Christ's Holy Blood obtained by the Weingarten monastery in the eleventh century.*

of distance related to modern transportation, and the importance of mass tourism including religiously oriented tourism (Table 3-1).

Regardless of distance, there is an important difference between pilgrimage perceived as an individual act and pilgrimage undertaken as a corporate enterprise. In the former case, the journey—whether real or symbolic—is made by a particular person who may be seeking health for himself or loved ones, fulfilling a vow made during a time of personal crisis, or responding to a personal need to express thanksgiving or devotion. Although the pilgrim may be (and usually is) accompanied by members of his immediate family or by close friends, the relationship of the pilgrim and the holy person to whom the shrine is dedicated is a highly personal "I/Thou" association (figures 3-2, 3-3). The timing of the journey is not necessarily determined by any special day or activity at the shrine, and the group with which the pilgrim chooses to travel is not directly related to the purpose or meaning of the pilgrimage.

Communal pilgrimage, in contrast, is essentially a "We/Thou" relationship. Health and salvation from catastrophe may lie at its roots, but it is the community rather than the individual that seeks protection or pays homage. Pilgrims approach the shrine in an act of corporate thanks for salvation from plague, war, natural disaster, or as a community act of tribute and devotion. In difficult times they ask for deliverance, not solely as individuals, but for a community which they see as an extension beyond the span of their personal lives. This sense of community underlies many pilgrimages and inspires individual participation even in a modern age.

There are also long-distance pilgrimages in which the devotees travel more as members of a corporate body than as individuals. The pilgrims may represent a particular community such as a diocese, a village, an urban neighborhood, or the congregation of a parish church (Figure 3-4). Each pilgrim may have personal reasons for making the journey, but all share the collective view that their shrine visit will benefit the entire community. For example, participants in the fiftieth anniversary pilgrimage from Liverpool to Lourdes, whom we encountered in 1980, said that the primary purpose of their journey was to affirm a special relationship between their English city and the French shrine, although some individuals in the group expressed personal reasons for joining that particular annual delegation.

Another type of pilgrimage group is composed of the members of a brotherhood or a pilgrimage association. These people may be, and often are, neighbors in a spatially defined community, but the pilgrim group is defined in terms of organizational membership rather than the community as a whole. In Assisi, Italy, we shared accommodations with members of a French pilgrimage association. These people from suburban Paris had prepared for their tour of holy places associated with Saint Francis of Assisi by attending weekly meetings over a two-year period. The sessions involved lectures and discussions of readings on the saint's life and teachings. During their pilgrimage, group members traveled in a caravan of private automobiles, shared evening accommodations, and worked together to prepare meals. Each morning of the journey began with prayer and song accompanied by tape-recorded music. The enthusiasm of this intellectually oriented, generally well-educated group extended beyond a shared devotion to Saint Francis toward a feeling of unity with other members of the pilgrimage association. Their pilgrimage was a climax of interpersonal communion as well as a reward for two years of devotional preparation.

Table 3-1 *Types of Contemporary Pilgrimage*

Shrine Importance	Distance Traveled	Traveling Group
International, National, or Major Regional	Long distance. Hundreds to thousands of miles beyond pilgrim's ordinary range of circulation.	Individuals, often with kinsmen or friends.
		Groups from the same community (town, parish, organization members).
		Package tour groups.
Minor Regional or District	Medium distance. Ten to 100 miles. Generally somewhat beyond pilgrim's normal range of circulation or toward its margin.	Individuals, families, groups of friends.
		Community and organizational groups.
Local or Immediate Vicinity	Short distance. Within about 10 miles of home. Well within the normal field of circulation, but sometimes to place not regularly visited.	Local individuals
		Tourists visiting area
		Emigrants visiting hometown
		Community members

Participants on a religious tour make up a third type of group frequently encountered at European pilgrimage centers. Such tour groups are usually ad hoc composites of travelers with specific interests. Just as pilgrims in the Middle Ages sought protection in each other's company, so modern pilgrims seek the convenience and cost advantages of traveling together as members of a packaged tour. It may be an expensive air tour from the Americas, a hospital train from Denmark, or a West German package involving travel by bus and nights at campgrounds sleeping in accompanying dormitory trailers. Tour groups may be made up of people who had never previously met or of people largely collected from the same town or parish. Some of these travel packages are conceptualized, or at least promoted, as pilgrimages whereas others are viewed only as religiously oriented tours.

Motive for Trip	Seasonality	Processions
Personal. Highly varied. Vows, search for aid, to pay respects.	Any time of year; may be at a special time.	May take part in processions organized at the shrine.
Largely to pay respects/ promote group solidarity.	Likely to be at a special time of year.	Processions from transport stop to shrine are common.
Varied. May be largely recreational.	Likely to be any time of year.	May take part in processions organized at shrine.
Personal, highly varied.	Any time, although often at a special time.	Unlikely
To pay respects, honor community vows, promote group solidarity.	Usually at a special time.	Likely
Personal, varied	Anytime	No
To watch	Special time	Participation as spectators
To renew ties, visit kinsmen. Vows.	On arrival and at special times.	Likely to participate
To pay respects, honor community vows; promote group solidarity.	Special occasions	Pilgrimage likely to take the form of a procession, pardons, romerías, rogations, etc.

Many shrines are visited by pilgrims who travel as individuals as well as by those who arrive as members of corporate groups. Some shrines, however, tend to emphasize one end of the spectrum. Many minor shrines, especially in southern Europe, are rarely visited except by community groups on special days of pilgrimage. In Germanic lands, however, numerous small shrine chapels in remote areas remain open throughout the year and are frequently visited by individuals and small family groups. Unless they are also the settings for group pilgrimages, such places are difficult to distinguish from other small country chapels and there is not always a consensus as to which should be considered pilgrimage places. The handbook of the Diocese of Speyer, West Germany, for example, lists the Maria Herzeleid chapel, located on a hill overlooking the town of Hauenstein, as a *Wallfahrtskapelle*, or pilgrimage

Figure 3-2 *At Fátima, Portugal, a pilgrim accompanied by her family approaches the site where three shepherd children reported visions of the Virgin Mary in 1917.*

chapel. The local priest, however, wrote that the place was only a "prayer chapel" and had never been a pilgrimage center. The caretaker, who was cleaning the chapel when we arrived on a windy March day in 1981, first told us that the chapel was not a place of pilgrimage. Then she decided that maybe it was for some people. Certainly it was well maintained and often used. Fresh flowers and many candles surrounded an old, very worn natural wood image of the Virgin Mary with the dead Christ. According to diocesan information and the caretaker, it is considered miraculous.

Strictly individual pilgrimage often marks the declining stage in the life cycle of a shrine. This happens when special personal and family devotions linger for years after community pilgrimages cease.

Pilgrimage and Religious Tourism

Many shrines attract large numbers of people who visit for reasons having little to do with traditional expressions of pilgrimage. As expressed by Monsignor André Lefèuvre of the Pontifical Commission on the

Figure 3-3 *A German pilgrim at Altötting, West Germany, fulfills her vow to carry a cross several times around the chapel containing a dark image of the Madonna that has been considered miraculous since 1489. The paintings on the chapel walls provide graphic documentation of miracles attributed to the intercession of Our Lady of Altötting.*

Pastoral Care of Migrants and Tourists, people who visit sanctuaries today have many different motivations, "and it would be rash, indeed erroneous, to attach the label of 'pilgrim' indiscriminately to all of them."[4] European churchmen frequently use the phrase "religious tourism" as a way of discussing the prospects and problems offered by the large numbers of people who visit the subcontinent's pilgrimage shrines and other religious attractions. The term has fewer theological and traditional implications than the word "pilgrimage" and encompasses a broader range of motivations for visiting places associated with religious history, art, and devotion. Use of the term also has a kind of neutrality, avoiding implications that pilgrims are somehow better than tourists, for, as shrine administrators sometimes point out, it is entirely possible for a visitor to come as a casual tourist and, because of emotions experienced at the shrine, return for another visit as a pilgrim.

Figure 3-4 *Members of the delegation from Boston, Massachusetts, arrive at Knock, Ireland, to represent the archdiocese at the 1979 centenary of the Knock shrine, established as a result of visions of Mary and several saints reported by villagers in 1879. This shrine, which now draws approximately a million pilgrims per year, is understandably popular with Irish-Americans.*

Among the mix of travelers who might be found at a famous shrine on any summer day, some may be pilgrims in the traditional sense. They have come to pay their respects, give thanks for favors granted, or seek divine assistance. Others are members of packaged religious tours that focus on places with religious associations and are often accompanied by a member of the clergy. Still others are merely vacationers seeing the sights, which in Europe inevitably include places of both historic and religious significance in Christendom. Some of these visitors are heirs of religious traditions other than Christianity, and many are Protestants with little personal awareness of pilgrimage as a part of their religious backgrounds. Thus, busloads of tourists from Japan, the Islamic world, and the bastions of American and northwestern European Protestantism periodically inundate the shrine cathedrals of Chartres, Notre-Dame de Paris, and Cologne and the great monastic shrines such as Ettal and

Kloster Andechs in Bavaria, Heiligenkreuz in the Vienna Woods, or Italy's Montecassino.

From the perspective of clerics with the responsibility for providing pastoral care at historically or architecturally significant pilgrimage centers, the variety of visitor motivations provides some difficult challenges. As the Vatican official, Monsignor Lefèuvre, views the problem, a distinction should be made between pilgrims and religious and secular tourists on the grounds that differently motivated visitors have different needs. Nevertheless, he feels that all should sense the sacredness of the place. There are, he argues, important values in a tourism that brings people to holy places because of their interest in art and history rather than religion. In his words, "Beauty, art, the rediscovery of a need for lyricism through its sensible expression are an opening to the sacred, a reflection of the God they are groping towards! History, the revived consciousness of their belonging to the life of a people, the memory of a past which continues to exist in the present, but still more, an opening to the sacred, the sign and witness of God's design which is embodied and manifested in it, transforming it into sacred history! The stones speak."[5]

The monsignor's message reaches beyond narrow definitions of pilgrimage toward a meaning of sanctity in place which can be shared by people of many religious persuasions, as well as those who do not identify with formal religious systems. For example, at Saint Benedict's first monastery of Subiaco east of Rome a monk told us about a Japanese architectural student of Buddhist background who spent two years detailing every feature of the ancient monastic buildings. The oriental scholar's love for his work, and the sensitivity with which he touched stones that must have been speaking to him from an ancient time in a different cultural tradition, convinced the monk that this man was among the most genuine pilgrims to visit Subiaco in decades.

The monastic complex of Subiaco primarily attracts visitors interested in the evolution of Western art and the history of Western monasticism, although a few people leave silver hearts and other offerings of the kind often displayed at shrines where miracles are expected to happen. These are something of an embarrassment to the resident monks who prefer to think of their ancient monastery as a haven of meditation and a site of great historical and artistic significance rather than a place of miraculous cures. The unrequested ex-votos are kept in the vestry, perhaps to remind the monks that Benedict, the founder of Western monasticism, is a saint, and that one cannot deny the possibility of miracles associated with an important place in his lifework.

In northern Portugal, however, numerous statues of Saint Benedict are considered miraculous. Carried in processions on days of pilgrimage, these effigies are decked with offerings of money and are followed by devotees carrying wax replicas of body parts or narrow wax tapers the length and width of their bodies (Figure 3-5). Such a procession may wind through a bustling market where vendors of food, drink, and assorted items ranging from live chickens to plastic toys do a brisk business. The blare of rock music advertising cassette tapes for sale may compete with the staccato beats of a Boy Scout drum corps leading the procession. Dancing and general revelry continue long into the night until the festivities end in a brilliant display of fireworks. The miraculous statues that are the focal points of the devotions and festivities are not great works of art, and generally they are housed in architecturally unremarkable churches. In contrast to Subiaco, tourists and folklorists are attracted to the Portuguese shrines by the festivities, not the churches.

The difference between the Subiaco monastery and a Portuguese São Bento romería site, such as Sexias, Ermelo, or the crossroads hamlet of São Bento de Porto Aberto, is substantial. In terms of the model presented in Chapter 2, Subiaco lies on the margin between pilgrimage shrines per se and historical-religious tourist attractions that are not generally thought of as pilgrimage centers. The Portuguese village church of Sexias lies on the border between a pilgrimage shrine and the site of a religious festival. In their varied ways, however, both Subiaco and Sexias can be considered centers of pilgrimage because they are goals of religiously motivated journeys related to special devotions which draw adherents to particular places. Both also represent places where the sacred and the secular are so intertwined that it is difficult to specify just how much visitation is specifically religious in nature.

The Sacred-Secular Mix

The mixtures of sacred and profane that characterize many European celebrations make it impossible to separate pilgrimages from other activities by virtue of exclusiveness or intensity of religious behavior. Pilgrimage events range from starkly serious occasions to near-riotous explosions of human activity during which carnival rides stop for no more than the five minutes it takes for the honored saint's image or relic to pass by their immediate location along a procession route (Figure 3-6). The same range of behavioral variation characterizes holy day observations held at places other than pilgrimage shrines. Often the most extreme manifestations of religious behavior occur at the very places where profane activities such as getting drunk, having fights, and flirting with members of the opposite sex are simul-

Pilgrimage in the European Tradition

Figure 3-5 *This wonder-working statue of Saint Benedict (São Bento in Portuguese) is carried in an annual pilgrim's procession at Sexias, a town on the south bank of the Minho River which forms the northern boundary of Portugal with Spain. One of the long candles typically carried by pilgrims in this region can be seen on the right.*

Figure 3-6 *Carnival thrills and intense expressions of religious devotion occur simultaneously during the July Romería of São Torcato near Guimarães in northern Portugal. This festive pilgrimage honors a saint believed to have been a companion of Saint James the Greater during the apostle's legendary mission work in first-century Iberia. The discovery of Saint Torcato's incorrupt (mummified) body in the late eighth century preceded the discovery of bones claimed to be those of Saint James (Santiago) in nearby Galicia.*

taneously taking place. Nor does there appear to be any particular link between events that are devotionally somber to the point of penitential boredom and the degrees of religiosity expressed or felt by the participants.

Major events at great pilgrimage shrines combined devotional, commercial, and recreational activities during the Middle Ages. Pilgrimages with strong festive and/or folkloric dimensions are still found throughout much of Europe, although they are most prevalent in the Mediterranean peninsular countries. In more northerly regions there is a greater tendency to separate religious and secular celebrations. West German, Austrian, and French communities sometimes hold civic or folkloric festivals concurrently with the main week of pilgrimage at a nearby shrine while maintaining a definite spatial and social-psychological distance between the two sets of activities.

Individuals move back and forth between the event settings but are reminded that they should shift from secular to religious behaviors and attitudes. In other cases, communities celebrate well-publicized secular festivals at one time of year and unadvertised pilgrimages on a different date, thus separating the sacred and the profane in time as well as space.

A list of festivals compiled by the Portuguese National Tourist Office in which events are categorized by type and degree of religiosity provides insights into the southern European tradition (Table 3-2). Pilgrimages and romerías comprised about 25 percent of the 597 events listed for July, August, and September 1981. Romerías were somewhat more likely to be considered strictly or essentially religious than were festas without romerías, but a substantial majority of both combined sacred and profane activities. No romerías were described as purely secular, and only 18 festas were classified as having no religious implications. Fairs were more likely to be secular, and all expositions and folkloric festivals fell into that category. Although only 48 of the events were described as exclusively or primarily religious, nearly three-quarters had a religious dimension.

The level of association between religion and festive special events in Portugal is high for modern Europe, as indicated by a comparison of the Portuguese data with a classification of events presumed to be of touristic interest on Spanish, French, and West German event lists. Whereas 72 percent of the Portuguese celebrations and 67 percent of the Spanish events had some kind of religious connotations, this was true of only 41 percent of the French events. The West German list emphasized secular occasions; only 16 percent, including such affairs as Christmas markets and sacred music concerts at abbeys and cathedrals, had any religious significance. The proportion of religiously associated events, which were described as pilgrimages or romerías, was about the same for Portugal (36 percent) and France (33 percent), and somewhat lower for Spain (26 percent). In West Germany, however, only 5 percent of the small number of religiously related events were described as pilgrimages.[6]

In order to provide a more comprehensive overview, we categorized 650 events in study area countries that were described in a secularly oriented guide to European festivals.[7] Eighty-three percent of the events described for Portugal had a religious dimension, as was the case for well over one-half of the events described in Spain and Italy. More than one-third of the French, Belgian, and Austrian events had religious connotations, followed by West Germany at 23 percent of the events, Switzerland at 18 percent, and Ireland at 14 percent. Only 10 to 12 percent of the events listed for the predomi-

Table 3-2 *Religiosity of Special Events in Portugal*

Degree of Religiosity for Each Event	Pilgrimages and Romerías	Festas	Fairs	Expositions	Total
Strictly religious	8 (5%)	4 (2%)	0	0	12
Essentially religious	17 (11%)	19 (8%)	0	0	36
Religious/ profane mix	129 (84%)	191 (82%)	59 (30%)	0	379
Secular	0	18 (8%)	135 (70%)	17 (100%)	170
Total	154 (100%)	232 (100%)	194 (100%)	17 (100%)	597

nantly Protestant countries of the United Kingdom, Scandinavia, and the Netherlands had any association with religious traditions.

Religious celebrations described as pilgrimages and romerías made up nearly one-quarter of the Portuguese and Italian events and were fairly important among events listed for Spain (15 percent), France (12 percent), and Belgium (9 percent). The proportion of pilgrimages dropped to 7 percent in Austria, 4 percent in West Germany, and 0 percent in Switzerland. Ireland's Catholic heritage was reflected in a description of the famous Croagh Patrick pilgrimage, which, like most Irish pilgrimages, is not especially festive.[8] The lack of pilgrimages among events listed for lands where Protestants are in the majority is not especially surprising. Far more interesting is the additional evidence of a Germanic tendency not to promote pilgrimages as tourist attractions.

The Roman Catholic parts of Western Europe's Germanic countries have very high densities of shrines and are characterized by numerous pilgrimage events. The relative lack of touristic emphasis on pilgrimage has a twofold explanation. First, most Germanic pilgrimages, as well as many in France, are quiet affairs with little pageantry or folkloric display. A special pilgrim's mass featuring a homily by the abbot of a nearby monastery or a lecture by a renowned theology professor from a university has relatively small value for attracting tourists, even when followed by an afternoon organ concert. Second, many events at West German, Austrian, and Swiss shrines that do involve processions in traditional costume or other colorful displays of potential touristic interest are not advertised as attractions. In some cases, any publicity that might draw onlookers, whether from abroad or from a nearby city, is deliberately avoided. Sometimes processions are not even announced in the weekly bulletin of the shrine church. As a consequence, such pilgrimages are not listed by national or regional tourism agencies and are virtually unknown except to the participants, their friends and kinsmen, and the people of the immediate shrine vicinity.

Several unpublicized pilgrimages, which feature splendid folklore displays, occur each year at shrines in the Bavarian alpine area south of Munich. One, which we were invited to attend by the local priest, involved a procession of approximately 2,000 traditionally dressed pilgrims from 32 neighboring communities (Figure 3-7). The procession was followed by an open-air Mass. There were no on-site festivities before or after the event. A few dozen pilgrims stayed in the hamlet long enough to drink a beer at one of the two local inns, but most left immediately after the Mass. The costume display featured many well-preserved antique garments, and some of the jewelry was probably several hundred years old. Each village was marked by slight differences in dress, and there were different costumes for each age and sex group within the communities. The spectacle of this multitude of beautifully dressed Bavarians carrying community banners uphill to the shrine had obvious tourist attraction value, especially for folklore enthusiasts.

The reason for the lack of publicity was obvious. The pilgrimage takes place annually on a South German religious holiday when most business establishments are closed, and the shrine hamlet is less than an hour's drive from the city of Munich. Far too many pilgrims came in procession to be accommodated in the small pilgrimage church, and there was barely room for the 2,000 marchers and the additional worshipers at the adjacent site of the outdoor Mass. As it was, many people could not see the altar and could follow the service only because of a public address system. Clearly, this pilgrimage would be vulnerable to total inundation by genuinely religious Munich citizens on a devotionally appropriate holiday outing if it were publicized.

Promotion of this colorful, but exclusively religious event as a tourist attraction probably would result in major modifications such as those that appear to be affecting the extensively advertised pardons of Brittany in France. Many Breton pardon journeys from towns and villages to shrines, including the July 26 pilgrimage at Sainte-Anne-d'Auray, have been replaced by short processions on the shrine grounds with participants in ordinary, modern clothes. In other cases, processions have been given up entirely, and, as in many Germanic areas, the pilgrims arrive by car or tour bus, attend Mass, and leave. Some small pardons have died out entirely under the impact of over-promotion, while others have lost most of their religious meaning and

Figure 3-7 *Village pilgrims in Bavaria, West Germany. Pilgrimages characterized by beautiful displays of traditional dress are often completely unpublicized in southern West Germany, Austria, and Switzerland.*

have become largely secularized folkloric festivals for the participants as well as the onlookers. The nonpromotional solution, fairly common in Germanic alpine areas, also appears to be making an appearance in Brittany and other parts of France.

These and other responses to what anthropologist Davydd Greenwood refers to as the "commodization of culture"[9] suggest that relatively small festive and/or folkloric pilgrimages are especially vulnerable to promotion as folkloric events in the interest of encouraging mass tourism. Larger shrines generally have more resources for sponsoring a series of events to meet diverse visitor expectations. They are better equipped to provide interpretive programs which educate tourists as to the religious significance of the place, and the site is more likely to be designed to accommodate large crowds. In addition, administrators at major shrines have long had to deal with cultural diversity, including a large variety of specific reasons for visitation. This knowledge is passed on through generations of persons responsible for the shrine, and disruptive effects stemming from sudden "discovery" of the place by promoters of the mass tourism industry is less likely than is the case at minor shrines traditionally visited from a small, fairly homogeneous area.

The Annual Cycle

Because of its strong event focus, European pilgrimage activity is highly seasonal. Numerous minor pilgrimage chapels stand locked and seemingly abandoned most of the time. Their significance becomes evident only once or twice each year when devotees traveling some distance by automobile and bus join pilgrims walking in procession from nearby communities. A day or two later, little remains to recall the convergence of the faithful except some shreds of paper decorations or a tattered poster advertising the event. Many important regional and international shrines are scenes of season-long or year-round visitation, but even the great shrines usually have special pilgrimages highlighted by intense activity and larger-than-usual crowds of devotees and onlookers. Viewed collectively, the dates of primarily pilgrimage celebrations display a pattern of pilgrimage seasonality that varies in intensity from month to month, with a particular concentration in frequency of events during the warmer periods of the year.[10]

The fourteenth-century English poet, Geoffrey Chaucer, expressed the seasonal nature of pilgrimage to the holy shrines of Europe in the opening lines of *The Canterbury Tales*:

> When April with its gentle showers has pierced the March drought to the root and bathed every plant in the moisture which will hasten the flowering; when Zephyrus with his sweet breath has stirred the new shoots in every wood and field, and the young sun has run its half-course in the Ram, and small birds sing melodiously, so touched in their hearts by Nature that they sleep all night with open eyes—then folks long to go on pilgrimages, and palmers to visit foreign shores and distant shrines in various lands.[11]

Chaucer's emphasis on April may reflect earlier starting dates for pilgrim journeys in the Middle Ages, or even a bit of poetic license. At present, the spring peak of pilgrimage comes in May, and more pilgrimages take place in the late summer and early fall than during the spring. Pilgrimages, of course, require some time for the journey as well as participation in events at the shrine goal. Modern pilgrimage events have different durations. Many last only for a day or a weekend. Others take place throughout a novena, a nine-day devotional period which usually ends with a special celebration that draws the greatest numbers of visitors. At some shrines, intense special activities take place for an entire month, as at Italy's Incoronata shrine where pilgrimages occur all during May. A few shrines sponsor so many special events of approximately equal importance throughout the year, or the warm season, that their celebrations provide no highly specific insights into the seasonality of pilgrimage.

Functionality of Event Focus

Shrines that serve a series of villages in rural districts generally celebrate only one special day or week of pilgrimage each year. The stress on a single pilgrimage time serves important social functions at such shrines by drawing together the people of several nearby communities in an emotionally charged display of common cause. As is also true for local or vicinity-wide religious festivals, celebrations at shrines with a small range of drawing power affirm the essential unity of the town and its hinterland or the communities of the district. A single time of pilgrimage, especially if it corresponds with a vacation or holiday period, also offers an opportunity for the widely scattered offspring of the shrine region to return home at the same time. Thus, urbanites and workers in foreign places mingle not only with the folks at home but also with each other. Contacts, friendships, and marriages result from these periodic reunions and serve to perpetuate a sense of place and communal roots in an increasingly urban world.

The focus on visitation during a single time of year also serves as a way of setting the local or district shrine apart as a special destination. At some shrines greater emphasis is placed on a special date and event than on the place itself. In such cases, the shrine takes on its strongest character as a special holy place during the days of pilgrimage. At certain holy wells in Ireland the curative waters are thought to be effective only at one time of year, indeed often a particular day and sometimes an hour.[12] Although some small shrine chapels draw individual devotees year-round, others are rarely visited except during a pilgrimage event when groups come from one or several communities. Individual visitation tends to be especially discouraged if the chapel is locked except on these special occasions. The most obvious reason for keeping such structures closed is to discourage vandalism or theft at sites where no caretaker is available. In some cases, however, local people explain that no one ever visits the chapel except during pilgrimage days so there is no need to keep it open. Although no special rule of avoidance was articulated, if the shrine is only visited during a time of pilgrimage, then it lies outside the regular circulation field of its devotees even though it may be quite nearby in terms of physical space. This, in turn, would tend to increase the sense of periodic pilgrimages as true journeys beyond the bounds of the mundane world.

Important shrines, which draw pilgrims from extensive regions, are more likely to be visited on a year-round basis or throughout the warm season. Even the major shrines, however, usually focus on one or a few special dates when visitation peaks to extraordinary highs. These occasions are important for the maintenance of pilgrimage cultus that thrives on the experience derived from being caught up in mass celebration. However, visitation peaking creates much the same problems at pilgrimage centers as at secular tourist destinations.[13] If there are enough accommodations for visitors during one or two great celebrations, then there are bound to be facilities little used during the rest of the year. Labor shortages at one period give way to times of slack employment during other seasons. Thus, administrative goals at some of the major shrines are directed toward spreading visitation through much of the year for the benefit of both shrine and community, as well as for the convenience of pilgrims whose travel plans are dictated by work and school vacation periods. At important shrines, events are often scheduled at intervals throughout the season or the year and many pilgrimage tour operators prefer to schedule arrivals during times of relatively light visitation when accommodations are not a major problem.

Some shrines have special days of pilgrimage for people from different communities or nations. A Saint Roch shrine on a hill overlooking the town of Bingen, West Germany, for example, celebrates religious and secular events during a nine-day period in August, and pilgrims from the various towns and urban neighborhoods in the region come on different days of the novena period. At the great French shrine of Lourdes, the character of the town changes in late July when trainloads of pilgrims from the Naples area leave and are replaced by busloads of the faithful from Belgian and English cities.

Patterns of Seasonality

Not a week passes without some kind of pilgrimage taking place somewhere in Europe, and at least 200 different dates serve as annual focal points for pilgrimage events. In general, however, pilgrimage celebrations tend to be concentrated at specific times of the year. A majority of special events at European shrines are celebrated within a week of six holy days, and most of these events are directly related to the symbolism of the feast days involved. These include the movable spring feasts of Easter, Ascension, and Pentecost, and the celebrations of the Virgin Mary's Nativity on September 8, her Assumption into heaven on August 15, and her Visitation, or visit with Elizabeth, on July 2. In contrast, relatively few pilgrimages are celebrated on or near Christmas Day, during Lent, or at the times of year devoted to three of the five traditional major feasts of the Virgin. These are the Purification, now celebrated as the Presentation on February 2, the Annunciation on March 25, and the Immaculate Conception on December 8. Thus, the warm season bias of pilgrimage seasonality is obviously not directly related to the times of highly important religious celebrations.

Months provide the most practical unit for general comparisons of seasonality, although interpretations are complicated by the fact that more than one-third of the spring pilgrimages are held on movable feast days that take place in different months depending on the date of Easter. Of the months from March through May, only May has a substantial number of fixed-date pilgrimage events. In accordance with a lunar calendar, Easter can fall on any Sunday between March 22 and April 25. Three of the possible variations in the annual cycle are evident in Figure 3-8. When Easter is celebrated in March, which happens about 23 percent of the time, this month is an important time for shrine celebrations.[14] In these years there are few pilgrimages in either April or June. If Easter is assigned the date of April 8 at the midpoint of the Paschal cycle, Palm Sunday and Holy Week celebrations take place in April as do the pilgrimages on Low Sunday after Easter. In such years, pilgrimage celebrations traditionally scheduled on Ascension Day, 40 days after Easter, and Pentecost or Whitsunday, 50 days after Easter, take place in May. When Easter is celebrated on or after April 6, the pilgrimages of the Trinity feast day, on the Sunday after Pentecost, take place in June. The relatively few Corpus Christi pilgrimages, generally celebrated in Europe on the Thursday after Trinity Sunday, occur in June whenever Easter comes on April 2 or later. When Easter falls very early in April, Palm Sunday and most Holy Week pilgrimages actually take place in March.

A third type of cycle occurs when Easter is celebrated between April 13 and April 22. In these years, the numerous pilgrimages of Pentecost take place in early June, giving this month nearly as high a proportion of pilgrimage celebrations as May. June becomes even more important as a pilgrimage month on the rare occasions when Easter falls on April 23, 24, or 25, because

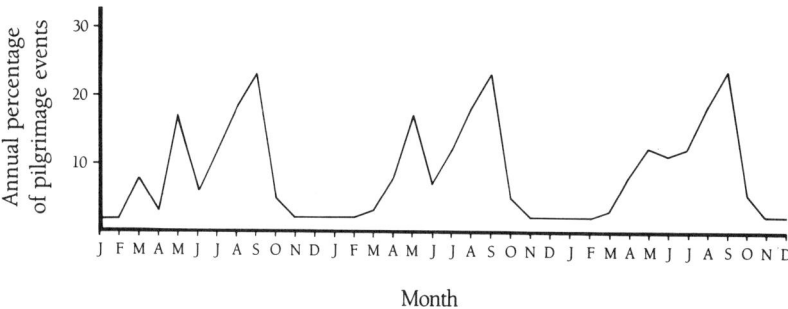

Figure 3-8 *Patterns of pilgrimage seasonality in various years depending on the date of Easter.*

in these years Ascension Day pilgrimages are also celebrated in June. Easter falls on April 13 or later about one-third of the time; thus, on the average of one year out of three, pilgrimages are fairly numerous during the early part of June. From July on, most dates or weeks of pilgrimage show no change from one year to the next except for the variations that occur from celebrating main events on the Sunday before, the Sunday after, or the Sunday nearest the traditional pilgrimage day.

The most obvious feature of pilgrimage seasonality in any year is the concentration of activity in the warm months of late spring, summer, and early fall. Many important, but remote countryside shrines are inactive throughout the winter and in some cases the roads are closed once the snows begin. Even when shrines remain open through the winter, the colder months are usually times of individual pilgrim visits. Although there are some winter pilgrimages, these events are most often celebrated at shrines located in or near population centers. For example, approximately 57 percent of the January pilgrimages are made to shrines in or on the outskirts of cities with populations of more than 25,000. In contrast, only 38 percent of the far more numerous September pilgrimages are made to shrines located in or on the outskirts of cities. Similarly, 54 percent of the January pilgrimages are made to shrines located within the confines of settlements as compared with only 36 percent of September pilgrimages.[15]

The simplest explanation for the seasonal pattern is that pilgrimage is an essentially outdoor activity, best undertaken in warm weather. Whether pilgrimage involves a long journey to a distant shrine or a procession to a nearby hill-top chapel, summer is better suited than winter in all but the southernmost parts of the subcontinent. However, the pattern is not quite so easily explained. June marks a decided low point during the warm season about two-thirds of the time; and although July is as satisfactory in terms of weather as August and September, it is less important as a month for pilgrimages. Throughout much of Western Europe, October weather is not unreasonably intemperate, yet pilgrimage activity shows a dramatic decline in that month.

Pilgrimage and the Liturgical Year

The warm season concentration of pilgrimage events takes on a different kind of significance when the pilgrimage year is compared with the emotional highlights of the "temporal" liturgical year. This temporal year consists of a series of feasts and seasons celebrated by the Roman Catholic church in honor of events related to the life of Christ. The temporal cycle overlaps with the sacred cycle of feast days dedicated to the saints and the Virgin Mary, but this cycle is generally considered less important.[16] Christmas and Easter can be thought of as the most emotionally charged periods of the temporal year throughout Europe. The Christmas season begins with Advent in late November or early December and lasts until the day after Epiphany on January 6. Carnival celebrations, which technically begin in early winter, are usually well under way by mid-January. Thus, the Carnival period corresponds with one of the two "neutral" or "ordinary" periods of the temporal liturgical year. These celebrations, important throughout Catholic Europe, have strong pagan undercurrents, but are immediately followed by the fasting and penitence beginning on Ash Wednesday and lasting though the 40 days of Lent in preparation for Easter.

The Paschal, or Easter, cycle of the temporal liturgical year begins with Ash Wednesday, continues though Holy Week and Easter Day, and ends on the day after Pentecost. The first part of the Lenten period is not an important time for pilgrimage in Western Europe, but activity increases considerably during Holy Week. The famous penitential processions of Spain and Italy customarily take place on Good Friday, although these events are not ordinarily considered pilgrimages by Europeans unless they are specifically related to a pilgrimage center (Figure 3-9). Low Sunday is a popular time for pilgrimage events, as are Ascension Day, Pentecost, and the days immediately before and after these feasts.

The year's longer "neutral" period begins after Pentecost and lasts until Advent. August and September, which lie midway between the end of the

Pilgrimage in the European Tradition

Figure 3-9 *Penitential processions, such as this one at Assisi, Italy, take place on Good Friday in many Italian and Spanish communities. Only a minority of these events are conceptualized as pilgrimages.*

Paschal cycle and the beginning of the Christmas cycle, can be conceptualized as a kind of psychological low point in the temporal liturgical year. The experiences of Holy Week have faded into memory and Christmas is far in the future. Thus, the numerous pilgrimages of August and September tend to fill a gap in the liturgical year by providing an emotionally charged religious activity during the midpoint of a season not characterized by major feasts related to the life of Christ.

The long neutral period is also characterized by two months that are low points in both the temporal liturgical year and the annual pilgrimage cycle. Two-thirds of the time, June marks a low point in the emotional pitch of both the temporal liturgical year and the pilgrimage year. This is always the case with October, although increasing numbers of shrines are promoting rosary or Fátima day pilgrimages in the early part of the month. It is, therefore, interesting that Mid-Summer's Eve in late June and All Souls' Eve in the last part of October are both occasions when folklore allows the demigods of smothered paganism to ride abroad in their post-Christian interpretations as witches and demons. Carnival, with its pagan overtones, takes place during the winter neutral period, further adding to the suggestive nature of an apparent relationship between ancient expressions and low points in both the liturgical and pilgrimage cycles.

The gap-filling functions of Europe's pilgrimage cycle, however, do not adequately account for the seasonal patterns. If that were the case, then August and September pilgrimages should be proportionately numerous throughout the Christian world, even in regions with very different climates and agricultural cycles. Data from tropical and subequatorial temperate zones in Latin America suggest that climatic factors are a more important determinant of seasonality than the social-psychological functions of late summer pilgrimage in the Christian tradition. For Latin America as a whole, December is the peak month of pilgrimage. Lenten pilgrimages are numerous, and the major celebration at subsidiary Lourdes shrines usually takes place on the February holy day celebration of the Lourdes apparitions rather than in August as is the case at Lourdes, France, and at most of Europe's subsidiary shrines. In tropical regions there appears to be little of the seasonal concentration of events that characterizes Europe. Some months have more pilgrimages than do others, but the pattern fluctuates throughout the year. In southern South America, where warm and cold seasons are reversed from what is found in Europe, there is a slight concentration of pilgrimage events during the warmer months of November through March.[17]

Regional Variations in Pilgrimage Seasonality

Additional complexities are introduced by noting that seasonal patterns of pilgrimage vary substantially within Europe. Comparisons can be made by fixing the date of Easter on April 8, reflecting a monthly seasonality of spring pilgrimage that occurs about half of the time. In French-speaking lands, August and September have by far the greatest number of pilgrimage events. Although May is the most important spring month, it is much less frequently a time for pilgrimage than late summer and early fall. Neither June nor July is especially important. Activity in Italy also peaks in September, and there are numerous August pilgrimages as well. In Italy, however, there are more pilgrimages in May than in August, and April pilgrimages are fairly frequent whenever Easter falls within that month. Thus, spring is a more important season for pilgrimage in Italy than in France. The Spanish pilgrimage cycle is similar to the Italian pattern with a high point in

September, a strong emphasis on May, and a greater-than-average number of April events. In Spain, however, August is decidedly less important as a time for pilgrimage than in either Italy or France, and more events are celebrated in June than July, a reversal of the pattern found in the other two countries where there is a rise from a warm season low in June to increasing activity through July and August to the September peak.

Considerably more divergent patterns characterize the annual cycles in Portugal and Germanic Europe. By April, Portuguese events increase in frequency from the winter low, maintain nearly the same level in May and June, increase sharply in July to peak in August, and decline slightly in September. The generalized Germanic pattern shows relatively little difference in frequencies of pilgrimage from May through September, except for a sharp decline in the number of events during June, a condition that occurs in two out of three years on the long-term average. A slightly greater number of events are celebrated in May than in the peak late summer month of September, and there are more pilgrimages in July than in August. The decrease in the number of pilgrimage events in October and November is far less dramatic than in the other European regions.

When pilgrimages in West Germany alone are considered, an even different pattern emerges with three annual peaks of high pilgrimage separated by months of much lower activity levels. The spring peak in May is followed by the usual drop of activity in June. There are slightly more pilgrimages in July than in May, then a definite decline of activity in August, followed by the events of September which are somewhat more numerous than in July. April, October, and November have about the same number of events as the low summer month of June, leaving only November through February as a period of very infrequent pilgrimage. This is particularly interesting in that West Germany has a more severe climate than most parts of the other countries considered.

Irish, and to a lesser extent British, patterns are unique to those areas. In Ireland, the cycle tends to replicate very old pre-Christian patterns of religious seasonality. July, marking the time of the ancient Celtic harvest festival, is the most important month and there are greater-than-average proportions of winter events, particularly in February.[18]

Cultural Variables

The most divergent patterns from the generalized European norm are found in regions that are characterized by a relatively strong continuity of pilgrim devotions to saints. Shrines dedicated to the Virgin Mary and to Christ show somewhat similar pilgrimage cycles, with a spring emphasis on May and a late summer emphasis on September (Figure 3-10). August is more important than May as a time for Marian pilgrimages, but Christ-centered events are primarily May and September activities. In contrast, events at saints' shrines, although still primarily concentrated between April and October, show much less dramatic fluctuations in monthly frequencies. Thus, countries with high proportions of saints' shrines, such as Portugal, West Germany, and Austria, should be expected to show less monthly variation in the number of pilgrimages than is the case in France, Italy, Spain, and other countries with a strong Marian focus. Specific regional devotions to certain saints whose days fall at a particular time of the year are also factors in accounting for variations in seasonal cycles.

The importance of July pilgrimages in Germanic lands, however, is also related to an especially strong focus on the minor Marian feast day of the Visitation as a time for pilgrimage. This feast, commemorating the visit of Mary with Elizabeth, was of some importance in the Roman church as early as the eighth century; it was, however, originally celebrated in November. In its current form and date of expression, the Visitation is unusual among the more important Marian feast days in being of essentially Medieval Western European origin. Franciscans celebrated the Visitation in summer by 1236, and the date of July 2 was fixed by the Council of Basel in 1431.[19] As a time for pilgrimage, it tends to be associated with shrines established after the mid-fifteenth century and is most often an occasion for pilgrimage in the Germanies where it is particularly important toward the north.

The importance of July, combined with a relative neglect of August as a pilgrimage month in northerly regions, supports the idea that regional differences in European pilgrimage cycles are, as has long been suspected, closely related to traditional labor demands of the agricultural year. The generalized pattern of pilgrimage seasonality tends to reflect the importance of late summer as a major time for pilgrimage in Mediterranean lands since pre-Christian times. In these regions, the wheat is generally in by August and the grapes are not ripe. The month was presumably less suitable as a time of pilgrimage for a largely agricultural society in more northerly regions where it corresponds with the time of the wheat harvest and other important agricul-

Pilgrimage in the European Tradition

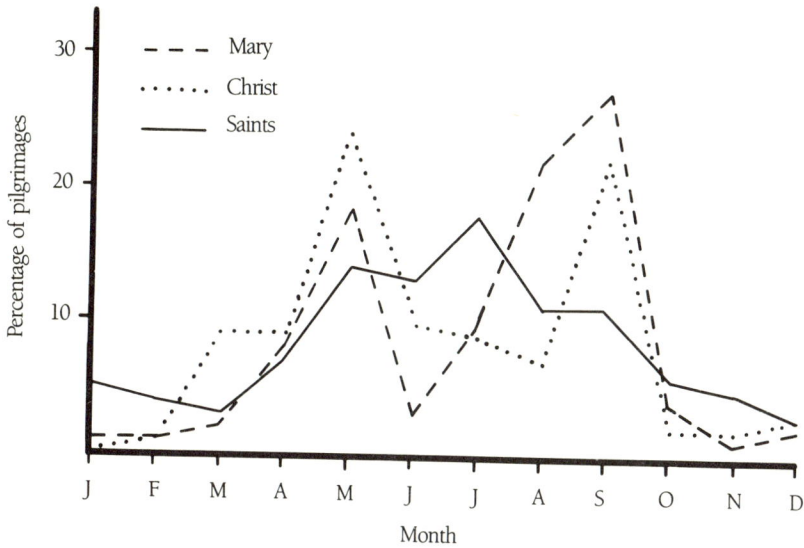

Figure 3-10 *Pilgrimage seasonality related to different subjects of devotion.*

tural activities. It is specifically in those Continental regions where the wheat harvest begins after mid-August that substantially more pilgrimages are celebrated in July than in August. Most regions where the wheat harvest begins late, however, have few pilgrimages because the zone corresponds closely with those parts of Europe where pilgrimage was curtailed after Protestantism took root in the sixteenth century.[20]

Although relatively few Europeans are now engaged as agricultural workers, and machines decrease the time needed for harvest and seasonal demands for many laborers, pilgrimage seasonality probably reflects a time when most people were agriculturists. These same patterns, however, have influenced the establishment of school and work vacation periods, so that the traditional annual cycle remains largely functional in a modern world. During the past few decades, numerous shrines have changed their date of pilgrimage from the traditional day of celebration to the weekend before, after, or closest to that day, an obvious adjustment to modern patterns of work and leisure. At shrines with several special events, the traditionally most important day of celebration may draw smaller crowds than a less significant event held during a more convenient time of year. At Fátima, for example, the holiest days are the beginning and ending dates of the apparitions on May 13 and October 13, but the crowds are large on August 13 because the month corresponds with Europe's major vacation period. Many district and regional shrines, especially in areas of substantial out-migration, have either shifted their main pilgrimage dates to August or added a special event during that month to honor visiting emigrants and their families. This redefinition of pilgrimage dates is part of the process whereby even minor shrines retain their vitality in a modern age.

The Continued Vitality of Minor Shrines

The dense concentrations of minor pilgrimage sites found in such regions as northwestern Portugal and adjacent Galicia, central Switzerland, southern Bavaria, and much of Austria indicate particularly vigorous traditions of vicinity and district pilgrimage, but substantial numbers of active minor shrines are found throughout most of Catholic Europe. This raises questions about a presumed decline of minor pilgrimage as large, important shrines become more easily accessible. Such a trend may have been fairly important earlier in the twentieth century and has been attributed to improvements in transportation, the rise of incomes relative to transportation costs, and sociocultural variables including emigration that, as the Turners observed, may undermine "village and intervillage corporateness."[21] At present, however, similar factors plus new interpretations of the meaning of pilgrimage appear to be favoring an increased emphasis on minor pilgrimage centers.

Of particular interest is a late twentieth-century rediscovery of the values of foot pilgrimage, a phenomenon particularly apparent in France and West Germany and especially expressed by affluent urban dwellers with ample leisure time. Although some of these pilgrimages focus on major shrine goals and involve journeys of several days or weeks, many others are directed toward less important shrines within range of a day or weekend hike.[22] Also, of course, long-distance foot pilgrims now as in Medieval times generally stop at several relatively minor holy places along their route. In addition to walking pilgrims, increasing numbers of religiously oriented "recreational" hikers visit minor shrines as they travel along Europe's ancient pilgrim paths. Unless inquiries are made, it is often difficult to distinguish recreational hikers who visit shrines en route from people engaged in a long-distance foot pilgrimage. Although some foot pilgrims march in sizable processions complete with

Pilgrimage in the European Tradition

flying banners, others, not desiring to attract undue attention, deliberately blend in dress and behavior with the general hiking public, at least until approaching their shrine goals. This presents a fascinating reversal of the well-known Medieval strategy by which secularly oriented travelers dressed and behaved like pilgrims in order to move unnoticed and with greater safety along the roads of Europe.

It should also be considered that the very ease and affordability of rapid transport, which makes possible the journey to a distant shrine in hours or days rather than weeks or months, may increase pilgrimage activity nearer home. Travel to a great shrine such as Lourdes may heighten the pilgrim's sense of special devotion, thus stimulating a desire to more frequently visit a small Lourdes grotto nearby. Other pilgrims and religious tourists return from an extended shrine tour with a newly kindled desire to become better acquainted with the "shrine-scape" of their home regions. Some may become enthusiastic collectors of shrine experiences, an activity encouraged by numerous recent publications describing shrines in specific regions or countries, especially in Germanic lands. In this manner, minor shrines are, to some extent, maintained and even revitalized because of the relative ease with which major shrines can be visited during longer periods of leisure time.

Ease of travel, affordability, and rapidity of transportation, whether or not supplemented by inspiration derived from occasional visits to great shrines, has stimulated an increasingly important phenomenon sometimes referred to as the "day pilgrimage." A typical such "journey" originates in a city or large town and combines attendance at Mass at a rural shrine with an excursion into the countryside, valued in its own right as a temporary escape from the stress of urban life. Even when one or more major shrines lie within easy day-trip range by car or bus, holy day services at a relatively minor shrine in a pretty setting are sometimes thought of as especially compatible with the country outing aspects of the experience sought by many religious excursionists. Group trips of this type by chartered bus seem to be especially popular with youth organizations and collections of elderly parishioners. Probably more important for maintaining the vitality of minor shrines are family "day pilgrimages" by automobile, an activity which, not unexpectedly, seems to have increased with the rising rates of private car ownership in Europe over the past several decades. This, in turn, reflects a difference in kind from the rapid mobility represented by the spread of railroads in the nineteenth century.

The different implications of train travel versus private car travel for choice of leisure-time destinations may, in fact, be part of the explanation for a possible nineteenth- through mid-twentieth-century trend toward visiting major shrines at the expense of nearer minor pilgrimage places. As a general rule, primary reliance on train travel tends to cluster people at a relatively small number of destination points. In contrast, a strong emphasis on travel by private vehicle, and to a lesser extent by chartered bus, seems to spread tourists—and no doubt pilgrims as well—over a much broader range of destinations. Automobile ownership particularly seems to implement day-trip and weekend travel, often of a fairly spontaneous nature and focused on nearby places.[23] What is true for such attractions as beaches, mountains, parks, or quaint villages within about an hour's drive of the excursionist's home is probably equally true for shrines, at least for that segment of Europe's population that is interested in shrines and pilgrimages. Thus, to the extent that analogues from studies of secular travel patterns by train versus car apply to pilgrimage and religious tourism, one should expect to find a decline in visits to minor pilgrimage centers not located near rail lines, and a corresponding increase in visits to a smaller number of important shrines as long as most travel is by train. By the same token, an increase in visitation at relatively minor shrines is an "expected" result of increasing reliance on road travel, particularly when associated with high levels of private vehicle ownership.

A considerable amount of urban-to-rural day and weekend pilgrimage travel by car involves the maintenance of family and community ties, and the district shrine visited on a special day is the shrine traditionally visited by the people of one's home community. This is especially true in West Germany and other urban-industrialized areas where rural-to-urban migration often involves moving to a city located within an hour or so by car from the community of birth. Thus, out-migration from rural areas to cities, suggested by both Christian and the Turners as an explanation for a decline in emphasis on district and local pilgrimage centers, may have the opposite effect of maintaining, or even strengthening or reviving, district pilgrimages.

Local or district shrines can benefit from out-migration even when long distances are involved. Restorations of some Spanish, Italian, and Portuguese shrine churches, many of which were in danger of crumbling into ruin only a few years ago due to the lack of local resources, have been made possible by contributions from emigrants who have worked in the industrial centers of northern Europe. For example, in the province of Huelva in southeastern Andalucía, ornate German-made candles dominate the votive collections at some district romería chapels, and special celebrations are held in honor of vacationing emigrants in August. Major restorations had recently been completed, or were in progress, at four of the six district shrines we visited in 1983. Several persons mentioned the contributions of emigrants from the district, not only in helping to repair the churches but also in sponsoring celebrations. We found much the same thing at district shrines from Tuscany to Apulia in Italy and, of course, in Portugal. Indeed, for some who must earn a living in cold, alien northern lands, the most important shrine in all of Europe is the pilgrimage center especially sacred to their ancestors, their kinsmen, and the people of their home communities. It seems likely that the district shrine, with its intimate symbolism and roots in place and community, will continue to thrive in a highly mobile modern world.

Pilgrims' Offerings

Pilgrims keep shrines vital as pilgrimage centers by visiting them. The gift of their presence is the most essential offering for the maintenance of cultus. In addition, pilgrims customarily leave some token of their visit at the holy place.[24] Offerings often take the form of monetary donations, gifts in kind, or gifts of labor, each an increment for the building or maintenance of the shrine complex, for underwriting the cost of special celebrations, or for promoting some cause sponsored at the shrine such as support for overseas missions or aid for the poor or sick.[25]

Although monetary gifts may be employed in a variety of ways, the pilgrim sometimes has an opportunity to express the desire for a particular use, at least in a symbolic sense. At the Catholic shrine by the Slipper Chapel near Walsingham, England, for example, pilgrims and tourists alike are encouraged to help pay for a large new basilica expressed in terms of cost per brick or roof tile. Thus, the contributor has the satisfaction of knowing that he or she has paid for a specific part of the structure. Gifts of money take on a visually symbolic value when bills are attached to images or when coins are tossed onto the tombs of saints or into the waters of holy wells. Although such practices are frequently viewed as unsophisticated by shrine administrators and often discouraged in a modern age, these customs have a strong persistence, especially in parts of southern Europe.

Gifts in kind persist in certain rural areas, often less from the lack of a basic monetary economy as from the strength of old traditions. At northern Portuguese romería centers, for example, devotees who exchange cash for food, drink, and goods at the festa market may donate eggs, wine, farmyard animals, or even large livestock as offerings. In parts of rural Europe certain kinds of gifts have a strong symbolic value over and above their monetary value, and it is not unusual for pilgrims to bring offerings "in kind" that have actually been purchased and that are auctioned off at the close of the pilgrimage event in order to reconvert the gift to cash.[26]

Gifts of time and labor include work to maintain or restore shrine facilities and create new additions to a shrine complex. Such offerings are particularly important at district and vicinity shrines in poorer rural areas. The gift of service to other pilgrims is especially important at the great curative shrines, such as Lourdes and Banneux, where there are many medically trained devotees among the laypersons who tend the sick, handicapped, and aged pilgrims.[27] The recently established special pilgrimages for the sick or handicapped at numerous other shrines depend heavily on volunteer services, as, for example, at Walsingham, England, where the annual "Faith and Light" pilgrimage for severely retarded young people involves nearly as many volunteer helpers as handicapped children.

Many offerings, such as the flickering flames of votive candles and the fresh bouquets of flowers, are ephemeral. The flame dies when the fuel is gone and the flowers fade soon after picking; but because such offerings are deeply rooted in tradition, they are continually renewed (Figure 3-11). Equally as ancient is the urge to leave more permanent marks of one's presence. At Monte Sant'Angelo in southern Italy, for example, twentieth-century pilgrims have scratched their handprints on the ancient stones of the church, just as handprints were left on the walls of European caverns during the Upper Paleolithic. Similarly, Medieval pilgrims carved crosses in the stones of churches along their routes. At some Irish holy wells, pilgrims still use pebbles to deepen carved crosses and circles in ancient stones as part of the ritual of making the rounds. Initials are also found carved or painted on the stones of sacred places, although the practice is generally discouraged. Modern pilgrims are invited to sign visitor books, or write requests for favors or notes of thanks for favors received in books of intentions. Monks once kept such records in "Miracle Books," an unnecessary task in an age of near-universal literacy throughout most of Western Europe.

Irish holy wells may be marked by nails or coins driven into the bark of trees, by pins or coins in the well, and by crosses made of twigs. Twig crosses and nail heads driven into church doors to form crosses are occasionally found at rural shrines on the Continent, particularly in Austria. Another ancient type of offering is a "rag," traditionally a strip of the pilgrim's clothing. Such rag offerings are found at shrines in India and the tombs of Moslem holy men in parts of North Africa. Once common in many parts of Europe,

Figure 3-11 *Candles at Lourdes, France. Flickering flames and fresh bouquets of flowers are ancient types of offerings that share the quality of being highly ephemeral. Thus, offerings of this kind must be continually renewed and their constant presence, as here at Lourdes, indicates a highly active shrine with year-round visitations. The absence of such offerings during off-seasons does not necessarily indicate a fading cultus, especially in the case of rural shrines that serve as pilgrim goals on only one or a few occasions per year. At some shrines, especially in Germanic lands, large elaborate candles given as ex-votos are not burned, but are kept on display as at Altötting, Bavaria, where some of the candle offerings date back to the sixteenth century.*

rag offerings are displayed today only at certain holy wells in Ireland and Scotland. Here, rags customarily are hung on a thorn tree beside a spring or well, although barbed-wire fences may substitute for the traditional rag repository (Figure 3-12).

Most Irish and Scottish "rag wells" are hidden away in remote areas and such offerings are not encouraged at the more important shrines.[28] In Highland Scotland, local people, who claimed not to participate themselves, explained that the rags are left at ancient holy places on the first of May in order to appease the spirits of the well. Irish folklore suggests that the offering allows the pilgrim to transfer his or her bodily ills to the tree, or presumably, nowadays, to the barbed-wire fence. Although rags are no longer acceptable

Figure 3-12 *Rag offerings at Saint Bridget's Well, Fauchart, Ireland.*

offerings for display at Continental shrines, offerings of entire garments such as wedding gowns, military uniforms, and christening gowns are still common in southern Europe. These may be kept with other types of votive offerings in special rooms assigned for that purpose at a shrine. Bloodstained garments worn when the pilgrim was injured in an accident or a war are also found in Continental votive collections.

Pilgrims also leave numerous other types of personal objects, each of which probably had a symbolic significance for the donor. Some of the remote Irish holy wells are heaped with a jumble of ballpoint pens, broken eye glasses, rosary beads, tobacco tins, broken plaster statues, devotional cards, plastic flowers, needles, pins, costume jewelry, baby pacifiers, toys, and numerous other personal articles. Braids and strands of hair, which were considered especially appropriate gifts for the gods in pagan times, are still found as votives at some shrines, especially in southern Europe (Figure 3-13). Photographs of pilgrims adorn shrines, and these can be viewed as the modern equivalent of the portrait busts and other personal likenesses frequently left by devotees at pagan Greco-Roman shrines. Crutches, braces, bandages, and other tokens of an injury or illness survived are left as thank offerings at shrines throughout Europe. Whether or not these items, or any other kind of votive offerings, are on public display at a shrine is a matter of individual administrative policy.

Replicas of afflicted body parts similar to those left at Mediterranean healing shrines during the first millennium B.C. are still found at many Italian, Spanish, and Portuguese shrines. Wooden models of body parts were once common at shrines in Switzerland, but metal is the traditionally preferred medium for small arms, legs, torsos, and other body parts left at shrines in Spain and Italy. Wax body parts, probably as ancient as the metal versions but much less durable, are most commonly found in Iberia (Figure 3-14).

Portuguese pilgrims often carry wax votives in processions as part of the request for a cure, or in fulfillment of a vow to make a pilgrimage if a cure is granted. At small Portuguese romería centers, wax votives may be recycled. A devotee buys the appropriate item at the shrine, carries it in procession on a day of pilgrimage, then leaves it as a votive. When the votive collection grows overly large, some of the items are removed from display and resold to a new set of pilgrims. At the great shrine of Fátima, the wax offerings include life-sized wax images of small children. Wax offerings may also take the form of long narrow candles the length and width of the devotee's body. Although this custom is now largely restricted to Portugal, such candles were commonly offered at shrines throughout Europe during the Middle Ages. In Ger-

Figure 3-13 *Braids of hair and photographs mingle at the shrine of Santa Casilda in Old Castile, Spain. Hair was offered as a votive long before the advent of Christianity. Photographs, while technologically modern, also reflect an ancient tradition. Greek and Roman pilgrims often donated portrait busts or other likenesses of themselves at the shrines of their gods, although the likenesses of supplicants, other than important members of the upper classes, do not appear to have been left at Christian shrines prior to the Renaissance.*

manic lands, particularly Bavaria, wax offerings have long taken the form of large, elaborately decorated candles that are displayed rather than burned. Shrines such as Kloster Andechs near Munich and Neukirchen bei Heiligenblut in the eastern Bavarian forest display hundreds of these candles, some dating back to the fifteenth century.

Elaborate silver hearts, fringed with cutwork and looking much like lace-trimmed valentine cards, are numerous at Italian shrines (Figure 3-15). These represent generalized thank offerings rather than a specific reference to the heart as an afflicted organ. Similarly, engraved marble plaques are common in the pilgrimage churches of France and adjacent regions. The custom seems to have developed in the late eighteenth century and become widespread during

Pilgrimage in the European Tradition

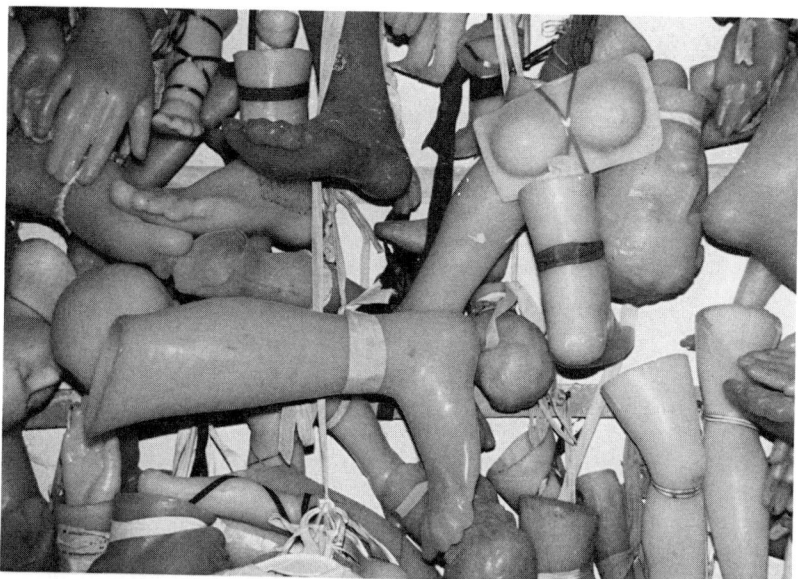

Figure 3-14 *Several of these wax body parts on display at the Spanish shrine of Nuestra Señora de Cortes are almost life-sized. Wax offerings representing an afflicted part of the body are most prevalent today in Spain and Portugal, although the custom was once more widespread. Wooden body parts were once common at shrines in Switzerland, and metal replicas of afflicted body parts, almost identical with those offered at Mediterranean healing shrines centuries before Christ, are common in Italy and Iberia.*

the nineteenth and early twentieth centuries. Some French and Belgian shrine churches are literally walled with marble plaques. Other votives of the type may be of wood or stones other than marble, but the vast majority are characterized by a written rather than a graphic symbol, usually a word for thanks and sometimes a date. Votives of this type, whether silver hearts or engraved plaques, are generally quite uninformative about the nature of the problem for which thanks is given and the marble plaques are more depressing than inspiring to some late twentieth-century observers. As expressed by the French scholar, Bernard Cousin, sanctuaries covered with this type of offering take on something of the air of a cemetery.[29] Walls covered with votive plaques tend to acquire emotional power only when they are allowed to serve

Figure 3-15 *Elaborate silver hearts are sometimes mounted on handworked pieces of cloth, as here at Montenero near Livorno, Italy. Votives of this type are by far the most common in Italy where they sometimes cover large sections of the walls of pilgrimage churches.*

as a backdrop for other offerings such as flowers, personal items, or the small wax figures hung on a wall of votives at the shrine of Our Lady of Oudenberg in Belgium (Figure 3-16).[30]

Among the most evocative offerings left at shrines are small ex-voto paintings indicating a special favor requested or received (Figure 3-17). As is the case with so many types of votives, the custom has roots in antiquity. Graphic expressions suggesting a personal relationship between heavenly beings and individual mortals date back to relief carvings and paintings from Greek and Roman shrines of the first millennium B.C. Some offerings found at pagan shrines suggest the direct intervention of a deity on behalf of a mortal by showing a god of war aiding an individual in combat or a god of healing standing beside the bedside of a sick person.[31] Christian paintings with an ordinary mortal included in the scene date from at least the sixth century, and occasional Medieval paintings indicate divine intervention on behalf of an embattled community or suggest a special relationship between a sacred persona and one or more mortals of high social status.[32]

Ex-voto paintings depicting the direct intervention of holy persons in the solution of specific problems encountered by individuals of relatively ordinary social status appeared in Renaissance Italy. Some of the oldest known examples, from such shrines in central Italy as Cesena and Madonna della Quércia near Viterbo, date from the fifteenth century. The earliest votives of the type are small versions of the old theme of the donor/supplicant kneeling before, or otherwise included in, a portrayal of the holy being. Yet, even in the scenes showing only the holy being and the supplicant mortal, changes were occurring by the 1400s. The mortal no longer had to be a great or famous person in order to appear in the scene, as had been the case during the Middle Ages. In addition, as Cousin has pointed out, the relative size of earthly and heavenly beings underwent a fairly rapid and dramatic change.[33] During Medieval times, the nobles and high churchmen represented in the same paintings with heavenly persons were relatively small, even when they were in the foreground. During the fifteenth century, mortals attained the same size as the holy persons of veneration and, as the concept of perspective spread through the world of Renaissance art, it seems to have become increasingly acceptable to portray the holy persons as small figures surrounded by heavenly clouds in the upper part of the picture. The usual placement in the upper right-hand part of the painting indicates a heavenly being looking down on the scene from the right.

The painted votive, as it has evolved since the fifteenth century, sometimes expresses a devotee's desire for future assistance, or is meant as a generalized

Figure 3-16 *The custom of leaving engraved marble plaques, such as these on the wall of the shrine church of Our Lady of Oudenberg near Grammont in Flemish Belgium, is most common in France where the innovation seems to have originated. Similar votives may be of other stone or wood, but all are characterized by a written rather than a graphic symbol of thanks and are sometimes inscribed with a date.*

Pilgrimage in the European Tradition

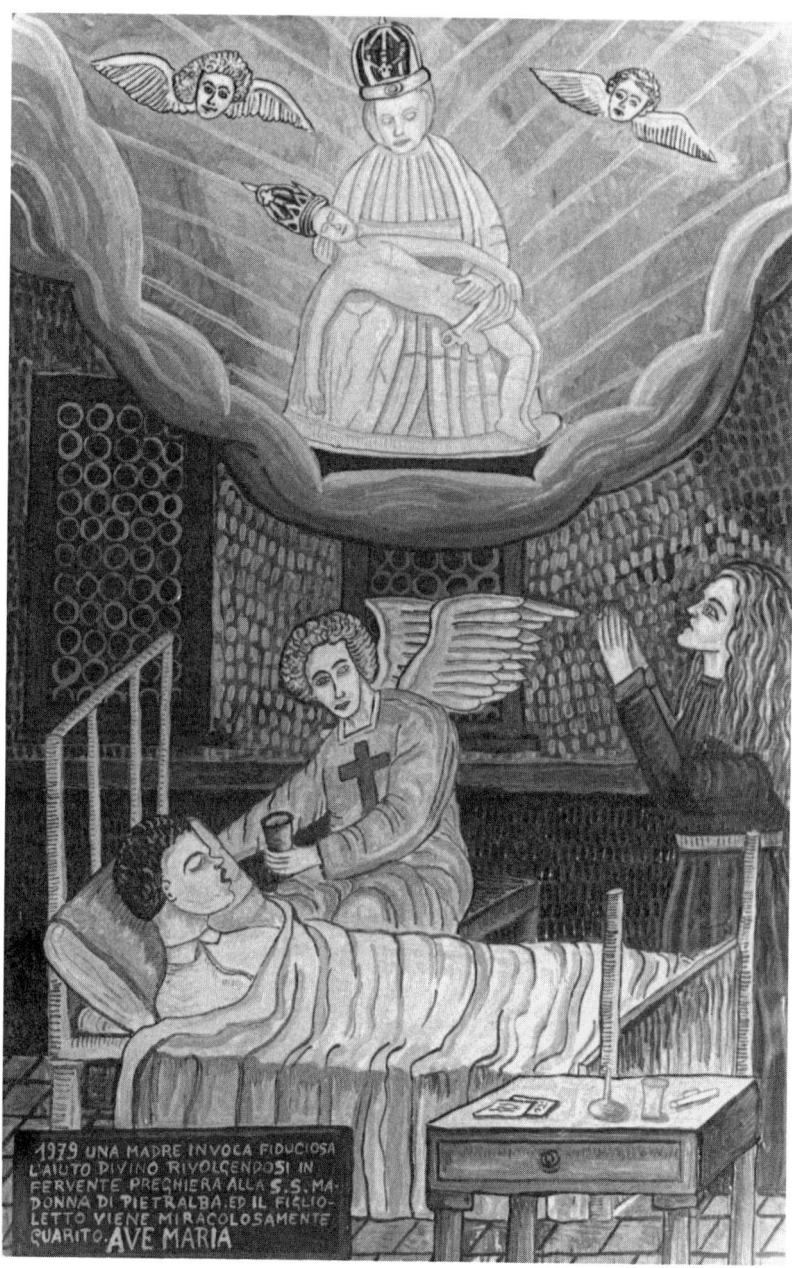

Figure 3-17 *Painted votive offering at Pietralba, Italy. Painted ex-votos usually indicate particular situations that have led people to seek divine intervention.*

graphic comment on the power of the shrine's subject of devotion, but the majority appear to be tokens of answered prayers (Figure 3-18). Frequently a vow of pilgrimage is made during a crisis, and the votive is left when the vow is fulfilled. Nearly all such votives include a representation of the divine being hovering above the human supplicant. Many, especially from the past two or three centuries, include a legend providing details of the circumstances leading to the pilgrimage. Painted votives became popular among sailors at an early date, and it seems likely that mariners were instrumental in spreading the custom from Italy to shrines along the Mediterranean shores.[34] The terror of sea storms combined with the need to avoid panic among the crew has long presented a situation in which a vow of pilgrimage made under desperate conditions may be especially effective as a means for increasing the chances of survival. Offerings in the form of painted votives spread northward to Germanic lands during the sixteenth through eighteenth centuries and westward across the Atlantic to become one of the most popular types of votive offerings at the Christian shrines of Latin America.

Many of the older votive paintings have been lost through the accidental or deliberate destruction of shrine churches, or because they were disposed of by nineteenth- and early twentieth-century shrine administrators who sometimes considered such offerings to be old-fashioned and of no particular value. During the past few decades, there has been an increasing awareness of the importance of the painted votives as a popular art form, as social-historical documents, and, among churchmen, as a psychologically useful means of expressing thanksgiving. Many of the shrines that maintain large painted votive collections display numerous recently placed examples depicting salvation from modern versions of centuries-old problems related to illness, accident, war, environmental hazard, and other threats to human well-being.

Pilgrimage in the European Tradition

Figure 3-18 *Sometimes the symbolism is ambivalent. The pilgrim who left this votive at the French shrine of Laghet was clearly a laborer, as indicated by the tools of rural and urban work. The mountains of home contrast with, yet repeat, the shapes of urban high-rise structures. A line across the heart suggests that he chose the city, but only at a great psychological cost. The note of thanks in the lower right-hand corner indicates that he is thankful for the Virgin's intercession, possibly in providing comfort and support during the period of choice and readjustment to a new environment. In many parts of southern Europe, it is the people who have made such emotionally rending choices who, today, reaffirm their roots in the countryside by providing money for the restoration of local and district pilgrimage chapels and by assuming much of the cost of festive pilgrimages in their home regions.*

four

Periods of Pilgrimage

Shrine Formation

The shrine landscape of modern Western Europe is a complex amalgam of pilgrimage places dating from different times of cult establishment (Figure 4-1). New shrines, currently in formation, join those that have endured for centuries. The mix of shrines from different historical periods varies from region to region within Europe and contributes to regional variations in aggregate attributes of modern cultus. These include differences in emphasis on subjects of devotion, the relative importance of sacral site features, and variations in the most common types of pilgrimage origin stories. We therefore agree with the Turners' thesis that "the epoch of genesis is of crucial significance in determining the lines along which a specific pilgrimage has developed."[1] According to these authors, pilgrimage centers change through time as old shrines acquire new attributes, but "each pilgrimage continues to maintain a subsystem of beliefs and symbols derived from its historical origin." These original ideas concerning the cultus are interpreted by the Turners as exerting a "selective pressure on all subsequent borrowings."[2]

This chapter provides an overview of the temporal dimension of modern European pilgrimage as it has evolved to the present. Because the analysis is limited to surviving shrines, many of the considerations that should be incorporated into a specifically historical study of Western European pilgrimage over the past 2,000 years are not adequately represented in the data base. This is particularly the case for early periods. After about 1400, and to a greater extent after 1530, the data presented here provide a reasonably good surrogate indicator of general trends in shrine formation and suggest leads for future historical investigation.

Figure 4-1 Old and new provide a dramatic contrast at Knock, Ireland, where an ancient bullaun stone of a type often associated with the activities of early Celtic saints landscapes a "garden of meditation" near the modernistic basilica built during the 1970s to commemorate visions of the Virgin Mary beheld by villagers in 1879.

Dating the Shrines

The temporal data base was developed largely from dates and/or periods of shrine formation provided in letters and interviews by shrine administrators or given in shrine-specific literature and compendia. Shrine-formative dates derived from these materials were drawn from a variety of sources including archaeological evidence, oral traditions, old accounts written decades or centuries after the shrine came into being, and, especially for more recent shrines, documents contemporary with the events being recorded. The quality of historical scholarship apparent in the available materials is uneven. Many early dates are merely a matter of tradition, and some exact dates for cult-formative events at old shrines may have been "invented" by chroniclers writing long after the pilgrimage was established.[3] Often, however, traditional dates that were passed on through oral history for long periods before they were recorded in writing probably place formative activities in the right general time period.

As a rule, the older an exact date given for shrine establishment, the less likely it is to be supported by extant documentary evidence contemporary with the time when the shrine is said to have begun attracting pilgrims. After about the fourteenth century, the dates of cult formation specified in shrine literature increasingly tend to be on firmer ground, although some cases are speculative and others are not fully supported by archival papers. Because our objective was to identify general patterns for comparative purposes, we accepted traditional and undocumented dates at face value except in cases where evidence presented by historians suggests major inaccuracies. If restricted to shrines with formative dates proven in documents contemporary with their establishment, the analysis would be limited, biased toward relatively recent cult formations, and weak for areas where warfare, iconoclasm, and other disasters have taken the greatest toll of records. The fact that the general temporal pattern remained highly consistent as we added information on well over 1,000 shrines after 1979 suggests an underlying historical reality of considerable importance for interpreting the evolution of modern pilgrimage.

For purposes of analysis, the date of cult formation at each pilgrimage center was operationally defined as the year or time period when pilgrims first began visiting the place for approximately the same reasons they now visit. This definition automatically placed all cult-formative dates in the Christian epoch, although about 4 percent of the shrines were probably pre-Christian holy places and, as discussed in Chapter 8, have special characteristics as a group. Shrines where the pilgrim focus gradually shifted in emphasis from one Christian holy person to another without any notable hiatus in pilgrim visits were dated from the period when the pilgrimage seems to have begun. Places associated with the lives of saints were dated from the saint's death year except where evidence suggested that the pilgrimage began later.

Many pilgrimage centers have undergone periods of waxing and waning activity, and some have lain dormant for many centuries before their restoration in new times under new circumstances. The problem of distinguishing between ancient holy places where new cultus has been generated and those shrines where revitalization has followed short-lived neglect was dealt with by assuming that a shrine was truly dormant if there was evidence that pilgrim visits had ceased for a period of 200 or more years. In such cases, the re-establishment date was considered to be the date of contemporary cult formation and the reasons for renewal of pilgrimage were recorded as the shrine-formative stories. It should, however, be kept in mind that initial cult-formative events are usually part of the contemporary mystique at such shrines, as emphasized in our discussion of British shrines later in this chapter. In cases where pilgrimages ceased for shorter times, as happened at many French shrines during the late eighteenth and early nineteenth centuries, the shrines were dated from their original Christian formations. The application of the 200-year dormancy criterion to areas where Protestantism was imposed by edict placed most pilgrimage origins in these regions in the nineteenth and twentieth centuries. It also put the origins of most Iberian shrines in Post-Reconquest times.

Exact dates of cult establishment were recorded for 2,476 shrines, and 3,120 were dated by century of formation. An additional 929 shrines were assigned to general time periods of cult formation for a total of 4,049 cases. Percentages given in the text and tables refer only to those shrines that could be assigned to a time period. More than three-quarters of the shrines in Italy, Switzerland, Britain, and the Scandinavian countries were dated by period, as were 69 to 71 percent of the shrines in Austria, France, and West Germany. Nearly two-thirds of the Belgian shrines were dated by period, but this was the case for slightly fewer than half of the Spanish and Dutch shrines. Portugal has the lowest proportion of dated shrines at only 22 percent of the cases.

The Shrine-Formative Cycle

When the shrines are dated by year of establishment and plotted by decade, as in Figure 4-2, a cyclical pattern appears in the formation times of contemporary pilgrimages. Clusters of decades accounting for substantial numbers of active shrines are followed by periods during which relatively few pilgrimages with longtime survival potential came into being. Few shrines deriving from the first ten centuries of the Christian Era can be dated with any precision, and exact dates for the establishment of many Medieval shrines are either unavailable or questionable. Also, because the graph is based only on datable shrines that have survived to the present, it does not directly indicate actual cult-formative levels in past decades. In addition to the lack of precise dating information on many early shrines, substantial numbers of once-important pilgrimage places no longer draw pilgrims. We doubt that the graphed highs and lows of surviving cult formations are of much value for interpreting actual cycles of Medieval or even Renaissance shrine formation due to the unusually large die-outs of shrines with no immediate replacements in areas that became Protestant. From about 1530 to the present, the graph is probably a good indicator of temporal patterns of variation in enthusiasm for shrine establishment and may also suggest general cycles of pilgrimage activity.

Rates at which new shrines are created tend to vary in space and time, as do rates of decline and extinction of older shrines.[4] Whenever new shrines are being established at about the same rate as older shrines become dormant or extinct, the pilgrimage system can be conceptualized as being in balance. There is little change in the number of pilgrimage places available to the faithful of the region in question. Occasionally, however, the rate of new shrine creation seems to exceed the rate at which older shrines decline so that the actual number of pilgrimage centers increases. At other times, the rate of decline exceeds the rate of new pilgrimage formation and the number of shrines decreases. Thus, one can think in terms of periods of pilgrimage florescence and decline that may be partially reflected in the origins of existing shrines.

Pilgrimage probably drops off during low periods in cult-formative cycles and picks up again at older shrines during periods of marked new cult-formative activity. It seems likely that new cycles of pilgrimage florescence begin with a series of adaptive transformations that improve the fit between pilgrimage and a changed socioeconomic, intellectual, and technological order. The adaptations often begin at newly established shrines, but are soon

Periods of Pilgrimage Shrine Formation

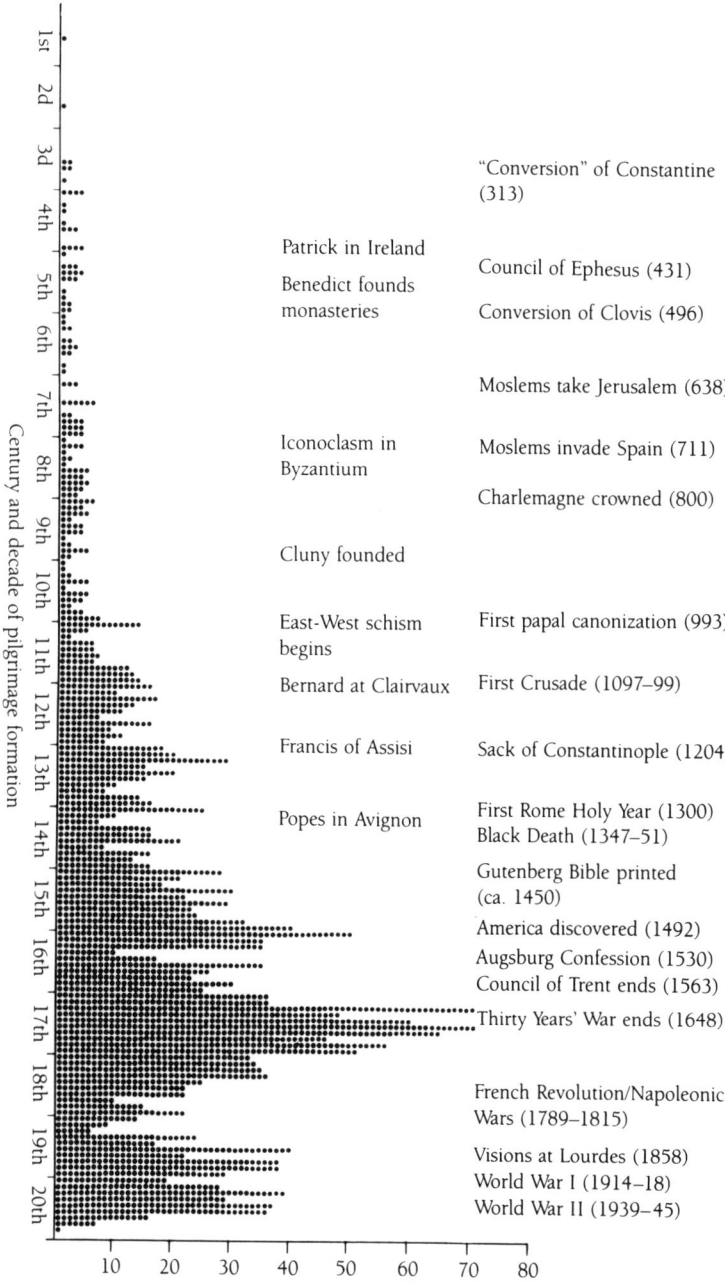

Figure 4-2 *Cyclical patterns of pilgrimage formation.*

selectively grafted onto expressions of pilgrimage at older shrines that subsequently experience renewed vitality.

The most striking graphed pattern, suggesting such a cult-formative cycle, is the near bell-shaped curve of new shrine formations rising from a low point during the troubled Protestant Reformation years of the 1530s to a high in the mid-seventeenth century, a time when the creation of hundreds of microstates following the Thirty Years' War and unsettled conditions related to the Turkish threat resulted in especially propitious conditions for new shrine establishment in the Germanies. The seventeenth-century high was followed by a slow decline during the eighteenth century to a low point in the decade immediately preceding the French Revolution. This Post-Reformation period of shrine formation is obviously a major seedbed for contemporary European pilgrimage and is also critically important for interpretation of Christian pilgrimage in Latin America and other parts of the world missionized by Roman Catholic Europeans during the sixteenth through eighteenth centuries.

Shrine-Formative Periods

Ebb points in the graphed cycle were used as a basis for defining cult-formative periods (Table 4-1). Because fewer than half of the shrines established before 1400 could be assigned to a specific decade, the first three periods were ended at the turn of the nearest appropriate century rather than at apparent cycle low points. This permitted inclusion of the largest possible number of shrines for each period. The periods are of unequal duration so, it is important to note that the relatively small number of Renaissance shrines reflects the brevity of a 130-year period characterized by high average-per-annum shrine formation. Table 4-2 indicates the relative importance of each of the seven regions in accounting for active shrines from different time periods. Maps 4-1 through 4-6 illustrate the distribution of shrines from the various periods.

Early Christian Period, First Century to 699

The seven-century Early Christian period accounts for slightly more than 6 percent of the shrines assigned to periods. It began in the first century with the earliest stirrings of a Christian pilgrimage tradition and continued through nearly three centuries of sporadic persecution to blos-

Table 4-1 Shrine-Formative Periods

Period	Number of Dated Shrines	Percent of Dated Shrines
Early Christian (to 699)	248	6.1
Early Medieval (700–1099)	407	10.1
High Medieval (1100–1399)	893	22.0
Renaissance (1400–1529)	623	15.4
Post-Reformation (1530–1779)	1,308	32.3
Modern (1780–1980)	570	14.1
Total	4,049	100.0

Table 4-2 Dated Shrines in Each Time Period by Region

	Time Period										
	Early Christian		Early Medieval		High Medieval		Renaissance		Post-Reformation		Modern
Region	N	%	N	%	N	%	N	%	N	%	N	%
Italian	61	25	68	17	187	21	207	33	289	22	141	25
French	63	25	143	35	211	24	100	16	167	13	117	21
Iberian	12	5	82	20	209	23	77	12	140	11	29	5
S. German	16	7	80	20	214	24	196	31	633	48	156	27
N. German	6	2	30	7	67	8	39	6	74	6	51	9
Irish	86	35	2	‹1	4	‹1	2	‹1	0	—	10	2
British	4	2	2	‹1	1	‹1	2	‹1	5	‹1	66	12
Total[a]	248	100	407	100	893	101	623	99	1,308	100	570	101

[a]In this and subsequent tables, percentages may not total 100 due to rounding.

som in the fourth century as the Roman world of late antiquity accepted, then officially adopted the Christian religion (Figure 4-3). The physical remains of Christians martyred during periods of Imperial Roman persecution provided the most important focus for shrine establishment in western continental Europe during the first four to five centuries after Christ. During the late fifth century, the Eastern cultus of the Archangel Saint Michael reached southern Italy's Gargano Peninsula at the still much-visited shrine of Monte Sant'Angelo. Spreading westward along the pilgrim routes, this devotion gave rise to the French pilgrimage center of Le Mont-Saint-Michel in the eighth century and eventually spread to Britain and Ireland.

Other Eastern Mediterranean ideas related to pilgrimage moved from east

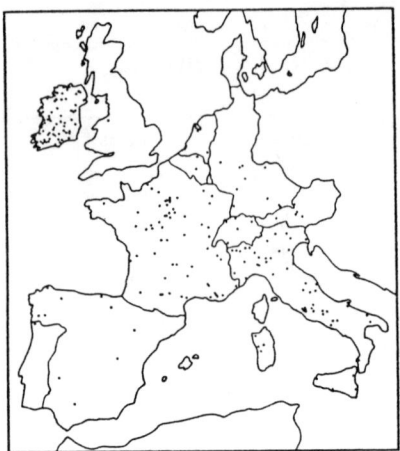 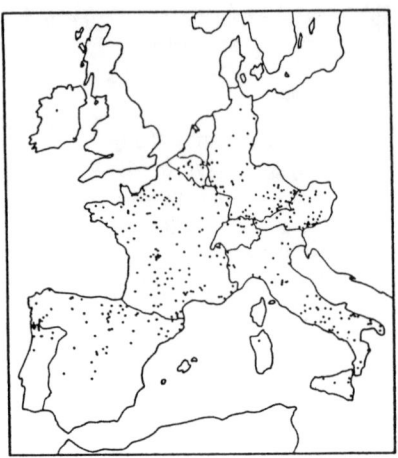

Map 4-1 *Distribution of Shrines Dating from the Early Christian Period*

Map 4-2 *Distribution of Shrines Dating from the Early Medieval Period*

Each dot on these maps represents one shrine. The datable shrines surviving from the different time periods show marked variations in distribution patterns. The importance of Ireland, France, and Italy as places where Early Christian shrines have survived is notable, as is the southward spread of new cult formations in Medieval Iberia. Surviving shrines from the High Middle Ages show a remarkably even pattern of distribution as compared with those from later periods, although they are absent or relatively few in those areas where the Protestant interpretation of Christianity was enforced by edict. Italy and the southern Germanic lands appear to have been especially important areas for Renaissance cult formations with long-term survival value, a pattern that becomes much more pronounced in the Post-Reformation period. Shrines established during the Modern period show a similar clustering, but to a much lesser degree. Several of the most important shrines established during the past 200 years are in France and Belgium, and the revitalization of pilgrimage in Britain and Scandinavia is obvious.

Periods of Pilgrimage Shrine Formation 89

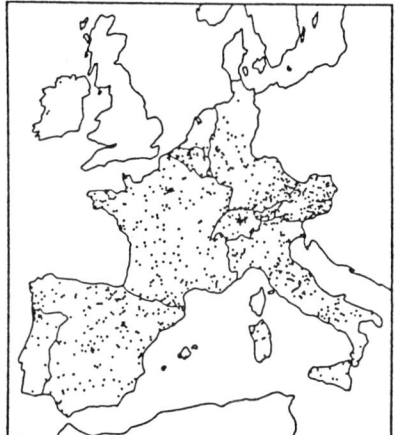

Map 4-3 *Distribution of Shrines Dating from the High Medieval Period*

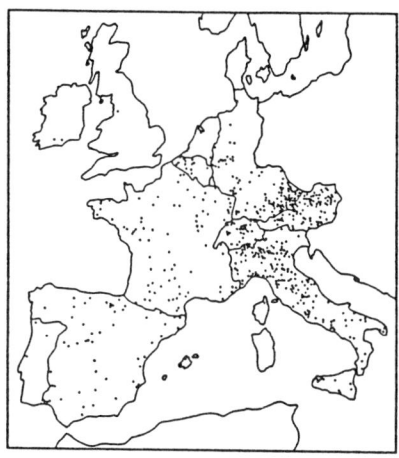

Map 4-4 *Distribution of Shrines Dating from the Renaissance Period*

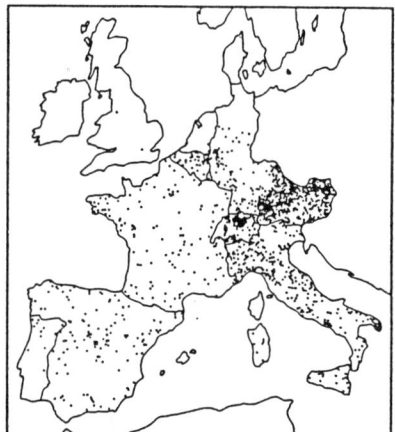

Map 4-5 *Distribution of Shrines Dating from the Post-Reformation Period*

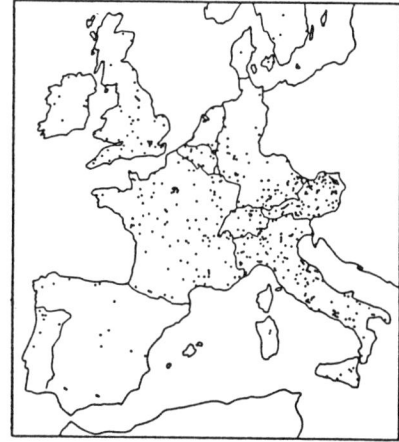

Map 4-6 *Distribution of Shrines Dating from the Modern Period*

to west during the same time period. The proclamation of the Virgin Mary as the Mother of God at the Council of Ephesus in Turkey in 431 affected, or reflected, pilgrimage developments in the Eastern Mediterranean long before Marian pilgrimage became important in the West. However, this council, held in a place formerly sacred to a powerful pagan mother goddess, marked the beginnings of a diffusion wave that transformed interpretations of pilgrimage in twelfth-century Western Europe. By the end of the Early Christian period, Marian shrines may have existed in Byzantine-influenced parts of southern Italy at such places as Conversano and Casarano in Apulia, near Viggiano in Basilicata, and Madonna di Novi Velia on Monte Sacro, Campagna. Oropa, Crea, and Varese are examples of northern Italian shrines from the period originally associated with early bishop-saints, but transformed into Marian centers during the Middle Ages or later.

By the early fifth century Christianity had spread beyond the confines of the disintegrating western Roman world to Celtic Ireland. There, to a greater extent than had been the case on the Continent, shrines of the new religion were superimposed on natural site features already thought of as sacred.[5] Saint Patrick, and other less demonstrably historical holy persons, baptized the old holy wells, drove the pagan demons from mountaintops, and established monasteries where learning thrived during an otherwise dark age. By the sixth and seventh centuries, Irish Celtic Christians were traveling eastward as missionaries, leaving in their wake such shrines as Iona off the Scottish coast, Saint Columban's at Bóbbio, Italy, and Sankt Gallen in Switzerland. One such Celtic saint, born in Munster, Ireland, in the early seventh century, became the bishop of Táranto on Italy's southern shores after his return from a pilgrimage to Jerusalem. His relics lie in the Táranto Cathedral where he has been venerated as Saint Cathaldus since his death in about 685.[6] Thus, an important counterflow of ideas from west to east also influenced Continental interpretations of pilgrimage and the nature of holy places. An increased Continental tolerance for the often nature-oriented shrines of the pagans is evidenced by the early seventh century in Pope Gregory the Great's famous letter to Mellitus of Canterbury advising the Christianization of pagan holy places in Britain.

The sixth century, which accounts for more Early Christian shrines than any other in the period, also gave rise to the Benedictine monastic order. Early in the century, Saint Benedict of Nursia retired to Subiaco near Rome, and later to Montecassino, to develop a Benedictine rule that established the foundation for most early, non-Celtic monasticism in the West. Shrines sprang up in the footsteps of the Benedictines just as they did along the

Periods of Pilgrimage Shrine Formation

Figure 4-3 These marble footprints, probably once left as a votive offering by a Roman pilgrim in a pagan temple, are now enshrined in the Quo Vadis Church on the Appian Way near Rome. The footprints mark the spot where, according to tradition, Saint Peter stood when Christ appeared to him on his flight from persecution in the city. As told in a second-century apocryphal account, the great apostle was inspired by this vision to return to Rome and to his death on Vatican Hill.

routes of the Celtic saints. During the seventh century, Christian pilgrimage traditions were strongly affected by an expansion of Moslem power that reduced the size of Mediterranean Christendom and restricted pilgrim access to the Holy Land.

Shrines of the Early Christian period are most numerous and proportionally far most important in Ireland, where a considerable majority of surviving shrines appear to have roots in the florescent period of Celtic Christianity. Many similar early shrines were also established in Britain, but few survived the Reformation. On the Continent, the period is best represented in France and Italy. Several Early Christian Italian shrines, including the four major basilicas of Rome—Saint Peter's, Saint Paul's, Saint John's, and Saint Mary Major (Santa Maria Maggiore)—remain extremely important to modern pilgrims. Some of the great saints' shrines of early Gallo-Roman Christendom, such as those at Tours, Toulouse, and Marseilles, are still visited but are no longer of major significance. A few places such as Chartres, Le Puy, Lyon, and Orléans have legends of ancient Christianized mother goddess traditions. Whether or not these places qualify as very old centers of Marian devotion, they were important centers of Gallo-Roman Christianity and are sites of great Marian shrines at present.

Early Christian shrines are not especially numerous in the Germanies because many Germanic areas were Christianized rather late. However, several fairly important pilgrimage centers in modern-day Belgium, West Germany, Austria, and Switzerland, such as those at Banz, Augsburg, Gheel, Sankt Gallen, Sankt Wendel, and Rülzheim, were probably attracting some pilgrims by the seventh century or earlier.

Most early Iberian shrines were either extinguished or relegated to a long period of dormancy by the Moslem conquest of the peninsula, which began at Gibraltar in 711 and soon overwhelmed the Christian Visigothic ruling class. Iberian Christianity, not subject to Moslem restraints, survived only in and beyond the mountains of the north and northwest. Shrines at Mérida and Toledo were never completely forgotten during centuries of Moslem control, although continued Christian pilgrimage seems to have been problematical.[7] Zaragoza, Spain, claims a sanctity of place dating from a mythical visit of the Virgin Mary with the Apostle Saint James the Greater during his legendary first-century missionary work in Iberia, but there is no evidence for a Marian cultus there prior to the ninth century.[8]

Early Medieval Period, 700 to 1099

About 10 percent of Europe's datable shrines were established during this 400-year period (Figure 4-4). In several respects, the eighth century marks a turning point in the development of Western Christianity. Even as most of Iberia was temporarily lost to invaders of the Islamic faith, missionaries were taking Christianity to previously unconverted Germanic peoples beyond the Rhine and the Danube. Other missionaries, mostly monks and hermits, were penetrating the remoter, sparsely settled hinterlands of modern-day France, Switzerland, southern West Germany, Austria, and Italy, where many people still retained their pagan traditions. By the ninth century, Christian shrines were being reestablished in Iberia as the Christian reconquest of the peninsula moved southward from its bastions in the Pyrenees, Cantabrians, and Galician hills. Of particular importance was the early ninth-century discovery in Galicia of bones believed to be those of the Apostle Saint James the Greater. Santiago de Compostela eventually became the third greatest shrine of Christendom and drew Medieval pilgrims from all of Europe into northwestern Spain.

Marian devotions received impetus in the West as late seventh- and early eighth-century popes, several of Eastern origin, incorporated Eastern holy days honoring the Virgin Mary into the Roman Catholic liturgical year. Saintly hermits, to whom popular piety now ascribes a special devotion to the Virgin Mary, began drawing pilgrims to such places as Montserrat in Catalonia and Sion in Lorraine by the ninth and tenth centuries, although it is not certain just when these shrines became full-fledged Marian pilgrimage centers. Also important was the Eastern campaign against the veneration of sacred images launched in 726 by the Byzantine Emperor Leo III. Possibly as a reactionary measure, image veneration was officially sanctioned for the Western church by Pope Gregory II in 731. Throughout the Byzantine iconoclastic period, which lasted until 843, Easterners who disagreed with iconoclastic principles fled to Italy and other parts of Western Europe. These refugees, who are said to have carried their icons with them in flight, undoubtedly played a role in a westward diffusion of early Eastern Mediterranean ideas about pilgrimage. Shrines at such places as Ascoli Satriano in Apulia, Tagliacozzo in the Abruzzi, Tropea in Calabria, and Itri in Latium trace their legendary origins as Marian shrines to the acquisition of holy objects brought westward by refugees from Byzantine iconoclasm.[9] A similar story is told about the famous dark Christ of Lucca in Tuscany.[10]

During the late eighth and early ninth centuries, the northern power center

Figure 4-4 *A dancing procession at Echternach, Luxembourg. Each year thousands of pilgrims from West Germany, Belgium, the Netherlands, and Luxembourg dance through the streets of Echternach to honor the eighth-century Northumbrian missionary, Saint Willibrord, whose body is entombed in the basilica. Pilgrims are thought to have prayed and danced here during an eighth-century cattle epidemic. The formalized dancing process has taken place since at least the mid-sixteenth century and probably dates from the plague years of the mid-fourteenth century.*

established at Aachen by Charlemagne was affecting the course of European history and resulting in a northward flow of important holy objects that continued through the Middle Ages. Portions of the relics of Christ's Holy Blood, supposedly found at Mantua, Italy, in the ninth century, lost in the tenth, and again found in 1045, were sent to southern Germanic lands soon after their rediscovery.

One of the more important pilgrimage-related events of the tenth century was the first official canonization of a saint, the Germanic bishop Saint Ulrich, by Pope John XV in 993. Increasingly centralized control over pronouncements of sanctity eventually had an impact on the way in which saints' shrines were officially established, although pilgrims continued to vote with their feet for popular deceased holy persons, as they still do.

A major watershed in pilgrimage establishment trends seems to have begun in the eleventh century with the Truce of God movement, the Cluniac reform of Benedictine monasticism, and the increasing numbers of shrines dedicated to the Virgin Mary from inception. In Italy, shrines were established at places sacred to holy men who can be thought of as predecessors of the thirteenth-century Francis of Assisi. Eleventh-century Italian shrines, where aspects of nature are important and about which cluster much the same legends as those associated with Saint Francis, are found at Cocullo in the Abruzzi, Camáldoli and Vallombrosa in Tuscany, and Serra San Bruno in Calabria. In the same century, the arrival of the bones of Saint Nicholas in Bari and the "rediscovery" of Christ's Holy Blood at Mantua gave rise to cults that soon spread far beyond peninsular Italy. The century closed with the First Crusade (1097–99), and the successful, although temporary, conquest of the Holy Land was a major turning point in Western European history.

The Early Medieval period is especially well represented in France and next most important in northern and central Iberia and in southern Germanic lands. The once-numerous Medieval shrines of Britain did not, for the most part, survive the Reformation, although several of modern Britain's shrines were reestablished in the nineteenth and twentieth centuries at the sites of Medieval and earlier pilgrimage places. The generally low proportion of Irish shrines dating from the eighth through the fifteenth centuries suggests that the later Protestant British repression was more successful in uprooting that Catholic island's Medieval shrines than in eliminating the earlier cults of the Celtic saints.

High Medieval Period, 1100 to 1399

The High Medieval period accounts for 22 percent of Europe's active shrines. These 300 years are usually thought of as the golden age of Western European pilgrimage, and considerably more English-language studies of European pilgrimage traditions deal with these centuries than with any others, before or since. The period encompasses the greatest days of the pilgrimage to Santiago de Compostela, Spain; the peak popularity of journeys to the shrine of Saint Thomas Becket, assassinated in Canterbury Cathedral in 1170; and the first great Holy Year pilgrimage to Rome in 1300 (Figure 4-5). The High Middle Ages also witnessed the establishment of pilgrimage-promoting religious orders such as the Franciscans, the Dominicans, and the Carmelites. Several of Italy's most important shrines from the period are found at places related to the lifework of Saint Francis of Assisi, founder of

Figure 4-5 *In this stained glass window in the thirteenth-century Trinity Chapel of Canterbury Cathedral, England, pilgrims are fixed in an eternal journey toward their religious goals. Chaucer's work, The Canterbury Tales, has made this High Medieval pilgrimage shrine famous throughout the English-speaking world.*

the Franciscans. The Padua tomb of his disciple, Saint Anthony, presently attracts several million pilgrims annually.

The northward movement of relics into the Germanies, and, to a lesser extent into other parts of Western Europe, continued to stimulate the rise of great new pilgrimage centers including the twelfth-century shrines of the Three Kings in Cologne and of Saint Matthew at Trier. The sack of Constantinople by Western European Crusaders in 1204 resulted in an even greater flow of Eastern holy objects west and northward.

The High Middle Ages are particularly noted for a Western European surge of pilgrimage centers devoted to the Virgin Mary. Among the Medieval Marian shrines currently drawing large numbers of pilgrims and other visitors are Loreto and Montenero in Italy, Ronchamp and Rocamadour in France, Scherenheuval in Belgium, Bornhofen in West Germany, Mariazell in Austria, and Guadalupe in Spain. During the period, many older saints' shrines seem to have stayed vigorous by a sometimes gradual, sometimes abrupt transformation into predominantly Marian shrines.

The High Medieval period, as here defined, opened with the temporary establishment of Christian control in the Holy Land resulting from the success of the First Crusade, and with Saint Bernard of Clairvaux's impassioned preaching of his devotion to the Virgin Mary. We ended it at the turn of the fifteenth century in order to include numerous fourteenth-century shrines that could not be accurately assigned to years or decades. In a social-psychological sense, the High Middle Ages drew to a close with the spread of the bubonic plague through Europe in 1348–49. Within a few years, the population of Western Europe was probably decreased by a third, and shrines dedicated to Saint Roch and other plague saints had become common by the end of the century. Religious uncertainty, generated by the residence of the popes in Avignon between 1308 and 1378, and the Western Schism, marked by numerous competitive claims of church leadership between 1378 and 1418, may have affected pilgrimage patterns, but we have found no evidence for this in cult-formative stories.

High Medieval shrines are fairly evenly distributed across the predominantly Roman Catholic parts of Europe. Near-equal percentages of shrines from the period are found in the Iberian, Italian, French, and South German regions.

Renaissance Period, 1400 to 1529

Fifteen percent of dated active cults were established during this 130-year period (Figure 4-6). This represents considerably more surviving shrines per annum than from the 300-year High Medieval period. The Renaissance period began with a large number of new cult formations in the early fifteenth century as Europe recovered from the trauma of fourteenth-century plagues and wars. The formation of cults with a survival value continued at high rates through the third decade of the sixteenth century, then precipitously declined all over Europe. The creation of pilgrimages that survive to the present tapered off in France and the Germanies during the second decade of the sixteenth century, but remained high through the 1520s in Spain and in an Italian peninsula that was racked by the French wars.

Although short, and therefore accounting for a relatively small proportion of dated shrines, the Renaissance period is critically important for interpretation of Europe's contemporary traditions. Pilgrimages, along with religious expressions in general, seem to have become more personalized in the sense of being more oriented toward individual interactions with divinity. This trend is reflected by a rise in origin stories related to individual thank offer-

Figure 4-6 *Santa María del Cubillo near Aldeavieja in the Spanish province of Old Castile. A typical Spanish story of pilgrimage formation is the shepherds' cycle legend that involves the appearance of the Virgin Mary to a shepherd and the subsequent finding of a long-lost statue of Mary holding the Christ Child. This is said to have occurred in about 1454 at the site of this shrine, where sheep still add a pastoral note to the scene. By the fifteenth century in Spain and Italy, however, a new type of Marian apparition was being reported: one in which Mary appeared alone and delivered an important message to a visionary who was often female, and for which no "proof" was found in the form of an image.*

ings and by the appearance of painted ex-voto offerings that vividly portray specific miracles for which individuals gave thanks.[11] Apparitions of the Virgin Mary to an elderly woman in 1426 and 1428 at Vicenza, Italy, to another woman at Caravággio, Italy, probably in 1432, and to female and child visionaries at several places in fifteenth-century Spain display all of the characteristics used by Victor and Edith Turner as indicators of a modern or "postindustrial" type of Marian vision.[12]

Italy's other great Marian shrines of the period include Genazzano, which has a more traditional origin story, and Madonna della Guárdia near Genoa, the scene of a predominantly modern-type apparition of Mary in 1490. One of Italy's greatest Renaissance saints' shrines is found at Cáscia near Spoleto where Saint Rita is entombed. Pilgrims also visit nearby Roccaporena where this essentially modern holy woman was born. Rita of Cáscia, abused wife, mother, and later religious social worker and visionary nun, has been honored by pilgrims since her death in 1457, although her cultus seems to have begun its spread beyond Italy after her canonization in 1900. It seems likely that the Italian region, which accounts for more than one-third of the shrines from the Renaissance period, was the area of origin for many of the most influential innovations in the manifestation of pilgrimage during this time.

A considerable proportion of Renaissance shrines are also found in southern Germanic regions. These include the famous Eucharistic miracle shrine at Walldürn and the great Marian shrine at Altötting, both in Bavaria. The French, Iberian, and northern Germanic lands are less important in accounting for active shrines originating from the period, although L'Épine in Champagne, Trois-Épis in Alsace, and Peña de Francia in Spain are examples of Renaissance shrines from these regions that are still of considerable importance as pilgrimage centers.

Post-Reformation Period, 1530 to 1779

The 1,308 shrines that can be traced to this 250-year period constitute 32 percent of the datable shrines and more than one-fifth of all shrines in the inventory. The dramatic 1530s' low point in the cult-formative cycle corresponds closely with the beginnings of the Protestant Reformation, triggered in 1517 when Martin Luther posted 95 theses calling for reform on the door of a church in Wittenberg, currently in East Germany. The Protestant movement accelerated when Luther's support from German princes led to the Augsburg Confession of a Lutheran faith in 1530. Three years later, King Henry VIII of England defied Rome by divorcing Catherine of Aragon and marrying Anne Boleyn. Henry was duly excommunicated and, in 1534, decreed an Act of Supremacy that made the sovereign of England the official head of the nation's church. During the same decade, John Calvin's influence in Switzerland laid the foundation for a version of Protestantism distinct from Lutheran theology. The Protestant reformers and their followers were generally hostile to pilgrimages, especially Marian pilgrimages, and those involving a perceived abuse of images. Even in England, where Henry VIII may have remained a Catholic at heart, the suppression of English monastic orders and the attacks of some of Henry's subordinates on the cult objects of England's pilgrimage places marked the beginning of the end for most English pilgrimage activity until the advent of the more permissive nineteenth century. In contrast to commonly held notions, however, the low point in surviving cult formations, corresponding to the crucial 1530s' watershed in European religious history, was short lived in regions that remained Catholic. A slight upswing in shrine establishment began in the 1540s, a decade that witnessed the first meetings of the Council of Trent, the beginnings of the Counter Reformation (or Catholic Reformation), and the dawn of a new age of European pilgrimage.

A higher-than-average proportion of the Post-Reformation shrines are minor, but the age, with its many cult establishments, is represented by a number of very important pilgrimage centers such as Kevelaer in West Germany's Lower Rhine; Montallegro near Rapallo, Italy; Pietralba in the Italian Tirol; Maria Taferl in eastern Austria; Sainte-Anne-d'Auray in Brittany; and the Holy Shroud chapel in Turin, Italy. Some Post-Reformation shrines were established or nurtured by such Catholic Reformation religious orders as the Jesuits, the Discalced Carmelites, and an autonomous branch of the Franciscan order known as the Capuchins. France's Saint Francis de Sales, Italy's Saint Charles Borromeo, and other leaders of the Catholic Reformation also promoted shrines. Additional pilgrimage centers sprang up in the wake of Catholic victory in religious wars. Many shrines from the period, however, seem to have developed in much the same manner as shrines of Renaissance times without any specific reference to the Catholic-Protestant conflict or the dynamics of the Catholic Reformation.

The age is characterized by higher-than-usual proportions of shrines developing around the veneration of images of Christ, particularly in Iberia and the Germanic lands. It is also noted for a higher-than-usual proportion of pilgrimage cults generated by reports of images that attested to their miraculous qualities by crying, bleeding, moving, or speaking, and for origin stories describing visions beheld in dreams that were not publicly announced until after the pilgrimage had come into being due to a series of wondrous events related to a place or an image.

Post-Reformation cult-formative activity appears to have been most prevalent in the southern Germanic lands, an area that accounts for nearly half of the surviving pilgrimage places established between the mid-sixteenth and late eighteenth centuries (Figure 4-7). The peak of surviving cult formations occurred during the sixteenth century in Italy and Iberia, whereas the seventeenth century was decidedly more important in French and Germanic regions. The period is characterized by virtually no overt shrine-formative ac-

Figure 4-7 One of the hundreds of Post-Reformation shrines found in southern Germanic lands is Sankt Anton's, located on an alpine height above Partenkirchen, West Germany. Built in the early eighteenth century as a thank offering to Saint Anthony of Padua for salvation from war, this shrine contains a votive painting showing citizens of the area in kneeling supplication as American tanks rolled into Partenkirchen during the latter days of World War II.

tivity in Britain and Ireland. This probably helps explain why the Post-Reformation florescence of pilgrimage shrine formation has generally been neglected in English-language literature.

The period is critically important for scholars interested in the roots of contemporary Christian pilgrimage in the Americas, as well as in Europe, because it corresponds with the time of the early missions to Latin America, French Canada, and other parts of the world colonized by Roman Catholics. The pervasive notion of a Medieval Hispanic pilgrimage tradition diffusing across the Atlantic needs serious reconsideration, because the transatlantic transfer of European religious ideas was undertaken by Catholic Reformation missionaries. Their concepts of divine manifestation, reasons for shrine establishment, and appropriate pilgrim behavior were based on the ideas of their own times and differed to a considerable degree from Medieval ideas. In addition to changes in ideas stemming from the Catholic Reformation, pilgrimage in Europe had undergone major reinterpretations during the Renaissance. The missionaries who carried Christian pilgrimage traditions across the Atlantic were not Medieval men, and they did not think like Medieval Christians. Even in Latin America they were not exclusively Iberian. Many of the missions on the frontiers of the Hispanic New World were, at least partially, staffed by men born and reared in Italian and Germanic parts of the Hapsburg Empire, and, in some cases during the eighteenth century, by English Catholics trained for the priesthood in Spain and Spanish Flanders.[13]

Modern Period, 1780 to 1980

Shrines established during the past 200 years account for only 14 percent of Europe's active shrines, or considerably less than half the number established during the previous period. However, great shrines are especially well represented. More than a quarter of the pilgrimage centers now drawing over 100,000 pilgrims per year from very extensive geographical areas have come into being since 1780. The most famous of these great modern-age shrines are church-approved sites of Marian apparitions such as Lourdes in France, Knock in Ireland, and Fátima in Portugal, along with several other intensively visited places of the same general kind in France and Belgium. Ecclesiastically unrecognized, or merely tolerated, Marian apparition sites of the past half century that now draw pilgrims on an international, and sometimes intercontinental basis, are found in such widely scattered places as Garabandal, Spain; Kerizinen in Brittany, France; Heroldsbach and Pfaffenhofen in southern West Germany; and San Damiano near Piacenza, Italy. Although none of these, nor others that are similar, yet qualify as truly great shrines, several are growing rapidly in importance and a few will probably gain full approval from future bishops.[14] Most of these developing shrines are similar in type to the accepted Marian apparitional shrines of the nineteenth and early twentieth centuries.

The publicity accorded to recently founded Marian apparitional shrines tends to obscure the fact that a substantial majority of pilgrimage centers established within the past 200 years are of quite different types. Even among the great shrines of the period, only about one-third are found at sites of nineteenth- and twentieth-century apparitions, although unpublicized visions are spoken of by pilgrims at a few other places such as Collevalenza, Italy.

Shrines at Pompeii and Trieste in Italy are representative of extremely well-visited modern Marian shrines that stem from cult-triggering events other than apparitions. Important modern-age pilgrimage centers dedicated to the Sacred Heart of Christ, a devotion springing from the visions of a seventeenth-century nun at Paray-le-Monial, France, are found at several places including the church of Sacré-Cœur de Montmartre in Paris and the shrine on the Cerro de los Ángeles at Getafe near Madrid, Spain. These shrines have strongly politico-religious overtones, which emphasize a conservative dimension of modern nationalism, and are more totally "new" in some respects than the Renaissance-based "modern-type" Marian apparitional shrine.[15]

The proportion of new shrines dedicated to saints has shown a marked increase, especially in the twentieth century and particularly among shrines that currently draw many pilgrims from distant places. These recently established saints' shrines are of three basic types: (1) shrines like those of Saint Theresa at Lisieux, France, and Saint Maria Goretti at Nettuno, Italy, that are dedicated to holy persons who have died within the past 200 years and were canonized rather quickly; (2) shrines that are dedicated to holy persons long deceased but only recently canonized, as at Wittem in the southern Netherlands where devotions to the seventeenth-century Italian Redemptorist holy man, Gerard Majella, were established in 1904 immediately after Saint Gerard's canonization; and (3) places, not yet officially shrines, that are dedicated to recently deceased holy persons now under consideration for beatification and/or canonization. Some of these latter sanctuaries are being popularized by active promotional efforts, heavy visitation, and testimonials of miraculous intercessions. Among the most important are the burial places of the reformed Irish drunkard, Matt Talbot (d. 1925), in Dublin; the Spanish Capuchin, Leopoldo de Alpandeire (d. 1956), in Granada; the German Jesuit, Rupert Mayer (d. l945), in Munich; and the famous stigmatized Italian Capuchin priest known as Padre Pio (d. 1968) in San Giovanni Rotondo. Also important is the birthplace of Pope John XXIII (d. 1963) at Sotto il Monte, a village near Milan, Italy.[16]

Finally, shrines have been reestablished in areas where nationalized Protestantism banned overt Catholic expressions of pilgrimage from the sixteenth or early seventeenth century until the nineteenth and, in Scandinavian countries, the early twentieth centuries. Most of these shrines are of no more than regional importance, but a few, such as Aylesford and Walsingham in England, are now counting more than 100,000 pilgrims per year (Figure 4-8).

Shrine establishment appears to have been uneven during the Modern period. A slight upsurge in cult-formative activity occurred during the French

Figure 4-8 Banners of the English martyrs are displayed at a youth pilgrimage at "The Friars," located at Aylesford, Kent, near London. A Medieval Carmelite monastery here was associated with Saint Simon Stock, who experienced a vision of Mary in 1251. The saint died at Bordeaux, France, and was buried there in the cathedral. Meanwhile, in 1538 the ancient monastery was sacked. The Carmelites returned to Aylesford in 1949, and in 1951 the archbishop of Bordeaux gave the skull and other relics of Saint Simon Stock to the fledgling establishment. The Friars now draws hundreds of thousands of pilgrims each year.

Revolution and Napoleonic Wars, but none of these shrines are important. A more pronounced high point came during the middle decades of the nineteenth century, a time marked by the Vatican proclamation of Mary's Immaculate Conception and the apparitions at Lourdes. Another peak seems to have occurred during the mid-years of the twentieth century. The relatively few new shrines plotted for the past two decades reflects only that it takes a number of years for a new pilgrimage to become firmly established and generally acknowledged. Several new cults, some of which show promise of longevity, have emerged since the early 1960s.

Of the 551 shrines from the Modern period that can be assigned to centuries, 330 date from the years between 1780 and 1899. These shrines are especially prevalent in France, Switzerland, and Austria. The twentieth century accounts for 231 widely distributed shrines. For the period as a whole, the Italian and South German regions account for the largest number of modern shrines. The relatively high percentage of modern shrines found in Britain includes revivals of Medieval and older pilgrimage centers as well as new cults formed after nineteenth-century Britain developed more permissive attitudes toward freedom of religious practice. The low percentage for Iberia probably reflects nineteenth- and early twentieth-century anticlericalism in Spain.

Regional Variations in Time Period Importance

Shrines from various time periods are better represented in some places than in others (tables 4-3, 4-4). Regional variations in modern pilgrimage traditions may be clarified by further consideration of these differences.

The *Italian region* is distinctive for its above-average proportion of Renaissance shrines. As in the fields of art, architecture, literature, diplomacy, classical scholarship, and scientific observation, Italy in the fifteen and early sixteenth centuries seems to have been a source area for innovations related to the establishment of shrines and the expression of pilgrimage. It has been suggested that "to this day, the social life of Western Europe is subtly molded by concepts adopted by Italians of the Renaissance, in their fusion of aristocratic and bourgeois societies."[17] This generalization applies to many aspects of social life expressed by and reflected in modern pilgrimage.

When viewed in terms of centuries, the great florescence of Italian shrine formation extends from about 1400 to the end of the seventeenth century with a slight peaking in the sixteenth century. The thirteenth century was the most important 100-year period in the Middle Ages, partly reflecting the influence of Saint Francis of Assisi and his followers. Near-equal numbers of surviving shrines date from the eighteenth, nineteenth, and twentieth centuries.

The *French region* is slightly above average in percentages of Early Christian shrines and has higher-than-average proportions of Early and High Medieval shrines. The most important 100 years of the Early Medieval period came in the ninth century, a time when several shrines are alleged to have been related to Charlemagne's activities. The twelfth century accounts for the greatest

Table 4-3 *Percentage of Dated Shrines in Each Region by Time Period*

	Region						
Time Period	Italian	French	Iberian	South German	North German	Irish	British
Early Christian	6	8	2	1	2	83	5
Early Medieval	7	18	15	6	11	2	3
High Medieval	20	26	38	17	25	4	1
Renaissance	22	12	14	15	15	2	3
Post-Reformation	30	21	26	49	28	0	6
Modern	15	15	5	12	19	10	83
Total	100	100	100	100	100	101	101

Table 4-4 *Percentage of Shrine Formations by Century*

	Century																	
Region	3	4	5	6	7	8	9	10	11	12	13	14	15	16	17	18	19	20
All Cases	1	1	1	2	1	2	2	2	4	6	7	6	12	10	19	9	8	8
Italian	1	2	1	1	1	1	1	1	4	4	10	6	16	17	15	7	8	7
French	1	2	2	1	2	2	4	2	6	11	9	5	8	8	15	6	12	5
Iberian	0	1	0	<1	0	3	2	3	6	12	17	8	10	17	10	6	1	4
S. German	0	<1	0	<1	1	1	1	2	2	4	4	7	11	8	29	17	8	5
N. German	<1	<1	0	<1	2	4	4	1	2	8	7	11	11	6	16	6	5	16

number of High Medieval shrines. The fifteenth and sixteenth centuries were less important for the establishment of surviving shrines than in most other parts of continental Europe and, although the years between 1600 and 1699 account for more active shrines in the region than any other century, overall Post-Reformation shrine-formative activity seems to have been relatively low. The spurt of activity in the seventeenth century was strongly concentrated in Brittany, Flanders, the area near Lourdes in the Midi-Pyrénées, and in linguistically Germanic Alsace. The region's importance in accounting for modern-age pilgrimages primarily reflects events of the nineteenth century.[18]

The *Iberian region* is distinctive for an unusually high proportion of High Medieval shrines and a low proportion of shrines established since the late eighteenth century. Iberia is also characterized by higher-than-usual percentages of Early Medieval shrines. The importance of the Early and High Medieval periods is apparently related to the southward thrust of the Christian reconquest of the peninsula which, according to tradition, began at Covadonga, Asturias, in 718, reached near-completion in the thirteenth century, and culminated with the conquest of the Moslem kingdom of Granada by the armies of Ferdinand and Isabella in 1492.

When viewed by centuries, the years between 1200 and 1300 appear to have been especially significant for the establishment of Hispanic shrines, although the sixteenth century, which straddles the late Renaissance and early Post-Reformation periods, was almost as important. The seventeenth and eighteenth centuries seem to account for smaller proportions of shrines than is the case in other parts of continental Europe, and the nineteenth century is unusually low in cult-formative events. This, however, appears to be a predominantly Spanish phenomenon because about 15 percent of the relatively few Portuguese shrines assigned to centuries came into being during the years between 1800 and 1899.

The *South German region* is remarkable for its Post-Reformation emphasis. The high point in the formation of existing shrines came in the seventeenth century, but, in contrast with other parts of Europe, the eighteenth century was also of considerable importance as a genesis period for contemporary pilgrimage. The region has average proportions of Renaissance shrines, largely reflecting the fifteenth century as an age of pilgrimage formation. A sixteenth-century decline in surviving formations is probably related to religious turmoil and confusion in the area during early Reformation times, whereas the importance of the seventeenth and eighteenth centuries partly reflects a response to the Thirty Years' War and the political fragmentation that resulted from the Treaty of Westphalia ending that war in 1648. In addition, numerous Austrian shrines developed during the struggle with the Ottoman Turkish Empire that culminated in the 1683 siege of Vienna.

The Catholic Reformation in the region stimulated a proliferation of secondary, or subsidiary, pilgrimage cults, reflecting both a revitalization of old traditions and the spread of newer devotions. For example, the ancient shrine at Loreto, Italy, which may have existed as early as the late twelfth century and was attracting numerous pilgrims by 1315, was popular in Germany by the fifteenth century. In its Post-Reformation Germanic form, the Italian cultus inspired the construction of numerous copies of the "Holy House," several of which became shrine centers in their own right and continue to attract pilgrims. According to Walter Pötzl, devotions to the Virgin of Loreto rose to a "new peak of fervour" after the Thirty Years' War and stimulated the construction of more than 50 copies of the Holy House within the boundaries of present-day Bavaria alone.[19] The Mariahilf cultus, which developed at Passau after 1622, eventually generated more than 500 secondary pilgrimage sites in Germany, Austria, the Italian Tirol, Switzerland, Alsace, and Czechoslovakia.[20] Some of these shrines survive as pilgrimage centers along with Post-Reformation centers subsidiary to the great Medieval Swiss Marian shrine of Einsiedeln; the fifteenth-century Bavarian shrine to the Virgin of Altötting and to a number of saints, including Saint Wendel whose burial place is in the Rheinland-Pfalz; and Saint Anthony, who is entombed at Padua, Italy.

Due to the large amount of Post-Reformation shrine-formative activity, the South German region has a considerably lower-than-average proportion of shrines dating from Medieval times and is slightly below the norm for the establishment of modern pilgrimage centers. As in the French region, the nineteenth century is of greater importance than the twentieth.

The *North German region* displays a very different pattern from that found in more southerly Germanic areas. Here shrines of the High Medieval and Modern periods are proportionally more numerous than in most other parts of Europe. The Post-Reformation period, so important in southern Germanic areas, is considerably less well represented, although more shrines date from the seventeenth century than any other 100-year period. The eighth and ninth centuries, corresponding with the Carolingian Renaissance, account for most of the Early Medieval shrines that can be assigned to 100-year periods. Elsewhere in continental Europe, shrines of this period tend to be clustered in the tenth and, especially, the eleventh centuries. As in the South German region, but in contrast to Italian, French, and Iberian patterns, the most important 100-year period of High Medieval times is the fourteenth century. The sixteenth, eighteenth, and nineteenth centuries are low in cult-formative events as compared with the fifteenth, seventeenth, and twentieth centuries.

The relative importance of the twentieth century is partly related to the reestablishment of shrines at old holy places or at new sites in areas that were formerly Protestant by edict. All of the shrines of Scandinavia, for example, have been created or reestablished within the past 60 years, and 65 percent of the relatively few Dutch shrines assigned to time periods have been established since the late eighteenth century. Increased mobility of modern populations is also a factor in the creation of new shrines in this region. Urban employment opportunities have tended to attract Roman Catholics to Protestant areas such as the West German Ruhr. A substantial number of the several million Germans who fled westward at the end of World War II were Catholics, and many of these refugees settled in parts of West Germany that had been predominantly Protestant. As a result, several North German shrines are visited almost exclusively by refugees from Eastern bloc countries and their descendants.

When the country of West Germany is considered as a whole, the temporal pattern is closer to that for the South German than the North German region. This should be expected because nearly twice as many shrines from the southern part of the country were analyzed by time period than was the case for the central and northern areas.

The *British region* is characterized by an extreme concentration of active shrines in the Modern period if the shrines of England, Scotland, and Wales that lay dormant during the Reformation are considered as new pilgrimage formations when revitalized in the nineteenth and twentieth centuries. Only a few shrines with initial origin dates prior to the gradual lifting of restrictions on Roman Catholic worship during the nineteenth and early twentieth centuries claim to have attracted pilgrims during the sixteenth, seventeenth, and eighteenth centuries. The best candidate for a holy place continually visited by Catholic pilgrims since its formation in Early Christian times is Holywell in Wales. The springs there, which had been venerated by pagans and attributed with curative powers, were Christianized through associations with Saint Winefride in the seventh century. Devotions continued throughout years of repression during which Jesuit priests disguised as innkeepers ministered to the Roman Catholic faithful.[21] A few other ancient holy places such as the Scottish island of Iona, Holy Island off the coast of Northumbria, and the tomb of Saint Candida at Whitchurch Canonisorm, Dorset, may have been visited by pilgrims throughout Reformation times. Several old English, Welsh, and Scottish holy wells, which may always have attracted a few devotees, have been reestablished as Roman Catholic or High Church Anglican centers of pilgrimage. Others, in the guise of "wishing wells," continue to be visited by people seeking cures or giving thanks for good fortune. In the Inverness region of Highland Scotland, people still place rags on trees or barbed-wire fences near certain small springs, as is also done at the folk Catholic rag wells of Ireland.

Some British centers of pilgrimage were secret places for Masses throughout the Reformation period so we have dated these from the time of inception as Christian holy places. Also, a few sites are said to have come into being as shrines during the Reformation because they were near older shrines, but remote and less suspect. At other places, there is fairly good evidence that relics of persons killed for their Catholic beliefs have been secretly venerated in the general area of the modern shrine since the time of these martyrs' executions in the sixteenth and seventeenth centuries.[22] Most British shrines, however, including the Early Christian religious center at Glastonbury, the eleventh-century Marian shrine at Walsingham, and the site of Saint Thomas Becket's twelfth-century martyrdom at Canterbury, apparently lay dormant from the sixteenth century until their reestablishment as centers of pilgrimage in the nineteenth and twentieth centuries.

When English, Scottish, and Welsh shrines are ascribed to the periods when they first acquired sanctity in the Christian tradition, there is a somewhat closer correspondence to overall European patterns. In terms of initial dates of revitalized cultus, British shrines tend to date from Early Christian and Early Medieval periods with a special emphasis on the eighth century. Possibly the earlier saints, many of whom were also British culture heroes, had a cultus deeply rooted in the folk tradition. Their shrines, therefore, were harder to stamp out and were more easily reestablished than was the case with many former High Medieval and Renaissance shrines. The sixteenth century accounts for the greatest number of places made sacred by the activities or deaths of Catholics martyred during the Post-Reformation period.

The proportion of truly new British shrines established during the nineteenth and twentieth centuries at places that had not previously drawn pilgrims may be artificially high. Several of these modern shrines are found at the sites of old abbeys or way stations along Medieval pilgrimage roads. Although in earlier times these places may not have been shrines per se, they clearly have strong associations with Britain's ancient Roman Catholic traditions. Pilgrimage formation in Britain seems to be on the rise and there are more new or revitalized shrines dating from the twentieth century than the nineteenth. Part of the resurgence can be explained in terms of a High Church Anglican rediscovery of the values of religiously motivated travel to holy places. Most of the Anglican shrines are devoted to early saints and are, at least theoretically, centers of ecumenical pilgrimage.[23] At the Medieval pilgrimage center of Walsingham there are two Marian shrines, one Roman Catholic and the other Anglo-Catholic.

The *Irish region* is unusual in that most shrines appear to be extraordinarily old. Indeed, Ireland's shrines are, for the most part, so old that their placement in time draws mostly from folkloric studies and archaeological evidence. It seems likely that several holy wells assigned to the Early Christian period may not have been "baptized" until the eighth or ninth century, and a few seemingly ancient legends may be related to shrines first visited in even more recent times. However, the many now dormant or extinct Irish shrines created after the Norman Invasion in the late eleventh century and Cistercian penetration of the island in the twelfth century mostly had formative stories and veneration orientations resembling those of continental Europe during the same period. They thus were quite different in mystique from Ireland's older pilgrimage places.

The Irish pattern is best understood in terms of differential survival. Very few of the island's Medieval shrines withstood centuries of British effort to uproot Irish pilgrimage traditions, and with a few exceptions, such as Holy Cross Abbey in County Tipperary, Ireland's eleventh- through fifteenth-century shrines have not been revived. Nor was the Post-Reformation period a propitious time for new shrine formations, although some of the Mass Rocks of penal times are now scenes of pilgrimage. What did endure in Ireland were the old, nature-centered shrines of the Celtic saints, many of which had been pagan holy places. New shrines, such as the Marian apparitional center at Knock and the tomb of the venerated Matt Talbot in Dublin, have been established during the more religiously tolerant Modern period, but the number of such shrines is not large. Thus, the Irish tradition, in the aggregate, was until recently the most archaic in Western Europe. In terms of many characteristics, the Irish pattern is the antithesis of patterns found on the Continent.[24]

The Periods in Perspective

Europe's pilgrimage centers range from extremely old shrines dating from the first centuries of Christianity to places where cultus is currently in formation. Although most English-language studies of Christian pilgrimage tend to stress periods prior to the Reformation or after the turn of the nineteenth century, the years between 1530 and 1779 are demonstrably of major significance as a seedbed for Europe's contemporary traditions.

The importance of this sixteenth- through eighteenth-century period in Europe should be stressed because the age is sometimes dismissed as relatively insignificant. For example, historian Jonathan Sumption refers to a "sharply reduced" popularity of real as opposed to imaginary pilgrimages in the wake of sixteenth-century satirists' taunts and the impact of the Reformation. In their influential book on *Image and Pilgrimage in Christian Culture*, Victor and Edith Turner contend that after the Reformation "pilgrimage was terminated in most of northern Europe and markedly curtailed in southern Europe."[25] Although the Turners' "Modern" pilgrimage type is described as growing "steadily in the post-Tridentine period of European Catholicism," the period is viewed by these authors as a predominantly nineteenth- and twentieth-century phenomenon within the European context.[26] Thus, in their typology of stages in the historical development of Marian pilgrimage, the Turners describe a "fourth stage" consisting of "colonial [American] shrines, which replaced, as it were, the shrines destroyed during the Reformation in Europe."[27] The development of Christian pilgrimage in Latin America is obviously important in its own right and has even had some impact on the continued evolution of pilgrimage in Europe. However, the hundreds of "replacement" shrines that sprang up in Catholic Reformation Europe are much more appropriate than Latin American shrines as examples of the precursors of the great nineteenth- and early twentieth-century Marian apparitional shrines of Europe that constitute the Turners' fifth and most recent developmental stage.

Unfortunately, the Turners' typologies tend to perpetuate a pervasive, but misleading, model which draws a kind of mental flat line between the low point of shrine-formative activity in the 1530s and the apparent drop-off in activity that characterized the late eighteenth century. Lack of information about the great Post-Reformation pilgrimage-creation florescence leads to overemphasis of what the Turners have referred to as a "dramatic resurgence" of Marian pilgrimage in the nineteenth and twentieth centuries.[28] By the same token, their argument "that there is a significant difference between pilgrimages taken after the Industrial Revolution and all previous types" seems to be based on comparing the obvious differences between High Medieval shrines and those of the nineteenth and twentieth centuries.[29] As previously mentioned and as will be more fully discussed in Chapter 7, all apparitional types and indeed most shrine-related characteristics described by the Turners as "postindustrial" are documented for Italy and Spain by the fifteenth century and have continued to occur in one part or another of Western Europe ever since.[30] Thus, the qualitatively different, "modern" type of pilgrimage essentially has its roots in the Renaissance rather than in the mass urban-industrial society that developed in the nineteenth century. Many of the changes occurring since the fifteenth century appear to be evolutionary rather than dramatically new.

As indicated by the creation dates for surviving shrines, models presupposing reduced shrine-formative activity during the Post-Reformation years are appropriate only for those parts of Europe that became Protestant and for British-dominated Ireland. The most important single century of formation for today's European pilgrimage centers was the seventeenth. The years between 1600 and 1699 were especially significant for the genesis of shrines in

Germanic regions; they were also of considerable importance in the French and Italian regions. In predominantly Catholic Europe, the century is of relatively minor importance in accounting for surviving shrines only in Spain, where many of the pilgrimages that emerged during the century appear to have had relatively low long-term survival value.[31] Even in Protestant Britain, covert cults were formed around relics and places associated with men and women executed on the grounds that administering sacraments or aiding a Roman Catholic priest engaging in such activities was an act of treason against the state.

The eighteenth century was a period of more or less steady decline in surviving cult formations from the marked mid-seventeenth-century high point. However, in southern Germanic lands and even in Iberia, the eighteenth century accounts for considerably more active shrines than the nineteenth century, and these two centuries account for about the same number of active pilgrimage centers in the Italian and North German regions. Therefore, the Turners' nineteenth-century "postindustrial" resurgence of pilgrimage in Europe is a peculiarly French, British, and Irish phenomenon. Several nineteenth-century cult-formative events in France became more famous than similar epiphanies in preceding centuries and have exerted a strong influence on the development of twentieth-century pilgrimage shrines throughout Western Europe and the rest of the Christian world. However, these influential new shrines, such as La Salette and Lourdes, did not emerge suddenly from a 300-year limbo of Pan-European pilgrimage decline.

Variability in times of genesis for shrines in different areas is important for interpreting regional differences in shrine characteristics. One should expect Irish shrines to differ as a group from those of other regions simply because the majority are of such great antiquity. More than half of the datable shrines of France, Spain, and Portugal were established before 1399, so Early and High Medieval themes should be especially apparent in the pilgrimage lore of these countries. In Italy and Belgium, the 50 percent mark occurs in the Renaissance period. Austrian, Swiss, German, and Dutch traditions are still more recent in the aggregate, with more than half of today's datable shrines coming into being after 1530. However, as will become apparent in the next few chapters, Germanic pilgrimages, especially in parts of Switzerland and Austria, display a fairly high proportion of traits often thought of as archaic. Very likely, many sixteenth- through eighteenth-century Germanic pilgrimage places developed as "replacements" for older shrines that failed to survive the turmoil of the Reformation and religious wars. Old stories may have been retold about the newly identified, or reidentified, holy places.

The shrines of England, Scotland, and Wales are interesting in that many are simultaneously very old and very new. To the extent that cultus at a recently reestablished shrine draws its mystique from lore surrounding its initial identification as a Christianized holy place, the shrine may be thought of as representing an ancient tradition. However, because many of these pilgrimage places lay dormant for so long, the stories of their re-creation as shrines are typically of a modern type. Thus, old and new often blend in curious ways, and, perhaps ironically, the old is often stressed more at those British pilgrimage centers maintained by the Anglican church than at the Roman Catholic shrines where emphasis is placed on the circumstances leading to reestablishment of the pilgrimage.

Shrines of all levels of current importance date from all periods. However, there are variations in the percentages of major and minor shrines from each period. Major shrines are more likely to derive from Early Christian, Early Medieval, or Modern time periods than are shrines in general. The years since the early nineteenth century are especially important in accounting for major pilgrimage centers of the present. This is probably because such shrines reflect fairly recent epiphanies and derive much of their drawing power from a mystique which asserts that miracles continue to happen in a modern world. Proportions of minor shrines reach a decided peak in Post-Reformation times; but because large numbers of shrines are involved, this period accounts for a greater number of Europe's major shrines than any other period except the High Middle Ages.

In conclusion, regional variance should be examined from the perspective of differential proportions of shrines reflecting Pan-European trends of the past. Aggregate differences between shrines of different regions are also rooted in the specific culture history of each area and sometimes in very ancient, regionally specific traditions of landscape sanctity. These and other themes will be further explored in the following chapters.

five

Holy Persons

The Subjects of Devotion

Pilgrimage shrines in Western Europe are centers of a special devotion, or cultus, focused on a particular holy person who is historically or symbolically associated with the pilgrimage place, or with an image or relic enshrined at the place. These subjects of devotion include the Virgin Mary, Christ, and the numerous holy persons—historical or legendary, canonized or not—whom we will refer to collectively as the saints. At some shrines, a group, such as the Fourteen Holy Helpers, Saint Leopold and Saint George as protectors of livestock, or Mary, Joseph, and the Christ Child as the Holy Family, is venerated as a unit. At most shrines, pilgrim attention is directed to a single individual or group, but at least 11 percent of Europe's shrines honor two or more individuals or groups which are considered to be distinctly separate subjects of devotion. In these cases one subject usually takes precedence in the pilgrims' frame of reference, so it is possible to define that subject as primary and the other, or others, as secondary. The person for whom the church or chapel is named, and thus to whom it is "officially" dedicated, is not necessarily a subject of pilgrim devotion although local festivals may be held in his or her honor in addition to the pilgrimages directed toward the shrine's subject of devotion.

Pilgrimage focus on holy persons is so pervasive at Europe's shrines that our inventory included only 99 cases where no subject of veneration was identified. A few of these shrines, such as a monastic ruin in Denmark where a modest pilgrimage began in the twentieth century, have no special subject focus. Other such cases reflect a lack of information. Shrines for which no subject focus was recorded make up 1.6 percent of the inventory and have not been considered in the development of the tables and maps for this chapter.

Relative Importance of Mary, Christ, and the Saints

European pilgrimage is predominantly Marian. Christ's mother, Saint Mary, is the principal subject of devotion at nearly two-thirds of today's shrines (Table 5-1, Figure 5-1). Her significance is followed by that of a multitude of saints whose 1,614 shrines make up 27 percent of the cases examined. Christ-centered pilgrimage cults are relatively rare, accounting for less than 8 percent of the shrines. These 453 shrines include 39 focused on the Trinity, usually represented by a carving or painting of the Father, Son, and Holy Ghost. This "three-in-one" subject usually emphasizes Christ, although in some cases the Holy Ghost depicted as a dove seems to be the subject of special pilgrim attention, whereas God the Father is apparently the primary subject of devotion at a few shrines. Among secondary subjects, the saints predominate, representing nearly 70 percent of the recorded cases. Mary accounts for less than 19 percent of the cases of shrines with secondary devotional subjects, followed by Christ at 12 percent of these shrines.

Primary and Secondary Devotional Subjects

When a shrine has a dual focus, the orientation toward more than one devotional subject sometimes dates from the time of cult establishment. This may happen when a saint's devotion to a particular Marian image gives rise to cultus directed toward both the saint and Mary as manifest in the saint's icon of inspiration. In such cases, the saint is likely to be the primary subject of a modern devotion embellished with a secondary Marian cultus if he or she lived during the past four to five centuries. In cases of earlier saint-Mary combinations of this type, the Marian cultus generally takes precedence unless the saint is an extremely powerful persona in his or her own right.

More often, shrines with a dual subject focus emerge as a result of the superimposition of a new devotion to a different holy person on an older cultus associated with a place that was already attracting pilgrims. During the Middle Ages many fading saints' shrines gained new vigor when an image of the Virgin Mary began drawing larger numbers of pilgrims because of various types of miraculous events. In these cases, Mary is usually the primary subject attraction for modern pilgrims while devotion to the saint around whose mystique the shrine first developed is now secondary.

Frequencies of relationships between various devotional subjects in pri-

Table 5-1 *Subjects of Devotion*

	Level of Devotion			
	Primary		Secondary	
Subject	N	%	N	%
Christ	453	7.5	82	12.0
Mary	3,984	65.8	127	18.5
Male saints	1,192	19.7	367	53.5
Female saints	361	6.0	74	10.8
Mixed saints	61	1.0	36	5.2
All saints	1,614	26.7	686	69.5
Total	6,051	100.0	686	100.0

mary and secondary roles indicate that the most prevalent combination is found at shrines where Mary is the primary subject and one or more saints are secondary (Table 5-2). The saint subordinate to Mary is usually a male, but she is also covenerated with female saints, particularly her mother, Saint Anne. At 14 percent of the dual-focus shrines a saint is primary and Mary is secondary, thus bringing the overall Mary-saint combination to nearly two-thirds of the cases. At shrines where Mary and Christ are viewed as distinct subjects of veneration, Mary is most likely to be the primary subject. But at shrines focusing on both Christ and a saint, Christ is more often the principal subject. Most shrines combining devotions to several saints do not appear to emphasize one saint over another, especially when the saintly subjects of devotion are of the same sex. These shrines were assigned to general male or female saint categories. Most of the multiple saint shrines listed in Table 5-2 reflect situations in which two quite different saints, often of the opposite sex, are honored at the same place in distinctively separate devotions.

Relative Importance of Male and Female Subjects

In the Christian tradition, Mary and the female saints may be thought of as representing womanly aspects of divinity, whereas Christ, the Trinity, and male saints presumably reflect more masculine traits.[1] Among the saints, males predominate. At least 1,163 active European saints' shrines are primarily dedicated to holy men, as opposed to 361 focused on female saints other than the Virgin Mary. However, as a result of Mary's importance as a primary devotional subject, modern European pilgrimage is strongly

Figure 5-1 *The Virgin Mary is the principal subject of veneration at 66 percent of Europe's shrines. Even in Ireland, where only a small proportion of active shrines are focused on Mary, devotions to Our Lady are strong. Here, an Irish pilgrim lays flowers at the feet of one of several outdoor statues decorating the grounds of the shrine at Our Lady's Island, County Wexford.*

Table 5-2 *Simultaneous Devotion to Holy Persons as Primary and Secondary Subjects*

	Primary Subject		
Secondary Subject	Christ	Mary	Saints
Christ	0	56 (8%)	26 (4%)
Mary	35 (5%)	0	94 (14%)
Saints	44 (6%)	353 (52%)	78 (11%)

oriented toward a female principle of divinity. More than 70 percent of the primary subjects of devotion are holy women, either Mary or a female saint. Among secondary subjects of devotion the pattern of sex emphasis reverses. Males, including Christ, the Trinity, and masculine saints make up nearly 66 percent of the secondary devotional subjects.

National and Regional Variations in Primary Subjects

Relative emphasis on Mary, Christ, and the saints varies considerably within Western Europe. As indicated in Table 5-3, high proportions of shrines dedicated to the Virgin Mary are especially characteristic of Italy, Spain, France, and Belgium. West German and Austrian shrines are predominantly Marian, but to a lesser degree, whereas in Portugal and Switzerland nearly as many shrines are dedicated to Christ and the saints as to Mary. Percentages of Marian shrines are low in countries once Protestant by edict. Catholic Ireland has a very low percentage of Marian shrines probably because Protestant British attempts to repress Irish pilgrimage eliminated most of the island's Medieval Marian shrines and suppressed the establishment of newer such shrines until the nineteenth century.

When proportions of Marian shrines are examined by subregion, the complexities of the distribution pattern become more apparent. Map 5-1 separates Europe into those areas that are well above average in proportions of Marian shrines, those that cluster around the Pan-European average of 66 percent of identified shrines with a known subject focus, and those that are clearly below average.

High proportions of pilgrimage centers devoted to Mary extend from

Table 5-3 *Subjects of Devotion by Country*

	Subject						
	Mary		Saints		Christ		
Country	N	%	N	%	N	%	Total[a]
Italy	920	77	232	20	40	3	1,192
France	742	75	236	24	18	2	996
Spain	754	75	154	15	100	10	1,008
West Germany	550	59	252	27	124	13	926
Austria	525	57	295	32	100	11	920
Portugal	168	52	124	39	29	9	321
Switzerland	142	51	104	38	31	11	277
Belgium	118	80	23	16	6	4	147
United Kingdom	34	41	49	58	1	1	84
Ireland	16	13	106	86	1	1	123
Netherlands	12	25	33	69	3	6	48
Sweden	2	40	3	60	0	0	5
Denmark	1	50	1	50	0	0	2
Norway	0	0	1	100	0	0	1
Finland	0	0	1	100	0	0	1
Total	3,984		1,614		453		6,051

[a]Totals reflect shrines where a devotional subject focus has been identified.

southern Portugal through most of Spain and southern France into northern and north-central Italy. Other areas with higher-than-average proportions of Marian shrines are in southern Italy and western France, and in a belt extending from Belgium through the French provinces of Lorraine and Alsace. A line of relatively low frequencies of Marian shrines extends through the French and Germanic regions of Switzerland, across alpine Austria, and into Niederösterreich. Limoges is the only French region with a below-average proportion of Marian shrines. Fewer than half of the shrines of the northwestern Spanish province of Galicia are Marian, in sharp contrast with the rest of Spain. This low emphasis on Mary combined with a high proportion of saints' shrines is also found in northern and central Portugal. The Mediterranean islands of Corsica and Sardinia have below-average proportions of Marian shrines in contrast to Sicily and the Balearics, which show above-average percentages. Lower-than-average emphasis on Marian shrines also characterizes central and northern West Germany except for the Münster region. Scandinavia, the Netherlands, Britain, and Ireland are substantially below average in proportions of Marian shrines. Discounting Norway and Finland, countries

Holy Persons

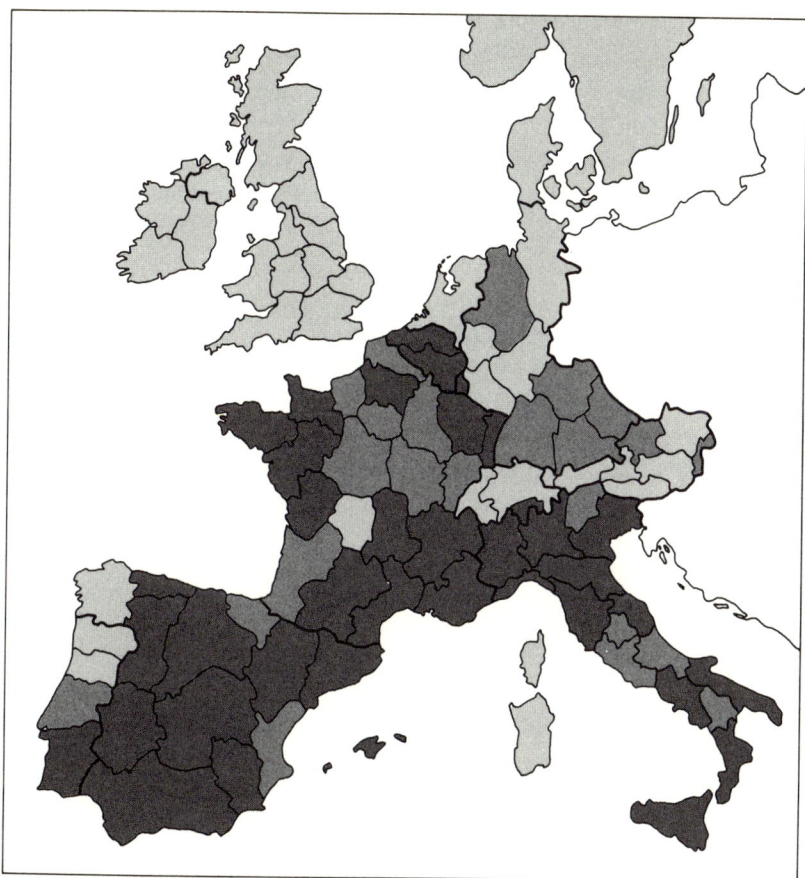

Key:

▢ Less than 60 percent of the shrines dedicated to Mary

▨ 60 to 71 percent of the shrines dedicated to Mary

▮ 72 percent or more of the shrines dedicated to Mary

Map 5-1 *Regional Variations in Percentages of Shrines Dedicated to the Virgin Mary*
The southern European tendency toward high frequencies of shrines devoted to the Virgin Mary is evident in this map. Regional subdivisions are based on standard political or economic units within European countries or on aggregates of such units.

with only one shrine dedicated in both cases to a male saint, frequencies of Marian shrines are lowest in Ireland where only 13 percent of the holy places with an identified subject of veneration are dedicated to the Virgin Mary.

Although Mary is the principal subject of devotion at half or more of the identified shrines throughout much of Europe, the amount of regional difference suggests caution in generalizing about the Marian orientations of Western European pilgrimage. A research focus on central Spain, for example, would present a different view of devotional subject importance than a study based in the northwestern Spanish province of Galicia and would be of no value for interpreting shrine subject focus patterns in Ireland.

Map 5-2 divides European regions into four categories of emphasis on saints' shrines. Areas with half or more of their shrines primarily dedicated to saints can be thought of as having a strong saint orientation within the modern European context. Regions with approximately one-third to fewer than one-half of their shrines dedicated to saints stand out as well above average in devotion to saints, while those with 20 to 29 percent are within the general range of the Pan-European average. Regions where fewer than one-fifth of the shrines are dedicated to saints can be conceptualized as generally weak in this type of devotion, although a few famous saints' shrines are found in such areas. Because the number of Christ-oriented shrines is fairly small, proportions of saints' shrines tend to be a reverse of the percentages for Marian shrines.

The map indicates that saints' shrines are proportionately most prevalent in Ireland and the predominantly Protestant areas of northern Europe. They are also important in northwestern Iberia, north-central West Germany, and along a transalpine belt extending from southeastern Austria westward through Franche-Comté and Burgundy to an outlier in the Limoges region of France. This region, with 45 percent of its shrines devoted to saints, is more saint-oriented than other areas along the central French-Swiss-Austrian line. The high proportion of saints' shrines in Limoges reflects the seventeenth-century institutionalization of an ancient, once widespread tradition of making pilgrimages with the relics and/or images of locally venerated saints to the shrine of the district's most important saint, often the patron of the district's major town. Community groups carrying their most sacred relics and images converged sporadically on these shrines in Medieval Limoges, as elsewhere in Europe, usually as part of the ceremonial reception for a visiting dignitary or during periods of stress induced by warfare, plague, or famine. During the 1600s this custom was regularized in Limoges into a series of once-every-seventh-year events known as *ostensions*. These periodic pilgrimages, which

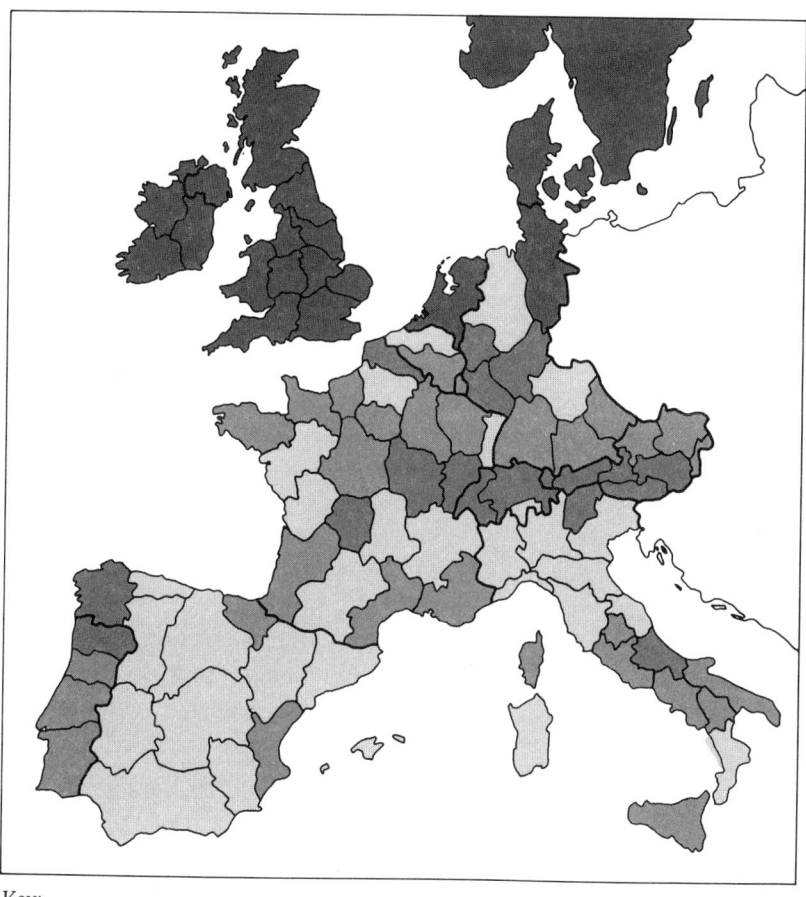

Key:

☐ 0 to 19 percent of the shrines dedicated to saints

■ 20 to 30 percent of the shrines dedicated to saints

■ 32 to 49 percent of the shrines dedicated to saints

■ 50 percent or more of the shrines dedicated to saints

Map 5-2 *Regional Variations in Percentages of Shrines Dedicated to Saints* Saints' shrines are relatively the most common in predominantly Protestant areas and Ireland. They also appear with higher-than-usual frequencies in a belt extending from central France through Switzerland and alpine Austria and in the northwestern corner of the Iberian peninsula. Because a substantial majority of the saints venerated at European shrines are males, areas with the large proportions of saints' shrines are also those with a stronger-than-usual focus on male as opposed to female subjects of devotion.

have continued ever since, are deeply ingrained in Limoges tradition and the civic pride of the region's communities.

Sixteen Limoges localities announced ostensions in 1981. Thirty-eight different community groups participated in the 1981 Le Dorat ostensions, where we witnessed the closing ceremonies. Most villages and towns of the region took part in at least one of the 1981 ostensions. Although many of the participant communities now place special emphasis on attending these celebrations with locally venerated images of the Virgin Mary, the focal point of nearly all these events is the shrine of a saint.[2] Similar periodic celebrations of old saint-oriented pilgrimages are found scattered in other parts of Europe, as for example at Maastricht in the Netherlands.

In Italy, the culturally Germanic Trentino-Alto Adige region forms a southward extension of the alpine belt of saint shrine emphasis. A similar pattern is found in the mountains of the Abruzzi-Molise region, an area of several rather curious pilgrimage cults including survivals of pagan Roman rites of spring with offerings of snakes to the tenth-century Benedictine, San Doménico Abate. Sardinia also has higher-than-average proportions of saint-focused shrines.

As illustrated by Map 5-3, Christ-centered cultus, although nowhere extremely common, is primarily an Ibero-Germanic phenomenon. Fifteen percent or more of the shrines in the Münster, Hildesheim, Baden-Württemberg, Munich, and Regensburg areas of West Germany are dedicated to Christ, as is also the case in the Spanish provinces of León, Extremadura, and Murcia. Christ cults appear to be generally unimportant in France, especially toward the west, and the Spanish provinces bordering France show low frequencies for Iberia. The current distribution of a relatively high emphasis on Christ can be largely accounted for by survivals of shrines created by an enthusiasm for miraculous images of Christ, reaching its greatest levels in Iberia and the Germanies during the Catholic Reformation. This idea of cultus, in contrast with earlier Christ-centered pilgrimages focused on relics of the Passion such as pieces of the True Cross, seems to have spread from the Germanies to Spain and from these regions to the Americas without making any obvious impact on shrine development in France prior to the late eighteenth century. These regional patterns are reflected in data on New World pilgrimage. More than 28 percent of the 970 active shrines that we have inventoried in Hispanic America are focused on Christ. However, in French-influenced Canada only 4 out of 95 identified shrines are places where Christ provides the focus for pilgrimage devotion. Three of these four Canadian shrines are dedicated to Christ's Sacred Heart, a modern Christ-oriented devotion that became im-

Holy Persons

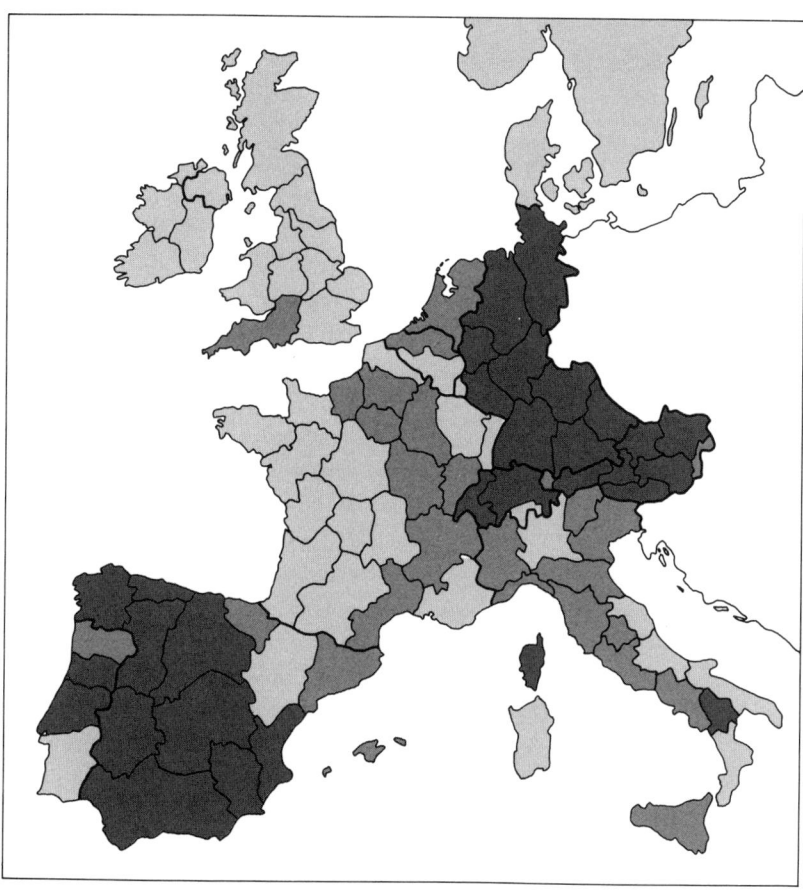

Key:

▢ 0 to 2 percent of the shrines dedicated to Christ

▢ 3 to 8 percent of the shrines dedicated to Christ

▢ 9 percent or more of the shrines dedicated to Christ

Map 5-3 *Regional Variations in Percentages of Shrines Dedicated to Christ*
There is a strong tendency toward higher-than-usual frequencies of Christ-focused shrines in Iberia and the Germanic lands. Such cults are notably uncommon in western France and the British Isles.

portant only toward the end of the eighteenth century although it can be traced to the visions of a seventeenth-century French nun whose burial place at Paray-le-Monial in Burgundy is one of the great pilgrimage centers of modern France.

The pattern for Belgium also reflects the difference between French and Germanic emphasis on Christ. Only 1 percent of the shrines found in Walloon Belgium are Christ-centered, as contrasted with Flemish Belgium where 8 percent of the shrines are focused on Christ.

England and Ireland each have one Christ-centered shrine, in both cases at recently reestablished pilgrimage centers which in Medieval times claimed to have pieces of Christ's Cross. The apparent sparsity of Christ shrines in these regions probably reflects the demise of Medieval and Renaissance shrines along with religious isolation from the Christ cults centered on images that flourished in Iberia and the Germanies during the Catholic Reformation. Christ-centered shrines are also low in frequency throughout much of Italy. In this area, the highest concentrations are in Basilicata where 9 percent of the identified shrines are Christ-centered and in the culturally Germanic Trentino-Alto Adige region where 7 percent of the shrines are focused on Christ.

Shrines where we found Christ cultus related to images of the Trinity are concentrated in Germanic alpine Europe, especially Austria and southeastern Bavaria (Figure 5-2). Trinity cultus in these regions primarily dates from the seventeenth and eighteenth centuries as at Sonntagberg in Lower Austria. This alpine site, probably sacred in pagan times, has attracted Christian pilgrims since at least the thirteenth century when the shrine was dedicated to Mary. The current cult object, however, is a large seventeenth-century painting of God the Father holding the crucified Christ. A form of Holy Spirit cultus appeared much earlier in Portugal, where it was introduced in the fourteenth century by Isabel of Aragon, known as Holy Queen Isabel.[3]

There is considerable variation among countries in the prevalence of female versus male devotional subjects. With the exception of Portugal, the strongest pilgrimage orientations toward a female principle of divinity are in France and the Mediterranean peninsulas. These are also the areas where ancient mother goddess devotions are most likely to have lingered in the countryside long after the impact of Celtic and Germanic migrations of peoples oriented toward a high god, and despite the later missionary efforts of early Christian churchmen who emphasized a masculine principle of divinity.[4]

Holy Persons

Figure 5-2 *This carving of the Trinity in a church in eastern Austria, although not a pilgrimage cult object, is typical of the baroque imagery that evokes Trinity devotions at approximately two dozen shrines. Note the Holy Ghost represented as a dove.*

Because regions with large proportions of saints' shrines are nearly always the most masculine oriented, Map 5-3 provides an idea of regional variation in the proportion of male and female devotional subjects. An exception to this rule is found in Wales, an area that is both saint-oriented and female-focused because most of the active saints' shrines are dedicated to holy women. Generally, however, there is no special pattern of regions with high proportions of female saints relative to male saints and the greatest concentrations of female saints' shrines are in areas with the most saints' shrines of any kind. Fairly high proportions of Christ and male saints' shrines tend to moderate female emphasis in Bavaria and the Münster region in West Germany, and in the Spanish province of Valencia. In general, however, regions with substantial percentages of Christ cults seldom coincide with those having many saints' shrines, so a combination of Christ with male saints rarely tips the balance toward a strong male orientation.

The Saints

Christ and Mary are symbolized in various ways at shrines focusing on different attributes of their human and heavenly personalities, but, no matter how manifest, the devotional subjects at these shrines are only one or another of two individuals. The saints, in contrast, are many. Some, particularly uncanonized folk saints, are virtually unknown beyond the districts of their single shrines. Others are famous canonized saints of the universal church to whom numerous chapels, parish churches, and even cathedrals may be dedicated in name, but whose cultus draws pilgrims to only a few of the active, greater-than-local shrines of modern Europe.

A considerable majority of the 1,614 active saints' shrines identified in this study focus on holy persons of vicinity or regional fame who have only one or a few shrines located in the region where they lived or where their relics are found. Saint Hervé provides an example of a saint who attracts pilgrims primarily from a single district. According to legend, this blind holy man was born to British emigrant parents in sixth-century Brittany. He founded a monastery at Lanhouarneau, Brittany, where he died in about 568. His relics were exhumed and placed on a church altar in 878, and his body, or most of it, was taken to Nantes Cathedral in 1002. It was hidden by a priest during the French Revolution and has never been relocated. Lanhouarneau, however, claims the saint's arm bone which is kept in the town church. At the saint's holy well, about two kilometers from town, the waters are still thought to be effective for curing eye diseases (Figure 5-3). A procession with the relic takes place each year on the Monday of Pentecost and a pardon to the holy well is held each June 17.[5]

Saint Hemma, an Austrian noblewoman who died in about 1045, is an example of a regionally important saint. She is venerated at five shrines in the southern Austrian regions of Kärnten and Styria. One of her shrines tops Hemmaberg, a hill near Globasnitz. Christian structures dating from the third to the fifth centuries are currently being excavated at this probable pre-Christian holy place. Another shrine near Edelschrott marks the spot where her husband, Saint Wilhelm, was saved from a wild boar. At the Marian shrine of Maria Elend in Rosental where the saint is said to have made a pilgrimage

Figure 5-3 *Saint Hervé's Holy Well is located in a field near Lanhouarneau in Brittany, France. Pilgrims come each year to pay their respects to this patron of musicians and protector of people in the region where he established a monastery in the sixth century.*

while pregnant, Hemma is currently the secondary subject of veneration, and she is venerated at Gräbern along with her husband who was buried at the site when he died on the way home from a pilgrimage to Rome (Figure 5-4). The best known center of Saint Hemma's cultus is at Gurk, another pre-Christian holy place where the saint founded a convent and monastery. Local devotees may have attributed some of the traits of the goddess Isis-Norica to Hemma, and one authority speculates that these pagan associations help explain why Hemma was not formally canonized until 1938.[6]

Several well-known saints also attract pilgrims to only a few sites. For example, we found Saint Mark, author of the second New Testament gospel, as the primary subject of devotion only at Saint Mark's Cathedral, Venice, which claims to have his relics, and at one other Italian shrine. Similarly, the Apostle Saint Andrew whose remains are said to be in Amalfi, Italy, was found as the devotional subject at only three other shrines, one in France and

Figure 5-4 *In this relief carving from the shrine church at Gurk, Austria, Saint Hemma bids a tearful farewell to her husband, Saint Wilhelm, as he prepares to leave on a pilgrimage to Rome. According to tradition, the journey was made in penitence for a bloodbath of workers ordered after the couple's two sons were murdered during an uprising at one of Wilhelm's mines. The landgrave died on his way home, and the widowed Hemma devoted the rest of her life to good works among the poor and the establishment of religious houses.*

two in Spain. Some of his relics may have been taken to Saint Andrew's, Scotland, in the fourth century, but this pilgrimage did not survive the Reformation. Saint Thomas, the doubtful Apostle, was identified as a subject of veneration at three shrines located in Italy, France, and Austria. The great evangelist, Saint Paul, has his only important Western European shrine at Saint Paul's Outside the Walls in Rome, and there is a minor shrine at the site of a sixteenth-century apparition of the saint to some shepherds near Albocacer in eastern Spain. The Three Kings of the Nativity story, beloved throughout Europe in their roles as bearers of gifts to children on January 6, draw pilgrims to the Cologne Cathedral where their assumed relics have been enshrined since 1164 (Figure 5-5).

Famous saints of more recent vintage are often honored at only one impor-

Figure 5-5 *The wonder of the Christmas season fascinates a tiny Spanish child of Barcelona who posed for a portrait on the lap of an elaborately dressed man representing Balthasar, one of the Three Kings, or Magi, described in the Gospel of Saint Matthew as coming from the East to offer gold, frankincense, and myrrh to the infant Christ. Relics, believed to be those of the Magi, were brought from the Holy Land to Milan during the Crusades and sent as a gift to the German city of Cologne in 1164. As a result, Cologne became one of the great pilgrimage centers of Medieval Europe, and the Magi are still honored there on January 6, a day when children receive presents said to have been brought by the Three Kings.*

tant pilgrimage center or at a small cluster of shrines in the region of their greatest activity. Thus, Saint Joan of Arc is especially venerated at Domrémy-la-Pucelle, France, where she was born and where her visions led her to assume command of French troops during the Hundred Years' War. A Counter Reformation saint, Francis de Sales, is honored at three shrines in and near Annecy, France, and the Loyola family castle in the Basque province of Guipúzcoa, Spain, is a center of pilgrimages to Saint Ignatius Loyola, founder of the Society of Jesus. Here in 1521, while recovering from battle wounds, Loyola experienced visions leading to his adoption of a religious life. Other examples include the Spanish mystic, Saint Teresa of Ávila, venerated at Ávila and at her burial place of Alba de Tormes, Spain; the twelve-year-old Italian rape victim, Saint Maria Goretti, venerated at Nettuno, Italy; the nineteenth-century Curé d'Ars, in France, who is the patron of parish priests; and Saint Bernadette Soubirous, the Lourdes visionary, who was canonized in 1933 and is honored at her convent tomb in Nevers, France.

A modern saint with relatively few shrines in Europe but several in the Americas is the young French nun, Saint Theresa of Lisieux, "The Little Flower." This model of late nineteenth-century piety died of tuberculosis in 1897 at age 23 and was canonized in 1925. Her basilica tomb draws more than a million pilgrims per year to Lisieux, France. The cultus provoked a particular response among North American Catholics and there are at least six active shrines focused on Saint Theresa in the United States and Canada.

Exemplary, but as yet uncanonized, holy persons such as Padre Pio and Pope John XXIII also draw pilgrims to only one or a few places. Indeed, such persons are not technically supposed to be venerated by the faithful because of their uncanonized status. However, pilgrimages to their tombs are often encouraged, possibly because canonization still requires proof of miraculous intervention, and pilgrimage experiences now as in the past tend to set the stage for wondrous events that can be attributed to the intercession of the exemplary person in question.

Occasionally, canonization procedures—which take place years or even centuries after a holy person's demise—lead to a rapid development of subsidiary shrine centers in regions far from the saint's homeland. This is especially likely if the saint's cultus is vigorously promoted by members of a religious order with branches in many lands. The spread of the cultus of the fifteenth-century Italian nun Rita of Cáscia after her canonization in 1900 was mentioned in Chapter 3. European shrines in her honor are now found in France, Spain, and the Netherlands; she is also venerated at several shrines in the Americas.

Another example is the spread of the cultus of Saint Gerard Majella from southern Italy to the Netherlands. This Italian holy man, who became a Redemptorist lay brother in 1748, was noted for an extraordinary number of prophecies, visions, and ecstasies and was credited with miraculous cures prior to his death in 1754. His burial place at Materdómini, inland from Salerno in southern Italy, has been a pilgrimage center ever since, but it was only after the saint's canonization in 1904 that the new Dutch shrines began

Holy Persons

to emerge as a result of their promotion by Redemptorists. The most important is at Wittem, but there are at least four others. This particular spread of cultus has resulted in some curious cultural incongruities. The Dutch churches where the saint is honored provide a totally different pilgrimage experience from his shrine at Materdómini. Here bills and coins lie on the floor of a grill-enclosed area surrounding the saint's wax effigy in a glass casket. Walls in the surrounding halls are covered with silver hearts, fading newspaper clippings describing auto accidents, and snapshots of southern Italians saved from various catastrophes through the saint's intercession. A great new basilica of modernistic style and stark interior was rising near the old, earthquake-damaged church when we visited the shrine in 1978.

Saint Gerard, or Gerardus, also provides an eighteenth-century example of an ancient phenomenon—the living person as a focus for pilgrimage. Such pilgrimages were common in the Greco-Roman world of pre-Christian antiquity. The custom was Christianized early and appears to have been commonplace by the fifth century as the faithful sought out wonder-working monks and hermits.[7] The practice is evident in every age, including the present. We have talked with people who made pilgrimages to San Giovanni Rotondo, Italy, in order to honor and be helped by Padre Pio, the stigmatized Capuchin priest, before his death in 1968. On the day of Padre Pio's death it is said that a visible stigmata appeared on the hands, feet, and side of another monk named Brother Gino who established a Fátima shrine at San Vittorino near Rome during the early 1960s. Shrine literature at the site emphasizes the Marian Fátima cultus, but some of the many pilgrims visit the place primarily to see and honor Brother Gino.

As seems to be occurring at present with such recently canonized saints as Rita of Cáscia and Gerard Majella, a few holy persons acquired a mystique that has given rise to numerous long-lived pilgrimage centers, frequently extending into regions never visited by the saint when he or she was alive. These major saints of European pilgrim devotion include some of the great saints of Christendom, although others are little known beyond the geographical range of their pilgrimage cultus. The most frequently encountered saints, listed in Table 5-4, are described in the following sections.[8]

Members of Jesus' Family

Among the most popular of Europe's pilgrimage saints are members of the earthly family of Jesus. Saint Mary, His mother, is of such importance that she is considered separately in this study. Next in order of

Table 5-4 *Important Pilgrimage Saints*

Saint	Shrines N	Saint Alone[a] %	Saint and Mary[b] %	Saint and Christ[b] %	Countries Where Found N
Anne	85	71	27	2	8
Leonard	77	70	22	8	4
Anthony of Padua	58	75	16	9	7
Joseph	32	50	47	3	9
Sebastian	30	84	13	3	7
Benedict	29	83	10	7	6
Michael	27	67	22	11	7
John the Baptist	24	58	25	17	7
George	23	87	9	4	6
14 Holy Helpers	22	72	23	5	3
Mary Magdalene	21	80	10	10	7
Wendel	21	71	19	10	3
Peter	20	40	35	5	9
Francis of Assisi	20	70	25	5	3
Valentine	19	74	26	0	4
Roch	18	78	22	0	6
Ulrich	18	55	39	6	3
James the Greater	16	62	38	0	4
Patrick	15	88	6	6	3
Wolfgang	14	86	14	0	2
Lucy	11	100	0	0	4
Christopher	11	82	18	0	6

[a]In a few cases the saint is co-venerated with another saint.
[b]Saint may be either primary or secondary as devotional subject.

significance, as indicated by numbers of shrines, is Mary's mother, traditionally known as Saint Anne, followed by Mary's husband, Saint Joseph, and Jesus' cousin, Saint John the Baptist. Jesus' maternal grandfather, referred to in European tradition as Saint Joachim, is occasionally found as a devotional subject, especially at shrines primarily dedicated to Saint Anne.

Saint Anne, as she is called in apocryphal writings, is obviously a historical rather than a purely mythical person despite the fact that nothing is actually known about her. Legends surrounding Saint Anne are numerous and sometimes fantastic. In Brittany she is supposed to have been a Celtic Breton princess who migrated to the Holy Land where she wed Saint Joachim and gave birth to Mary. Saint Anne is portrayed in a variety of ways. Occasionally, she is represented as a very large figure looming over a child-sized Mary holding a doll-sized infant Christ, perhaps the ultimate graphic expression of a grandmother cultus. Active Saint Anne shrines of the present often focus on images showing Anne teaching the child Mary to read; she may also be portrayed as a queen mother sitting regally beside her holy daughter, as at Annaberg in Austria (Figure 5-6).

We found Mary's mother as a subject of devotion at 85 shrines widely scattered across Western Europe. Areas of special concentration include Brittany, central Switzerland, and southeastern Austria. Apt, France, claims to be Saint Anne's oldest Western European shrine. This Provençal town had a Christian community by the fourth century and has been the seat of a bishop since approximately the year 314. Here, in about the twelfth century, the tomb of a woman believed locally to have been Mary's mother was "miraculously" discovered in the crypt of the local cathedral, and pilgrimages have taken place ever since.[9] Saint Anne's most visited Western European shrine is at Sainte-Anne-d'Auray in Brittany, where she appeared in 1623 to a local freeholding farmer named Yvon Nicolazic. The man's visions took place over a nine-month period and were finally accepted when an old statue of Saint Anne was found in 1625 near the site of a chapel that had fallen into ruin nearly 1,000 years earlier. Although the original statue was burned during the French Revolution, part of the head was saved and is enshrined in a reliquary at the base of the current devotional image. The shrine at Sainte-Anne-d'Auray claims an annual visitation of 800,000 pilgrims from all over the world.[10]

From France, Saint Anne's cultus spread to Canada where she is the primary subject of veneration at 16 percent of the 95 shrines we have identified in that country. Due largely to French influence, there are 11 shrines dedicated to Saint Anne among the 190 pilgrimage places we have located in the United States.

Saint Joseph, Mary's husband, is honored in at least 32 places in eight Western European countries. His veneration is often combined with a Marian devotion, and 6 of the shrines ascribed to Saint Joseph are actually dedicated to the Holy Family as a group. The Judean carpenter's cultus began in the East where the apocryphal *History of Joseph* was extremely popular from the fourth through seventh centuries. His veneration spread in the West during the fifteenth century, especially after 1476 when his feast was introduced into the Roman calendar. His cultus was vigorously promoted during the Catholic Reformation and has continued to increase in significance during modern times. Saint Joseph was declared "Patron of the Universal Church" in 1870, and he is regarded as a model for fathers of families, as a protector of work-

Figure 5-6 *Statues of Mary, the Christ Child, and Mary's mother, Saint Anne, provide a regal focus for pilgrim devotions at Annaberg, Austria. Saint Anne is frequently portrayed as an ordinary woman, often teaching the child Mary to read, as well as a huge figure holding a child-sized Mary with the infant Christ in her arms.*

men (related to his occupation as a carpenter), and as a patron of social justice.

One of the saint's more important European pilgrimages began in 1856 at Esplay-Le Puy, France, after a devout woman found a small statue of Saint Joseph. She placed it in a grotto near the ruins of the Medieval castle that had once served as a summer home for the bishops of Le Puy, and pilgrim visits began soon afterward. In addition to those places where Saint Joseph attracts pilgrims, his March 19 feast is celebrated enthusiastically in many communities, especially in Italy. Saint Joseph is also popular in North America, with at least four shrines in Canada and seven in the United States.

Saint John the Baptist, cousin of Jesus and first-century Judean hermit-preacher, was arrested by Herod Antipas, tetrarch of Perea and Galilee, and beheaded at the request of Salome. During his life he baptized Jesus and inspired many to follow the teachings of Christ. He is usually thought of as

Holy Persons

the last of the Old Testament prophets as well as the precursor of Christ, and at 17 percent of his shrines there is also a Christ cultus. Shrines dedicated to Saint John the Baptist are extensive in Western Europe and include at least 24 places of pilgrimage, mostly of fairly minor importance. The eve of his feast day of June 24, which falls at the summer solstice, is an occasion for celebrations at these shrines and throughout the subcontinent.

The Apostles

Two of Christ's original twelve disciples, Saint Peter and Saint James the Greater, are focal points of veneration at more than ten widely distributed shrines. Saint Jude, or Saint Judas Thaddeus, ranks third among the apostles as a pilgrimage saint with at least nine European shrines to his credit. Saint Jude also has at least five shrines in North America. The cult of this apostle, who replaced Judas Iscariot among the original group, developed slowly and became important only in the twentieth century.

Saint Peter is believed to have been crucified in about A.D. 64 during the reign of Emperor Nero and buried on Vatican Hill. Saint Peter's Basilica, the most important church of Western Roman Catholic Christendom, has risen on this site. At least 19 other shrines in nine Western European countries are dedicated to this saint, and his special day, along with that of Saint Paul, is widely celebrated in the Christian world.

Saint James the Greater is the primary subject of veneration at Santiago de Compostela, Spain. This Galician town was the third most important shrine of Medieval Christendom. While no longer third in rank behind Jerusalem and Rome, the shrine at Santiago remains one of the truly great pilgrimage places of the Western world (Figure 5-7). The shrine's fortunes have waxed and waned as its legends have been alternately accepted and rejected. The idea that the Apostle James the Greater ever went on a mission to Iberia is considered doubtful, and the notion that his bones could have been transferred from the site of his martyrdom, probably in Jerusalem, to the far northwestern corner of Iberia is generally thought to be a pious legend. The Santiago pilgrimage has been decreed dead or dying by numerous observers over the past several hundred years, but the Spanish cultus has been revived repeatedly through the centuries.[11]

Santiago de Compostela's most recent revival at the international level took place when Generalissimo Francisco Franco's government vigorously promoted the 1965 celebrations of the Santiago Holy Year, which occurs whenever the saint's day of July 25 falls on a Sunday. Holy Year pilgrimages since

Figure 5-7 *The elaborate granite carvings of the Obradoiro, or west-facing main facade of Saint James's Basilica in Santiago de Compostela, turn golden in the late afternoon light. This baroque masterpiece dates from the eighteenth century, but the tomb of Saint James the Greater has drawn pilgrims to this distant corner of northwestern Spain since its miraculous discovery in the early ninth century.*

1965 have been attended by well over a million devotees. Hundreds of thousands come during ordinary years and walking the ancient Way of Saint James, or at least the last 100 kilometers, has become a popular activity for those with time to make the effort.

We found Saint James as a subject of veneration at 15 other European shrines in four countries, with the majority in Spain and Portugal. His cultus is often found in conjunction with venerations directed toward the Virgin Mary. As might be expected, this saint is honored at several shrines in Latin America, but he does not seem to have emerged as a focal devotional figure for pilgrimage in the United States or Canada.

Other Biblical Figures

An angel, Saint Michael, and a presumably historical woman, Saint Mary Magdalene, have little in common except that both are mentioned in the Bible and are figures of ancient and widespread cultus in Western Europe. Both of these pilgrimage saints have greater-than-usual proportions of shrines at sites thought to be pre-Christian religious centers and a particular affinity for places marked by natural characteristics such as heights and grottoes. There is, however, no reason to think that the cults of the angel and the biblical woman are interrelated and the present-day pilgrimage centers have rather different patterns of distribution. They are grouped in the same section because neither fits well into any other category.

Saint Michael the Archangel, mentioned twice in both the Old and the New Testaments, is one of three angels, along with Gabriel and Raphael, whose veneration is customary. Of these, only Saint Michael is of any importance as a subject of pilgrim devotion. Except for a minor Saint Gabriel shrine we chanced upon in a remote district of northeastern Portugal, we found no evidence for contemporary European pilgrimage cultus related to the angels Gabriel and Raphael. The Western cultus of Saint Michael is apparently related to his ascribed role as captain of the Heavenly Hosts and as protector of Christians from the devil.[12] His pilgrimage cultus probably originated in west-central Asia Minor (ancient Phrygia) and was dramatically planted on Italy's Gargano Peninsula in the late fifth century at a site where the archangel is said to have appeared to several persons including the local bishop, who was a native of Asia Minor. The fame of the Monte Sant'Angelo pilgrimage soon spread widely and influenced the establishment of the great French shrines of Le Mont-Saint-Michel in the eighth century and Saint-Michel-de-Frigolet in the twelfth century. We found active Saint Michael venerations at

27 widely scattered European shrines, fairly often in association with cults focusing on Mary or Christ.

Saint Mary Magdalene, who is mentioned several times in the New Testament, was one of the three women to discover Christ's empty tomb and hear the angelic announcement of the Resurrection. An ancient popular belief identifies Mary Magdalene with the unnamed woman in the Gospel of Saint Luke who, when she anointed Christ's feet, was forgiven sins popularly presumed to involve prostitution. Some modern biblical scholars doubt that the Mary Magdalene of the Resurrection account is the same person as the sinful woman and point out that there is no evidence that Luke's unnamed woman beseeching forgiveness was a prostitute. There are, after all, numerous other ways to sin.

These scholarly arguments are somewhat irrelevant to the Western cultus of Saint Mary Magdalene, the penitent "fallen woman" who gained Christ's loving forgiveness. She is currently venerated in at least 21 pilgrimage places scattered through most of Europe. Her cultus in the West is related to a pious legend that tells of her journey to southern France with Lazarus, Martha, and other early Christians who were escaping persecution in the Holy Land. Once in France, the saint is supposed to have lived for thirty years in a cliff-side cavern where she practiced extreme penitence. In her old age she is said to have visited the missionary, Saint Maximinus, and died at the place now known as Saint-Maximin-la-Sainte-Baume in Provence. A more probable, if less fascinating, account places her Western European cultus in the eleventh century as a result of relic transfers from the East.

Whatever the origins of the cultus, pilgrims still visit several of the grottoes scattered through southern Europe that are claimed to have been the setting of Saint Mary Magdalene's penitence. By far the most famous is the cave-church high on a hill near Saint-Maximin-la-Sainte-Baume. Here, in a place that attracted pilgrims long before the advent of Christianity, modern devotees and tourists trudge up a path through a sacred forest, maintained by the French Forestry Service, to the grotto church. A few attempt the steeper climb to a cliff-top chapel marking a spot where angels are said to have flown the saint each day for her evening devotions.

Two other Mary Magdalene shrines are noted for a Medieval dispute over possession of the saint's relics. According to tradition, she was buried at Saint-Maximin-la-Sainte-Baume. When this settlement was abandoned in the mid-eighth century, her remains were said to have been taken to the Burgundian monastery of Vézelay which subsequently became a great pilgrimage shrine. Vézelay's fortunes declined in the thirteenth century, whereupon, in

1279, monks at a revived Saint-Maximin announced that they had found the "real" body in the crypt of their ancient church. An "odor of sanctity" in the rediscovered tomb was accepted as proof that the eighth-century monks had taken the wrong relics to Vézelay. Charles of Salerno, Count of Provence, promoted the Saint-Maximin claims and the Vézelay pilgrimage faded into obscurity. During the late Middle Ages the Saint-Maximin pilgrimage also faded as Saint Mary Magdalene's popularity waned. The contending shrines have been rediscovered by art history enthusiasts as well as by a new generation of devotees of this famous biblical saint.[13]

Early Christian Martyrs

Western Christendom's earliest shrines developed at the tombs of the apostles and other early Christians martyred during periods of Roman persecution. Many of these saints are no longer important as figures of pilgrim veneration, or have no more than one or two active shrines. Some, whose cultus continues to attract devotees to several places, have been venerated since early times. Others did not become widely known until centuries after their martyrdom and are legendary figures who may incorporate attributes of several individuals and perhaps a few pagan deities.

Those for whom we found five to ten shrines in more than one modern country include Saint Apollonia, an old deaconess supposedly killed in Alexandria, Egypt, in 249; Saint Catherine, also possibly of Alexandria and martyred in about 310; Saint Euphemia, presumably of Chalcedon, who is said to have been used as bear bait in about 310; and Saint Blaise, an Armenian bishop beheaded for his faith in about 316. Early martyrs with more than ten widely distributed shrines in the West are the saints Sebastian, George, Valentine, Lucy, and Christopher.

Saint Sebastian is a subject of devotion in at least 30 places scattered throughout much of Western Europe. He seems to have been an early Christian martyr who was buried along the Appian Way near Rome. This saint was venerated in Milan as early as the fourth century, and his cultus became very popular in Rome in the aftermath of a late seventh-century epidemic. Legends, none of which are reliable, suggest that he was a Gaul who became a Roman soldier in about 283. After accepting Christianity, he is said to have made many converts even as he advanced in his military career. When his faith was discovered during Emperor Maximian's persecution of Christians, Sebastian was condemned to death. Shot full of arrows, he was left for dead but was rescued and nursed back to health by a Christian widow. Not content to leave well enough alone, Saint Sebastian then denounced the emperor for his cruelty to Christians and was beaten to death.

Noted for his ability to protect communities from plague and enemy attack, Saint Sebastian became the principal devotional subject at numerous shrines, some of which are still active although mostly of minor importance. His best-known pilgrimage center is the basilica that rises above the catacombs of San Sebastiano in Rome.

Saint George, as a patron of knights and soldiers, was extremely popular during the Middle Ages. The story of his conquest over a dragon apparently dates from the twelfth century and was popularized in the thirteenth-century *Golden Legend*.[14] His veneration in the West, however, originated in about the sixth century when myths and legends related to his exploits began to emerge. All that is known about this saint is that he was martyred in Palestine prior to the reign of Emperor Constantine. Legends suggesting that he was a soldier in the Roman army may be based on reality and he has been pronounced a patron of England, Portugal, Aragon, the Germanies, Genoa, and Venice.

We found 23 active Saint George shrines in five countries, with the largest number in Austria. Sankt Georgenberg near Schwaz in the Tirol provides an example (Figure 5-8). There was a chapel on this remote mountain bluff by the tenth century, and a Benedictine abbey was established in about 1138. A Saint George pilgrimage developed after the monks obtained a bone fragment believed to be a part of the martyr's body. This shrine is also noted for a fourteenth-century Eucharistic miracle. According to tradition, white wine used to celebrate the Mass turned bloody red and boiled when a priest expressed doubts about the doctrine of transubstantiation in about 1310. Thousands of pilgrims each year still climb the long, steep mountain footpath to this shrine, but at present their devotions are oriented primarily toward the Virgin Mary who is symbolized by a miraculous statue. Most of the shrines primarily dedicated to Saint George are currently of minor importance.

Saint Valentine, or at least one or another of the Saint Valentines, is venerated in at least 19 minor pilgrimage places in four countries. One of the two Italian Valentines honored on February 14 was a physician and a leader in the Christian community of third-century Rome; he was beheaded in about 269 and buried on the Via Flamínia where a basilica was erected in his honor in 350. The other Italian martyr named Valentine was an early Christian bishop of Interamna, now Terni, a community about 60 miles from Rome. Some scholars think the two are actually the same man, perhaps condemned at Interamna and taken to Rome for execution. Another Valentine was a fifth-

Figure 5-8 *Austria's Sankt Georgenberg, dedicated to Saint George and the Virgin Mary, provides a good example of a remote shrine reached only by footpath.*

century abbot who died at Mais in the Tirol while carrying out missionary work. He seems to account for the stories told at two or three of the Saint Valentine shrines in Germanic lands.

The saintly Valentines have been invoked against epilepsy as well as epidemic diseases affecting either humans or livestock. They are also associated with fertility, a tradition that has evolved into the custom of sending Valentine Day greetings on February 14. At one Austrian shrine, probably dedicated to the fifth-century missionary Valentine, couples are said to get their children out of a well behind the church.

Saint Lucy was one of the many devout young Christian girls who, according to tradition, chose a brutal death rather than the loss of virginity through forced marriage to a pagan nobleman. Her martyrdom is said to have taken place in Sicily, the land of her most important pilgrimage shrine at Siracusa. She is a subject of veneration at a minimum of 11 shrines in four countries.[15]

Saint Christopher, patron of travelers and, in recent years, special protector of motorists, is a largely mythical saint. He is thought to have lived in Asia Minor during the third century. Christopher is usually portrayed as a huge man carrying the Christ Child across a river, an iconography that reflects an ancient legend. He was stricken from the official Roman calendar in the wake of Vatican II reforms, but his cultus is still permissible at the discretion of local bishops. We found him as a subject of veneration at 11 shrines where the blessing of automobiles in his name continues to be popular.[16]

Early Church Leaders

Several somewhat diverse persons living during the fourth through eighth centuries have a substantial number of currently active shrines. Among those honored at five to ten pilgrimage centers are Saint Martin of Tours, a bishop and early proponent of Western monasticism who died in about 397; Saint Silvester, a fourth-century pope; and Saint Odilia, an Alsatian noblewoman and abbess who died in about 720 and whose most important shrine is located on a dramatic height in the Vosges Mountains. Saint Hubert, an Ardennes nobleman, also has a number of shrines, the most important being at Saint-Hubert, Belgium, near the site where this early eighth-century holy man is said to have been hunting when he saw a cross glowing between the antlers of a stag. As a result of this vision, Saint Hubert is the patron of European hunters and his day of November 3 is often celebrated with the Saint Hubert's Mass played on hunting horns.

Another saint from this period is Saint Nicholas, a bishop of Myra in Asia Minor, who died in about 350 and whose cultus became important in the West after his relics were taken to Bari, Italy, in 1087. European children receive small gifts on his day of December 6, and his Dutch name of Sint Klaes ultimately gave rise to the American Santa Claus who seems to be a symbolic combination of Christian saints with Germanic gods.[17]

Holy persons from the Christian Era prior to A.D. 900 with more than ten active shrines in several lands are discussed below in order of their date of death.

Saint Patrick, patron of Ireland, was probably born in Roman Britain in the late fourth century. According to tradition he was captured as a young lad and carried off to slavery in Ireland. Eventually he escaped to Roman Gaul. After years of study in Continental monasteries and possibly one English monastery, he was consecrated a bishop in about 432 and sent as a missionary to Ireland. He died in about 461, perhaps at Saul in Downpatrick, Northern Ireland. Patrick was considered especially holy long before his death, and a wealth of myths and legends has grown up around his activities.[18] Most of the 15 pilgrimage places we found dedicated to Saint Patrick are in Ireland, but he is also venerated at shrines in England and Austria. The Celtic saints, Bridget and Gobnait, also have numerous shrines in Ireland but are not generally found in other parts of Europe.

Saint Benedict of Nursia, founder of Western monasticism, is honored at 29 Western European pilgrimage places. This young man of good family was born in about 480 at Nursia, or Nórcia, in Umbria, and educated in Rome. In about the year 500 he retreated to a hermit's life in the mountainous district of Subiaco. For three years he lived in a cave where he was fed by a monk named Romanus and, as the story goes, by a raven. He attracted growing numbers of disciples whom he organized into monasteries under individual priors. In approximately 525, Saint Benedict left Subiaco to create a new monastic foundation at Montecassino. Here he wrote his famous rule prescribing a life of prayer, study, and work in balanced proportions. His sister, Saint Scholastica, who founded a convent at Plombariola near Montecassino, is considered the first Benedictine nun. Saint Benedict died at Montecassino in about 547.

The Italian sites of Nursia, Subiaco, and Montecassino are important to devotees of Saint Benedict. Montecassino and the ancient Abbey of Fleury, now Saint-Benoît-sur-Loire, France, both claim the saint's mortal remains in a feud that has endured for more than a millennium.

A few minor Saint Benedict shrines are found in Germanic regions. However, Galicia in Spain and the provinces of northern Portugal, where he is called São Bento, have the largest number of pilgrimage centers dedicated to this saint (Figure 5-9). Thus, Saint Benedict, along with Saint Leonard who is discussed next, provides an example of a saint whose most numerous shrines are concentrated in an area far from his lifework.

The Saint Benedict cultus appears to have been established in northwestern Iberia by tenth- and eleventh-century Benedictines who worked to restore order in the hilly territories that had suffered Moslem invasion but had not been occupied by followers of the Prophet. Pilgrims still bring wax, salt, and eggs as offerings to several shrines at the sites of old monasteries. The custom suggests something of the nature of early symbiotic relationships between the monks and the region's people. Probably the Benedictine establishments were largely self-sufficient, but away from the sea the monks would need salt. Wax served as a source of light and egg whites were used as a binder for paints employed in the illumination of manuscripts.[19]

Saint Leonard, known as Leonhard in Germanic regions, is a subject of devotion in at least 77 places, mostly in Austria and southern West Germany. None of these numerous shrines are important beyond vicinity or minor

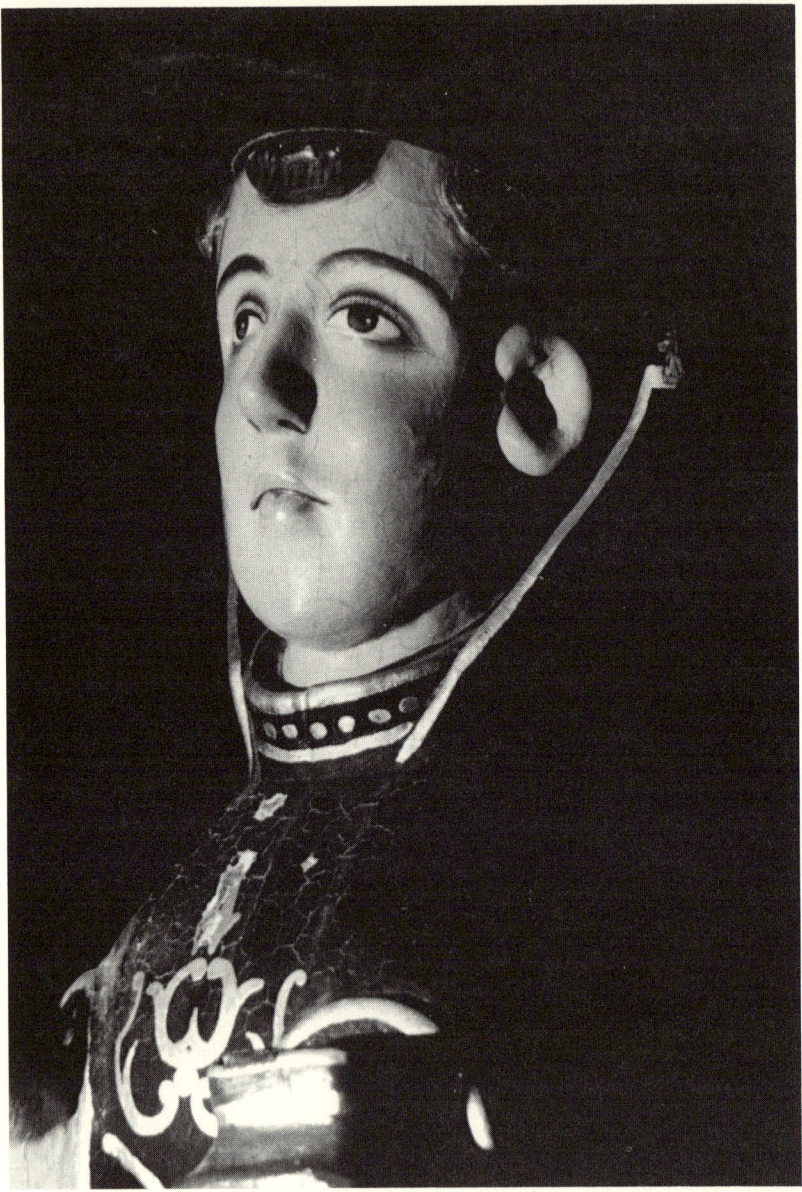

Figure 5-9 *An old statue of Saint Benedict is a focus of pilgrimage at the remote northern Portuguese village of Ermelo on the Rio Lima. The site, which was probably a pre-Christian holy place, contains the ruins of a Benedictine monastery dating from about the tenth century.*

regional levels. The saint's extensive cultus in southern Germanic lands is somewhat curious because the holy man apparently never visited these regions. Legends suggest that he was the godson of the sixth-century Frankish King Clovis I. According to tradition, the saint prayed for the queen's safe delivery of a child and was rewarded with a grant of all the land he could traverse on a donkey in a day. The monastery he founded on this land formed the nucleus of the town of Saint-Léonard-de-Noblat in the Limoges region of France. Clovis supposedly also promised to release every captive whom the saint visited, thus making this remarkable holy man a saint whose aid is solicited by prisoners of war as well as women in labor. Saint Leonard's powers are invoked to protect horses, cure cattle diseases, end plagues, cure insanity, ward off infidel Turks, and alleviate other such pervasive human problems. At Geiersberg near Ried, Austria, he appeared to a knight who was lost in a forest, saving the man from what otherwise might have been a most unfortunate end.

Saint Leonard, who died in about 559, seems to have remained an obscure local holy man until the eleventh century when the fortuitous position of his shrine town on a main pilgrims' route to Santiago de Compostela generated increasing interest in his cultus. Reports of the saint's miracles began to circulate in the early eleventh century. A highly imaginative biography was written in 1030 and during this period the devotion spread to Germanic regions. A shrine legend from Kundl in the Austrian Tirol suggests that Holy Roman Emperor Henry II may have played a role in promoting the Germanic version of the cultus. The saint's reputation for securing the release of Crusader knights captured by infidels probably increased his popularity in the Germanies during the twelfth century.

By the early fourteenth century, if not sooner, feasts of Saint Leonard provided an occasion for the southern Germanic horse pilgrimage.[20] One of the best known Saint Leonard pilgrimages of this type takes place each November 6 at Bad Tölz, Bavaria. Saint Leonard of Limoges has probably melded with a Saint Leonhard who was an early archbishop of Salzburg. This man, in turn, may have acquired some of his attributes from pagan deities. The one pilgrimage shrine clearly ascribed to Saint Leonhard of Salzburg is at Waitschach, Austria, and the pilgrimage was once locally referred to as the "Sacrifice for Thor" (Figure 5-10).[21]

Saint Wendel, a saint little known in English-speaking lands, is currently a subject of devotion in at least 21 places. This saint was probably an abbot of the Benedictine house at Tholey in the Rheinland-Pfalz not far from Trier. He died in the early seventh century and remained a local folk hero until the

Figure 5-10 *The chapel of Saint Leonhard at Waitschach, Austria, rises above an underground ossuary containing thousands of neatly stacked skulls and bones. Nearby is a later pilgrimage church dedicated to the Virgin Mary with Roman carvings built into the exterior walls. The only settlement within miles of this alpine site consists of a farmhouse and a guesthouse, which share the hilltop with the two churches.*

High Middle Ages. The first mentions of pilgrimage date from the tenth century, and his burial place at Sankt Wendel in present-day West Germany seems to have become fairly important by 1192. The cult spread rapidly in the fifteenth century due to the saint's reported effectiveness in curing livestock diseases, and most Wendelan legends developed during this period. Saint Wendel's cultus nearly died out during the sixteenth century but resurfaced in the early eighteenth century. In addition to scattered minor shrines in West Germany, Austria, and Switzerland, this patron of farmers and herders is honored at his basilica in the small city of Sankt Wendel.[22] During the 1960s, yearly pilgrimages were made to this shrine by members of about 100 parishes. The basilica was undergoing major renovation in the early 1980s, and local authorities expected increasing crowds after the completion of repairs.

Early Medieval Saints

Two tenth-century Germanic bishops were among the first officially canonized saints and still attract pilgrims to a considerable number of shrines.

Saint Ulrich, or Ulric, became bishop of Augsburg in 923 and led the community in rebuilding after the city was ravaged by the Magyars. He retired to the abbey at Sankt Gallen, Switzerland, in his old age. After his death in 973, he was buried on a hill overlooking Augsburg, West Germany, beside the bones of the early fourth-century martyr, Saint Afra. Saint Ulrich, who was canonized by Pope John XV in 993, is the first saint on record to be officially canonized by a pope.

Some of the 17 other, very minor, shrines we found dedicated to Saint Ulrich may be focused on another German saint of the same name. This Ulrich was born about 1020 in Germany. He chose a religious life after a pilgrimage to Rome and Jerusalem and became a Benedictine monk at Cluny, France, in 1052. His remains were buried under the altar of the monastic church he founded near Zell in the German Black Forest. This church was once a regionally important shrine but the pilgrimage is now considered extinct.

Saint Wolfgang, with at least 14 active shrines, is another of the Germanic agricultural saints. His folk connections with pre-Christian deities are reflected in the location of his shrines, nearly all of which seem to have been pagan holy places. The historical person around whom the legends developed was a Benedictine monk of Swabian origin. He did the usual things required for sanctification in tenth-century Germanic regions, meaning that he was of noble parentage, studied in monasteries as a youth, was ordained, and subsequently founded monastic establishments. He was officially canonized in 1052. His active shrines are of minor significance. The most important are his burial place at Regensburg, West Germany, and the shrine at Sankt Wolfgang am See in the Salzburg region of Austria. The latter shrine ranked with Cologne, Einsiedeln, and other great Germanic pilgrimage places during Medieval times; it is currently visited by an estimated 7,000 to 8,000 people per year, of whom about 2,000 come as pilgrims in a formal sense.

The Fourteen Holy Helpers sometimes included Saint Wolfgang among a mixed group of Early Christian through Early Medieval saints. They are still important as a focus for pilgrimage in southern Germanic lands, where we found 22 such shrines. The Holy Helpers generally include three bishops, Denis of Paris, Erasmus, and Blaise; three virgins, Barbara, Margaret, and

Catherine of Alexandria; three saintly knights, George, Achatius, and Eustace; one physician, Pantaleon; one monk, Giles; the deacon Cyriac; the martyr Vitus; and the giant Christopher. In some localities, the saints Nicholas, Leonhard, Sixtus, Wolfgang, Sebastian, or Oswald may be substituted for one or more of the Holy Helpers. The cultus was apparently first promoted by Dominicans in the fourteenth century and probably spread during the mid-century plague years. The earliest known representation of the Fourteen Holy Helpers dates from about 1320 and comes from the Dominican church of Saint Blaise in Regensburg.

The most important shrine dedicated to the Holy Helpers is found at Vierzehnheiligen near Bamberg, West Germany, where the son of a shepherd working for the Cistercian monastery of Langhein experienced a vision of 14 children surrounding the Christ Child in about 1445. The Child explained that the other children were the fourteen helper saints and that they wanted a shrine established on the site. The small chapel built by 1448 has been replaced several times, most recently by a late eighteenth-century baroque basilica which was being renovated in the early 1980s.[23]

Other Early through Medieval saints with numerous shrines are named Bernard and Stephen. However, because there are at least 12 saintly Bernards and 16 Saint Stephens, it is not always clear which Stephen or Bernard is venerated at a given shrine.[24]

High Medieval and Renaissance Saints

Twelfth- through fifteenth-century saints with between five and ten widely scattered shrines are the Englishman Saint Thomas Becket, whose principal shrine at Canterbury is again attracting pilgrims, and the Italian Saint Rita of Cáscia. The High Medieval personalities with the greatest number of active shrines at present are Saint Francis of Assisi, Saint Anthony of Padua, and the "Plague saint" Roch, probably of Montpellier, France. Each of these holy men has a distinctive type of cultus.

Saint Francis of Assisi, the great thirteenth-century Italian mystic and founder of the Franciscan order, is principally honored at his tomb-basilica in Assisi and at the Portiuncula in nearby Santa Maria degli Angeli where he died. Most of his other shrines are found at places that he visited during his wanderings through central Italy. Religious tours and pilgrimages in the footsteps of Saint Francis are popular at present, especially among French and West German devotees. Saint Francis's role as patron of ecology, advocated in a 1965 essay by historian Lynn White, Jr., and proclaimed by the Vatican in

1980, reflects a special twentieth-century devotion to this saint as an advocate of sanctity in nature.[25]

Saint Anthony of Padua, an early disciple of Saint Francis, is honored at a minimum of 58 shrines in seven Western European countries. Born in 1195 at Lisbon, Portugal, as Ferdinand de Bulhoes, he was the son of a knight at the court of King Alfonso II. As a young man, the future saint was schooled by Augustinian monks. He was ordained an Augustinian in about 1220 but transferred to the newly established Franciscan order in 1221. After a short stint of missionary work in Morocco, he moved to Italy where he became famous for his eloquent sermons. He settled in Padua in about 1226, but his brilliant career of preaching and good works among the poor ended with his death in 1231 at age 36. Saint Anthony was credited with numerous miracles during his lifetime, and stories of miraculous events stemming from his intercession multiplied after his death. Alms are often called "Saint Anthony's bread" in token of his role as patron of the poor. He is also called upon for help in finding lost articles, and perhaps there is a connection between that power and his special efficacy in helping young women find husbands. Anthony of Padua is also the only male saint other than Saint Joseph who is ordinarily depicted holding the infant Christ. This iconography is explained in several ways, including a tale that it represents a vision beheld by one of his early devotees.

Part of Anthony of Padua's success as a focus for widespread shrine formation may relate to the fact that other saints named Anthony were already established as protective saints in Western Europe by the time he appeared on the scene. The charismatic preacher of Lisbon and Padua apparently preempted cultic identification at a number of older shrines originally dedicated to Saint Anthony Abbot, who is possibly the same person as the fourth-century Egyptian hermit-saint; he also absorbed cults originally directed toward a number of minor saints named Anthony, Antony, and Antoninus. Anthony of Padua's special effectiveness for protecting livestock probably derives from his folk identification with the powers of the earlier Saint Anthony Abbot.[26] Saint Anthony's most important shrine is his tomb-basilica in Padua, Italy.

Saint Roch is claimed as a native by Montpellier, France. In 1315, when he was 20 years old, this holy man made a pilgrimage to Rome. In Italy he devoted himself to the care of people stricken by a plague. He became sick at Piacenza, but recovered, and is said to have miraculously cured many people. His ministrations to the sick continued through the worst onslaught of the Black Death in 1348–49 and afterward. Toward the end of his life he was arrested on a charge of spying, either at Montpellier or at Angers, Lombardy, and is said to have died in prison in 1378. A popular cultus developed soon after his death when numerous miracles were reported as a result of his intercession. Saint Roch, known as San Roque in Spain and San Rocco in Italy, is frequently invoked against plague and pestilence not only at his 18 greater-than-local pilgrimage centers but also at countless local votive chapels and parish church altars scattered throughout Europe (Figure 5-11).[27]

Later Saints

No saint who lived after the fourteenth century seems to be the primary subject of devotion at more than ten shrines. Catholic Reformation saints with more than five shrines in geographically diverse regions are the Jesuit Saint Francis Xavier and the Redemptorist lay brother Saint Gerard Majella. Of course, many holy men and women of the sixteenth through twentieth centuries are honored at one or a few shrines, some of which are very important. Several of these persons are also honored in side chapels at many churches.

Subjects of Devotion and Periods of Shrine Origin

Historians suggest that most Christian pilgrimage centers in Western Europe were focused on saints during the first millennium of the Christian Era. Toward the end of the eleventh century, however, a Westernized "Cult of the Virgin" made a rather sudden appearance in the documentary record. Stimulated by vigorous Cistercian promotion and the Crusading experience, the growing popularity of Marian pilgrimage became a revolutionary force for change in the shrine landscape of the West. During the same High Medieval period emphasis on Christ as a pilgrim's devotional subject also increased, especially in the Germanies, although to a much lesser extent than was the case for His mother's cultus. Historical studies dealing with European pilgrimage since the Reformation do not present a comprehensive picture of pilgrimage developments on a Pan-European basis, but Christian's work on Spain suggests a considerable amount of Christ-centered cultus in that area during the seventeenth and eighteenth centuries followed by a modern-age decline in such emphasis.[28] Most other regionally specific historical

Figure 5-11 *The people of Gioviano, Italy, a Tuscan hill town, and their neighbors celebrate the 450th anniversary of San Rocco's salvation of the district from the plague in 1528.*

studies of post-Medieval shrines stress the importance of Marian pilgrimage, particularly during the nineteenth century.

Our data on devotional subject focus at active shrines and the time periods during which these shrines were established reflect the patterns suggested by historians. Because cultus at some shrines has shifted from a primary focus on one subject of devotion to another since the period when the places first began attracting pilgrims, a cross-tabulation of current subjects of primary devotion and time period of formation does not necessarily indicate the devotional subject around whom cultus initially developed. All saints are subsumed under one category, so shifts from one saint to another, apparently fairly common in certain times and regions, present no interpretive problems. The fairly large-scale High Medieval and later replacement of old saints' cults with new Marian devotions must, however, be considered when examining information on current devotional emphasis at Early Christian and Early Medieval shrines. We have attempted to compensate for this problem by separating out those currently Marian shrines dated from periods before the twelfth century at which it seems likely that Christian pilgrims initially began arriving to pay their respects to holy hermits, missionaries, monks, and other early saints. At some of these places, the saint is still venerated as a secondary devotional subject and pilgrimage seems to have been more or less continuous even as the shift toward a predominant Marian cultus occurred.

A few High Medieval and later shrines now dedicated to Mary also originated as centers focused on saints, and occasional shrines dating from the Catholic Reformation have undergone a shift in primary devotional focus from Christ to Mary during modern times. There have been occasional changes in devotional focus from Mary to Christ, as happened at Cerro de los Ángeles near Madrid in the early twentieth century. Shifts from Mary to a saint have also occurred, as at Nettuno, Italy, where Saint Maria Goretti, canonized in 1950, was entombed in a church visited by pilgrims devoted to an image of the Virgin brought from Britain during the sixteenth century to prevent its destruction by Protestant iconoclasts. However, except for the Medieval and later replacement of very old saints' cults with Marian devotions, the number of cases in our data base suggesting transfers of devotional focus across major categorical lines appears to be small, and thus of too little consequence to have much effect on the overall time-space patterns indicated in Table 5-5.

The overwhelming importance of saints during the Early Christian period has survived at the shrines of the era that remain active in the late twentieth century. At nearly three-fourths of these shrines, modern cultus is still primarily focused on early saints. An additional 18 percent, now Marian, were probably developed around veneration of saints at the time of their formation. Thus, at least 92 percent of the active shrines from the period originated as centers of saints' cultus. Almost half of the Early Christian shrines still dedicated to saints are located in the British Isles, primarily in Ireland. Most of the rest are in Italy and France along with nearly all that were once saints' shrines but later became Marian. The few Early Christian shrines in Germanic lands are dedicated to saints. In those areas, we found no indications of Marian or Christianized mother goddess pilgrimage cults prior to the turn of the eighth century.[29]

During the Early Medieval period shrines dedicated to saints seem to have begun a proportional decline as increasing numbers of new shrine formations with survival value were dedicated to Mary. This change is particularly evi-

Table 5-5 *Devotional Subjects and Shrine-Formative Periods*

	Time Period										
	Early Christian		Early Medieval		High Medieval		Renaissance		Post-Reformation		Modern
Subject	N	%	N	%	N	%	N	%	N	%	N	%
Mary	14[a]	6	92[a]	23	654	73	479	77	955	73	400	72
Saint, then Mary[b]	45	18	155	38	—	—	—	—	—	—	—	—
Saints	184	74	143	35	176	20	104	16	211	16	125	23
Christ	5	2	17	4	63	7	38	6	142	11	31	6
Total	248	100	407	100	893	100	621	99	1,308	100	556	101

[a]These shrines, which were not necessarily Marian at the time of establishment, represent cases for which no particular evidence for an initial saint's cultus was found.

[b]These shrines were dedicated originally to saints in the Early Christian or Early Medieval periods, but now focus on Mary as the primary subject of devotion.

dent among surviving cult formations after the turn of the eleventh century. A higher proportion of saint-focused shrines founded in this period eventually became Marian than seems to have been the case for saints' shrines surviving from Early Christian times. Although near-equal numbers of Early Medieval shrines devoted to Christ are found in Romance-language and Germanic areas, the emphasis on Christ is higher in the Germanies. Such shrines appear to have focused on relics of Christ's Passion such as pieces of the True Cross and Holy Blood from the Crucifixion rather than on images. However, the iconography of a suffering, as opposed to a triumphant, Christ on the Cross was present in the German Rhineland by the ninth century.[30]

The great change in devotional emphasis becomes apparent, as should be expected from historical studies, during the High Middle Ages. The proportion of surviving saints' shrines drops to 20 percent overall, whereas the proportion dedicated to Mary rises to 73 percent. This High Medieval shift to an emphasis on Marian cultus is most pronounced in Romance-language regions where 82 percent of the shrines from the period are currently Marian. In Germanic lands, she accounts for only 55 percent of the High Medieval shrines. In these regions, 16 percent of surviving High Medieval shrines are focused on Christ, a very strong time-space concentration. Historian Lionel Rothkrug and the German writer Karl Kolb relate the Medieval rise of Christ-centered pilgrimage in Germanic lands to the largely Germanic Marian cultus of the suffering mother holding her dead son as expressed in the pietà.[31]

Seventy-seven percent of active shrines established during the Renaissance are focused on Mary, with those emphasizing devotion to the Virgin continuing to be more common in Italy, France, and Iberia than in the Germanies. Christ cults established during the period account for 6 percent of the cases overall.

The low point in the relative importance of surviving saints' shrines comes during the Post-Reformation years at 16 percent of the period's shrines. However, for this period, Mary accounts for a slightly smaller proportion of shrines than during the preceding period, and the proportion of surviving shrines dedicated to Christ reaches its highest Pan-European level at 11 percent of the cases. In the Romance-language world, Catholic Reformation Christ cultus appears important only in Iberia where it accounts for 9 percent of the shrines from the times. In Germanic lands, 15 percent of the period's shrines are focused on Christ. Indeed, the Post-Reformation Germanies, with 18 percent of all dated shrines, account for 36 percent of all dated Christ-centered shrines, another example of an extremely high-time space concentration among surviving examples of this particular cultus.

Figures for new formations since 1780 suggest that saints have made a slight comeback in relative significance. Twenty-three percent of the shrines established during the past 200 years are primarily dedicated to saints, and nearly 30 percent of those founded since 1900 are saints' shrines. Many of these persons lived during this period, suggesting that contemporary pilgrims tend to especially identify with holy persons whose lives indicate the potential for sanctity in a modern world. This recent emphasis on saints is of a modest dimension in continental Europe when compared with Britain and Ireland where 46 percent of the shrines established since 1780 are dedicated to saints.

Shrine Rank and Devotional Focus

The saints are sometimes interpreted as being predominantly local helpers when compared with Mary, whose cultus is considered more generalized and thus more suitable for regional, national, and international pilgrimage centers.[32] We initially thought there might be a progression in emphasis on Mary from a relatively lower importance at minor shrines to the highest importance at great shrines, but this does not appear to be the case. Of the 139 major shrines of Rank I (as described in Table 2-2), 58 percent are Marian, whereas 66 percent of shrines at all importance levels center on Mary (Table 5-6). An unusually high 12 percent of the Rank I major shrines focus on Christ, and 30 percent are saints' shrines. Of the Rank II major shrines, however, 70 percent are Marian, so it seems to be at this second level of importance that the Virgin's cultus is most pronounced. Shrines of this rank are the least likely to be dedicated to saints. There is no difference in the frequency of saints' cults among the two ranks of minor shrines which, because of the numbers involved, are close to the general European pattern. Support for the thesis that saints are relatively more important at the local level throughout Europe would require a comprehensive survey of the purely local pilgrimages that merge with other types of saints' day celebrations.

As a check on the possibility of a greater-than-usual emphasis on saints at the local pilgrimage level, we examined the 300 Continental shrines in our inventory that seemed, based on available information, most likely to be representative of purely local rather than vicinity places of pilgrimage. A vast majority of Irish shrines of all importance levels are saint-oriented. We therefore considered only Continental cases, because inclusion of a considerable number of very minor, probably local, Irish holy wells would unrealistically bias the data toward an emphasis on saints. The pattern that characterizes the most localized Continental shrines in our inventory is 12 percent focused on Christ, 57 percent focused on Mary, and 31 percent focused on saints—a curious reflection at the bottom of the importance scale of the percentages found for the top-ranked category of great shrines. Although more research on highly localized pilgrimage patterns would be of interpretive value, European pilgrimage appears to consist of a strongly integrated, although regionally varying, system in which minor shrines reflect much the same principals of subject focus as do major shrines. We conclude that the European pilgrimage tradition as a whole does not display a hierarchy of holy persons corresponding with a hierarchy of shrine importance.[33]

Regional and Temporal Variations in Subject Focus

Mary, the saints, and Christ, in that order, serve as subjects of pilgrim devotion at Western European shrines. At greater-than-local shrines there is relatively little variation in subject emphasis except for the

Table 5-6 *Devotional Subjects and Rank of Shrines*

Subject	Major Shrines by Rank					
	Rank I		Rank II		All Major Shrines	
	N	%	N	%	N	%
Mary	81	58	482	70	563	68
Saints	42	30	161	23	203	24
Christ	16	12	48	7	64	8
Total	139	100	691	100	830	100

Subject	Minor Shrines by Rank					
	Rank III		Rank IV		All Minor Shrines	
	N	%	N	%	N	%
Mary	824	66	2,596	65	3,420	66
Saints	336	27	1,075	27	1,411	27
Christ	87	7	303	8	390	7
Total	1,247	100	3,974	100	5,221	100

few great shrines where Mary is somewhat less frequently found as a primary subject of pilgrim devotion than is otherwise the case.

There is, however, substantial regional and temporal variation in subject focus. Christ-centered pilgrimage is primarily Germanic, with a secondary emphasis in Iberia among shrines of the Post-Reformation times. Mary is the primary subject of veneration at a majority of shrines in continental Europe and for the shrines from all time periods since the High Middle Ages. However, her cultus is, for all periods of shrine formation, relatively more important in French and Mediterranean peninsular regions than in Germanic lands. The saints, considered as a general category of devotional subjects, take numerical precedence over Mary and Christ only in the largely Protestant areas of northwestern Europe and in Ireland. Saints' shrines are proportionately best represented among pilgrimage places dating from the years before A.D. 1100, although new saints' shrines with survival potential have emerged in all time periods and the percentage of Modern shrines focused on saints is higher than for any era since the end of the High Middle Ages. Most saints are venerated at only one or a few shrines, but some, such as Mary's mother Saint Anne and Saint Anthony of Padua, are focal points for devotion at numerous pilgrimage centers distributed throughout Western Europe and, indeed, large parts of the Christian world.

The subjects of devotion described in this chapter are usually represented or symbolized by relics or images. These cult objects, and the importance of iconographic variations in the symbolism of Christ and Mary, are considered in Chapter 6.

six

Sacred Objects

Focal Points for Veneration

*I*n the dim light of a crypt at Nettuno, Italy, pilgrims kneel devoutly before a wax effigy of a young girl lying peacefully in a glass casket. Nearby, at Genazzano, a monk pushes a hidden switch. Panels covering a sacred painting of the Madonna and Child glide back silently as he tells the story of the miraculous transfer of the icon from Albania. Northward, at Einsiedeln, Switzerland, a black carved wooden statue of the Virgin displayed for veneration has a wardrobe fit for a queen. The statue's garments are changed regularly and a colorful book illustrating the gowns is sold at the shrine gift shop. Far to the west in Drogheda, Ireland, the mummified head of the decapitated seventeenth-century bishop, Saint Oliver Plunket, stares from a glass reliquary at the flickering lights of candles and fresh bunches of flowers left by the faithful.

Such evocative images and relics are found at shrines throughout Europe where they serve as a visual focus for pilgrims, directing their attention to the heavenly qualities and special powers of the person to whom the shrine is dedicated. These sacred objects share three basic characteristics. First, they are intrinsically human in that they are either the mortal remains of human beings or objects made by human hands. Natural landscape features including springs, hills, trees, and stones may also serve as cult objects, but shrines that focus only on such site features are rare in the Christian tradition except in Ireland where they are common.

Second, relics and images that serve as cult objects are considered to be miraculous, either through association with wondrous events or because they invoke special admiration or awe. A miraculous quality is attributed to the mortal remains of saints because these relics are the earthly remnants of exceptionally holy persons believed to be spiritually influential in heaven.

Noncorporal relics may acquire such qualities through association with the holy person during his or her lifetime or by being touched to a saint's mortal remains. Images may also acquire special sanctity by being touched to relics or other venerated images, but more often they develop their miraculous qualities through legendary or historically documented events associated with them or with some lost or destroyed statue or painting for which the current cult object has been substituted. Occasionally the present cult image serves as a reliquary for a fragment of an older one, just as many saints' relics are kept in reliquary images. The events credited with giving especially miraculous qualities to specific images usually presuppose divine intervention, but are not restricted to happenings that modern Europeans consider to be understandable only through invoking supernatural explanations. Some cult images are said to have bled, cried, mysteriously returned to the places where they were found, or otherwise demonstrated highly unusual qualities; others have acquired the power of the apparitions they are believed to symbolize.[1] Many images, however, are thought of as "miraculous" primarily in the sense of being extraordinarily important because of the historic-symbolic meanings that have become associated with them since the time of the shrine's formation.[2]

A third characteristic shared by venerated images and relics in contrast to natural site features is potential mobility. Although small sacred stones and pieces of holy trees can be removed from their natural surroundings, the stone or wood is often transformed into an image or placed in a reliquary image when this occurs. Some miraculous images, particularly frescoes and other wall paintings, are difficult to move. Nevertheless, portions of walls decorated with images that acquired miraculous qualities have been relocated, as at the shrine of the Madonna della Orto in Chiávari and several other places in Italy. Thus, even wall paintings can be considered potentially movable and are not tied to the mystique of a specific site in the same way as are natural objects. The fact that images and relics can be and occasionally are relocated has considerable importance for understanding pilgrimage in the West. In some cases, the importance of a relic or image outweighed the significance of place to such an extent that pilgrim destinations changed when the cult object was relocated.

The pilgrim focus on images and relics is so pervasive in continental Europe that William Christian defined Spanish pilgrimage shrines as places "where there is an image or relic that receives a particular devotion."[3] Similarly, Hans Dünninger, in his study of the Catholic Reformation emphasis on images in the Germanies, suggests that "in our own time a pilgrim shrine without a cult image is virtually unthinkable."[4] Table 6-1 shows the variation among countries in terms of object-focused shrines. The Continental tendency toward object focus is evident in the low percentages of shrines without either images or relics. In the aggregate, excluding the few cases in Scandinavia, about 96 percent of the mainland shrines contain especially venerated images or relics with a range of 91 percent in Switzerland to 98 percent in Spain and Portugal. At Continental pilgrimage centers where there is no special image or relic, administrators sometimes make a point of their shrine's atypical nature.

The United Kingdom and Ireland present a different picture. In Britain, where many Medieval cult objects were destroyed during the Reformation, only about two-thirds of the present shrines focus on an object. In Ireland only about 12 percent of the shrines have venerated images or relics. Irish pilgrimages mainly focus on one or more sacral site features such as springs, trees, sacred stones, or mountain heights. These are often located at places where a Celtic saint is said to have established a monastery, performed wonders, paused while wandering through the land, or died and was buried. At some of these places, a type of relic cultus survives in the form of a special efficacy attributed to the earth from the grave site of a saint.

Only a small proportion of Europe's innumerable religious statues and paintings fall into the category of pilgrimage cult images. Important shrines are often virtual museums of iconography where the image to which pilgrims pay their respects may be artistically inferior to surrounding images that serve merely as decoration. For example, the Italian shrine of Madonna della Quércia near Viterbo directs pilgrim attention to a painted board that was attached to the trunk of an oak tree by a farmer in about 1417. The simple painting, associated with miracles since 1467, is decorated with offerings of jewels and has visual power, but it is not a great work of art, even in the context of a folk art tradition. The shrine church, however, is noted for several very fine works of art including a terra cotta by Andrea della Robbia.[5] Even shrines with no wonder-working images or relics are usually decorated with graphic representations of Mary, Christ, and the saints. In Ireland, where a Medieval orientation toward miraculous images was virtually eliminated by Protestant British repression, simple white statues of various holy persons are found at many holy wells where they are often treated by pilgrims as if they were some new form of holy thorn tree springing from the sacred soil.

Similarly, few of the many mortal remains of saints found in Roman Catholic churches throughout Europe are popularly thought of at present as having any extraordinarily miraculous qualities. Because relics were required for new

Table 6-1 *Object Orientations by Country*

Country	Shrines with Object Data N	%[a]	Images %[b]	Human Remains %[b]	Other Relics %[b]	No Objects %[b]
Italy	1,029	86	87	7	2	4
Austria	854	92	92	4	1	3
Spain	645	64	92	4	2	2
France	619	60	80	13	2	5
West Germany	586	62	77	13	7	3
Switzerland	191	67	70	16	4	9
Portugal	156	47	96	3	0	2
Belgium	110	73	82	9	6	4
Ireland	103	76	6	5	1	88
United Kingdom	82	95	32	33	0	35
Netherlands	19	38	58	21	16	5
Scandinavia	6	60	17	17	0	67

[a]Percentage of inventoried shrines in each country for which the presence or absence of an object has been determined.

[b]Percentage of each type of cult object, or no object, for the cases in the inventory for which this information was obtained.

church consecrations by the Second Council of Nicaea in 787, all Catholic churches would, theoretically, be pilgrimage shrines if all relics were considered equally miraculous.[6] Some churches in the Germanies are virtual mausoleums of elaborately dressed skeletons lying forlornly neglected in glass caskets. These forgotten saints molder in baroque splendor, with no candles or flowers to suggest that anyone really cares who they were or what they may have symbolized.

Origins of Object Veneration

Relics were the earliest form of potentially movable cult objects because Christian pilgrimage on the Continent grew out of a tradition of veneration for the mortal remains of saints. The earliest shrines in the West developed in the urban-edge cemeteries of the Roman world where Christian martyrs were buried. From very early times Christians assembled at the tombs of their martyred fellows to celebrate the saint's death date as his or her heavenly birthday. Miracles occurred and votive offerings were left as these early pilgrimage centers evolved. Devotional focus was supposed to be directed to the saint's bodily remains rather than to the place of burial, and the miracles were expected to "proceed from the person of the saint, not from his impersonal surroundings."[7] The saint was believed to be present in his mortal remains and the power attributed to these relics was so great that it could be transferred to any object that touched the saint's body. Only in the Celtic tradition does emphasis on sacred natural site features appear to have been promoted during the initial period of Christianization.

Although disinterment and dismemberment of the dead violated traditional Roman law and custom, saints' bodies were being removed from their original tombs before the end of the fourth century. From about that time through the eleventh century, the usual way of inaugurating a holy person as a saint was by "elevation" of his or her relics, a practice initiated by a local bishop's decision and involving disinterment of the body and placement of the relics on an altar within a church. This practice continued after centralized procedures for canonization were developed in the eleventh century. Especially miraculous qualities were, and still are, attributed to exhumed bodies that proved to be "uncorrupt." Such mummified bodies, displayed in glass caskets, are objects of devotion at several European pilgrimage centers, including the Italian shrines of Saint Zita in Lucca, Saint Clare in Assisi, Saint Margaret in Cortona, and the Portuguese shrine of a São Clemente in the church of Bom Jesus do Monte near Braga (Figure 6-1).

By the late fourth century, the remains of saints were being sent as gifts from Italy to regions north of the Alps where their arrival led to the development of new pilgrimage shrines. Because the saints were believed to be physically present in their bodies when their relics were moved, the saints moved with them. As the demand for relics grew, the division of saints' bodies into fragmentary pieces became increasingly prevalent. The saint could thus be present in many places because, in the words of Theodoret of Cyrus, "in the divided body the grace survives undivided and the fragments, however small, have the same efficacy as the whole body."[8] Possibly the reduction of many early saints to piles of disarticulated bones and dust through purely natural processes made the dismemberment of saints' bodies seem less distasteful by the time the demand for relics reached major proportions in the eighth century. After the Second Council of Nicaea in 787 required relics for church consecrations, a virtual flood of bone fragments poured forth from the Roman catacombs for the benefit of new churches in recently converted regions with few indigenous martyrs.

Figure 6-1 *The mummified body of São Clemente, elaborately dressed and displayed in a glass casket, is venerated at the church of Bom Jesus do Monte near Braga, Portugal.*

During and immediately after this period, the urge to amass enormous collections of relics affected kings and noblemen as well as the keepers of religious establishments, placing a further premium on the bones of holy persons. Fake relics and thefts of real relics multiplied as a profitable traffic in holy objects developed.[9] During the Early Middle Ages increasing numbers of Eastern saints' relics appeared in the West, as did pieces of wood believed to represent Christ's Cross and chalky stones from the Milk Grotto in Bethlehem symbolizing Mary's milk that nurtured the Christ Child. Despite theological contentions that tiny bone fragments were as holy as entire bodies, saints' relics may have begun to lose some of their efficacy, not only because some were of doubtful origin, but also because they were altogether too common and losing ground to an increasing number of objects related to Christ and Mary.

Fragmentary relics, whatever their associations, all had the advantage of being considerably easier to move around than were mummies and skeletons. Housed in elaborate reliquaries, such fragments could be placed on the main altar during times of special celebration and easily carried in religious processions (Figure 6-2). As the flow of relics from the Roman catacombs and the Eastern Mediterranean made dismemberment of bodies an ordinary custom, selected body parts of local saints were taken from their shrine tombs and placed in reliquaries for ease of display and procession.[10]

The presence of saints in their bodily fragments was enhanced when representational reliquaries came into use during the ninth century.[11] These reliquary heads, busts, and full statues, which combined the efficacy of saints' bones with the visual power of three-dimensional imagery, had become common in southern France by the mid-tenth century. The famous reliquary statue of Saint Foy, the head of which dates to the fifth century, was venerated in this region where there is also early documentary evidence of a venerated statue of the Virgin Mary in the form of a seated figure created in 946 by order of the bishop of Clermont as a reliquary for some tokens of the Virgin.[12] From that time on, relic cultus often combined with image veneration, although there may have been other sources for the rise of image cultus in the West that were independent from the cults of relics.

The extent to which images were venerated by Western Christians prior to the period when reliquary statues made such venerations fully acceptable is uncertain. The earliest known portrayals of Christian holy persons in the West have been found in Roman catacombs of the late second or early third centuries, but it seems likely that Christian art was initially conceptualized as decoration, perhaps with instructional value. Image worship was deeply implanted in pagan tradition and for that reason seems to have been rejected by early Christians who were influenced by Judaic injunctions against the worship of graven images. By the early third century, however, both Christian and Jewish places of worship were being decorated with biblical scenes that included representations of sacred persons.[13] Some early churchmen felt that Christian acceptance of devotional images could open the floodgates to image veneration. Epiphanius of Salamis in Cyprus, an iconoclastically oriented cleric of the fourth century, was one of the first to comment on the images of

Figure 6-2 *Bejeweled gold reliquaries display a collection of saints' relics at Rochechouart in the Limoges region of France on the occasion of the town's 1981 ostensions celebrations.*

Christian holy persons already abundant in his day. As he put it, "When images are put up the customs of the pagans do the rest."[14]

From an iconoclastic viewpoint, Epiphanius may have had reason for concern because Christian practices involving the veneration of images seem to have developed by the late fourth century. During the sixth century, devotions related to images became prevalent in Eastern Mediterranean regions and included such practices as carrying images in processions, claiming that miracles were performed by holy persons as represented in their images, and venerating personal devotional images in the home. A few, still-visited, early shrines focused on images of Mary may have emerged by the seventh century in parts of the Italian peninsula that were strongly influenced or controlled by the Byzantines and even in Rome. The painting called La Madonna della Clemenza venerated in the Roman church of Santa Maria in Trastevere, for example, proved to be of seventh- to early eighth-century origin when overpainting was stripped away during a 1953 restoration.[15]

Some of the earliest venerated images appear to have acquired their powers through direct contact with holy persons or their mortal remains. In a sense, these were little different from the cloths called *brandea* which were sanctified by being touched to the mortal remains of saints. Such cloths were frequently venerated at early Christian shrines, especially before the disinterment and dismemberment of saints' bodies became commonplace.

In the case of Mary, the idea of a "True Icon" in the form of a portrait painted from life by Saint Luke gradually took root and became a cornerstone of the Western iconophiles' arguments against eighth- and ninth-century Byzantine iconoclasm. Paintings popularly attributed to Saint Luke are found at several European shrines and include the famous Salus Populi Romani icon venerated at the Roman basilica of Santa Maria Maggiore, the La Bruna of Naples, Bologna's Madonna di San Luca, which was brought from the East in the twelfth century, and the Notre-Dame de Grace icon of Cambrai, France. The famous dark Virgin of Częstochowa, Poland, is also associated with the legend of Saint Luke's portrait of Mary, whereas the Lucas story told about the statue at Montserrat in Spain presumes that the author of the third Gospel was a sculptor as well as a painter. The fact that none of these images dates from the first century is considered irrelevant by those who are inclined toward the Lucus tradition on the grounds that copies of images traditionally have, or soon acquire, the same value as the originals. In some cases, copies have become more important as pilgrimage cult objects than the originals even when the prototypes still exist. As Karl Kolb points out, "Whether or not Luke actually had Mary sit for a portrait is far less important than the undeniable fact that it has been believed for many hundreds of years."[16] The possibility of a portrait from life, even if copied 100 times over, represents the *Vera Icon*, the likeness of an important once-living person which should not be destroyed even in a campaign against "idolatry." Kolb suggests that the power of such an idea may have contributed to the sixteenth-century and later Protestant conviction that Saint Luke could not possibly have produced a portrait of Mary and a special Protestant abhorrence of such images.[17]

In the case of Christ, it was argued from early times that He could be graphically portrayed in spite of Old Testament injunctions against graven images of God, because, in at least one dimension of His nature, Jesus had been a living man. Miraculous images of Christ were venerated in Jerusalem and Memphis by the late sixth century.[18]

Documentary evidence for early image veneration west and north of Italy appears to be scant until the emergence of reliquary images in the ninth and tenth centuries. However, there are indications that the Eastern cult of images spread to parts of France relatively early along with other aspects of Eastern devotion. The sixth-century bishop, Gregory of Tours, referred to a painting of the Crucified Christ at Narbonne that asked to be covered and to an image of Christ that bled when pierced by Jews. Also, the late sixth-century Bishop Serenus of Marseilles was apparently so disturbed by the adoration of images in his churches that he ordered their destruction or removal, a decision disapproved by Pope Gregory the Great.[19]

A plausible story of an early Marian pilgrimage stemming from Eastern influences comes from the shrine of Notre-Dame des Miracles in Orléans, France. According to this tradition, a group of Syrian merchants settled at Avenum, near Orléans, in the late fifth century. The colony, which was mentioned by Gregory of Tours, seems to have been augmented by substantial numbers of new arrivals from the East during the sixth century and probably remained an ethnic enclave until the eighth century Moslem occupation of their homeland in present-day Lebanon ended the flow of immigrants and cut the trade links on which the settlement depended. During this period, the Syrians apparently began to integrate with the Orléans community through a search for new means of livelihood and intermarriage. According to oral tradition recorded in the tenth and eleventh centuries, the initial immigrants arrived with an ebony statue of the Virgin Mary, which was placed in an oratory and was soon honored by many inhabitants of the area. When Normans ravaged the countryside and besieged the village in 897, the people of Avenum successfully defended their walls both through defensive warfare and by means of a procession with the old image, which thus came to be considered miraculous. The first written mentions of the episode, although much embellished in later accounts, date from within living memory of the Norman attack. Whether the image was actually of fifth-century origin or of ebony, or even honored very early by people of the area, cannot be known. It is, however, far more likely than not that members of the Syrian enclave acquired one or more venerated images of the Virgin Mary from their homeland by at least the sixth century. The spread of such devotions beyond an ethnic community is most likely to have occurred during the eighth century as a normal consequence of disenclavement. Stories of the miraculous intervention of images during enemy attack date back to at least the sixth century in Eastern Mediterranean lands, so it is likely that descendants of the Syrian colonists had retained the idea of evoking the power of an icon in response to impending catastrophe as part of their cultural heritage. The wooden statue venerated at Orléans during the Middle Ages was burned by Huguenot soldiers in April 1562 and replaced, probably in the last quarter of the sixteenth century, by a statue carved from black stone.[20]

The Orléans story suggests a somewhat different diffusion model from the simple east to west spread of image veneration usually implied in generalized accounts. Instead, it is useful to conceptualize the possibility of image-centered Marian devotions spreading out into nearby districts from a series of Eastern ethnic enclaves scattered along the shores of the Western Mediterranean and, in the case of Orléans, sometimes far beyond the coastal fringes.

French oral traditions also suggest that a few pagan mother goddess statues may have been Christianized. The famous legend of a pagan mother goddess venerated by early Christians in a cave at Chartres is of Medieval origin and probably has no historical foundation, although speculation about possible pre-Christian origins continues to appear in shrine publications.[21] There are, however, other stories. At Longpont-sur-Orge, near Paris, a statue of a woman and child is said to have been found in an oak tree beside a spring dedicated to Isis. According to tradition, Saint Denis used this statue to explain the story of the Virgin and Child during his conversion work in the third century, and a pilgrimage is said to date from that time. Kolb reports that until 1514 the Church of Saint Germain in Paris displayed a black image of the Egyptian goddess Isis as a Madonna; and at Château-Quinipily near Baud in Brittany, a stone statue, possibly of Isis, stands forlornly on an old fountain. According to tradition, it was once so venerated that ecclesiastical authorities twice threw it into the Blavet River, from which it was retrieved by the local people.[22]

Many representations of Mary bear strong resemblances to pagan images, and problems related to the mistaken identification of pagan mother goddess images as representations of the Christian Virgin and Child were mentioned in the ninth century by Théodulf of Orléans.[23] It seems likely that veneration of mother goddess statues had not disappeared completely in France prior to the development of a widespread Christian version of image veneration.

In Iberia, where numerous statues of Mary are said to have been miraculously unearthed in the wake of the reconquest of the peninsula from the Moslems, traditions were long based on the supposition that such images must have been hidden during the early eighth-century Moslem invasion or during ninth- or tenth-century Moslem raids. Most statues about which such stories are told are no older than their presumed dates of finding, mostly in the eleventh through thirteenth centuries, and this stylistic evidence combines with the lack of documentation to support historians' contentions that

Sacred Objects 171

there were no Marian pilgrimage cults in Spain before the Moslem invasions. However, Christian images of Mary were present in Spain by the fourth century and a strong devotion to Mary in the early Spanish church can be traced to the mid-seventh-century writings of Saint Ildephonsus, bishop of Toledo. Therefore, it is at least theoretically possible that a few Early Christian images, or perhaps pre-Christian mother goddess figures, were discovered and considered miraculous by Medieval Spaniards.[24]

In southern France, increasing use of reliquary images during the tenth century seems to have led rather rapidly from relic veneration per se, through a short transitional period of devotions directed toward reliquary statues, to veneration of statues not containing relics. This and other influences were apparently operating in other areas to lay the foundations for a widespread devotional focus directed toward images. This was especially the case with the growing cultus of Mary, because she could not be represented by her corporal remains without denying the ancient belief in her bodily assumption into Heaven. Although the same principle applies to Christ, relics associated with His Passion, such as pieces of the Cross and earth supposedly sanctified by the spilling of His blood, seem to have arrived in Europe from the East in sufficient quantities to satisfy the demand for relics necessary for the development of Christ-centered shrines. Veneration of Christ images, particularly those representing the suffering of the Crucifixion, may have received impetus from association with relics of the Passion, particularly in Germanic regions where numerous such items had been collected by the twelfth century.[25]

However it happened, during the High Middle Ages images began to replace relics as the most common type of movable cult object, and a substantial proportion of shrines from that period now have images containing no relics as their primary cult object. This emphasis on images has continued to the present.

Cult Objects in Modern Times

Among the cult objects most venerated at European shrines today, there are approximately eight miraculous images for each relic of any kind, and the ratio of images to the bodily remains of saints is approximately ten to one (tables 6-2, 6-3). This emphasis on images is further enhanced by the display of many saints' relics in some type of effigy figure. Thus, the pilgrims' primary visual experience with a cult object is directed

Table 6-2 *Objects of Devotion*

Object Type	Number of Shrines with Data	Percent of Object-Oriented Shrines	Percent of Shrines with Data
Images	3,635	88	83
Human remains	373	9	8
Other relics	110	3	3
Subtotal	4,118	100	94
Shrines with no cult object	282	—	6
Total	4,400		100

Table 6-3 *Representations of Subjects at Object-Oriented Shrines*

	Subject						
Object Type	Mary N	%	Christ N	%	Saints N	%	All Subjects N
Two-dimensional images	626	21	31	8	103	14	760
Three-dimensional images	1,690	56	196	51	224	31	2,110
Unclassified images	676	22	69	18	20	3	765
Total images	2,992	99	296	77	347	48	3,635
Mortal remains	0	0	0	0	373	51	373
Other relics	18	1	89	23	3	1	110
Total relics	18	1	89	23	376	52	483
Total cases	3,010	100	385	100	723	100	4,118

toward an image or an image containing relics at a substantial majority of shrines.

Types of Relics

Of the relics currently serving as primary objects of veneration, more than 77 percent are the mortal remains of saints (Table 6-4). Various parts of an individual saint's body may serve as a focus for pilgrimage at several different places, as has been the case for at least 1,500 years. For example, although the tomb of the thirteenth-century Franciscan, Saint Antony, is in Padua, Italy, at least five other European shrines dedicated to this saint claim fragmentary relics of his body. Relics believed to be those of Saint

Table 6-4 *Types of Relics*

Relic	Number	Percent of Relics	Percent of All Cult Objects (N = 4,118)
Human remains	373	77	9
Pieces of True Cross	38	8	1
Blood from Holy Land	10	2	‹1
Other Passion relics	12	3	‹1
Eucharistic relics	24	5	1
Bandera, strands of hair, drops of milk and other similar relics	26	5	1
Total	483	100	12

Anne are venerated at Apt and Sainte-Anne-d'Auray in France, Annaberg and Vienna in Austria, and possibly at some of her other European shrines. This saint's relics also provide a focus for Canadian pilgrims at the Quebec shrines of Sainte-Anne-de-Beaupré, Sainte-Anne-de-la-Rochelle, and Sainte-Anne-de-Micmacs and at Lac-Sainte-Anne in the province of Alberta. In the United States, her relics are venerated at shrines in Saint Anne, Illinois; New Orleans, Louisiana; Detroit, Michigan; New York City; and Isle La Motte, Vermont.[26]

Relics are often displayed in reliquary images including the traditional busts, wax effigies lying in glass caskets, and full statues with a glass-covered cavity to allow for relic viewing as is the case with the reliquary image of the Italian San Doménico Abate carried in procession each May with an offering of tame snakes writhing around its neck and head (Figure 6-3). When no reliquary image is used, fragments of the saint's remains may be displayed in other types of reliquaries ranging from simple miniature coffins to elaborately wrought examples of goldsmith art. If the body is "incorrupt" or reduced to an articulate skeleton, it may be displayed for veneration in its entirety, although in many of these cases a few tiny fragments may have been detached and sent elsewhere. Holy persons whose case for official sainthood is pending ordinarily lie in closed tombs because it is not considered appropriate to display the relics of a person who has not been canonized. At certain other shrines, including the basilica of Saint Francis at Assisi, the pilgrim's attention is directed primarily toward a tomb rather than a visually displayed relic or reliquary image.

In a few places, miraculous fluids are associated with relics or tombs. The

Figure 6-3 *For more than 1,000 years the people of Cocullo, Italy, and the faithful of surrounding districts have honored San Doménico Abate with offerings of live snakes such as those writhing around the image's head in the 1981 celebration of this event. A fragment of this tenth-century Benedictine saint's body is contained in the round, glass-covered cavity seen in the chest of the seventeenth-century statue. The mule shoe in the statue's left hand is also a powerful relic reputed to cure snakebites and prevent rabies.*

tombs of Saint Nicholas at Bari and Saint Andrew at Amalfi, both in Italy, and the English-born eighth-century Saxon nun Saint Walburga at Eichstätt, West Germany, periodically emit a clear liquid believed to have great curative powers. Reports of a marvelous liquid exuding for a time from the bones or incorrupt bodies of saints are associated with several other holy persons including the seventeenth-century Italian, Saint Gerard Majella, and the Spaniard, Saint Pascual Bailón. An empty fourth-century marble sarcophagus called La Sainte-Tombe, kept at an old Benedictine abbey in the French Pyrenean town of Arles-sur-Tech, accumulates a considerable amount of clear water that is pumped out each July 30 in a special ceremony and is occasionally collected for individual purposes at other times. This water has been considered especially sacred since its application cured a nobleman's face cancer in 1204. The best known example of a blood relic that periodically turns from a coagulated to a liquid form is that of Saint Januarius, preserved in the Cathedral of Naples. The phenomenon of liquefaction was first observed during a procession in the late fourteenth century and since then has occurred on several special days each year. Those occasions when the blood has failed to liquefy on schedule are said to have coincided with the onslaught of major disasters.[27]

A form of saints' relic cultus fairly common in Ireland, and to some extent elsewhere, is represented by soil taken from places where holy persons were either buried or traditionally supposed to have been buried that is presumed to have a curative efficacy (Figure 6-4). This earth-from-holy grave focus is more site-oriented than the more usual emphasis on the mortal remains of deceased holy persons.

The emphasis on corporal relics as cult objects at saints' shrines reflects the early Christian heritage of veneration of a holy person's mortal remains, and indeed only the saints can be so represented at their shrines. According to biblical accounts, Christ ascended into Heaven 40 days after the Resurrection. There has never been any reason for nonheretical Christian pilgrims to assume that they could be in Christ's presence by going to a place claiming to have his mortal remains. To be able to do so would destroy the reason for going. The belief that Mary was bodily assumed into Heaven is also extremely ancient, although the Assumption of Mary into Heaven was not pronounced as Roman Catholic dogma until 1950. The desire to venerate Mary's mortal remains was occasionally expressed in Early Christian times, but her body was never found.[28] Given the numerous "inventions" of other saints' relics, one may safely suppose that strong cultural pressures operated to prevent acceptance of a "miraculous" discovery of Mary's body.

Christ and Mary may, however, be represented by other types of relics. Those associated with Mary are usually pieces of clothing, especially her sash or "girdle" and her veil, along with strands of her hair and drops of the milk with which she nourished the Christ Child. These milk relics are often pieces of chalky rock from the Milk Grotto in Bethlehem, a site visited by Western pilgrims from early Christian times. Pilgrims visiting the Basilica of Notre-Dame in Évron, France, still venerate such a rock, brought from the Bethlehem grotto by a pilgrim who returned from the Holy Land in about 648.[29] Relics associated with Mary are found in numerous shrine and cathedral treasuries, but only 18, including the sashes venerated at Prato, Italy, and

Figure 6-4 A priest's grave at Saint Gobnet's, County Cork, Ireland. Only a few saints' relics have survived in Ireland, but earth from holy graves is thought to have curative powers. In this case, the bones of a locally beloved priest, who served the needs of his rural flock during the years when Britain attempted to repress Irish Catholicism, disappeared from his County Cork tomb about 30 years ago. A countrywoman encountered at the place suggested that a dog may have carried off the bones. This, however, was not considered important because dirt from the grave still has curative properties.

Tortosa, Spain, appear to be of current importance as primary cult objects. Often, as at Chartres, France, Marian relics are one of several objects of devotion and share attention with one or more miraculous images.

The situation is different in the case of Christ. About 23 percent of the currently active Christ-centered shrines focus on artifactual relics or images containing relics (Table 6-3). Most are "Relics of the Passion," including pieces of the True Cross, nails from the Cross, thorns from the Crown of Thorns, rods from the beating, garments worn during the Passion, earth soaked with Holy Blood spilled during the Crucifixion, and the famous Shroud of Turin. Veneration of the blood-soaked earth stimulated theological debates on the compatibility of the doctrine of Christ's bodily ascension into Heaven with the notion that corporal relics detached from His body continued to exist on earth. By the High Middle Ages, it was more or less agreed that Christ's foreskin, umbilical cord, milk teeth, and shed blood could have remained on earth, a conclusion possibly reached because all such objects were already well established as focal points of pilgrimage cultus. Of these, only relics of the Holy Blood, which are essentially Passion relics, are of much importance in late twentieth-century Europe. Famous shrines focusing on Holy Blood of the Crucifixion are found in several places including Mantua, Italy; Bruges, Belgium; Fécamp, France; and Weingarten, West Germany.[30]

Other Christ-centered shrines developed around relics of Eucharistic miracles including remnants of a bleeding or otherwise miraculous Host and stains on cloth left by Communion wine said to have turned to blood. Reports of such miracles go back to very early times and pilgrims still visit Lanciano, Italy, to venerate five small pellets of blood and a strip of flesh said to have been formed from consecrated bread and wine during the celebration of the Mass by a doubting monk of the Basilian order in the eighth century. Most such shrines, however, seem to have sprung from a High Medieval intensification of piety directed toward the Eucharist as a true relic of Christ. According to Rothkrug, "Just as a bone from the physical remains of a saint, in popular belief, *was* in fact the saint himself, so the Eucharist, believed to be the physical and spiritual presence of Christ, constituted the ultimate, the most precious, of all relics."[31] Requests for elevation of the Host so that the faithful could actually see the body of Christ became increasingly common during the twelfth century. Transubstantiation, the dogma that bread and wine actually became the body and blood of Christ through the miracle of the Mass, was proclaimed by Pope Innocent III in 1215, and the feast and processions of Corpus Christi were established in the mid-thirteenth century. This devotional milieu generated numerous reports of incidents proving that Eucharistic elements actually became the body and blood of Christ during the Mass and these accounts, along with relics of Eucharistic miracles, provided the basis for establishing many new shrines.[32] Although many of the Medieval shrines established in this manner have ceased to draw pilgrims, at least two dozen shrines in contemporary Europe focus on mementos of Eucharistic miracles; others that originated because of such miracles now have only cult images, as is the case at Erding, a small Bavarian village near Munich, West Germany (Figure 6-5).

Several Eucharistic miracle shrines are of considerable importance in modern times. For example, Walldürn, Bavaria, is visited by more than 100,000 pilgrims per year, many of whom journey several hundred miles on foot in

Figure 6-5 "Blood" made of carved, red-painted wood attached to wires dramatically spurts forth from this miraculous seventeenth-century image of Christ enshrined at Erding, West Germany. According to the cult origin story, a poor farmer stole a consecrated Host in 1417 in hopes of using it to work magic. On his way home, the thief dropped the Host which became impossible to pick up. Not even the bishop could move the sacred object, so a church was built at the site. The present pilgrimage church dates from 1675.

order to venerate an altar cloth on which stains formed an image of Christ when sacramental wine was spilled in about 1330. The pilgrimage developed after the cloth was taken to Rome for examination in 1445.[33] Other Eucharistic pilgrimage centers include Orvieto, Italy, where the cathedral enshrines a blood-stained altar cloth as a relic of a miracle that took place in 1263 at nearby Bolsena, and at Cebrero, Spain, where a doubting fourteenth-century monk witnessed a miracle while saying a Mass requested by a Santiago-bound pilgrim. More recently established shrines include an abbey church shrine at Faverney, France, where two Hosts were miraculously saved from a fire in 1608, and the Church of Saint Francis in Siena, Italy, where a large number of consecrated Hosts stolen in 1730 proved fresh upon recovery and are said to have remained in a good state of preservation ever since.

Shrines focused on Passion relics and mementos of Eucharistic miracles are found in many parts of Europe, but are most prevalent in Germanic countries (Map 6-1). Possibly cults based on relics related to Christ have had a higher survival rate in the Germanies than elsewhere, but this may merely reflect the strong roots of such devotions in a region where the pilgrimage focus on Christ appears to have been especially intense since Early Medieval times.

Major shrines are more likely to focus on relics than are less important pilgrimage centers, especially among those shrines dedicated to saints. Certainly, the more important the shrine of a particular saint, the more likely it is to have his or her body or some part of it as a focus for pilgrim devotions. Often a shrine becomes highly important because it has a relic, especially in the case of shrines where saints are entombed. Occasionally, however, a saint's shrine that originates without a relic becomes so popular and well visited that a fragmentary relic is sent to the shrine from Rome or from some other shrine as a token of its importance. Pieces of the Cross and other relics associated with the Passion of Christ also influence the importance level of shrines through their perceived power, although several shrines with such relics are of only modest importance.

Miraculous Images

As a class of objects, miraculous images generally have certain things in common. First, they tend to represent a more limited range of symbolic portrayals than is the general case for graphic representations of holy persons. Second, they are rarely great works of art and some do not even qualify as good folk art. As a corollary, works by famous artists hardly ever

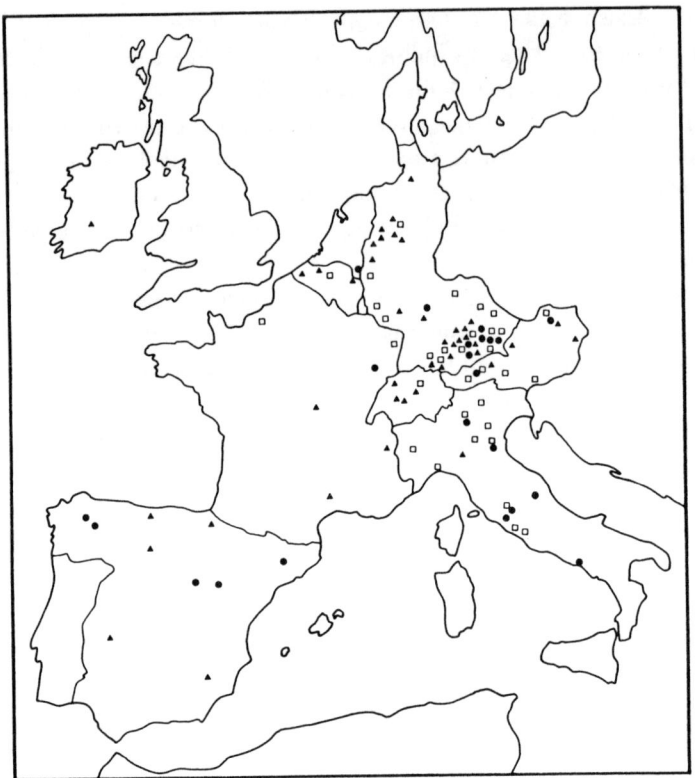

Key:

▲ Piece of the True Cross
☐ Holy Blood from the Holy Land
● Relic of a Eucharistic miracle

Map 6-1 *Distribution of Venerated Relics of the True Cross, Holy Blood from the Holy Land, and Remnants of Eucharistic Miracles*
Shrines at which pieces of wood thought to represent the True Cross and other relics of Christ's Passion serve as primary objects of veneration are primarily found in a north-south belt extending from northern West Germany to central Italy, with the zone of greatest concentration in southern West Germany. Shrines where mementos of Eucharistic miracles are still venerated as cult objects show a similar distribution pattern.

become the objects of cultus, although there are a few exceptions to this rule, especially in Italy.[34] Third, cult images are not ordinarily treated as art forms to be preserved for their intrinsic aesthetic or graphic historical value. Instead, they have often been dressed in assorted garments, embellished with crowns, modified dramatically in restorations that suited the popular tastes of the day, chipped at for talismans, and sometimes replaced altogether when considered inappropriate or out of date. Yet, in spite of this, their perceived power is such that iconoclasts may formally execute them as if they were living beings, and some among the faithful in most generations seem willing to die to save them, or at least have died because they tried.

The importance of cult images is usually dramatized by their placement within the sanctuary. The most common location is high on the retable behind the main altar where the image provides a powerful visual focal point. There is, however, considerable architectural diversity in the interior of churches visited by pilgrims and no general rule of image placement.[35] Cult images may also be located at the end of a side nave, usually to the right of the main altar, or on a pedestal slightly in front of the altar toward one side, again, usually to the right. At other shrines cult images are kept in side chapels that may be virtually anywhere around the church's interior periphery and a few are found in crypts, although this type of object placement is more commonly associated with tombs containing relics. At some shrine complexes, particularly in West Germany, as at Kevelaer, Telgte, and Altötting, the venerated image is displayed in a small separate chapel around which pilgrims walk as a part of their devotional exercises. At some Iberian shrines where the cult image above the main altar is much too high for pilgrims to reach from the main sanctuary, stairs lead to and from a small catwalk that allows a closer approach. In other Spanish churches stairs provide entrance to a small upper chapel behind the image, which is kept on a turntable so that it may be viewed from the main sanctuary on special occasions and more intimately from the chapel at other times.

At a majority of shrines, the cult object is kept on permanent display and may be seen whenever the church is open. Pilgrimage churches and chapels, particularly in Iberia, sometimes have special viewing holes in their exterior walls where pilgrims can kneel and pray outside, but within sight of the venerated image when the structure is locked. Similarly, many baroque-period churches in the colder Germanic lands are equipped with an antechamber which is separated from the main sanctuary by iron grills that may be locked without denying pilgrims visual access to the cult image. However, cult objects are not always on display at all shrine locations even when the structures are open. Images are sometimes hidden away within the church or even kept someplace other than the shrine structure except during times of special celebration, particularly when the shrine is a remote country chapel or a church in a poor inner-city district.

Many cult images are periodically taken from their shrine churches for use in processions, although some shrines have a special processional image that is usually a replica of the principal cult image. When carried in procession these images seem to acquire the power of the originals, but at other times they are relegated to a secondary position. The Fátima processional image is particularly interesting in that it has been taken as a "pilgrim Virgin" to many parts of the world and was even reported to have shed tears in New Orleans, Louisiana, during such a journey.

A number of cult images traditionally remain away from their main shrine churches for fairly long periods of time. Some, especially in mountain districts of France and Spain, are transhumant like the flocks and herds that provided traditional subsistence for their devotees. During the winter months they reside in a valley parish church. In spring or early summer, these images are carried in jubilant procession to their shrine chapels high in the mountains where they receive visitors throughout the warm season or on a special day of pilgrimage, often in August. In the fall, they are returned to their winter homes. For example, on July 2 the image of Notre-Dame de Font Sainte is taken from Saint-Hippolyte in the Auvergne to a mountain chapel located near springs considered sacred in pagan times. Pilgrimages take place on July 26, August 15, and September 8 and the image is returned to the valley town in mid-October. Most cases of moving images from place to place on a regular basis come from southern Europe; the custom is also found in Latin America.

In southern Spain, images of the Virgin Mary travel to fulfill multiple obligations. These Virgins are focal points for district or minor regional pilgrimages and are also considered to be the patronesses of particular towns, generally the most important settlement in the area. For most of the year they are kept at shrine chapels in the countryside and are honored by one or more pilgrimages from the district. Once a year, for a period of two weeks to a month, they are transported to a church in the town for which they are thought to provide special protection. Here, amid much festivity, they are honored by the local citizens with special Masses for the children born during the year, the newlyweds of the town, and for all who died since their last visit.

Still other cult images in Spain and Italy are periodically taken to each of the communities where they are especially venerated. For example, the Madonna di San Luca, enshrined in a hill-top basilica on the edge of Bologna, is taken annually to the central city church of Saint Peter's; it also makes the rounds of various parish churches in the suburbs of this large Italian city. Similarly, the image of the Madonna del Terzito, venerated in the Lipari Islands off the coast of Sicily, makes a two-month journey by boat each year to communities on the various islands of the chain. A few images spend time in a different town or parish in the devotional zone each year on a rotational cycle that varies in years with the number of communities claiming the privilege of such a visit. Some miraculous images encountered in southern Europe are so peripatetic that they do not really qualify as shrine images because they have no special place of veneration and are constantly rotated from one church to another within their spheres of influence.[36]

Statues and Paintings

Images may be represented on a flat or two-dimensional surface, or they may be entirely or partially three-dimensional. Of the 3,635 images indicated in Table 6-3, 3,129 can be classified by type (Table 6-5). Of these, 74 percent are essentially three-dimensional, either fully rounded statues or figures at least half carved in relief. Statues are usually of wood or stone and may be painted or left in a natural state. A few statuettes are made of terra cotta or some other ceramic material, and some of the more recent examples are made of plaster.

Paintings on canvas or wood are the most common type of two-dimensional cult objects (Figure 6-6). Most of the other two-dimensional images are wall paintings, usually frescoes, and are especially common in Italy. In addition, a small number of imprints on cloth serve as cult images and a few prints and lithographs are especially venerated. These generally originated as pilgrim souvenirs from some other shrine where a painting or statue was enshrined as a cult object. Such devotional prints have circulated widely since at least the fifteenth century and most have not survived. Once in a while, however, an example of such usually ephemeral memorabilia has acquired miraculous qualities and provided the focus for a great new pilgrimage cultus.

Two such events occurred in northern Germany during the seventeenth century. At Kevelaer, in 1647, a pious man heard a voice telling him to build a chapel in a particular place. Meanwhile, Mary appeared to his wife in a dream and instructed the woman to purchase a tiny print of the Luxembourg image of Our Lady of Consolation of the Afflicted that some soldiers passing

Table 6-5 *Types of Images*

Images	Number	Percent of Classified Images	Percent of All Cult Objects (N = 4,118)
Three-Dimensional Images			
Statues	2,288	73	56
Relief carvings[a]	21	1	‹1
Total	2,309	74	56
Two-Dimensional Images			
Paintings	702	22	17
Frescoes and wall paintings	102	4	2
Prints/lithographs	10	‹1	‹1
Imprints on cloth	6	‹1	‹1
Total	820	26	20
Total classified images	3,129	100	76

[a]This subcategory is probably underrepresented. Several of the images classified as statues are more likely high relief carvings.

through the town had attempted to sell her a few days earlier. The devotional picture was obtained and the shrine established. This great shrine of the Lower Rhine draws more than 800,000 pilgrims annually. A second example, the Neviges pilgrimage, originated with the dream vision of a Franciscan friar who did as instructed by taking his personal devotional lithograph of Mary to the largely Protestant Hardenberg area in 1681. Soon afterward a desperately ill nobleman was cured and a shrine was established. This shrine, still maintained by Franciscans and noted for a modernistic church, draws from the populous Ruhr Valley and is visited by 150,000 to 200,000 pilgrims per year. At both Kevelaer and Neviges, the tiny prints are displayed as if they were priceless jewels and are viewed as great cult objects despite their size and mundane origins.[37]

The spatial distribution of two-dimensional cult images indicates a much stronger orientation toward paintings as miraculous images in eastern regions than is found along Europe's western margins. Highly venerated three-dimensional images are abundant in all Western European areas where image cultus thrives. Two-dimensional shrine images are very strongly concentrated in Italy, where they make up nearly half of the images that could be classified. They are also common in southern Germanic lands, particularly Austria, but are seldom seen in France or on the Iberian peninsula. The reasons for this remarkably different pattern of distribution are unclear, especially since

Sacred Objects

Figure 6-6 *A crowned painting of Mary with the Christ Child provides an object of cultus near Cori, Italy, at a site sanctified by a 1521 apparition of Mary as a child. Miraculous paintings are particularly common in Italy where they make up nearly half of the country's venerated images.*

France and Spain have important traditions of religious painting as well as sculpture. Perhaps part of the explanation relates to closer ties between Italy and the Germanic lands and the Byzantine East where a focus on two-dimensional icons has prevailed at least since the end of iconoclastic times. Some of the cult images of Italy and the Germanies are Byzantine imports, and others are in the Eastern style. However, many images venerated in these regions, such as the famous Mariahilf painting by the sixteenth-century artist Lukas Cranach along with its numerous wonder-working copies, are of local origin and bear little resemblance to Eastern icons.[38]

The question of why flat-surface images so frequently serve as cult objects in Italy and the Germanies is less important than the question of why they are so rarely found in Spain, Portugal, and France. In Spain, 96 percent of the classified cult images are statues or relief carvings; in France, the figure is 97 percent. We found no two-dimensional cult images in Portugal, although there may be a few among the many not classified by type. A number of Spanish shrine stories relate the substitution of a statue for a painting around which a pilgrimage initially developed, further indicating a strong preference for three-dimensional cult images. In some of these cases, as with the Virgen de Almudena in Madrid, the original painting or a copy of it has recently replaced the statue. Among the few other relatively well-known two-dimensional Spanish cult objects is a very large painting of Christ carrying the Cross venerated at Moclín, Andalucía, as the Cristo del Paño. Nevertheless, the exceptionally strong emphasis on three-dimensional cultic imagery toward the western margins of the Continent suggests a cultural bias against accepting paintings as miraculous. [39]

It is tempting to speculate that the roots of this spatial difference come from very old traditions involving the Christianization of pagan statues toward the West. Art historian Kurt Weitzmann points out that the pagans preferred sculpture in the round for cult objects, but that painted panels depicting gods and goddesses were becoming more popular in late antiquity especially among the adherents of Eastern mystery religions.[40] Perhaps a tradition of preference for three-dimensional cult objects had remained stronger toward the western part of the Empire during the waning days of paganism. Possibly, also, the evolution of acceptable image veneration from reliquary images, which seems to have occurred in parts of France, made paintings, which could not easily serve as reliquaries, somewhat suspect. A more mundane explanation for three-dimensional image preference might be the Medieval rise of the custom of embellishing images with crowns and dressing them in elaborate garments—clearly an easier procedure with statues than with two-dimensional objects. This thesis is questionable, however, because Germans and Italians adapted such practices to paintings by attaching flat-sided crowns to their surfaces and decorating the figures with ropes of jewels.

Pilgrimage Iconography of Christ, Mary, and the Saints

Christian art is rich in variety. Christ, His mother, and the more popular saints have been portrayed in numerous ways, representing different events in their earthly lives along with symbolic interpretations of their heavenly powers.[41] Images that have acquired the status of pilgrimage cult objects, however, are generally limited to a small number of basic types representing only a few aspects of the life experiences and/or spiritual symbolism of the holy persons portrayed. In other words, miraculous images tend to be popularized clichés focusing pilgrim attention on only a few manifestations of the rich symbolism surrounding these holy persons.

Saints' Images

Cult images of the more popular pilgrimage saints generally emphasize some outstanding characteristic or symbol that makes the saint of devotion easily recognizable among his or her many fellow saints. Saint Anne, for example, is usually portrayed with the child Mary who sometimes holds a tiny Christ Child. Cult images of Saint Joseph and Saint Anthony of Padua are usually depicted as holding the Christ Child in their arms, while Saint Christopher is always an old man with a staff bearing the Child on his back or shoulders. The martyr Saint Sebastian is typically portrayed as pierced by arrows, and Saint Lucy usually holds a tray containing her eyeballs which she is said to have plucked out so as not to be attractive to a suitor who admired their beauty. Saint Benedict is easily recognized, despite many variations on the theme of his physical appearance, by the raven that appears somewhere in the imagery. There is somewhat more variety in the case of Saint James the Greater, Spain's great Santiago. Outside of Iberia, this saint is typically represented in pilgrim's garb with staff, gourd, and scallop shell on his hat. In the Iberian homeland of his cultus, shrine images of the saint are more likely to show him mounted on his trusty steed vigorously riding down hapless Moors—still with a scallop shell on his hat.[42]

If reliquary images are discounted, saints are somewhat more likely to be represented by two-dimensional cult images than are Christ and Mary. Also, a higher-than-usual proportion of saints are venerated at shrines where there is no relic or image. This partly reflects the large number of Irish saints, only a few of whose shrines display a corporal relic or miraculous image.

Images of Christ

Miraculous crucifixes are the most common cult images at Christ-centered shrines. Early Western European portrayals of Christ on the Cross generally showed a "triumphant" figure depicting a body against a cross with no sign of suffering or approaching death. Such images are sometimes included in the collections at pilgrimage shrines, but crucifixes venerated as cult images nearly always show a man in agony or death. This type of imagery existed by at least the ninth century in the Rhineland, where some surviving examples are thought to have been created by Byzantine artists employed by Carolingian kings, nobles, and abbots.[43] A twelfth-century example of Byzantine-influenced carving in northern West Germany is found in the Tuetoberger Wald at the Externstein, a rock formation of pre-Christian religious significance that attracted Christian pilgrims in Medieval times. Most extant cult images of the suffering Christ on the Cross, however, appear to date from the Renaissance and the Catholic Reformation (Figure 6-7).

The crucifix is only one of many ways in which Christ's last week may be graphically portrayed. Christian art details the triumphant ride on a donkey into Jerusalem on Palm Sunday, the overturning of the money changers' tables in the temple, the Last Supper with the disciples, the prayers in the Garden of Gethsemane, the betrayal kiss of Judas Iscariot, the trial before the Sanhedrin, the torture by Roman soldiers, the presentation to the public by Pontius Pilate, each step in the progress of the death march to Calvary, and the nailing to the Cross, as well as the Crucifixion, death, burial, and Resurrection. In the Stations of the Cross, prominently displayed at many shrines as well as in most Catholic churches of any type, Passion symbolism is simplified by reduction to fourteen categories of graphic display. The strong emphasis on crucifixes as pilgrimage cult objects thus represents a further iconographic reduction to a single, powerful symbol.

The greatest variety in especially venerated images of Christ is found in the Germanies, as might be expected given the strong concentration of Christ-centered cultus in these lands. Here, and to a lesser extent in Iberia, representations of other episodes in Christ's Passion still serve as visual symbols for pilgrim veneration. Some shrines, including the well-known, touristically

Figure 6-7 *This miraculous crucifix in the Santuario del Crocifisso de Valcalda at Pieve de Cadore, northeastern Italy, is said to have been found in 1540 when a farmer's oxen refused to move after the plow struck a coffin containing the image. The symbolism of a suffering Christ on the Cross provides the central imagery for most contemporary Christ-centered shrines.*

promoted Wies church in Upper Bavaria, focus cultus on a statue of Christ chained to a column while undergoing the torture of flagellation.[44] Representations of Christ tortured seem to have been fairly common as pilgrimage cult objects in Germanic areas during the Catholic Reformation, but many of these baroque images have lost much of their power to attract pilgrims. There are also a few extant *ecce homo* shrines in the Germanies and Iberia. At these places, Christ is shown as He was presented by Pontius Pilate to the Jerusalem population while the crowds call for His execution. Occasionally, as at Moclin in southern Spain, the cult image shows Christ carrying His Cross toward Calvary. Images of Christ in the tomb, carried in Holy Week processions in many southern European communities, are found in numerous Germanic, Italian, and Iberian churches, but miraculous "Holy Grave" representations of Christ serve as cult objects in only a few places such as Heiligengrab, Austria; Deggendorf, West Germany; and Pardo, Spain.

The most famous and influential visual symbol of a crucified Christ is the Holy Shroud venerated in Turin, Italy, since 1578 and last displayed in 1978. This famous relic is an ancient linen burial cloth on which can be seen full-length images of the back and front of a crucified man. The negative of a photograph made in the late nineteenth century proved to be a "positive" image, meaning that it looked like a print from a negative, thus suggesting that the figure on the Turin Shroud is a "negative" image in a photographic sense. The image, thought by some to be the *Sideon* venerated in Constantinople from about the sixth century, is not a painting, and is perhaps best explained as a kind of photographic negative, a technology nonexistent in Western Europe or elsewhere before the nineteenth century.

The interpretive program at Turin in 1978, while not taking a position on whether the figure on the Shroud actually portrays Jesus, emphasized the trauma of Christ's torture and ultimate death by crucifixion. Detailed photographs of parts of the linen cloth indicate that the man had been brutally whipped, and a cap of thorns had been placed on his head prior to his death. His shoulders were bruised as if from carrying a heavy burden and he had been nailed to a cross through his wrists as was the Roman custom, rather than through the palms as is usually, but unrealistically, shown in most Medieval and later representations of Christ Crucified. Probably the most emotionally impressive attribute of the Turin Shroud is the shock of recognition. Whether or not the Shroud actually portrays Jesus after His crucifixion, it has almost certainly served as a model for many graphic representations of Christ in Western Europe since the thirteenth century when this relic turned up in France, possibly as Crusaders' loot taken from Constantinople in 1205.[45]

Although the suffering, dying Jesus of the Crucifixion is by far the most common portrayal of Christ, even at Trinity shrines, where cult images usually represent a sorrowing Father God holding His dead Son, there are exceptions to the rule. A few shrines focus pilgrims' attention on statues of Christ in Majesty as at Nievenheim, West Germany. Several fairly recent cult images, including those found at Sacré-Cœur de Montmartre in Paris, Cerro de los Ángeles near Madrid, and Kloster Arnstein on the Lahn River in West Germany, show Christ exposing His "sacred heart" in accordance with a vision experienced by Saint Marguerite-Marie, a seventeenth-century French nun.

There are also at least six cult images of the Christ Child in Western Europe, the most famous of which is an early fifteenth-century olive wood statue of the Child Jesus venerated in the Basilica of Santa Maria de Ara Coeli in Rome. Three of the Child images are considered miraculous because they are thought to have come to life and carried on conversations with devout nuns. The earliest such story comes from thirteenth-century Sarnen, Switzerland, and the most recent from Collevalenza, Italy, in the 1950s. The "Little Jesus" of Espinheiro, Portugal, is said to have saved the region's people from French troops during the Peninsular Wars, and another famous Child figure is venerated along with a Madonna with Child at the Portuguese shrine of Quintela da Lapa. The famous Christ Child of Prague, Czechoslovakia, is of Western origin. The Spanish statue was brought to Prague by María Manriquez de Lara when she married a Czech nobleman in 1556.

The Child may be represented as a very young boy, as at Prague, or as a baby of the type frequently displayed in manger scenes during the Christmas season. The Christ Child cultus was more important in Catholic Reformation Europe than at present. The devotion is common in Latin America where, according to the oral traditions of preconquest Indian civilizations, gods often assumed the forms of children when they took the trouble to confront or instruct mortals. Therefore, the relatively numerous Latin American Christ Child shrines suggest the sprouting of European cultus seeds laid on fertile ground.[46] Of course, the infant Jesus frequently is represented in European cult image symbolism as a babe in His mother's arms, but at these shrines the devotional focus is directed toward Mary.

Marian Images

In the Christian pilgrimage tradition, the oldest and by far the most frequently found image of Mary is the Madonna with Child. Approximately three-quarters to five-sixths of Western Europe's present Marian cult images show Mary with the infant Jesus. Styles of representation have changed through the centuries. The stiffly erect, seated posture of a Medieval figure of Notre-Dame found at a French alpine shrine (Figure 6-8) and the elaborately vested eleventh-century image venerated at Tongre, Belgium (Figure 6-9), contrast vividly with the baroque image representing Notre-Dame de Vie at Villefranche de Conflent in Languedoc (Figure 6-10). In the Belgian example, the vestments virtually overwhelm the Mother and Child. In the early French image, the Christ Child, looking like a miniature adult, gives a formal blessing; in the baroque example, the Child appears as a lively baby whose fluid movements provide counterpoint to His mother's gesture of concern for humanity.

Since the Renaissance, miraculous images of the Madonna have tended to display regional ideals of maternal womanhood. The fifteenth-century Hohenpeißenberg Madonna, for example, is a stereotypically blond, plump Ger-

Figure 6-8 *Marian cult objects of the Romanesque period typically show a seated Madonna with Child. This old image is one of several venerated at Notre-Dame-de-la-Gorge in the French Alps. The Child blesses humanity with his right hand and holds an adult male head, presumably that of the Crucified Christ he will become, in his left hand.*

man hausfrau in spite of her crown and the baroque embellishments of her setting (Figure 6-11). In Spain, where the majority of miraculous Madonnas are still elaborately vested in dazzling garments, the mystique of Mary as a heavenly persona seems stronger, especially when such an image is carried from the pilgrimage church in a rain of rose petals as at Agreda in Castile (Figure 6-12). As this image moves forth from the church in procession, pilgrims crowd around, reaching out to touch the hem of the Madonna's garments (Figure 6-13).[47]

The most common representation of the Madonna shows Mary, either seated or standing, holding the Child in her arms or on her lap. Seated images are, on the average, considerably older than standing images in Western Europe, although standing representations of the Madonna and Child are

Sacred Objects

Figure 6-9 *The eleventh-century Madonna and Child venerated at Tongre-Notre-Dame, Belgium, appears to stand in elaborate cloth vestments. Mary is actually seated on a throne and holds the Child on her lap.*

Figure 6-10 *This standing baroque image of Notre-Dame de Vie is currently kept in the principal church of Villefranche de Conflent, a walled town in the French Pyrenees. At one time the image had its own pilgrimage chapel outside the town.*

of great antiquity in the East. Tenth-century copies of the famous Hodegetria of Constantinople, which was lost when the city fell to the Turks in 1453, show Mary standing with the Child in her left arm.[48]

Detailed photographs of 1,196 currently venerated Marian images in our files provided the basis for a rough estimate of the relative importance of various iconographic themes. Cult images show Mary with the Christ Child in more than three-fourths of the cases. Of these images, 847 focus only on Mary and the Child; no other persons are represented in the immediate scene. Thirty-six of these images are Byzantine or Byzantine-style icons. In most cases, Mary simply holds the Child, but 39 images show her either offering her breast or feeding the infant. This was a popular iconography in Medieval Europe that became outmoded during the late Renaissance.[49] Most examples still serving as cult images appear to be in Italy, although we found a few venerated at shrines in Spain, West Germany, and France.

At least two cult images show Mary holding the hand of a walking toddler. A small number of cult images showing Mary with the Child include Saint

Sacred Objects

Figure 6-11 *The German-looking Hohenpeißenberg Madonna dates from about 1460. It was donated to a hill-top chapel in present-day West Germany in 1514 by a ducal administrator, and cultus was promoted when a monastery was built at the site in 1608. The pilgrimage grew rapidly during the Thirty Years' War. The image was once elaborately vested, but has been displayed without cloth garments since its restoration in 1959.*

Joseph and tend to focus devotion on the Holy Family as a group. Sometimes other saints either flank or kneel before the Mother and Child. In twenty-two cases, mostly Italian, images venerated at shrines established because of an apparitional event include one or more visionaries along with the graphic symbolism of the Madonna and Child. In seven cases, Mary kneels before the Child in awe or lovingly tends a baby lying on a table or in a crib. At three minor Italian shrines the cult image shows an embattled Mary holding the Child in one arm while thrashing a horrid-looking Devil into submission with a weapon in her other hand. In two other Italian cases, Mary holds the Child while spreading her cloak over tiny kneeling figures of humans. Another such image, venerated at Jesi in the Italian province of the Marches, shows Mary with the cloak as pregnant with the Child glowing in her womb. Little of this imagery survived the Reformation, but at least one other image

Figure 6-12 *An elaborately garbed image of the Madonna is carried from the pilgrimage church at Agreda in New Castile, Spain, in a flurry of rose petals. The custom of vesting miraculous statues dates from at least the fourteenth century in Spain. It was especially widespread during the Catholic Reformation period and is still fairly common throughout the Continent.*

showing the Christ Child in Mary's body is said to be venerated at Malta in southern Austria.[50]

The Child is usually of appropriate size relative to the size of the Mother, although the baby often has relatively mature facial features, especially in some of the older representations. There are also a few curious examples of Mary holding an extremely large baby with the bodily proportions of an infant but the relative size of a four- to six-year-old child.[51]

The reasons for the evocative power of the Madonna with Child as a cult object are obvious. Mother goddesses have been portrayed in Europe and southwestern Asia in similar ways for thousands of years. Such graphic symbols represent a quality of sacred motherhood that cannot be reduced to purely masculine terms, even in cultural traditions emphasizing male figures

Figure 6-13 *Pilgrims at Agreda, Spain, reach out to touch the hem of the Virgin's gown as the image is carried in procession. The Agreda cultus dates from 1357 when a shepherd is said to have found a statue of Mary floating in a nearby stream.*

of divinity. As pointed out by Sharbrough and other students of religious symbolism, only women can bear children and nurse them with the milk of their breasts.[52] Thus, while the symbolism of the mother goddess may sometimes be denied or reduced to a very unimportant level in a pantheon or theological scheme, she rarely disappears.

The earth mother as a giver of life was also the death goddess in many early religious traditions. The myth of a virgin mother bearing a child who later dies in her arms can be traced back 5,000 years to ancient Sumerian civilization and the story of Inanna, Queen of Heaven, mother and bride of Dumuz, weeping for the son she gave over to torture and death. The symbolism extends through time from Inanna to the Babylonian Ishtar and to the Egyptian Isis, alternatively represented as nursing or mourning for her son Osiris.

Such Eastern goddess figures were venerated throughout the Roman world by the first few centuries after Christ, and the last temple of Isis at Philae in Egypt was closed in the sixth century A.D. many years after Mary's lamentations for Christ had been dramatized in Eastern Mediterranean poetry.[53] Unlike Isis, the Hindu Shiva, and some Greco-Roman interpretations of goddesses, however, Mary has never been a death goddess. In the pietà, where she holds the body of her dead Son, she is the sorrowing Mother who did nothing to bring about the death of her beloved Son.

At least 185 active shrines are primarily focused on a cult image depicting Mary with the dead Christ. Although examples are found in most parts of continental Europe, 70 percent are concentrated in culturally Germanic areas including France's Alsace region and Italy's Trentino-Alto Adige region. Several very old pietàs are venerated in southwestern France, but the cult of the sorrowing Mother sank its deepest roots into the folk tradition of Germanic lands. Rothkrug traces the Germanic spread of the cultus to promotional efforts of South German Dominican nuns beginning in about 1300. The center of activity appears to have been Baden and Swabia, where Rothkrug found 64 out of 71 Medieval German shrines dedicated to the sorrowing Mother.[54] According to Kolb, "The pietà was so popular in Germany for hundreds of years that she came to be considered typically German." He adds that pietà cultus was declining in the sixteenth century, but made a comeback in the seventeenth century due to the traumas of the Thirty Years' War.[55] Losses of young men and ultimate defeat in two twentieth-century world wars have undoubtedly helped keep the symbolism of the sorrowing Mother extraordinarily powerful in the Germanies and Austria as well as Alsace where men were drawn, sometimes involuntarily, into the German army in both wars.

Among the 68 images of Mary with the dead Christ of which photographs are on file, 4 show Mary, usually with others, standing by the Cross. In 3 cases, including cult images at Notre-Dame du Bischenberg in Alsace and the important West German shrine at Klausen in the Diocese of Trier, Mary is one of a group of people clustered around the body taken from the Cross. Most pietàs, however, show Mary alone with the body of her tortured Son. The majority of pietàs serving as cult images show a woman of a more-or-less appropriately mature age, assuming that Mary was very young when her Son was born. In some cases, however, the sorrowing woman looks much too young to be the mother of a man in his early thirties. At the Austrian shrine of Maria Dreieichen, a seventeenth-century polychrome wood carving shows a very young woman holding the body of Christ in a manner suggesting the agony of a newly bereaved widow mourning a dead husband-lover rather than a middle-aged mother sorrowing for the loss of her son.

In about two-thirds of the images in the photo file, the figure of the dead Christ is the size of an adult male, relative to the size of the Mother. The other pietàs show a relatively small Christ, usually with the proportions of a twelve- to fourteen-year-old adolescent boy, although generally with the figure's adult status represented by a full beard (Figure 6-14). In some cases, the Christ figure is very small indeed, as at the shrine of Maria Luggau in the out-of-the-way Lesachtal region of Ost Tirol, where the dead Christ in the arms of the sorrowing Mother is the size of a four- to six-year-old child. One possible explanation for such symbolism is that the small Christ places the visual focus on Mary as the subject of pilgrim devotions. Such imagery also evokes the probability that most mothers never cease thinking of their adult offspring as the children they once were. Thus, these disproportionate images reflect the cry of countless generations of women mourning their dead sons: "My son—my child—my baby!" While realistically the child becomes socially more important as he reaches adulthood, the mother's sense of loss reduces him in size to an earlier time when she could more easily enfold him in her arms.

In four cases we know of, the cult image shows Mary with the Risen Christ, or with the Father, Son, and Holy Ghost who are crowning her as Queen of Heaven. Such iconography is not uncommon in Europe, but rarely seems to serve as a focus for shrine devotion. Cult images may also show Mary without Christ but with other persons, or, more often, completely alone. At least 293 shrines found throughout Western Europe have images of this general type. The 194 examples for which photographs are on file represent a fairly wide range of portrayals although the majority show Mary in representations symbolizing the Immaculate Conception, the Assumption, the Annunciation, or as she was described by visionaries after an apparitional event as in the case of the widely copied Fátima and Lourdes images. In the latter case, the visionary, Saint Bernadette Soubirous, is usually included, often in a three-dimensional scene showing the Lourdes Grotto. In Italy, where apparitions of Mary without the Christ Child have been fairly common since at least the fifteenth century, the most important image at several apparitional shrines depicts Mary without the Child appearing to one or more visionaries. Sometimes these images seem to be true cult objects, although in other cases, as at Caravággio in Lombardy, the image seems to serve merely as a documentation of the event.

Eight photographs of cult images on file show Mary with the Angel of the

Figure 6-14 *The vested pietà venerated at Theirenbach in Alsace, France, dates from about 1350. The cultus originated in 1130 when a young lawyer was cured at a Benedictine monastery that had just been established at the site. Note the maturity of the Mother and the disproportionately small size of the dead Christ.*

Annunciation, and another eight show her standing majestically with her cloak extended over small supplicating humans. This imagery of the Madonna della Misericordia, or Our Lady of Mercy, has long been promoted by the Servites, a religious order founded at Florence, Italy, in 1233. One such image serves as the current cult image at the fifteenth-century Marian apparitional shrine of Monte Bérico on a hill overlooking Vicenza, Italy, a shrine administered by Servites. There are also a few Byzantine-style images showing only Mary's face, and thirteen sorrowful mother images of Mary as a middle-aged woman with her heart pierced by one or by seven swords.

A cultus of the infant Mary was promoted by a seventeenth-century abbess of Poor Clares in Todi, Italy, and Italian shrines at Forno Canavese and Monte Oliveto Maggiore focus pilgrims' attention on statues of Mary as a baby. This symbolism was found fairly often in a role of secondary importance at several southeastern French and northern Italian pilgrimage centers. Visionaries in Spain and Italy have reported apparitions of Mary as a little girl. Although the cult images at such shrines generally show an adolescent girl or a young woman, an image of Mary as a child is said to be the principal cult object at Linares de Río Frío in the León region of Spain.

A very old form of Marian imagery, not commonly found as a cult image in Western Europe, shows her "Dormation" or "the falling asleep" on her deathbed. A well-known example is found at the shrine of Montallegro high in the hills above Rapallo on Italy's Ligurian coast. Here, a poor but devout man experienced a vision of Mary surrounded by a host of angels while he was walking back to his home village of Canevale from Genoa in 1557. As a token, the Virgin is said to have given the man a small Byzantine-style picture of her dormation that is still venerated.[56] Another example is a fifteenth-century fresco venerated at the sanctuary of Canóscio near Città di Castello in Umbria.

Although venerated images of Mary without Christ are quite diverse, for the past century or so they have tended to be figures of a devout young woman characterized by eyes rolled up toward Heaven in an expression of obvious piety. In Figure 6-15, a German pilgrim carries such an image from his local church to its meeting with a similar image enshrined in the branches of a pine tree at San Sebastián de Garabandal, Spain.

Dark Images

Some representations of the Virgin Mary take the form of images with dark skin tones ranging in color from sooty, to medium and dark brown, to jet black. We identified 172 currently venerated examples of dark images through observations and descriptions in shrine literature. Of these, 2 represent Christ, 3 are portrayals of saints, and 167 represent the Virgin Mary, usually as the Madonna with Child. When a dark Madonna holds the infant Christ, the baby is nearly always the same color as the mother, although in two curious cases, one at San Severo in southern Italy, and the other at Chipiona in southwestern Spain, black or very dark images of Mary hold pink-toned babies. Despite the dark skin tones, the features are inevitably those of a Caucasian mother and child.

Although dark images are often regarded as a predominantly southern European representation, they are currently venerated throughout most of Western Europe (Map 6-2). At least two dark representations of the Virgin are said to be venerated in England, and the cult object at a shrine in Wetten, Netherlands, is a dark Christ. A beautiful Medieval representation of the Madonna and Child, carved in dark walnut, is honored by nuns and pilgrims at a convent shrine near Copenhagen, Denmark. This image was found in an antique shop in Jutland by a twentieth-century bishop of Copenhagen, and it was his gift of the image to the convent, about four decades ago, that generated the pilgrimage. Although one of the nuns pointed out that "we Danes are too practically minded" to think of the image as miraculous, the Sisters guard their treasure from the acquisitions program of a major museum.

Dark images are particularly prevalent in France, where nearly 11 percent of the identified cult images were described as dark and where more than 30 percent of the examples were found. Chartres, Boulogne, Le Folgoët, Font-Romeu, Le Délivrade, Le Puy, Myans, and Rocamadour are among the French shrines famous for their dark images of the Virgin Mary. Halle, in Walloon Belgium, also has a noted black Virgin. Eighteen percent of the dark images were found in Iberia. Among the most renowned are the cult objects at Montserrat, Guadalupe, Nuestra Señora de la Cabeza, and Peña de Francia—all in Spain. The image at the Catalan shrine of Nuria was also dark until restored to a lighter color after the Spanish Civil War. Italy has 12 percent of the dark images, including such famous examples as those at Loreto, Incoronata, Santuario di Monte Vérgine, Oropa, La Bruna of Naples, and the dark Christ of Lucca. Austria, Switzerland, and West Germany combined account for about one-third of the cases. Among the best known are the images

Figure 6-15 *Images of Mary alone have gained popularity as cult objects during the past two centuries. Here, at San Sebastián de Garabandal, Spain, a German pilgrim carries such an image on his devotional rounds.*

venerated at Einsiedeln, Switzerland, and at Altötting, Marienbaum, and Telgte in West Germany.[57]

Cult images described as "dark," "brown," or "black" may be the same shade all over or they may be displayed so that only the dark face and hands of the image can be seen. Others are polychrome images with the skin tones painted a dark color. The Romanesque "Black Virgins" venerated at Rocamadour and Font-Romeu in France, along with the fourteenth-century pietà at Telgte in northern West Germany, are examples of statues carved from a dark, or age-darkened, natural wood and unembellished with colors. Such images are monochromatically dark all over, garments as well as skin tones; many, nowadays, are displayed without cloth garments or vestments. Most, if not all, were once painted, and may have initially been characterized by light skin tones. The image at Rocamadour was originally covered with thin silver strips, a few of which remain in a tarnished state thus blending with the

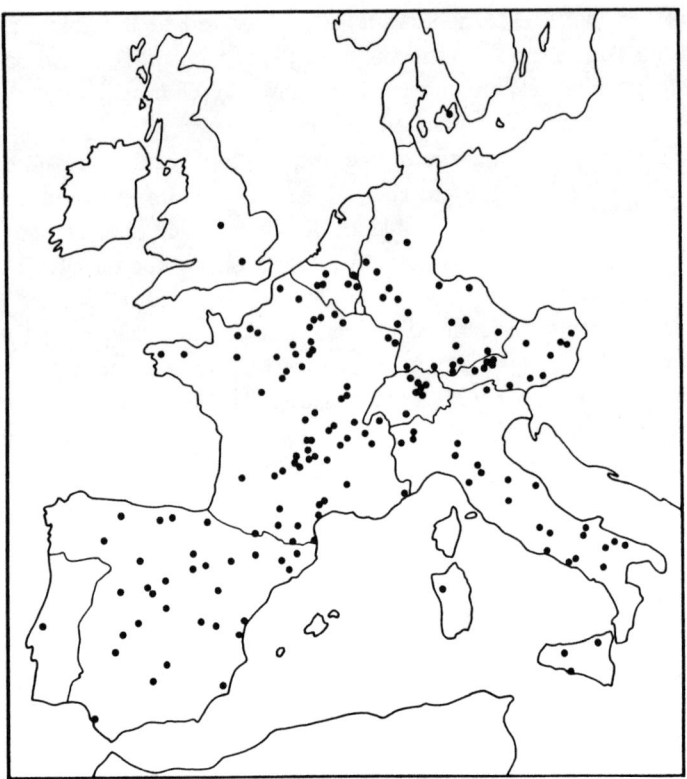

Map 6-2 *Distribution of Dark Images*
Pilgrimage centers at which the primary cult object is a black or dark-skinned image, usually of the Virgin Mary, show notable concentrations in France and Spain. For the most part, the French and Iberian images have their own unique traditions. Those in Germanic regions are mostly found at shrines subsidiary to a few great pilgrimage centers famous for dark images, particularly the Italian shrine of Loreto and less frequently the Swiss shrine of Einsiedeln and the West German shrine of Altötting.

wood. Similar in type are dark stone images, such as those venerated at Orléans and Le Folgoët in France. As with the wooden versions, the skin color results from the material of which the image is made and is no different from the color of the garments.

Other dark images, such as the famous Loreto Madonna, which is a twentieth-century copy of an image destroyed in a fire, as well as many of the

Spanish examples at such places as Guadalupe and de la Cabeza, are displayed in elaborate cloth vestments so that only the dark faces and hands of the Mother and Child are on view. In the case of such usually vested images, the skin tones may be of a natural dark material or may be painted in a dark tone. The garments under the vestments may also be natural or painted.

At Altötting in southeastern Bavaria, the venerated image is a polychrome wood carving that is usually vested for display but often photographed without the cloth garments. The skin tone is sooty, supporting the story of darkness acquired by centuries of exposure to candle smoke, but the carved wooden garments are rendered in brighter colors, thus contrasting with the darkened facial features. Einsiedeln, Switzerland, represents a case of a usually vested image, originally said to have been darkened by candle smoke, but now with garments refurbished with fresh paint and features painted an even black tone. Other images, including the Christ of Lucca and several of the Spanish *morenas*, have skins painted in various shades of brown. Some of the dark paintings, which are usually Byzantine or Byzantine-style icons, appear to have been darkened by smoke or merely indicate aging of the pigments; as with the statues, they may be restored so that the garments are brightened while the skin tones remain dark.

There does not appear to be any connection between the degree of darkness and the image's reputation as a powerful cult object, although dark images, as a general class, are often considered to have esoteric or highly unusual powers. Marina Warner exemplifies this theme in her comment that "In Catholic countries, where blackness is the climate of the devils, not the angels, and is associated almost exclusively with magic and the occult, Black Madonnas are considered especially wonder-working, as the possessors of hermetic power and magic."[58]

In shrine literature and speculative writings, this special power is sometimes related to the presumed antiquity of these images, and several accounts of the manner in which particular images supposedly became dark, such as the story of soot from centuries of candle smoke, emphasize veneration over long periods of time. Antiquity is also suggested by stories of images that are said to have darkened during periods of burial from which they were later retrieved, generally under miraculous circumstances. How many actually were buried for a period of time is unknown, although 43 are associated with legends of loss and mysterious rediscovery in such places as caves, crypts, trees, wells, or simply underground. Salvation from fire, which supposedly charred the images, is evoked as a reason for the darkness of 4 images. In at least 16 cases, darkness is related to presumed Eastern Mediterranean origins, although why images from the East should be dark is not entirely clear because most extant old Eastern icons are not characterized by dark skin tones. Darkness is also sometimes viewed as representing Marian symbolism interjected into the Song of Solomon, as in "I am black, but comely, O ye daughters of Jerusalem." As the Turners suggest, "this association is probably a fallacy of the *post hoc, ergo propter hoc* variety," although it could also relate to the twelfth-century Saint Bernard of Clairvaux's frequent use of the imagery in the Song of Solomon in his praise of the Virgin.[59]

A number of twentieth-century writers have argued that some images may always have been dark and suggest that the roots of such iconography reach far back into an Indo-European tradition in which goddesses, including the powerful Diana of Ephesus, have often been represented as black. Other writers, in contrast, maintain that most images now represented as dark were originally light, that there is no special connection between the age of an image and the degree to which it is considered especially powerful, and that there is little or no evidence for veneration of images noted for dark skin tones during Medieval times. In addition, William Christian has raised questions about the assumption that dark images, as a type, are more powerful or miraculous than light-skinned images and has demonstrated that pilgrims devoted to the dark image of the Virgin at Montserrat rarely mention darkness as a special attribute of this famous cult object.[60]

The question of whether dark images really have any special powers vis-à-vis light-skinned images is important, because if darkness is not an attribute of special power, then it is largely irrelevant except as a curiosity. The answer lies mostly in how the data are interpreted. Assuming shrine importance as a measure of image power, there are far more very miraculous light images than dark images. Many of Europe's most powerful cult images—including those venerated at Mariazell in Austria, Genazzano in Italy, and many other places—are not dark. Indeed, about 90 percent of the images venerated at major shrines are light. In addition, not all dark images are powerful. Many, not counted in this study, either receive no special cultus or serve as objects of local cultus. Others, although venerated at shrines, are secondary in importance to other cult objects including light images and relics. Of the dark images identified as primary or coequal cult objects at active shrines, 60 percent are venerated at minor places of pilgrimage. Thus, an image need not be dark to be considered especially miraculous and a majority of dark images have limited powers in terms of their ability to attract large numbers of pilgrims from extensive areas.

This line of analysis, however, does not adequately reveal the pattern, partly because there are so many more light than dark images currently serving as cult objects. Of the dark images identified as cult objects, 18 percent are found at the shrines identified as the most important in Europe in terms of visitation and drawing power. This compares with slightly over 2 percent of the light images. Forty percent of the dark images are venerated at shrines classified as major pilgrimage centers, in contrast with 15 percent of the light images. Thus, a cult image characterized by darkness of skin tone is well over twice as likely as a light image to be venerated at a shrine with substantial visitation from an extensive area, and even more likely than usual to be found as a primary cult image at an extremely important shrine.

Some dark images are more likely than others to generate subsidiary shrines. Of the 172 dark images identified, 38 are at shrines dedicated to the Italian Madonna of Loreto and are located primarily in Germanic lands.[61] These images are not all copies of the Loreto original, and it seems likely in some cases that the identification with Loreto resulted because an existing cult image was already black or very dark. There are a number of other subsidiary Loreto shrines, not counted in this analysis, where light-skinned images are venerated. In another 53 cases, subsidiary shrines focus on dark images that are copies of the famous Madonnas at Altötting, West Germany; Einsiedeln, Switzerland; Montserrat, Spain; and Częstochowa, Poland. It seems likely that a relatively small number of important dark image cults may also have given rise to a focus on dark images not identified as directly subsidiary. For example, the French art historian Émile Mâle has suggested that the very ancient dark image venerated at Le Puy before its destruction in the French Revolution probably served as a model for a number of the Black Virgins found in southern France.[62]

All but two of the shrines known to be directly subsidiary to other dark image shrines are currently of minor importance as pilgrimage centers. If these shrines are discounted, the proportion of dark images at major pilgrimage centers reaches 54 percent. It is obvious that a dark-skinned image, assuming it attains the status of a pilgrimage cult object, is far more likely to be considered especially powerful or miraculous than one that is not dark. Or, perhaps, as Christian has suggested, very important cult images at very important shrines are less likely than others to have their skin tones lightened during restoration.[63]

Subsidiary shrines, where copies of black images are venerated, are not only unlikely to be important, but are also much more recent on the average than other dark image shrines. The oldest date from the fifteenth century, and 89 percent of the 43 that could be assigned to time periods were established after 1530. None are located at places that were sacred in pre-Christian times. In contrast, of the 89 nonsubsidiary dark image shrines that can be assigned to periods of cult formation, 67 percent were drawing pilgrims before 1399, or before the establishment of the oldest of the subsidiary shrines. Only 20 percent were founded after 1530. Images were not always venerated from the beginnings of pilgrimage at these places, and, when they were, the images were not necessarily dark in skin tone. The general pattern, however, is one of substantially greater-than-average antiquity as Christian holy places. In addition, 10 percent of these shrines are thought, based on archaeological or other evidence, to have been centers of worship in pre-Christian times. This compares with only about 4 percent of all inventoried shrines and an even smaller proportion of those shrines where images are presently the primary object of cultus. Thus, the general notion that dark images are especially powerful, and that the shrines where they are venerated are of great antiquity, is supported in the aggregate.

Dark images also differ substantially from other images in the relatively small number that are said to have initially attested to their miraculous qualities by weeping, bleeding, moving, rolling their eyes, or calling attention to themselves as special among other images through association with unexpected miracles. There are exceptions to the rule, as in the case of the soot-darkened Virgin of Altötting that began attracting pilgrims after a drowned child was revived in the fifteenth century. The proportion of such cult-formative miracle stories associated with dark images is only 6 percent, however, as compared with 18 percent of all stories explaining how particular images came to be considered as especially miraculous. Maybe being dark is enough—one of several, alternative ways in which the special powers of a particular image may be manifest or symbolized.

When, where, and why this particular association was initially made or how it came to be widespread is uncertain. The idea of an initial connection between dark-skinned pagan goddesses and dark Madonnas remains speculative. Mâle suggested that the original Le Puy image might have been an Egyptian Isis figure brought from Egypt by legionnaires, but most extant dark images appear to be no older than about the twelfth century. Several of the more famous older examples, including the Virgin of Montserrat, are portrayed as light-skinned in early illustrations, and some scholars claim that there is little evidence for the attribution of special qualities related to darkness during Medieval times. It is tempting to speculate that a generalized association of dark skin tones with miraculous qualities was yet another Renaissance innovation. This would help explain the proliferation of shrines subsidiary to dark images during and after that period. It would also provide insights into the reasons why post-Columbian missionaries from Europe were so accepting of cults developing around dark-skinned images of Christian holy persons in the Americas and other parts of the world where the native peoples were dark in skin tone relative to Europeans.

Dark images of the Virgin were almost certainly venerated in Europe before the American discoveries. The situation is more problematic in the case of dark images of Christ, which are rarely found as primary cult objects in modern Europe. Some of the Cristos of Spain are fairly dark, and we watched pilgrims paying special attention to a jet black image of Christ on the Cross at the Marian apparitional shrine of Madonna della Guárdia near Genoa, Italy. However, we found only two Christ figures that were specifically mentioned in shrine literature as miraculously dark. One, venerated in the Netherlands since the early nineteenth century, is said to be derived from the other, the famous Volto Santo of Lucca, Italy. Lucca, a small Tuscan city west of Florence, celebrated the twelfth centennial of the acquisition of its dark-skinned, fully robed image of Christ in 1982. According to tradition, the image was brought to Lucca in 782 in order to save it from Byzantine iconoclasm, although the earliest documentation of the pilgrimage dates back to the eleventh century. The Lucca image was a highlight of the journey for Rome-bound pilgrims by the twelfth century and was famous throughout much of Europe during the Middle Ages.[64] There is some question as to the image's original darkness of skin tone because a Medieval fresco in one of Lucca's numerous churches shows a light image in a scene portraying the legendary arrival by ox cart. If, however, the Lucca image has been dark since at least the late Middle Ages, it indicates that a European association of a dark Christ with special powers predates the American discoveries. In Latin America, black or very dark images of Christ are fairly common as pilgrimage cult objects and are often found at shrines previously sacred to indigenous Latin American gods. Possibly these images represent cases of pre-Columbian survivals not stamped out because Christian missionaries were familiar with a European precedent.

Image Modification and Replacement

In spite of the mystique associated with dark skin tones, images have sometimes been changed from dark to light, although recently in France the trend seems to have been toward restorations that change the skin color from light to dark. This is sometimes done on the grounds that the image was originally "black" and was lightened during the course of an earlier restoration. In some cases, a lost or destroyed dark image was replaced by a light-skinned image that in turn has been changed to look more like the original dark image. Some cult images, through a series of restorations or in a series of copies, appear to have changed the color of their skin tones several times over the centuries. Thus, the Black Madonna, that most curious form of Marian iconography, tends to come and go.

Color is not the only way in which images are changed. Cult images have been modified by recarving, repainting, or stripping off previous coats of paint to expose the original wood or stone of a statue. Sometimes old images or some part thereof have been placed inside "prettier," or otherwise more acceptable, statue reliquaries. New images are created when the originals are lost or destroyed by accident or deliberately; in some cases, older images are simply cast aside when a new image is enshrined.

Duplicates of lost or destroyed cult images have been reconstructed from old seals or prints, as at Walsingham and some of the other revitalized English shrines. More recently, as in the case of several images destroyed during the Spanish Civil War, copies have been made from photographs. In other cases no attempt was made to copy the appearance of a lost original and the replacement looks quite different, although it may still be thought of as if it were the original. There have been numerous debates about proposed changes in the aspect of a cult image. Occasionally, a major change proved disadvantageous for the shrine because alteration so diminished an image's perceived power that pilgrims stopped coming. In other cases, the restoration of an image seems to have given it an increased power, or at least generated publicity resulting in more pilgrimages. Except in the immediate aftermath of notable changes, most pilgrims seem to accept the cult image as it is at any given point in time.[65]

At some shrines, the original image has been recarved or repainted beyond any semblance of its initial appearance and, in some cases, restorations look very much as if they are actually replacements. At Puig near Valencia, Spain, the shrine story of a thirteenth-century unearthing of a sixth-century Byzantine-style marble relief carving of Mary on her deathbed is not especially improbable. For several centuries, however, the principal cult object was a fifteenth-century Florentine statue that obviously could not have been hidden under a bell or in any other way in 712 to prevent its desecration by invading Moslems, anymore than it could have been rediscovered in 1237 as the troops of Jaime I of Aragon prepared for the conquest of Valencia. Eventually, an older cult object, presumably the original, resurfaced and the Italian statue was demoted to a position of decorative art. However, the "original" image was damaged during the Spanish Civil War, and in its restored form is a brown-toned bas-relief of Mary holding the Christ Child.[66]

These frequent replacements and modifications suggest the futility of attempting to disprove the origin date of a pilgrimage cultus from the stylistic age of the shrine's current cult image, even when pious traditions claim that the pilgrimage began when the image was found or otherwise acquired. Many cult images have been accidentally lost, often in fires; demoted and consigned to a side chapel or storage room; or deliberately, sometimes brutally, destroyed in periodic waves of iconoclastic fury. Indeed, cult images, along with pilgrimage churches, are often prime targets for attack by iconoclastic revolutionaries or enemy soldiers of a different religious persuasion. During the French Revolution, for example, the ancient "Black Virgin" of Le Puy was blindfolded, put in a cart, taken to the central square, guillotined, and then burned, in an example of iconoclastic image personification that would be amazing were it not so common. More recently, on July 28, 1936, at Cerro de los Ángeles near Madrid, a monumental outdoor stone statue representing the Sacred Heart of Christ was sentenced to death by Spanish Republicans and "executed" by firing squad. This, of course, proved rather ineffective, so the monument was dynamited on July 31. It still stood, so dynamite experts were called in on August 1, but to no avail. On August 6, the Republicans tried to pull the statue down with a cable attached to a tractor, but the cable broke. Finally, on the next day, symbolically a Friday, the monument was leveled and broken into fragments with sledgehammers. The bullet-pocked heart and the mutilated head are preserved as relics. The episode is photographically documented.[67]

Images also tend to disappear during times of war or iconoclasm, when they are taken away or hidden by the faithful in order to prevent their destruction. Sometimes they are later returned to the shrine, but in other cases they are never found again, or found only by accident many years later, often in poor condition. Some of the images hidden during the Spanish Civil War and not immediately recovered may yet turn up.

The shrine of Notre-Dame de Lumières near Goult in southern France provides an interesting example of shifting image orientations. A shrine was established here because of apparitions and cures occurring between 1661 and 1663. The earliest graphic representation of the apparitions was an engraving in a book published in 1666 and showed a Madonna standing with the Child in her arms. Between 1669 and 1846, however, the primary cult object seems to have been a seventeenth-century polychrome wood statue of a seated Mary holding the dead Christ. Although still kept at the shrine, the image was demoted in the mid-nineteenth century and replaced with the statue currently described as "miraculous" in shrine literature. This image, carved in 1856, is a polychrome wood Madonna standing with the Child in her arms and is supposed to represent the apparitional events of nearly 200 years earlier. The shrine also has an image carved from natural dark wood that dates from the mid-nineteenth century. This image is at least as important to pilgrims as the "miraculous" one in the main church, judging from the many marble plaque ex-voto offerings on the walls of its special grotto dug into the shrine's hillside foundations.[68]

Another example of changing imagery is found at the shrine of Notre-Dame de Dusenbach in the Vosges Mountains near Ribeauville, Alsace. Pilgrimages are said to have begun here when a local nobleman returned from a Crusade in 1221 and gave an image of Mary to a hermit who lived at the site. The original image is thought to have been an oriental-style icon obtained in the East, but may soon have been replaced with a statue of the Madonna and Child carved in thirteenth-century Lorraine. Whatever cult object was venerated in the fourteenth century was destroyed by English troops in 1360. In 1475, two Madonnas of apparently equal importance were venerated at the shrine. However, in 1484 Maximin II de Ribeaupierre, a descendant of the Crusading nobleman, returned from a Holy Land pilgrimage and encouraged a greater emphasis on Christ's Passion. A pietà became the most important cult object, and an image of Christ in the tomb was added for the pilgrims' further edification. Later, however, the local lords adopted the Protestant faith and the shrine was destroyed in 1632. Nevertheless, the fifteenth-century carving of Mary with the dead Christ was saved by being hidden in a catch in the rocks and was recovered in 1656. New construction began at the site of the shrine ruins and Notre-Dame de Dusenbach became one of the most important Marian shrines in Alsace during the latter part of the seventeenth century. When the shrine was again destroyed in 1794, most of its images were demolished or badly damaged, but the pietà was taken to the parish church and thus was saved to serve again as a major cult object after the shrine was rebuilt and pilgrimage reestablished in 1894.[69]

Image Embellishments

An early twentieth-century picture of the Dusenbach pietà shows the statue elaborately vested in a bejeweled gown, although at present it is displayed without vestments. The custom of dressing images in elaborate costumes may have originated in Medieval Spain where a few shrine legends hint that it was practiced by the twelfth century, and more certainly by the fourteenth century. The custom seems to have spread widely during the Renaissance, and was apparently being practiced at some English shrines on the eve of the Reformation. It seems to have become even more widespread during the sixteenth through eighteenth centuries, a time when most Marian cult statues were probably vested.[70] Although less common than during the last century, vested statues of Mary are still found throughout most of the Continent. Some have extensive wardrobes and the garments are periodically changed to fit an annual cycle of occasions. At present it is fairly common for an image to be vested for special occasions, but presented without cloth embellishments at other times.

Numerous images have crowns that are carved or painted onto the figure, but these and other images may also be displayed with detachable metal crowns on their heads. Paintings may have finely worked, crown-shaped metal strips attached to their flat surfaces and be further decorated with necklaces and other jewels as a kind of vestment. Byzantine-style icons are sometimes covered with silver or gold "garments," cut away in appropriate places so that the faces and hands of the painting may be seen. Vested images are nearly always crowned, although an image bearing a crown need not be vested. Images referred to as "coronated" are those that have been officially crowned in a special ecclesiastically approved ceremony symbolizing their special importance. Such events date from the Catholic Reformation period. Many occurred in the nineteenth century when a number of previously coronated images were recrowned and others were so honored for the first time. An image, however, need not be officially coronated to bear a crown.

At present, regular use of the full regalia of crown and vestments seems to be most common in Iberia, where well over half of the Marian images for which we have photographs appear to be so embellished (Table 6-6). Vestments are emphasized at about one-quarter of the Marian shrines in France, Austria, and Italy, declining to 13 percent in West Germany where totally unadorned images seem to be especially in vogue. Old prints and devotional cards suggest that most German images were vested and crowned in the past. The restoration of images to their presumed original states is a recent fashion

Table 6-6 *Estimated Emphasis on Adornment of Marian Images*

Country	Vested and Crowned	Crowned Only	Unadorned
Spain	58%	21%	21%
Austria	29	45	26
Italy	26	47	27
France	25	44	31

and often leads to the elimination of vestments and crowns in a modern version of the urge to constantly reinterpret cult images as times and styles change.

Images as Reliquaries for Older Images

Current cult images sometimes serve as reliquaries for tiny fragments of much older images. Examples can be found at Arroyo de San Servan in Extremadura, Spain, where a nineteenth-century image houses a late twelfth-century statue, and at several Spanish shrines where fragments of ancient images broken or burned during the Spanish Civil War have been incorporated into replacement images. At Angely in southern France, a crude seven-inch clay figure of a Mother and Child is kept inside a baroque image of the Madonna. The clay figure is generally supposed to be an early Gothic image dating from about the fourteenth century and is said to have been found by a plowboy in the early sixteenth century. At Josselin, Brittany, a tiny piece of a wooden statue burned in 1793 is kept in a casket reliquary and is said to represent a image found in the early ninth century in the ruins of a church that had been destroyed by Viking raiders. A modern statue carved from ebony venerated at Liesse, France, contains fragments of an old statue said to have been brought by knights returning from a Crusade in the thirteenth century. At Benoîte-Vaux in Lorraine, a seventeenth-century statue presumably has a very old hand. The original cult image is said to have been found by woodcutters on the roots of a blown-down tree in the twelfth century. It was saved during Post-Reformation religious wars, recrowned, and enshrined after being restored in 1641. However, it burned with the shrine church during the French Revolution. One charred hand, or a piece of it, was saved and attached to a seventeenth-century statue that survived because it decorated a fountain some distance from the destroyed church.[71]

Sacred Objects

When a new image contains some part of an older image, it would seem especially easy to conceptualize it as being "the same" as the original image. An image's miraculous qualities can also be transferred by touching a new image to an older one, as is often done when image copies are sent to daughter shrines. Power can also be transferred by touching the new image to something associated with the original—just as from early Christian times the miraculous power of saints' relics could be transmitted by touching an object to them. By the same token, an especially miraculous object seems to endow the place where it is venerated with a special power that extends beyond the mere presence of the object. In other cases, the object seems to acquire much of its power from association with the place, perhaps because the shrine site in itself has some special tradition of sanctity, or was indicated as the appropriate place for the shrine in some mysterious manner. Indeed, for a pilgrimage shrine to develop, the sacred object usually needs to be identified with a particular place. The objects are movable. Relics are almost infinitely divisible, images infinitely duplicable, and powers easily transferable from one object to another. How, then, do cult objects come to be associated with the specific places where pilgrimage shrines develop? The following chapter dealing with shrine origin stories explores the ways in which places come to be identified as particularly sacred.

seven

Wondrous Events, Miracles, and Legends

Origin Stories Examined

*P*ilgrimage centers come into being and are maintained as religious travel goals through traditions that associate a holy person, and usually an object symbolizing that person, with a particular sacred place. A fundamental part of the tradition is related to pilgrimage origins, generally expressed in the form of a story explaining how and why the shrine came to be established. The story may be supported with extensive historical documentation of the events in question, as is the case with the famous nineteenth-century Marian apparitional shrine at Lourdes. Other origin accounts are probable but undocumented by written records from the time when the events are said to have occurred. In some cases, once-existing records have been lost or were deliberately destroyed during outbursts of iconoclastic fury. Copies of old records have sometimes been modified by later writers who interjected their own interpretations of how shrines should be established. Many stories, especially those told at older shrines, are clearly legends, often embellished with mythical elements much too fantastic to have anything to do with what actually happened during the period when the cult was in formation. The analysis presented in this chapter, however, is based on the shrine stories as they are told, because our primary concern is with patterns in the types of origin stories that give meaning to present-day pilgrimages rather than with a historical examination of "what really happened." In this context, legends are data in their own right.[1]

The 3,126 origin stories in our inventory are highly varied in detail, but the majority center on one or another of several basic themes. Saint Peter's

Basilica rises on the traditional site of his execution in Rome. The site is significant in the development of Christianity in the West. Lourdes, France, became a shrine in the nineteenth century because people were impressed with the testimony of a girl who experienced visions of a beautiful young woman who called herself the "Immaculate Conception." Montserrat, in Spain's Catalonian region, derives much of its power from the story of a black image of the Virgin said to have been discovered under mysterious circumstances. Pilgrims flock to a chapel attached to Italy's Turin Cathedral because it contains the "Holy Shroud," acquired as a gift in the sixteenth century. The Saint Anthony chapel near Partenkirchen in Bavaria was established in thanks for salvation from war, and many other shrines originated as votives for salvation from various perils. Limpias, a shrine in northern Spain, represents a miraculous occurrence with little relation to great events; each year it draws thousands of pilgrims who venerate an image of Christ reported to have moved its eyes in the early twentieth century. A few shrines appear to be purely devotional, founded because an individual or a group decided that there should be a pilgrimage center in a particular place.

The repetition of variations on these themes makes it possible to identify the seven basic types of origin stories outlined in Table 7-1. Most shrines for which origin stories were collected were easily assigned to one or another of the seven categories. A few shrines were difficult to categorize because of complex or conflicting stories. Contemporary shrine literature often gives two origin accounts—one essentially historical and often well documented and the other presented as legend. These accounts are frequently of the same general type, but discrepancies between history and legend sometimes complicate the process of classification. In such cases, the historical version was chosen as the basis for classification except when the legend is clearly more important in the contemporary maintenance of the mystique of the pilgrimage cultus. When different stories appeared in several sources, emphasis was placed on accounts provided by shrine administrators or publicized in shrine literature.

A few shrines might have been categorized under two or more basic types because of complex cult-formative stories. The pilgrimage center of Nuestra Señora de la Cueva Santa in a mountain cave about 14 kilometers from Altura in eastern Spain provides an example. Here, according to tradition, early fourteenth-century shepherds who used the cave for shelter asked Fray Bonifacio Ferrer, brother of the famous preacher, Saint Vincent Ferrer, for an image of Mary to put in the cave for veneration and protection. The request was granted, but the image was eventually forgotten. Then, in the first decade

Table 7-1 *Types of Origin Stories*

Shrine Story Type (listed in the order discussed)	Number	Percent
Significant Site Shrines Places related to events in a saint's life or to the historical development of religion in a given region.	542	17
Ex-voto Shrines Created as a thank offering for group or individual salvation from catastrophe.	600	19
Devotional Shrines Created as a result of human action unrelated to miracles or unusual events.	161	5
Spontaneous Miracle Shrines Cultus developed around an object already at the site that proves to be miraculous, or as the result of a revelation of sacred power other than an apparition or the finding of a holy object.	459	15
Acquired Object Shrines Developed when a holy relic or image is brought from another place and proves to be miraculous in its new setting.	454	15
Found' Object Shrines Cultus developed after an image or relic is found in generally mysterious circumstances.	563	18
Apparitional Shrines Cultus developed as the result of an apparition or other vision. An object may be found as confirmation of the apparition.	347	11
Total	3,126	100

of the fifteenth century, a shepherd dreamed that the Virgin Mary wished to be visited in the cave. He went there and found the old image. The cultus spread rapidly, but the nascent pilgrimage seems to have died quickly; by the latter part of the century it appears to have been virtually forgotten. However, in 1574 a leper was expelled from his town, so his wife set forth to pray for his cure at the Catalonian shrine of Montserrat. On the way she visited the cave and was inspired to send her husband there. The leper claimed a complete cure after daily baths in the water from the cave walls. The pilgrimage was established firmly enough to survive to the present. The shrine's fame has grown since the Virgin of the Sacred Cave was declared patroness of Spanish speleologists by papal brief in 1955 and patroness of the region in 1960.[2]

Depending on which episode of its story is emphasized, the Cueva Santa shrine could be classified as having originated because an image was acquired as a gift, because a forgotten image was found as the result of a vision, or as the consequence of a miraculous cure. In such complex cases, shrines were categorized in terms of the theme that appeared to be most strongly stressed in shrine-related literature. In the case of Cueva Santa, the miraculous cure event appears to be the foundation of the modern cultus. The complexity of several origin stories and the judgmental element involved in the classification of such shrines suggest that the following analysis of origin stories should be viewed as a generalized examination of sometimes overlapping patterns.[3]

Some types of origin stories have stronger mythical qualities than do others. For example, most accounts of shrines established as votive offerings are reasonably matter of fact, whereas stories involving the discovery of holy objects are often poorly supported in written records and are often embellished with a multiplicity of mysterious events. However, fully documented examples exist for each type of story.

All categories of cult-formative stories are associated with shrines from each time period. Certain types of stories, however, are more frequent among shrines from particular periods than for those founded at other times (Table 7-2). Early Christian shrines are predominantly located at sites of significance in the lives of saints or in the development of the Christian religion, but this is true of only a few Renaissance shrines. Nearly one-third of the High Medieval shrines have origin stories emphasizing the miraculous discovery of a holy object as compared with only 6 percent of the shrines established since 1780. The Renaissance seems to have been a particularly efficacious time for apparitional shrine formation.

Most types of origin stories are Pan-Western European in distribution, or nearly so, but there are marked regional variations in the frequencies of different kinds of stories. Nearly three-quarters of the British and Irish shrines fall into the significant site category, as compared with only 12 percent of the Iberian shrines. Stories describing the finding of objects are considerably more common in Iberia than elsewhere. Stories of object acquisition are most frequently told at shrines in Germanic lands, and apparition stories are twice as commonly told at Italian shrines than at shrines in French culture regions (Table 7-3).

Christ, Mary, and the saints are the principal subjects of pilgrim veneration at shrines with all types of origin stories, but there are major proportional differences (Table 7-4). About 61 percent of saints' shrines were classified as significant sites, but this was the case for only 4 percent of the Christ-centered shrines and 5 percent of the Marian shrines. In some cases of current

Table 7-2 *Time Period Distribution of Origin Story Types*

Story Type	Time Period					
	Early Christian (N=178)	Early Medieval (N=271)	High Medieval (N=625)	Renaissance (N=446)	Post-Reformation (N=934)	Modern (N=417)
Significant site	76%	31%	13%	8%	7%	21%
Ex-voto	2	10	17	21	25	20
Devotional	1	3	2	2	5	20
Miracle	4	3	13	20	21	10
Acquired object	10	20	16	10	15	14
Found object	1	24	30	22	16	6
Apparitional	6	10	9	18	11	9
Total	100	101	100	101	100	100

Table 7-3 *Regional Distribution of Origin Story Types*

Story Type	Regions				
	Italian (N=878)	French (N=545)	Iberian (N=472)	German[a] (N=1,097)	British/Irish (N=134)
Significant site	14%	19%	12%	14%	74%
Ex-voto	14	23	14	25	1
Devotional	5	6	2	7	2
Miracle	18	12	7	18	3
Acquired object	13	10	14	19	10
Found object	15	21	36	13	4
Apparitional	21	10	14	4	6
Total	100	101	99	100	100

[a]The North and South German regions are combined here and in subsequent tables.

Mary or Christ focus, the shrine originated with devotions to a saint who remains important as a secondary subject. Well over twice as many Christ-centered shrines have stories involving the acquisition of a holy object as do Marian or saints' shrines. Marian shrines are much more likely to have stories involving apparitions and discoveries of holy objects than are shrines devoted to Christ or the saints.

Various kinds of cult objects are also more likely to be found at shrines with certain types of origin stories than those with others (Table 7-5). Over

Table 7-4 Origin Story Associations with Subjects of Devotion

Story Type	Christ (N = 229)	Mary (N = 2,212)	Saints (N = 685)
Significant site	4%	5%	61%
Ex-voto	19	21	14
Devotional	3	7	2
Miracle	25	17	5
Acquired object	35	13	11
Found object	11	23	5
Apparitional	3	15	2
Total	100	101	100

two-thirds of the shrines with a relic of a saint's body as a primary devotional object were classified as significant sites. Most of the rest of these relics were acquired in one way or another by the places where they are now enshrined. Almost two-thirds of non-corporeal relics, including relics of Christ's Passion, were brought from afar to the shrine where they are now venerated, and most of the rest are said to have been discovered under mysterious circumstances. Nearly three-fourths of the shrines with no devotional object are significant sites. Images make up the only category of primary devotional objects at shrines with all types of cult-formative stories, although it should be pointed out that the cult images at devotional shrines are considered to be merely inspiring rather than specifically miraculous.

Types of Origin Stories

Significant Site Shrines

Places visited primarily because of associations with the earthly activities or deaths of saints, or because of traditions of importance as regional centers of religious activity, are combined in the category of significant site shrines. The major basilicas of Rome exemplify this type, as does the shrine of Saint Winefride at Holywell in Wales where a sign clearly proclaims the association between the saint and the place (Figure 7-1). The type encompasses the category that anthropologists Victor and Edith Turner viewed as "prototypical" pilgrimages, or those that "were established by the founder of a

Table 7-5 Origin Story Associations with Types of Devotional Objects

	Object of Devotion			
Story Types	Human Remains (N = 309)	Other Relics (N = 96)	Images (N = 2,242)	Site Only (N = 195)
Significant site	68%	4%	7%	73%
Ex-voto	3	3	21	6
Devotional	—	—	5	5
Miracle	2	15	18	7
Acquired object	21	64	14	—
Found object	6	14	24	—
Apparitional	1	1	12	9
Total	101	101	100	100

historical religion, by his first disciples, or by important national evangelists of his faith."[4] However, our significant site shrine category also includes places associated with several early saints who acquired attributes of pagan deities and inherited holy places formerly associated with their cults. Thus, the type overlaps, to some extent, with the Turners' "archaic" pilgrimages or those "which bear quite evident traces of syncretism with older religious beliefs and symbols."[5]

Actually, the Turners' prototypical and archaic categories are not mutually exclusive. Saint Patrick, for example, was a historic early evangelist whose mission helped establish the Irish Celtic church, but who also is regarded as a near-mythical figure of pagan-Christian syncretism. In addition, our category has a much broader temporal scope than the Turners' prototypical and archaic pilgrimages because it includes places associated with the activities of saints from all periods, as well as shrines not specifically related to saints but fairly recently established or reestablished at sites noted for an antiquity of Christian religious significance. Selected attributes of these shrines are summarized in Table 7-6.

As at Holywell, shrine sites traditionally associated with early saints are often characterized by sacred site features, particularly, although not exclusively, in the case of Celtic saints. The story of a well or fountain springing up where the blood of a martyred saint was spilled is not only found at the Welsh shrine, but is also told at several holy places on the Continent. For example, at Alise-Sainte-Reine in Burgundy a fountain supposedly sprang forth where a third-century Christian girl was beheaded for refusing to marry

Wondrous Events, Miracles, and Legends 223

Figure 7-1 *Saint Winefride's Well at Holywell, Wales, provides an example of a shrine that was located in a place with historical significance because of a saint's activities. Protestant authorities were never able to completely stop pilgrimages to this ancient holy place.*

a pagan Roman governor. Similarly, five wells are said to have bubbled forth from under the head, hands, and feet of Saint Landolin when he was murdered in about 640 at Ettenheim in Germany's Black Forest. At other shrines, the water of a curative spring or well is said to have been called forth by a living saint, and a number of pagan holy wells were baptized as Christian by missionary saints. Caves where saintly hermits sought solitude, mountain heights where they were inspired or resisted temptation, stones marked by their footprints, and trees—or descendants of trees—that sprouted from their staffs are also fairly common at shrines dedicated to early through Medieval saints.

Pilgrimage places associated with more recent saints are less likely to have natural site feature associations. These sites often resemble the museums found at places of significance in secular history. For example, at the village of Ars-sur-Formans near Lyon, France, over 100,000 pilgrims each year visit a number of places associated with Saint Jean Baptiste Marie Vianney, the Curé

Table 7-6 Characteristics of Significant Site Shrines

Regional Distribution	N	%	Time Period	N	%
Italian	125	23	Early Christian	136	28
French	105	19	Early Medieval	83	17
Iberian	57	11	High Medieval	81	17
German	156	29	Renaissance	35	7
British	53	10	Post-Reformation	61	13
Irish	46	8	Modern	89	18
Total	542	100	Total dated	485	100

Time/Space Distribution of Significant Site Stories

Region	Early Christian	Early Medieval	High Medieval	Renaissance	Post-Reformation	Modern
Italian	7%	3%	5%	2%	3%	3%
French	6	5	3	1	3	3
Iberian	1	2	3	‹1	3	‹1
German	4	7	5	4	4	4
British/Irish	10	‹1	‹1	—	1	9

Devotional Subject	N	%	Devotional Object	N	%
Christ	10	2	Human remains	209	42
Mary	117	22	Other relics	4	1
Saints	411	76	Images	148	29
No subject	4	‹1	Site only	142	28
Total	542	100	Total classified	503	100

Types of Significant Sites

	N	%
Place of saint's death, usually burial site	186	35
Place of saint's tomb, other than death site	31	6
Place of saint's birth	27	5
Place founded by saint or site of saint's inspiration	152	28
Shrine reestablished at ancient holy place	37	7
Miscellaneous traditions of ancient sanctity	109	20
Total	542	101

d'Ars who lived from 1786 to 1859, was canonized in 1925, and was named patron of parish priests in 1929. His humble parish church is incorporated into a large modern basilica where his wax-covered body lies in a glass casket. Nearby one can see the priest's kitchen and bedchamber, which are filled with articles he used during his life. Similarly, at Weng, near Passau in Bavaria, tens of thousands of pilgrims visit the farmstead where Saint Conrad of Parzham was born in 1818, and where he lived until he became a monk at age 30. In addition to the home containing objects used or touched by this saint, who was canonized in 1934, pilgrims inspect his parents' graves and the place where he attended school. Similar shrine complexes are found at the birthplaces of the fifteenth-century Saint Nicholas of Flue in central Switzerland and the seventeenth-century Saint Vincent de Paul in a hamlet near Dax, France.

Significant site shrines not specifically associated with saints' activities include those established at places of historic religious significance, such as old monastic establishments and former Medieval pilgrimage centers in Protestant lands where activity was interrupted for centuries after the Reformation. Kaltenbrunn Chapel near Ranschbach in West Germany's Rheinland-Pfalz provides a clear example. Here, religious activity centered on a cold spring seems to have occurred as early as 1200 B.C., and archaeological evidence for a Celtic cult site continued to about 600 B.C. The initial Christian pilgrimage seems to have been established by the mid-eleventh century, but the chapel was destroyed in the sixteenth century when the area became almost entirely Protestant. Nevertheless, pilgrimages to the healing spring continued, and in 1928 a Lourdes grotto was built near the site. The shrine was publicized in connection with excavations of the Celtic Iron Age site along with a celebration of its 700th year as a Christian pilgrimage site in 1975, and in 1976 the chapel was restored. The shrine's long history as a holy place was promoted by the writings of a retired priest in the early 1980s, and by 1982 large numbers of pilgrims were visiting this Marian shrine following a series of "miraculous" cures that had been reported in West German periodicals.[6]

Significant site shrines are widely distributed in Western Europe. Modern countries with the largest number of these shrines are Italy and France, but Irish and British shrines are the most likely to be located at significant sites, although for different reasons. In Ireland these places are mostly associated with the activities of early Celtic saints, whereas British significant site shrines are primarily pilgrimage centers reestablished in modern times at the locations of pre-Reformation ecclesiastical structures, including places where Medieval pilgrimages were terminated during the Reformation.

On the average, significant site shrines tend to be old. Forty-five percent of those that can be dated were established prior to 1099, and 62 percent were founded before 1399. Relatively few date from the Renaissance and Post-Reformation periods, but 18 percent have been established since 1790, reflecting both the use of the category for classification of pilgrimage sites chosen because of pre-Reformation importance and because of a modern increase in the proportion of shrines focused on saints. Time-space concentrations of significant site shrines include Ireland, Italy, and France in the Early Christian period; Germanic lands during the Early Medieval period, when much of the mission activity in these areas was taking place; fairly high German and Italian concentrations during the High Middle Ages; and a Modern concentration in England, Scandinavia, the Netherlands, and northern West Germany.

The category's definition determined that most such shrines would be devoted to saints, and several of the 22 percent where Mary is currently the primary devotional subject were originally saints' shrines. Because many are located at places where saints were martyred or otherwise died, a high proportion of the primary devotional objects are saints' relics. The fairly large proportion of these shrines with no venerated relics or images reflects a strong emphasis on natural or cultural site features associated with saints' activities, especially in Ireland. In a sense, of course, the house where a saint was born, the bed where he slept, or, indeed, the tree or spring that came forth where he planted his staff in the ground might be considered forms of noncorporal relics.

The significant site type is more likely to be of major importance than are shrines generally. This reflects the use of the category for many of Western Christendom's great shrines of considerable antiquity, as well as the focus on places most directly associated with the lives of important saints. Significant site shrines are also more likely than usual to be located in cathedrals, in contemporary monastic churches, or at the sites of former monasteries.

Votive Shrines

More of today's shrines were created as votive offerings than for any other single reason. These origin stories are usually factual accounts of how the shrine and its pilgrimage tradition originated as an individual or group thanks for salvation from personal threat or general catastrophe. Often the shrine was created as the result of a vow made during a period of stress. Although numerous, relatively few of these shrines are important beyond a fairly small geographical area.

Most of the events associated with the founding of votive shrines can be subsumed under three basic categories: (1) problems related to health, (2) those related to threats of human violence, and (3) those related to accidents and natural hazards. The remainder of the votive shrine origin stories either made no reference to the reason for the thank offering or indicated that the shrine had been established in response to a variety of other problems related to human well-being. The number of shrines established as thanks for salvation from illness, accident, natural hazard, violence, and other problems is, of course, small compared with the number of votive offerings placed at preexisting shrines by individuals and groups in thanks for help. Alleviation of peril has often helped to trigger the beginnings of cultus at shrines we have placed in other origin story categories. For example, we considered a visionary's encounter with an apparition of the Virgin Mary to be the primary reason for a shrine's existence even though that vision may have been accepted as real because of cures that soon took place at the site. The figures given in Table 7-7 are based only on the events that led to the establishment of votive shrines per se.

Problems related to health, violence, and hazard can be subdivided into events affecting individuals or small, interpersonally related groups, and those threatening larger numbers of people, such as the members of a community, the people of a region, or an entire nation. Votive shrines are more likely to be established by communities than by individuals or small groups, as indicated by the finding that 61 percent of the problems giving rise to shrines as ex-votos were of a kind that threatened large numbers of people rather than only one or a few individuals (Figure 7-2).

The tendency for votive shrines to be community rather than individual projects is partly explicable in terms of the costs involved in establishing a religious center with sufficient power to attract pilgrims from beyond the immediate locality. For the most part, only the pooled resources of a community or the wealth and fund-raising ability of rich and/or influential individuals could pay for the establishment of a new shrine of this type. Shrines initiated as ex-votos, in contrast with vows of pilgrimage to existent shrines, often involve the expenses of building a shrine church, decorating it in a suitable fashion, and obtaining an appropriate image or relic for pilgrim veneration.

It is also probable that during much of European history only those indi-

Table 7-7 Characteristics of Ex-voto Shrines

Regional Distribution	N	%	Time Period	N	%
Italian	126	21	Early Christian	4	1
French	126	21	Early Medieval	26	5
Iberian	69	12	High Medieval	106	19
German	278	46	Renaissance	92	17
British	—	—	Post-Reformation	236	43
Irish	1	‹1	Modern	84	15
Total	600	100	Total dated	548	100

Time/Space Distribution of Ex-voto Stories

Region	Early Christian	Early Medieval	High Medieval	Renaissance	Post-Reformation	Modern
Italian	‹1%	1%	3%	5%	8%	5%
French	‹1	3	7	3	6	3
Iberian	—	1	4	2	3	‹1
German	—	‹1	6	7	26	7
British/Irish	—	—	‹1	‹1	—	—

Devotional Subject	N	%	Devotional Object	N	%
Christ	44	7	Human remains	8	2
Mary	456	76	Other relics	3	1
Saints	97	16	Images	462	95
No subject	3	‹1	Site only	12	2
Total	600	100	Total classified	485	100

Problems Alleviated

Health		Violence		Accident/Hazard	
Illness/handicap	83	Attacks	49	Accidents	79
Plague	143	War	123	Natural hazard	59
Total	226	Total	172	Total	138

Table 7-7 (continued)

Individual Votive Donor Characteristics (N = 214)							
Poor or Humble		Middle Class		Nobles		Religious	
Men	19	Men	54	Men	94	Priest, monk,	
Women	1	Women	5	Women	15	bishop	26
Sex		Social Status					
Males	90%	Poor or					
Females	10	humble	9%				
		Middle	28				
		Nobles	51				
		Religious	12				

vidual or family-specific events affecting nobles, or other reasonably influential persons, were considered sufficiently important to attract pilgrims unless a spontaneous mass movement and numerous cures immediately suggested that the place also provided salvation from problems experienced by common people. Most shrines where pilgrimage was triggered by the amazing cure of a poor person were not created as votives by the individual saved from illness or handicap, nor by his or her relatives. These shrines have been placed in the category of "spontaneous miracle" stories and are discussed later in this chapter.

The importance of the rich and/or powerful is evident in figures on the social status of 214 individual founders of votive shrines. More than half were members of the upper classes, ranging in status from knights and other representatives of the lesser nobility to members of royal families. An additional 12 percent were priests, monks, and bishops, who, although not always wealthy, were presumably influential in religious matters. Twenty-eight percent were persons representing society's middle sectors, some of whom, including ship captains and merchants, were probably wealthy. Only 9 percent of the individual votive shrine founders might, on the basis of such relatively humble occupations as shepherd, peasant, sailor, or common soldier, be considered to have been poor. It is doubtful, however, that many of these people were extremely poor in the socioeconomic context of their times. Men have been more likely to establish votive shrines than women. When all social levels are considered together, nine votive shrines have been established by men for each one sponsored by a woman. More cases are credited to males of humble station (9 percent) than to noblewomen and queens (7 percent).

Figure 7-2 At Archidona in southern Spain, the pilgrimage church of Nuestra Señora de Gracia shares a hilltop with a Medieval Moorish fortification. Pilgrimage began in the fifteenth century in thanks for divine aid in the Christian reconquest of this region, which was once part of the Moslem kingdom of Granada. Each August 15, pilgrims from all over the district walk up to the shrine to make or keep "promises." Some hike without shoes as an act of penance.

Presumably thousands of peasants believed they had been saved by prayers and vows when they fell under the wheels of their ox carts, and sick peasant children probably recovered at more or less usual rates after their parents called out for divine intervention. However, prior to socioeconomic changes beginning in about the fifteenth century, such people generally could not afford to build shrine churches. If they did put up tiny chapels or roadside markers, no one seems to have cared much unless something remarkable soon happened at the spot. But a nobleman or king who vowed a shrine to mark the spot where he fell off his horse, or to celebrate the recovery of his daughter from a fever or the regaining of his little lame son's ability to walk, could not only pay all or part of the costs for an impressively splendid shrine, but also was so important socially that any divine benefits realized by him or members of his family were accepted as part of the common good. In Renaissance Italy, however, and elsewhere soon afterward, this near-monopoly on shrine sponsorship by either communities or nobles, including noble churchmen, became relatively less pronounced as greater numbers of pilgrimage centers developed from votive shrines established by middle-class and even fairly humble individuals.

During the past several centuries, numerous shrines have been created by more-or-less ordinary individuals. In a fairly recent case, Anton Bolte, a priest from Fulda who taught German at a Catholic secondary school in Immense, Switzerland, became ill and resigned his position in 1925 to take charge of a small church built three years earlier by the tiny Catholic minority at Egg in Canton Zurich. Extremely ill at the time of his arrival in Egg, Father Bolte vowed to conduct pilgrimage services each Tuesday if he recovered. The cure was immediate, and the charismatic priest kept his vow until his death in 1952. His immediate successor, who was still in charge of the shrine when he corresponded with us in 1980, kept up the tradition and reported that pilgrims were coming year round from all over Switzerland.[7] A shrine at Marterle near Rangersdorf in Austria's Kärnten province provides an example of a fairly important minor regional pilgrimage center established by an ordinary layman as a votive for a cure. The site was originally marked by a shepherd who became lost in the mountains while looking for his flock and who later put up a wayside cross in gratitude for his survival in bad weather. Such votive markers are extremely common throughout Catholic Europe, especially in Austria and Bavaria, but rarely become centers of special devotions or pilgrimages even at the local level. An exception occurred at Marterle in 1854, however, when a sick farmer vowed to build a little chapel to shelter the old weather-beaten image of Christ on the Cross if he recovered. Soon afterward the place began to attract pilgrims from the Moll Valley who still come in considerable numbers on the second Sunday in September.[8]

In keeping with the votive shrine emphasis on problems affecting communities, those related to health are nearly twice as likely to have been established as thank offerings for the cessation of epidemics than as votives for individual cures. Pilgrimage shrines established by individuals as thank offerings for surviving epidemics are extremely rare, although there are a few cases as at Karnabrunn, Austria, where a seventeenth-century nobleman's votive chapel for personal salvation from a plague still attracts pilgrims. The substantial number and wide distribution of plague cults are particularly interesting because pilgrimages during epidemics are essentially disfunctional in a biological sense. Activities drawing together large numbers of people under crowded and generally unsanitary conditions intensify and spread disease.

There is some evidence that the death rate from bubonic plague in the mid-fourteenth century was especially high at pilgrimage centers and in communities along the main pilgrim routes.[9] Thus, the long-term survival and continued creation through much of the nineteenth century of votive shrines related to such epidemics as bubonic plague, cholera, and typhoid, along with events simply described as "plagues," is best interpreted in terms of the social efficacy of pilgrimage in the wake of an epidemic.

Students of human response to environmental hazard have demonstrated that disaster must be measured not only by the intensity of the impact event, but also in terms of human ability to withstand disaster and recover.[10] Plagues are particularly disruptive to social systems because fear of contagion leads to avoidance of others, sometimes even family members. Therefore, a community vow to build a shrine church or establish a pilgrimage to an existing sanctuary in the aftermath of plague serves to restore the social compact and accelerates recovery by unifying a shocked and frightened people around symbols of shared belief.

An interesting example of a plague vow that has continued to symbolize a strong sense of social unity in other times of threat comes from Tulle in the Limoges region of France. When the Black Death held the region in its grip in 1348, the people of Tulle and surrounding communities instituted a pilgrimage procession featuring an image of Saint John the Baptist. Records in the Tulle Cathedral, where the image is kept, indicate that this procession has been made every year since without fail, sometimes secretly and at great risk. During the French Revolution when the statue was temporarily hidden for safekeeping, people took turns imitating it along the route; and when the procession was banned by municipal edict during an anticlerical period beginning in 1899, the procession consisted of small groups quietly walking the route in the dark of night. When the ritual was banned again by German occupation forces in 1944, two vicars, an abbot, and some young boys placed the statue in a cart behind a bicycle, covered it with canvas, and cycled past the enemy guard. Once in the countryside, the canvas was thrown back to reveal the image as the brave little troop peddled past cheering farmers in the fields.[11]

The second most common type of hazard resulting in the creation of votive shrines is related to violence perpetrated by humans upon other humans. A considerable majority of these shrines are essentially community, regional, or national ex-votos for salvation from war and revolution although some were vowed and predominantly sponsored by rulers, military commanders, or the local bishop. Not all war-related shrines are in the votive category, however, because spontaneous miracles, findings of images, and apparitions all are common occurrences during or immediately after wars. Those that are votive shrines are widespread and date from all time periods. A few, especially among those vowed by military leaders, are thank offerings for great victories, and, as at Superga near Turin in northern Italy and Batalha in Portugal, are probably better thought of as religiously significant monuments rather than pilgrimage shrines per se. A greater number are expressions of gratitude for salvation from specific enemy attack. For example, a pilgrimage dedicated to Notre-Dame de Panetière dates from 1213 when citizens of Aire-sur-la-Lys near Calais, France, called on the Virgin Mary for help when the town was besieged and the people were dying of famine. The image venerated here was carved in the early sixteenth century, blasted to pieces by bombs in 1944, and restored when World War II ended. In other cases, as at Telgte in West Germany's Diocese of Münster, shrines were established as a more generalized thank offering for the end of a war. At Telgte, the local bishop promoted the development of cultus in 1651, partly as a means of restoring social and religious order in the wake of the terrible Thirty Years' War. A more recent case involving a bishop dates from the second decade of the twentieth century when the bishop of Speyer, West Germany, vowed to create a shrine in his largely Protestant hometown of Kaiserslautern if the region under his jurisdiction was spared damage during World War I. The vow was fulfilled by his successor with the restoration of a fourteenth-century church dedicated to Mary as protector of the city. Ironically, the church was heavily damaged by bombs during World War II, but it has been restored again.[12]

Other shrines were offered by communities in thanks for the return of at least some of their young men from various battlefields. These shrines, along with other war-related ex-voto shrines, often do double duty as memorials for those who did not return. The Saint Anthony chapel on an alpine slope above Partenkirchen, for example, was established as a votive shrine for salvation from an early eighteenth-century conflict. It now contains rows of fading photographs of young Germans who died in the Franco-Prussian War and the two world wars of the twentieth century.[13]

A large proportion of shrine origin stories—whether in the votive or other categories—that relate to warfare concern conflicts between protagonists of different religions. When wars between co-religionists are involved, origin stories tend to stress the general hazards of warfare. In wars with strong religious overtones, the enemy is more often specified as a particularly dangerous group of people. Moors in Medieval Spain, Saracens during the same general time period in southern France and Italy, and Turks in Austria during the fifteenth through seventeenth centuries were particularly threatening because they represented antagonists of the Islamic faith. Post-Reformation wars of religion between Catholic and Protestant Christians also had a particular propensity to generate shrines in Catholic areas. In parts of West Germany and Austria, "Swedes," a general term for the Protestant Scandinavian troops who ravaged several areas during the Thirty Years' War, are frequently referred to in much the same way as are Turks. Indeed, some Austrian stories deal more kindly with Turks, who are occasionally said to have been converted to Christianity, than with Swedes who represent a former friend gone bad rather than the old enemy whose predatory behavior is only to be expected. Also relevant are attacks by anticlerical, iconoclastically oriented revolutionaries as occurred on a widespread basis during the French Revolution and the Spanish Civil War.

Individually established votive shrines related to salvation from the threat of human violence include those sponsored by knights returning from the Crusades and soldiers arriving safely after various later wars. In a recent example, the shrine of the Madonna di Alpine near Boario Terme in Lombardy was built as the result of a vow made by a chaplain in Italy's World War II Alpine Division after being captured by the Russians. When the cornerstone of this votive shrine was laid in 1957, 15,000 Alpine troops took part in the ceremony.[14]

Other violence-related shrines came into being as thank offerings for salvation from attacks by marauding soldiers outside immediate battle zones and by robbers, pirates, or other outlaws. Villains also include cruel husbands noted for wife-beating, abusive masters who mistreated their servants, and brothers who abused handicapped sisters. In such cases, however, the victim is rarely in a position to create a votive shrine. Such accounts of violence are usually addenda to origin stories falling into different categories, as with the several shrines devoted to Saint Rita of Cáscia, whose mistreatment by her husband is an important element in the story of her struggle toward sanctity but not a primary reason for the creation of her shrines.

Falling into the same general category are threats of social violence related to miscarriages of justice, as when an innocent person is condemned to death. A Marian shrine at Lokeren, Belgium, for example, is said to have originated with a vow made by an officer to build a church if he was pardoned. According to tradition, the image venerated at this shrine cures headaches, reflecting the officer's good fortune in not having his head cut off.[15]

The third general category of problems leading to the creation of votive shrines includes individual salvation from accident or threat related to the impact of natural hazards, along with community offerings for the abatement of various environmentally hazardous conditions. Shrines established as personal votives include such places as Maria im Stein near Mitterndorf, Austria, where a man named Lobenstock built a chapel when he was saved from an avalanche; a shrine at Eberweis, Austria, where an early nineteenth-century tailor was saved after he swallowed a needle; and one near Zermatt, Switzerland, where two eighteenth-century merchants became lost in a fog on the Theodul Pass, but were saved when they stumbled onto a familiar wayside chapel and regained their bearings.[16] Several shrines, especially in Germanic regions, are related to salvation from hunting accidents. Riding accidents and travel-related problems also have prompted the founding of shrines. Others were established as thank offerings by ship captains, wealthy passengers, or all persons on board for salvation from perils of the sea. Stories of vows made to erect a shrine on the first point of land seen by fog-bound sailors are common, as at Perros-Guirec on the coast of Brittany where the chapel of Notre-Dame de Clarté stands on a cliff.[17]

Votive shrines of at least district importance may be established in the wake of such natural disasters as floods, severe storms, earthquakes, volcanic eruptions, droughts, and livestock epidemics. Two cases representing community action in the face of such threats are at Sannazzaro de'Burgondi, where pilgrims still visit a votive shrine built in 1705 after an antique fresco of Mary survived a Po River flood "miraculously" intact, and at Zafferana Etnea, Sicily, where a shrine was established in the aftermath of the 1852 eruption of Mount Etna. When lava threatened the town, the priest and local citizens carried a statue of Mary to the edge of the glowing flow and placed it in the path of the molten rock. The lava stopped, so a chapel was built on the site.

The responses to many natural hazards tend to be localized. As a result, relatively few such responses have led to the creation of shrines that attract pilgrims from outside the immediate locality. Community actions are more likely to result in small, locally visited votive chapels and in vows to stage special celebrations of a patron saint's day. If the potential affects of a hazard are more widespread, however, a shrine created through community efforts may have a broader devotional base. An example of this is a votive shrine established in 1857 by persons representing the Beaujolais winegrowers whose vineyards were being decimated by phylloxera. The Mont Brouilly chapel near Belleville in France's Rhône-Alpes region continues to be well visited.[18]

Some votive shrines have been established for a variety of reasons that do not fit well into the above categories. For example, at Hötting near Innsbruck,

Austria, it is said that in the seventeenth century a student fearful of failing his examinations attached a picture of Mary to a larch tree. He passed the exams, so other students have continued to seek equal favors by visiting the shrine. A number of shrines are especially visited by young women seeking husbands, while others are favored places for married women wishing to become pregnant. Such needs, however, do not ordinarily result in the establishment of new shrines. A few votive shrines are related to salvation from supernatural threats as at Kirchberg in the Austrian Tirol. Here, in about 1700, an innkeeper who was having an affair with a local girl was planning to visit her on a holy day when he should have been praying. As the story goes, a devil appeared to carry the innkeeper off to hell, but the man was saved when he vowed to build a chapel in honor of the Virgin Mary.[19]

An interesting case of a man whose vow to establish a shrine paid off in riches, comes from Sollheim, a suburb of Salzburg, Austria. In about 1680, a merchant ship with a number of Salzburg residents on board was reported overdue on a voyage from the Eastern Mediterranean. Johann Anton Kaufmann vowed a shrine to his favorite saint, Anthony of Padua, if the ship made safe harbor. Confident of divine aid, Herr Kaufmann used his life savings to buy the ship from its owners, who, believing the vessel to be lost at sea, were only too happy to sell. Thus, when the overdue ship arrived at Venice, Kaufmann became a very wealthy man and provided for the establishment of the Sankt Antonius church where he now lies buried.[20]

Votive shrines are widely distributed, although they are notably lacking in Catholic Ireland as well as in the Dutch, North German, and Scandinavian Protestant regions. The heaviest concentration is in Austria and the bordering regions of southern West Germany. Austria, with 174 cases, has the largest number of ex-voto shrines, followed by Italy with 126 cases. France is next with 112 ex-voto shrines. In terms of proportional importance, Austria again ranks first with 34 percent of the origin stories describing votive shrines. Examples of this type are next most prevalent in France followed by Switzerland, West Germany, Belgium, and Italy. Portugal apparently has a high proportion of ex-voto origin accounts, but the number of shrine origin stories collected there is too small to draw any conclusions about the type's relative importance in that country.

Shrines that originated as votives are predominantly Marian and focused on images. In sharp contrast with significant site shrines, votive shrines tend to be of fairly recent origin. Although the establishment of votive shrines is an ancient and, indeed, pre-Christian tradition, only 6 percent of those that can be dated were created prior to 1099. Well over half have come into being since 1530. Votive shrines, as a class, probably have fairly short life spans. The importance of particular events tends to fade through time, noble families die out, political alliances change, and new plagues, floods, and crop failures stimulate new shrines which draw pilgrims away from older district or regional votive shrines related to earlier occurrences of similar problems.

Devotional Shrines

Devotional and votive shrines are similar in that their origin stories both emphasize deliberate creation. The difference is that, in accounts of devotional shrine foundings, there is no mention of salvation from particular events. Rather, these shrines came into being because a pious individual or group decided that a pilgrimage center should be developed in a particular place. No miracles are invoked officially, although miracle stories sometimes circulate among the faithful. A chapel that tops a crest above the village of Kaulbach, West Germany, in the Rheinland-Pfalz provides an example of such a devotionally inspired pilgrimage place (Figure 7-3). The small sanctuary was constructed in 1875. Inspiration and fund-raising for the project are credited to a parish priest based in nearby Wolfstein who felt that the Catholics of his spatially extensive but largely Protestant parish needed a place to gather for special occasions. At present, the main pilgrimage events take place on Marian holy days in August and September. The chapel is also important to the dispersed Roman Catholic minority in the region as a place for baptisms, weddings, and funerals. This modest shrine claims no miracles in its century as a place of district pilgrimage. Its bells, however, are a constant part of life in the adjacent villages of Kreimbach-Kaulbach where they ring out at least as often, and quite as loudly, as the bells of the Lutheran parish church on a nearby hill. The drawing power of the Kaulbach chapel is related partly to its existence as a Catholic symbol in a Protestant region.[21]

One of Europe's most famous devotional shrines is Sacro Monte near Varallo, Italy. Here more than 40 chapels representing events in the life of Christ line a path that winds uphill to a pilgrimage church dedicated to Mary's Assumption. Work on this artistically important complex was initiated by Father Bernardino Caimi, who arrived in the region in 1478 after years of serving as the warden of the Church of the Holy Sepulcher in Jerusalem. The Franciscan priest wanted to reproduce in Italy the places and episodes of Christ's Passion. He is said to have been inspired to choose the hill where the shrine complex now rises because a nightingale began to sing there as he wandered in meditation through the countryside. People of the region, in-

Figure 7-3 *This pilgrimage chapel on the hillcrest above Kaulbach, in West Germany's predominantly Protestant Rheinland-Pfalz, was built in the late nineteenth century as a purely devotional offering. No miracles or other wondrous events are included in the formation story, but the little shrine serves as an important devotional and social center for the district's scattered Roman Catholic minority. The two main pilgrimage days are in August and September.*

cluding nobles and high churchmen, responded enthusiastically to his idea. The first chapels were built during the last decades of the fifteenth century, the project was promoted by Saint Charles Borromeo in the sixteenth century, and it was finally completed in the late seventeenth century. The story has elements found in other origin accounts, including initiation by a holy man, focus on an image of Mary brought from Jerusalem, and reports of miracles. The emphasis, however, is on the power of one man's devotional inspiration.[22]

Some shrines promoted as devotional in origin were founded by priests, monks, and nuns who experienced apparitions, but who chose not to proclaim them. Two examples are the shrine established by Saint-Louis Marie Grignion de Montfort near Pontchâteau, Brittany, in the early eighteenth century, and the pilgrimage center dedicated to Nossa Senhora do Sameiro on a hill near Braga, Portugal, developed by a priest named Martinho Antonio Pereira da Silva during the latter part of the nineteenth century. In each of these cases, the story of an unrecognized apparition of Mary is included in the current formative account, so we classified them as apparitional rather than devotional shrines.[23] In a more recent example, shrine literature obtained at San Vittorino near Rome states that on December 8, 1960, a humble monk called Brother Gino "came to understand that the Blessed Mother" wished him to create a shrine in honor of the early nineteenth-century apparitions at Fátima, Portugal. Pilgrims, nuns, and souvenir vendors all said that the "understanding" was actually an apparition that Brother Gino, now a priest, was too modest to proclaim publicly.[24]

About 45 percent of the devotional shrines were established by communities, members of religious associations, and other groups. Of those attributed primarily to the generosity or fund-raising abilities of individuals, half were the work of priests or members of religious orders. One-quarter were sponsored by nobles, and 18 percent were promoted by members of the middle classes. Only 7 percent are said to have been inspired by persons of humbler social ranks. Ninety-two percent of these shrines are said to have been created by males, including the husband-wife efforts of several middle-class founders (Table 7-8).

Devotional origin stories are most common in Italy and the Germanies, with the highest regional concentration in the central and northern Germanic areas. With few exceptions, shrines with this type of formation story are of relatively recent origin. Eighty-three percent were founded after 1529 and more than half have been established within the past 200 years. Twenty percent of these shrines were established in Germanic areas between 1530 and 1779. Nineteen percent date from the past 200 years in Germanic areas, while 16 percent were established in Italy after 1779.

There are several possible explanations for the time-space concentration of the type. For one thing, a substantial proportion of these shrines were established or promoted by priests, monks, or, much less frequently, nuns. Such persons, at least since the Reformation, and particularly in certain areas, may have felt it would be easier to win ecclesiastical acceptance for a new pilgrimage center if no miracles or highly unusual events were publicly proclaimed. In the case of the Fátima shrine at San Vittorino where a probable apparitional shrine is promoted as a devotional shrine, Brother Gino may have been less modest than knowledgeable about the furor that could result from public proclamation of an apparitional experience.

In other cases, shrine establishment was simply a devotional act, indicating that miracles are not a necessary element for attracting modern pilgrims. In regions where the majority of the population is Protestant, as in parts of West

Table 7-8 *Characteristics of Devotional Shrines*

Regional Distribution	N	%
Italian	42	26
French	30	19
Iberian	11	7
German	75	47
British	2	1
Irish	1	‹1
Total	161	100

Time Period	N	%
Early Christian	1	1
Early Medieval	8	5
High Medieval	11	7
Renaissance	7	4
Post-Reformation	50	31
Modern	84	52
Total dated	161	100

Time/Space Distribution of Devotional Shrines

Region	Early Christian	Early Medieval	High Medieval	Renaissance	Post-Reformation	Modern
Italian	—	1%	2%	1%	7%	16%
French	1%	3	2	—	3	11
Iberian	—	1	1	1	3	2
German	—	1	2	3	20	19
British/Irish	—	—	—	—	1	5

Devotional Subject	N	%
Christ	6	4
Mary	138	86
Saints	16	10
No subject	1	‹1
Total	161	100

Devotional Object	N	%
Human remains	—	—
Other relics	—	—
Images	116	92
Site only	10	8
Total classified	126	100

Individual Founder Characteristics (N = 92)

Poor or Humble		Middle Class		Nobles		Religious	
Men	6	Men	15	Men	19	Priest, monk	45
Women	0	Women	2	Women	4	Nun	1

Table 7-8 (continued)

Sex		Social Status	
Males	92%	Poor or humble	7%
Females	8	Middle class	18
		Nobles	25
		Religious	50

Germany, the devotional origin stories may be more appealing to many modern Roman Catholics than are stories that emphasize miracles. Concentration of devotional origin stories in modern times may also indicate a tendency toward relatively short life spans for such shrines unless miracles eventually occur. Or perhaps older shrines, founded for whatever reason, are likely to acquire more mystical origin stories as time passes. In cases where the founder is eventually canonized and devotion shifts toward his or her cultus, the shrine becomes a significant site establishment in terms of our classification system. Only 11 percent of the devotional shrines are of major importance, and many of these probably have some underlying story of a miracle or apparition not currently publicized in shrine literature.

Devotional shrines are predominantly Marian. None appear to have venerated relics, other than the usual kind with which all Roman Catholic church altars are consecrated. Most display one or more images in a manner suggesting a special focus of devotion, but these statues and paintings are not generally supposed to have any especially miraculous qualities.

Spontaneous Miracle Shrines

Shrines were classified as having been founded in response to spontaneous miracles if their origin stories centered on themes of wondrous events that attributed extraordinary holiness to familiar objects or places. Table 7-9 indicates some of the characteristics of the miracle shrines. These do not include shrines that are said to have originated with the finding of images or relics and those based on reports of apparitions, each of which are considered as separate categories to be discussed later in this chapter.

Shrines stemming from sudden miracles differ from votive shrines in being much more spontaneous in their development. Rather than stemming from a vow to create a shrine as an act of gratitude for salvation from catastrophe, the miracle shrine typically comes into being when the place is inundated by

Table 7-9 *Characteristics of Spontaneous Miracle Shrines*

Regional Distribution			Time Period		
	N	%		N	%
Italian	156	34	Early Christian	8	2
French	64	14	Early Medieval	8	2
Iberian	34	7	High Medieval	83	20
German	201	44	Renaissance	89	21
British	1	‹1	Post-Reformation	194	46
Irish	3	1	Modern	40	9
Total	459	100	Total dated	422	100

Time/Space Distribution of Spontaneous Miracle Shrines

Region	Time Period					
	Early Christian	Early Medieval	High Medieval	Renaissance	Post-Reformation	Modern
Italian	1%	‹1%	4%	10%	13%	6%
French	1	1	5	2	7	1
Iberian	—	‹1	3	1	3	—
German	—	1	8	8	23	3
British/Irish	‹1	—	—	‹1	—	‹1

Devotional Subject			Devotional Object		
	N	%		N	%
Christ	57	12	Human remains	5	1
Mary	371	81	Other relics	14	3
Saints	31	7	Images	392	92
No subject	—	—	Site only	14	3
Total	459	100	Total classified	425	99

pilgrims attracted by news of wondrous happenings. Although many images that eventually were considered miraculous originally came from some other place, the stories associated with these shrines differ from those subsumed under the acquired object category in that the accounts have little or nothing to do with how, or from where, the image was obtained. Also, the miracle that stimulated pilgrimage devotion to an image generally took place a considerable time after it had been placed in the spot where the wondrous event occurred. Because such images had never been lost, they could not be found. They were just there, perhaps venerated to some degree by many, or intensely by a few, but not noted for any special powers or the ability to attract pilgrims until after miracles indicated their importance.

The most common type of spontaneous miracle story involves wondrous events associated with an image that had previously served as a focus for personalized or highly local devotions. However, prior to the occurrence of the miracles that turned it into a pilgrimage cult object, the image was only one among many. In Catholic Europe, where images of Mary, Christ, and the saints have long been ubiquitous, it has not been unusual for individuals, neighborhood groups, or small communities to develop special attachments to particular statues or paintings among the many that adorn churches, mark crossroads, delineate field boundaries, or decorate the facades of town houses and farmsteads. The majority of images about which spontaneous miracle stories are told were originally located in local votive chapels, parish churches, cathedral side chapels, or other religious structures. Some, however, were paintings or statues displayed on simple roadside or field votive markers. Others had been attached to trees or walls for years before miracles made them famous, and a few were home devotional images. These images may not have lacked veneration, but before the onset of miracle reports they did not attract pilgrims from other places. They were essentially no different from numerous similar images honored by the local people. The frequent association of miracle stories with preexistent, and often well-known, images, churches, chapels, and countryside votive markers suggests that, in many cases, this type of origin story is best interpreted as an explanation for the expansion of a modest local cultus to the status of a district, regional, or even more important pilgrimage shrine.

The cult-triggering miracles associated with this type of shrine are of several kinds. Eucharistic miracles, which generally involve bleeding Hosts or sanctified wine turning into blood, fit this category. There are also stories of bleeding or oozing relics as well as images said to have bled, wept, or sweated. In other cases, images reportedly shifted position, changed expression, opened or shut their eyes, spoke aloud, or otherwise behaved in a manner not ordinarily expected of inanimate objects. Such wondrous events were often followed by cures or deliverance from plague, crop failure, or war.

Manifestations of this kind during wars have sometimes received direct credit for the salvation of a community. For example, in 1522 a French commander, Marshal Lautrec, is said to have ordered the massacre of the population of Treviglio, a resistant Po Valley town. When soldiers with weapons drawn entered the town at dawn, they were astonished to see "blood" sweating from the face and tears flowing from the eyes of a primitive image of the Madonna with Child painted on an exterior wall of a church. Word was sent to Lautrec who came to see for himself. Profoundly moved, the French commander sank to his knees, laid his sword and helmet at the foot of the weeping image, and ordered his troops to spare the people of the town.

Similar stories, ranging from historical to legendary, are told at several other shrines. For example, a legend from Bar-le-Duc, Lorraine, recounts the salvation of the city in 1130 when a statue of Mary located above the main gate of the castle of the Count of Bar shouted a warning as otherwise undetected enemy troops approached the city. When one of the soldiers threw a stone at the shouting statue, he was stricken dead, whereupon his comrades fled.[25]

A well-documented Renaissance episode of a bleeding image that led to the development of numerous subsidiary shrines comes from Re in Aosta's Val-Vigezzo. According to a report signed by several officials, including the governor of the valley, a man named Giovanni Zuccone threw a stone at a painting of the Madonna over the entrance of the parish church at five o'clock in the afternoon of April 19, 1494. The image began to shed bloody tears, a manifestation that continued for 20 days. This bleeding image attracted considerable attention and pilgrims soon began arriving from distant places. A young German from Bergatreute made the journey and returned to his Swabian village with a copy of the Re Madonna, which in its turn began to attract pilgrims when the figures of both Mary and the Child began bleeding copiously from the face in 1685 (Figure 7-4).

Several other shrines in Austria, southern West Germany, and northern Italy have copies of the Re Madonna as cult objects, although most of these images are not reported to have bled. As at Re, the bleeding manifestation is often initiated by a deliberate attempt to harm the image. An earlier Italian example comes from Madonna dell'Arco near Naples. Here, in 1450, it is said that a man who lost a turn in a game threw a ball at an image of the Madonna in a lime tree. The image bled and the man was saved from lynching by the Count of 'Sarno, who then sentenced him to death by hanging from the lime tree. In other cases, the image simply started sweating blood for no apparent reason.[26]

Siracusa, Sicily, has one of the most recent major shrines that developed after a report of a weeping Madonna. Here, in 1953, a home devotional image symbolizing Mary's Immaculate Heart cried for three days. In contrast with

Figure 7-4 *An example of a spontaneous miracle shrine is found at Bergatreute, in southern West Germany, where cultus focuses on an image that began attracting pilgrims when both Mary and the Christ Child are said to have started bleeding copiously from their faces in 1685. The wondrous painting is a copy of an image from Re, Italy, which, according to documents from the time, bled for 20 days after being struck with a stone thrown by a man named Giovanni Zuccone.*

most twentieth-century reports of this type, local church authorities encouraged the development of the pilgrimage cultus that stemmed from the spontaneous miracle.[27]

We collected 130 descriptions of bleeding, crying, moving, or speaking images. Several of these stories involved established shrines where the perceived image behavior served to reinforce the pilgrimage cultus rather than initiate it. When an image other than the principal cult object expresses curious behavior, the event often results in a shift of pilgrim focus to the newly miraculous one. Forty-eight percent of the stories concerning weeping, bleeding, or moving images are told at Italian shrines, making Italy by far the most important area for this type of miracle report. Most of the rest of the stories are Austrian, German, and Swiss. Only 9 percent are French, and 5 percent are Iberian. A considerable majority of these image manifestations have been reported since the fifteenth century. Somewhat similar are the reports of images talking to people, but in most of these cases the image was either newly discovered in some hidden place or was described as coming to life. Such reports fall in a difficult-to-classify area between apparitions and other epiphanies. Stories of shrines being established because an image spoke to someone are most common in Italy.

A related set of origin stories reported the miraculous salvation of images from accidental destruction. For example, an Austrian statue of Mary is said to have jumped out of a burning church into a nearby tree. Another supposedly flew out of the flames that engulfed its church at Walcourt, Belgium, in the fourteenth century and landed gracefully on a tree in the garden. Pilgrimages also have begun or have been intensified when images survived the demolition of churches not only by fire, but also by earthquakes, floods, volcanic eruptions, or bombs. In these cases, the images often came to be thought of as miraculous because they were found unblemished, or at least recognizable, amid the ruins. Other stories deal with image survival from deliberate attempts at destruction, such as those that would not burn when thrown into fires or sink when cast into rivers by Protestants or other iconoclasts. The important Swiss shrine at Bourgillon on the edge of Fribourg has such an origin story. Here, a fifteenth-century statue of Mary and the Christ Child was thrown into a fire by Protestants. When it failed to burn, it was rescued by Catholics and served as a symbol for a pilgrimage dedicated to preserving the Catholic faith in the region.[28]

A few origin stories deal with images that proved themselves miraculous by exacting vengeance on their tormentors. At Bernrain in Canton Thurgau, Switzerland, it is said that in the fourteenth century a boy from another town grabbed a statue of Christ and told it to blow its nose, whereupon the boy's hand stuck to the image and could be removed only after many prayers had been said by the faithful. A weaver was so impressed by the incident that he gave money to build a chapel, and a pilgrimage developed. In another Swiss case, this one in the late eighteenth century, a man mocked an old roadside crucifix as he passed by. A short distance down the road, he was stricken with severe pain. He piteously asked to be carried back to the image where he expressed his apologies and immediately recovered.[29]

A motif common to shrines in several countries begins with enemy soldiers or iconoclasts of various persuasions who shoot, stab, stone, or take an ax to an image that often bleeds as a result. The person who maimed the image then dies immediately or soon afterward, typically of a wound or wounds on the very parts of his body where the image was damaged. In one variation on this theme, a drunken soldier who shot an image on the day before a battle was immediately killed by his companions, a highly probable scenario.

Other pilgrimage-initiating events were more benign. At the Saint Séverin church in Liège, Belgium, pilgrims are said to have started venerating a Marian image in 1631 after some flowers that had been placed near it to decorate the church for Corpus Christi celebrations took on a more beautiful bloom rather than fading. In another peaceful case, the shrine of Notre-Dame du Chêne near Vion, France, is said to have been initiated in 1494 after the local priest put a small statue of Mary in an oak tree. As the story goes, the tree was immediately surrounded by doves during the day and a glow at night. Soon villagers and passersby began coming to the tree to pray, and miraculous cures began to occur.

In about one-third of the cases examined, the image's power was manifest initially through the cure of a humble person who had neither the money nor the influence to create a votive shrine. A fairly typical story of such a cure is told at Maria Eich on the outskirts of Munich. The sons of a local blacksmith placed a tiny image of Mary in an oak tree in 1710. As time passed, the tree's bark grew around the image, nearly obscuring it. The image apparently was not forgotten completely because, in 1735, a sick servant girl from a nearby farm vowed to crawl on her knees to the Madonna in the tree. Her report of a miraculous cure soon attracted others; and when a farmer's five-year-old daughter recovered from an illness, crowds grew and a chapel was built. More than 700 cures were reported between that date and 1800 when the statue was removed from the dying or dead tree and placed in a new stone chapel. The stump of the miracle tree is also enshrined in the chapel and kept behind glass to prevent pilgrims from carrying off splinters.[30]

Such stories have numerous variations, but the basic theme remains the same. The cure of a humble person, often with a well-known history of chronic illness or handicap, triggers the influx of pilgrims seeking similar benefits. One may conceptualize a kind of critical mass of sick persons. Once a certain level of visitation is reached, it is almost certain that cures will be credited to pilgrimages to the place. Cures will be said to stem from the journey in itself, from touching the cult object, or from drinking water from the shrine spring or well if there is one. Other cures will be reported when sick persons who stayed home are touched by objects brought by loved ones who made pilgrimages for them. As the stories are embellished and spread, there will be vows to make a pilgrimage to the shrine if one or one's loved ones get well. Among any large group of sick persons, some generally recover; thus, the shrine's ability to attract pilgrims grows.[31]

A few cases involve the resuscitation of an infant, either stillborn or dying before it could be baptized. These shrines, along with a few others initially established for different reasons, have traditionally been the scene of some of Europe's most pathos-filled pilgrim journeys as parents of dead, unbaptized infants have come to the holy place with the bodies of their babes in arms. Sometimes mothers are said to have walked four or five days so that the tiny corpse they carried might miraculously come to life just long enough to receive baptism and thus qualify for Christian burial. Rows of tiny churchyard graves at such shrines attest to a bending of church rules about baptism, and speak mutely of human sorrow and concern.

A few places classified as shrines with spontaneous miracle stories report site-marking manifestations that did not involve images. At the Swiss shrine of Maria Licht near Truns in 1660, for example, several people, including the local priest, claimed they saw a strange light on a rock outcropping. They took this as a sign that the Virgin wished to have a pilgrimage shrine on this spot. Construction of a chapel was approved by the abbot of the monastery at Disentis, and it is said that the entire hill was bathed in a mystical light when the cornerstone was laid in 1663. In another case, five farm workers were astonished to see five fountains of blood gush suddenly out of the ground near Kempten, Bavaria, in 1691. These "blood columns" continued to flow for 15 months, and after appropriate investigations in 1694 the Heiligkreuz shrine was built to mark the spot and succor pilgrims.[32]

Shrine stories emphasizing various types of miracles are broadly scattered throughout much of Europe, although they are especially concentrated in southern West Germany, Switzerland, Austria, and northern Italy. The largest number of cases are in Italy (153) and Austria (109). These countries also have the largest percentages of shrines of the type, followed closely by Switzerland and Belgium. The spontaneous miracle does not appear to be especially important in the cult-formative stories of surviving shrines in Spain, Portugal, or Ireland, and it is uncommon in areas where Protestant influences are strong. The major temporal concentration is Post-Reformation, although many such shrines also date from the High Medieval and Renaissance periods. Pilgrimages generated by instant miracle reports were quite common during the High Middle Ages and include many cases that did not survive as shrines to the present. Sometimes—then as now—reports of wonders drew thousands of supplicants and curiosity seekers shortly after the reporting of a miraculous event. The massive inundation peaked within weeks, months, or a few years, and the place was either forgotten or relegated to a modest district pilgrimage center shortly thereafter. Despite the early attrition rate for shrines of this type, many have become established and survived through centuries.

The greatest survival rate for High Medieval shrines of the type appears to be Germanic, with 8 percent of all miracle origin stories. The focus for surviving shrines shifted to Italy during the Renaissance, with 10 percent of all cases of the type. Post-Reformation Germanic lands, especially southern West Germany, Austria, Switzerland, and Flemish Belgium, account for 23 percent of all instant miracle stories, and the type was also important in Post-Reformation Italy with 13 percent of all analyzed cases. This particular cult-formative story has become relatively less important since the late eighteenth century, but remains vigorous in Italy, which accounts for more than half of the 40 reports of such shrine formations throughout Western Europe since 1780.

Perhaps reflecting the Post-Reformation concentration, along with the inclusion of most shrines related to Eucharistic miracles in this category, 12 percent of the miracle shrines focus on Christ, a higher-than-usual proportion. Eighty-one percent are Marian, and the small remainder are dedicated to saints. Because many of the stories directly involve images, it is not surprising that 92 percent of the shrines of this type have an image as the primary object of cultus.

Acquired Object Shrines

The stories of these shrines focus on the arrival of an image or relic brought from another place (Table 7-10). Fifteen percent of the acquired objects are the mortal remains of saints. An additional 13 percent are relics of Christ's Passion, plus a few garments, threads of hair, and milk relics representing the Virgin. The remainder are images. An unusually high 17 percent of these shrines focus on Christ. Seventeen percent are oriented toward saints and 65 percent are Marian. Some objects, particularly relics of various kinds, were considered to have especially miraculous qualities at the time of their transfer. Most images, along with relics of obscure nonlocal saints, gained their power to attract pilgrims by arriving in an unusual manner or by proving immediately miraculous in their new settings.

Some acquisition stories are ancient. The Cathedral of Xanten, West Germany, for example, claims the relics of the martyr Saint Victor, said to have been sent by Saint Helena in the fourth century. Archaeological work in the

Table 7-10 *Characteristics of Shrines with Acquired Objects*

Regional Distribution			Time Period		
	N	%		N	%
Italian	112	25	Early Christian	17	4
French	55	12	Early Medieval	53	13
Iberian	67	15	High Medieval	101	24
German	206	45	Renaissance	43	10
British	13	3	Post-Reformation	141	34
Irish	1	‹1	Modern	59	14
Total	454	100	Total dated	414	99

Time/Space Distribution of Acquired Object Shrines

Region	Time Period					
	Early Christian	Early Medieval	High Medieval	Renaissance	Post-Reformation	Modern
Italian	2%	4%	5%	2%	5%	4%
French	2	2	4	1	3	1
Iberian	‹1	1	6	3	7	3
German	‹1	4	10	5	20	6
British/Irish	—	—	—	—	—	3

Devotional Subject			Devotional Object		
	N	%		N	%
Christ	79	17	Human remains	67	15
Mary	297	65	Other relics	61	13
Saints	78	17	Images	326	72
Total	454	99	Total classified	454	100

Acquisition Circumstances for 286 Known Cases

	N		N
Gift of king or nobleman	48	Brought by soldiers, sailors, merchants, or migrant workers	33
Gift of queen or noblewoman	21		
Gift from abbot, bishop, or pope	32	Brought by refugees	5
Gift of middle-class man	8	Brought by monk, priest, or hermit	50
Gift of middle-class woman	3		

Table 7-10 (continued)

Washes up on seashore or riverbank	50	Brought by nun	7
Brought by animals that refuse to move further	9	Taken from ships that will not leave harbor	9
		Brought by mysterious stranger	9
		Flown to site by angels	2

early 1930s suggests that the cathedral site was a center of Christian cultus as early as the fourth century. More important to modern pilgrims, however, are the tombs of several Catholic priests who died in Nazi concentration camps, as well as relics of earth from each of the death camps preserved as memorials to all victims of Nazi persecution.[33]

Numerous acquisition stories are straightforward accounts that describe instances of the common custom of donating statues to churches and making gifts of relics. The shrine of Saint Marzellinus and Saint Petrus von Einhard at Seligenstadt on the still-popular foot pilgrimage route between Cologne and Walldürn contains relics said to have been brought from Rome in 828 by Charlemagne's private secretary.[34] The relic of Christ's Holy Blood venerated at Bruges, Belgium, is said to have been brought from the Holy Land by a count of Flanders, who, as a hero in the Second Crusade, received the precious item from the patriarch of Jerusalem. A piece of Christ's Cross venerated in Holy Cross Church at Donauwörth, West Germany, was probably brought to the West from Constantinople in about 1029 and given to the Benedictines at Donauwörth by Holy Roman Emperor Konrad II who reigned from 1024 to 1039. A Holy Blood relic along with a piece of the True Cross venerated at the monastery of Mittelzell on Reichenau Island are said to have been sent to Charlemagne by the prefect of Jerusalem and passed down through noble family lines until donated to the monastery by a duchess in the early tenth century.[35] The famous Black Virgin venerated at Halle, Belgium, was brought to the town by Princess Sophie, daughter of Saint Elizabeth of Hungary, when she married Henry II, Duke of Brabant, in the mid-eleventh century. The list is lengthy. Probably the most famous shrine with an object sent as a gift is the chapel of the Holy Shroud in Turin, Italy (Figure 7-5).

Of the 217 stories that specified the donor of the object or the person who brought it to the site of its current veneration, 80 described gifts from wealthy laypersons brought or sent to the place that became a shrine. Eighty-six percent of these donors were members of the royalty or the nobility, and

Figure 7-5 *Since the sixteenth century, the shrine of the Holy Shroud at Turin, Italy, has been one of the most famous examples of a pilgrimage established because of the acquisition of a particularly powerful holy object. Large numbers of people from all over the world visited Turin when the shroud was last displayed in 1978. The interpretive center set up for the exposition presented materials from several scientific studies of this unusual grave cloth with its essentially photographic image of a crucified man.*

the remainder were affluent members of the middle class. Largely because of the custom of including holy objects in dowries, 30 percent of these donors were women: 21 were queens and noblewomen, and 3 were middle-class women. An additional 32 objects were described as ecclesiastical gifts sent by abbots of great monasteries, bishops, or Vatican officials including the pope. Most of these objects were relics of saints, the Holy Cross, or earth saturated with Christ's blood. Priests and monks, often returning home from pilgrimages, brought 46 objects to the sites of current veneration. Seven were brought by nuns, generally as parts of the dowries they received on entering a convent.

In 33 cases, objects were brought to their present places of veneration by soldiers, sailors, merchants, migrant workers, and other persons with occupations that involved travel. As examples, a statue of Mary venerated at Trápani in Sicily is said to have been brought from Syria by Pisan seamen in 1244, and images of the Virgin, Saint Roch, and Saint Sebastian honored at Nettuno, Italy, were saved from destruction in sixteenth-century England and given to the Nettuno church by Neapolitan merchants in 1550. Several stories involving images brought by seamen include the motif of a ship that is becalmed or will not leave harbor. One such story begins with a fifteenth-century ship captain who was shown a pretty statue of the Virgin Mary by a local image vendor in Flanders. He decided to buy the statue, but forgot about it until he attempted to set sail and found that the ship would not leave the harbor. After the captain went back into town and purchased the image, the voyage began without further trouble and continued without incident until the ship reached a point off Chiávari, Italy, where it stopped. The captain noticed a little chapel on the cliffs west of Chiávari, so he and some sailors rowed ashore and placed the Flemish statue on the altar. After that, the voyage continued to a successful conclusion. Thus began the pilgrimage to the shrine of the Madonna delle Grazie near Chiávari, or so the story goes.[36]

A few stories involve images said to have been brought to their shrines by holy hermits. One is recounted at the isolated mountain pilgrimage chapel of Kirchwald, a Bavarian holy place accessible only by footpath and maintained by a Franciscan hermit who represents a long line of such caretakers dating back to early Post-Reformation times. As the story is told, a journeyman weaver from Bavaria made a pilgrimage to Rome where he was given a dark picture of Mary and some relics by a kindly church official whom he happened to encounter. The weaver was so inspired by his experience in Rome that he decided to become a hermit, and, on returning to his native land, found a cave in the mountain forest near a spring. It was an excellent retreat from the world, except that the water in the spring was bad. So, the former craftsman threw the relics into the spring and prayed before the image. The water became suitable for drinking as well as for working miracle cures. Pilgrims soon began hiking through the mountains, as they still do, to experience the beauty of the wooded path, pray before the image, and partake of the waters.[37]

Some objects reached their places of veneration by somewhat arbitrary relocation processes. An example was the transfer of Saint Benedict's remains from his tomb in the monastery at Montecassino, Italy, to Saint-Pierre-de-Fleury, a French monastery now known as Saint-Benoît-sur-Loire. A French version of the story stresses the seventh-century destruction of the Montecassino abbey church by barbarians. The abbot of the Fleury Benedictine monastery was so distressed to think of the great founder-saint's bones lying amid ruins that he sent some monks to find the bodies of Benedict and his sister, Saint Scholastica, and bring them to France where they might receive more appropriate veneration. Other examples, such as the transfer of the relics of Saint Nicholas from Myra to Bari by Italian merchants in the eleventh century, were clearly cases of theft.[38]

Fifty stories describe objects that washed up on seashores or river banks, or were discovered tossing in sea waves or drifting on river currents. Occasionally the object is said to have arrived in a small, unmanned boat, or to have just floated into shore. In some accounts, more common in southern Germanic areas than elsewhere, images defy the rules of nature by floating upstream. In several Bavarian stories, images swim upstream. A tale from Mariaort in the Diocese of Regensburg begins with an image of Mary supposedly thrown into the sea at Constantinople during the iconoclastic period. Instead of sinking, it floated into the Black Sea and then swam up the Danube. While the image was resting on the bank, it was found by German peasants who took it to their village and began to build a chapel to house it. However, angels carried the stones back to the place where the image had washed ashore so the church had to be built there. The current stone statue, which dates from the fourteenth century, shows Mary holding the Christ Child who is holding a frog.[39]

In nine cases, objects are said to have arrived on pack animals or in ox carts that, in some versions, were unattended by people. Resultant shrines developed where the animals stopped and refused to move farther, where the beasts fell and refused to get up, or where they dropped dead. Along with several of the stories of ships that would not leave harbors, most of the animal stories involve an object that was being transported to a place other than where it eventually came to be venerated. Stories of this type, incidentally, are far more common in Latin America than in Europe.[40] Putting a found or unexpectedly miraculous object on a pack animal or in a cart and letting the animal go seems to have been a fairly common way of deciding exactly where to build a shrine, at least since the tenth century in Europe.

An interesting story relating an acquired object with animal behavior comes from Loreto Aprutino in Italy's Abruzzi region. It seems that in about 1700, citizens of the town of Penne sent a priest to Rome to get some relics of a saint because they had only one saint and neighboring Loreto Aprutino had three. The priest looked around in the catacombs, as was the custom, and found a marble slab with the name "Zopytus" on it along with some bones. This presumed early Christian martyr thus became San Zopito. En route to

Penne, the relics were carried past Loreto Aprutino where an ox dropped to its knees. Nevertheless, San Zopito was enshrined in the Penne church, but the bones disappeared and turned up in the Loreto Aprutino sanctuary. The relics were taken back to Penne, only to return to Loreto Aprutino where they stayed.[41]

Several Italian shrines have origin stories describing the arrival of objects carried by angels through the air. The image of the Madonna del Buon Consiglio venerated at Genazzano, Italy, is said to have been flown from Albania where it appeared mysteriously on the wall of an unfinished Augustinian church. This story might better be classified as a case of cultus generated by a found or appearing object than as a tale emphasizing image acquisition, because the appearance of the fresco in 1467 seems to be a matter of record and occurred, most fortuitously, during a period when work on the church had ceased due to the lack of funds. The legend of the flight from Albania seems to have developed about a century later. The transfer theme, however, remains powerful at present and, according to a local monk, Albanian pilgrims still come to Genazzano, fall on their knees, and loudly beg the image to fly back home.[42]

An even more famous story concerns a small stone structure that, according to tradition, was the Nazareth home of Joseph, Mary, and Jesus. The Holy House was frequently visited at its original location by Christian pilgrims during the twelfth and early thirteenth centuries. However, during the troubled years that marked the end of the Christian Crusader states in the Eastern Mediterranean, the house disappeared. Then, in the late thirteenth century reports began to circulate about a Holy House in the Italian Marches. According to tradition, the Holy House was flown by angels from Nazareth to Dalmatia in 1291. From there it was carried to a forest on the Italian shore of the Adriatic, but after pilgrims were attacked by robbers in the woodland the house was taken to an open meadow. When members of a family of pilgrims had a big argument with each other instead of praying, angels are said to have picked the house up again and deposited it on a hill in the place that became Loreto, Italy. The small structure stands encased in an outer shell of elaborately carved marble inside of an enormous basilica, and the shrine attracts three to four million pilgrims per year. The little structure is probably a replica of the Nazareth house, possibly built of materials brought by pilgrims from the Holy Land. The legend of its transportation by air forms the basis of the Virgin of Loreto's role as the patroness of aviators, air travelers, and participants in hazardous sports such as motorcycle racing.[43]

Shrines with acquired object stories are concentrated in the Rheinland-

Pfalz, along the West German borders with Switzerland and Austria, and in central Switzerland. The type is broadly scattered throughout Italy, which has the largest number of cases. The highest percentages of acquired object stories are in Switzerland and West Germany, and in both of these countries they are the most frequently encountered of all origin story types.

About half of these origin stories specify the place or region from which the acquired object is said to have come. Many cases involve the transfer of objects from one place to another within the same general culture region, as, for example, the movement of San Zopito's relics from Rome to Loreto Aprutino. At least 215 objects reportedly came from distant places, although in some of these cases the current focus of veneration may be a locally made replacement for an older object of distant origin. Sixty-one percent of the objects from distant lands originated, or are thought to have originated, in the Holy Land or some other Eastern Mediterranean locality. Thirty-nine percent of these relics and images are venerated at Italian shrines, whereas 29 percent are found in Germanic lands. France has 17 percent, and 14 percent are found in Spain. Thus, the number of shrines with cult objects said to be from the East declines with distance from the source, as might be expected.

A number of the Eastern objects enshrined north and west of the Alps made their real or legendary journeys to their current places of veneration via the Italian peninsula. Rome and other parts of Italy have also served as an important source for relics and images that became objects of pilgrimage cultus in other lands. Nearly a quarter of the cult objects from distant lands are of Italian origin, and the direction of flow appears to have been predominantly northward to Austria, Switzerland, the Germanies, and Belgium. The number of cases declines with distance from Italy, and, when plotted on a map, shows a strong concentration in Austria, Switzerland, and southern West Germany. Indeed, one might almost speak of a flow of holy objects from Italy north to the Alps rather than to points north of the Alps.

Hints are provided of a number of other important interregional religious connections. Objects from the Germanies in Spain and from Spain in southern Germanic areas reflect Catholic Reformation transfers within the Hapsburg domains. Images from Eastern Europe are mostly found in Austria and southern West Germany, although one, which is venerated in Halle, Belgium, moved farther west as part of a medieval noblewoman's dowry.

Several cult images and relics from France and Belgium are venerated in England. All arrived during or after the French Revolution, a period when England provided refuge for French nobility who were Roman Catholic. The few cult images of English and Irish origin that serve as primary objects of veneration at continental European shrines are said to date from the Middle Ages. Most survived sixteenth-century Protestant iconoclasm by being smuggled out of Britain on ships bound for Catholic countries. One image of probable British origin, which is now venerated in northern Spain, is said to have washed up on the beach.

A few images made in Latin America were carried to Europe where they generated a new pilgrimage cultus. Not surprisingly, three of the five identified are enshrined in Spain. The other two are in Italy and Austria. At least one Spanish shrine developed after a returning emigrant brought an oriental statue of Mary from the Philippines.

Shrines said to have been generated by the acquisition of an object are proportionately highest among shrines from Early Medieval times, a period that accounts for 13 percent of the dated cases. Acquired object shrines from this period are more or less equally concentrated in Italian and Germanic areas. Forty percent of the cases from High Medieval times are in Germanic lands, followed by 23 percent in Iberia and 17 percent in Italy. Acquisition stories are not very common among Renaissance shrines, possibly reflecting a widespread skepticism of the times about the authenticity of holy relics and the efficacy of miraculous images. Forty-four percent of those dating from the Renaissance are German. The largest numbers of such stories date from the Post-Reformation period, and of these 58 percent are in areas where the German language predominates. In modern times, the concentration of shrines with object acquisition stories has remained Germanic (39 percent), but within this group there seems to be an increased emphasis on shrine development in the Netherlands and northern parts of West Germany. Nearly a quarter of the modern shrines with acquired object stories are in England.

Found Object Shrines

Several of Europe's most famous shrines have stories that emphasize the discovery of a holy object. During the first millennium A.D., the found object was usually a saint's body. The ninth-century discovery of a body presumed to be that of Saint James the Greater at Santiago de Compostela, Spain, is the root of the third most important pilgrimage center of Medieval European Christendom. Only Rome and Jerusalem were considered more important destinations in those days, and Santiago is still one of Europe's great shrines. From about the eleventh century onward, however, the emphasis shifted to miraculously discovered images of the Virgin Mary, mostly statues but occasionally paintings and fresco-embellished walls. One of the oldest and most famous of these shrines is found at Montserrat in Catalonia. Most formative stories of this type involve the finding of an image rather than a relic (Table 7-11).

There are five variations on the theme of cult formation related to holy object discovery. The most common story simply states that an object was found, or that it was found because of strange lights, celestial music, unusual animal behavior, or other curious manifestations. In a second type of story, particularly common in Medieval Spain, a visionary sees an image as if it were alive. We included simple stories of object findings, along with those involving sounds, lights, and appearing images, in the found object category because the main emphasis in such tales appears to be on the discovery rather than the events leading up to it.

In a third type of story, represented by a fourteenth-century legend from Guadalupe, Spain, and those of several other important Spanish shrines, a vision immediately leads to a discovery because the holy person tells the seer where to look for a lost image. Vision and image finding combine in these stories with a slight emphasis on the vision, at least as the tales are told at present. These stories have been included in the category of apparitional shrines although, structurally, they closely resemble the first two types.

A fourth type of found image story, recorded as early as the eighth century in England but increasingly evident after the turn of the fourteenth century, clearly separates the vision from the discovery of the object. In these accounts, the visionary describes his or her experience to other people before an image or other object is found. In some cases, the finder is someone other than the visionary who relayed instructions on where the image would be discovered. An example of such a legend comes from Nieva in Old Castile where the Virgin appeared to a shepherd in 1392 and told him to go to the bishop of Segovia to request a search for a long-lost image. Stories of this kind place primary emphasis on the apparition. The subsequent discovery or, occasionally, the mysterious acquisition of the image, serves as a kind of footnote to support the main event. These stories are also subsumed under the general category of apparition stories.

A fifth variant, particularly common in Renaissance and Catholic Reformation Germanic lands, begins with a dream or other vision during which the seer is instructed to go to a distant place and look for an image. The pilgrimage comes into being as a result of finding a holy object at the site revealed in the dream, often after the seer or someone else is cured. One of the earliest stories of this type, traditionally dating from the first decade of the fourteenth century, begins with Mary's appearance to a monk in León in northwestern

Spain. The Virgin told the seer to travel several hundred miles to Chipiona on the southeastern Andalucian coast, there to search for an ancient image that he subsequently found in a cedar box in a chamber five feet underground. The site had very old sacred connections: it may have been a Christian monastery as early as the fifth century, and it is close to the ruins of a Roman temple dedicated to Venus and Hercules.[44] Most of these stories are highly complex and thus difficult to categorize. Basically, cases in which the seer's experience was revealed after the shrine was established were subsumed under the found object category whereas the others were counted as apparitions.

A considerable majority of the 563 found object stories have a similar structure. The tale often begins with an account of how the object was lost. Usually it is said to have been hidden from iconoclasts. It is discovered much later, generally because of signs that lead the finder to its location. The relic or image proves itself miraculous either by the circumstances of its finding or by means of manifestations occurring soon afterward. These signs often include some indication of where the object is to be placed for veneration, usually the place where it was found. The place is often characterized by some natural feature such as a spring, a height, a cave, a curious stone, or a tree.

In the classic Medieval Spanish "shepherds' cycle" story, the object is described as a statue of Mary holding the Christ Child and is assumed to have been hidden to prevent desecration by Moslems. It is found by an adult male shepherd, often as the result of a dream, vision, strange lights, heavenly music, strange animal behavior, or some combination of these. Sometimes the image appears in an animated form, but becomes mute stone or wood thereafter. The shepherd either takes the image to a village church or notifies the local people who carry it to the community. The next morning, however, the image is gone and is rediscovered in the place where it was originally found. This usually happens three times, whereupon a chapel is built to house it at the place of discovery. Pilgrims come; and when additional miracles and wondrous events occur, the shrine becomes fully established. This, of course, is the stuff of legends, rich in a mythical symbolism that tends to obscure the essentially simple theme of loss and recovery. Many early stories of object discoveries may have been invented years after the pilgrimage began to illustrate the miraculous powers of cult objects or to explain the shrine's location.

Not all stories involving object findings are purely legends. Many of those with post-fifteenth-century dates are well documented. There is, for example,

Table 7-11 *Characteristics of Shrines with Found Objects*

Regional Distribution	N	%	Time Period	N	%
Italian	136	24	Early Christian	2	‹1
French	113	20	Early Medieval	67	13
Iberian	168	30	High Medieval	189	36
German	141	25	Renaissance	97	18
British	5	1	Post-Reformation	146	28
Irish	—	—	Modern	25	5
Total	563	100	Total dated	526	100

Time/Space Distribution of Found Object Shrines

Region	Early Christian	Early Medieval	High Medieval	Renaissance	Post-Reformation	Modern
Italian	—	2%	7%	4%	8%	1%
French	‹1%	4	7	4	4	1
Iberian	‹1	5	16	6	7	‹1
German	—	2	6	5	9	2
British/Irish	—	—	—	—	—	1

Devotional Subject	N	%	Devotional Object	N	%
Christ	26	5	Human remains	18	3
Mary	504	90	Other relics	13	2
Saints	33	6	Images	532	94
Total	563	101	Total classified	563	99

Individual Characteristics of 317 Finders of Objects

Male		Female		Males and Females	
Poor men	176	Poor women	10	Poor children	3
Poor boys	19	Poor girls	28	Villagers	8
Middle-class men	19	Middle-class women	6	Townspeople	6
Noblemen	18	Noblewomen	3		
Priests, monks	20	Nuns	1		

Table 7-11 (continued)

Sex		Age		Social Status	
Males	80%	Adults	84%	Poor or humble	77%
Females	15	Children and		Middle class	10
Both	5	adolescents	16	Nobles	7
				Religious	7

nothing legendary, or even especially mysterious, about a pilgrimage that may be forming around an old statue of Mary discovered in the attic of a German priest's house in 1978. A letter from the priest, whose retirement and move to other quarters resulted in cleaning out the attic, explained that a former pilgrimage died out two centuries ago. He hoped that a "scientific" examination of the image found in the attic would indicate that it was the authentic cult object so that it might provide a focal point for a pilgrimage revival.

It is entirely too easy to dismiss a shepherds' cycle story of shrine formation as a popular Medieval legend. William Christian, cautioning against undue skepticism about stories that seem to be legends, wrote: "That most of them were stereotyped or derivative by no means rules out the discovery of images or the historical phenomenon of apparitions. Real discoveries and visions were stereotyped: people organized these experiences into known patterns."[45] Assume that a region has experienced some kind of iconoclastic or other socioreligious disruption. Further assume that the area in question contains a number of images awaiting potential discovery. It is likely that some images will be found and that some discoveries will take on miraculous trappings.

Several stories of image finding describe actual rediscoveries of cult objects, lost or hidden during troubled times. Other found images were probably votives originally placed in obscure places such as rock shelters or tree hollows and eventually forgotten. Still others were lying around in unexpected places because they were misplaced, thrown away, or perhaps even buried for one reason or another. If it is anticipated that the finding of images under extraordinary circumstances is to be expected, such discoveries are likely to happen regardless of the local supply of hidden images. Judging from historical accounts of twentieth-century shrine formations in Latin America and southern Texas, a discovered "image" has sometimes been a curious stone or a twisted root that is thought to look like the Virgin Mary, Christ, or a saint. As the cultus develops such items are soon replaced by more acceptable man-made representations, a fate that seems to have befallen most of the pagan cult images that may have generated a number of the earlier, image-focused, found object shrines.

If the cultural tradition stresses an association between the discovery of images and the subsequent occurrence of marvelous events, the stage is set. The person who accidentally finds an image—especially in a mysterious place such as a cave, or in a totally unexpected place such as within the barked-over hollow of a tree being split for firewood—is likely to feel a special sense of awe. Because of the culturally assumed association between the discovery of images and wondrous events, initial reports of the finding create a general feeling of expectation among the local populace. With, and sometimes without, nurturing by local religious leaders, the expected scenario unfolds and a new place of pilgrimage comes into being.

The social psychology of such a situation was apparently well understood by sixteenth-century Benedictines at Saint-Avold, France, where an ancient pilgrimage cultus that focused on the bones of the Roman martyr Saint Nebor died out due to Huguenot influences in the region. As a means for promoting the Catholic faith and generating a new pilgrimage, these pious monks are thought to have hidden a statue of Mary in a place where they supposed it would be found "accidentally," and so it was. Although cultus at Saint-Avold faded when the image was hidden during the French Revolution, it was revitalized by a local parish priest in the late nineteenth century, and the shrine currently draws more than 10,000 pilgrims annually from Lorraine and the adjacent West German Saarland.[46]

The diversity in the details of found object stories suggests that many of these shrines really did begin with the chance discovery of an object considered to be especially holy. Relics, or at least human remains, are easy to find in areas where burial rather than cremation is the rule. Images of various kinds, including representations of mother goddess figures that bear strong resembles to some images of Mary with the Christ Child, have been made in Europe for thousands of years. In addition, almost anything—from a rock or a root to the pattern of browning on a piece of bread—can be conceptualized as a representation of a holy being and can generate an incipient cultus. The objects initially discovered are not necessarily, indeed probably not very often, the ones currently on display for veneration.

The first phase of the traditional story, or the explanation of how the image came to be in the place where it was eventually found, is generally speculative even when the events of the finding are well documented. The most common explanation is that the image was hidden to prevent its destruction or desecration by Byzantine iconoclasts, pagan Vikings, Moslems (variously described as Moors, Saracens, or Turks, depending on the time period and the place), or, after the early sixteenth century, Protestants. Several images, presumably hidden from Protestants, were found during the sixteenth through eighteenth centuries in France and Germanic lands. In Britain and Ireland, Protestant iconoclasts were especially energetic in their efforts to destroy Medieval cult objects, but a few were smuggled to safety on the Continent and others were hidden. One English shrine developed in the nineteenth century after an old statue of Mary was found under the floorboards of an ancient barn.

Numerous images also were hidden during the violent anticlerical and iconoclastic outbursts of the French Revolution and the Spanish Civil War. In most cases, these cult images were retrieved and reenshrined shortly after the troubles were over, but some, reportedly hidden or sent off for safekeeping during these crisis periods, have not been recovered. Thus, there is a continuing potential for the generation of a new cultus as a result of the discovery of an image thought to be one of those lost cult objects. Certainly, the hiding of holy objects threatened with destruction has long been a common human practice.

A fairly large number of stories, particularly from Germanic lands, presume that the found image was not actually hidden but merely placed in some remote spot as an individual votive and eventually forgotten. In other cases, the image was covered by flood-deposited sediments, rockslide debris, and, in at least one Italian case, ashfall from a volcanic eruption. Still others are thought to have been left in churches or chapels that fell into ruin after a war, a plague, or economic problems resulted in the depopulation of a village.

The next part of the typical story deals with the actual finding of the image, and there is enormous diversity in the places where images are said to have been found. Discovery locations may be in wild vegetation as, for example, in or under bushes, in brambles, in pasture weeds, in weeds grown up along old walls, in tree branches, in the roots of blown-down trees, in tree hollows, or inside trees split by woodmen. Some were found under leaves on a forest floor. Although oaks are the most frequently mentioned tree species, images have also reportedly been found in pine, fir, chestnut, laurel, linden, mulberry, hawthorn, apple, pear, and olive trees. The earth has yielded images from deep within caves, in shallow grottoes, or in narrow niches between mountain stones. Workers have found images while plowing, cultivating vineyards, cutting hay, and digging in the depths of mines. One image is said to have been found in a vulture's nest. In an Italian case, an image was supposedly found nine feet underground at the confluence of two streams during an excavation at the site that was inspired by a dream. In other cases images were dug up while the foundations for castles or churches were being excavated. Others were found buried in the sand and gravel of stream banks or as flotsam on sea and ocean beaches. Water is related to many found object stories. Some images were found in wells, and some turned up in pools by springs. Still others were found floating on streams or lakes, or being tossed in the waves of the sea; some were brought up in fishing nets. According to a macabre story from West Germany, the body of a man who died or was killed somewhere upstream came ashore near a village. The local people, not wishing to pay for the stranger's burial, cast the corpse back into the stream. But after it washed up over and over again in the same place, the villagers dug a shallow grave at the site, and it is said that their spades unearthed a long-lost image of Christ on the Cross.[47]

Miraculous images have also been found in attics; under barn floors; in wine cellars, castle dungeons, the foundations of old town walls, walled-over niches in town, castle, and church walls, ditches, cattle troughs, mill stones, closets, old chests; among the belongings of deceased hermits; and amid piles of junk in antique shops. Not infrequently images were found in or near the ruins of old churches, sometimes under earth and stones in the ruined interiors or in thorn thickets growing up around the ruins (Figure 7-6). Some were found in walled-up niches of churches being demolished, and others were frescoes found under layers of plaster during church restorations. During the 1930s, a pilgrimage developed in Bavaria's Ostrach Valley when a painting of Mary, which had hung in a damp, little-visited chapel for centuries, was taken out and found to be a work by Hans Holbein the Elder. Historically, the ruins of villages abandoned because of plague or war have been propitious sites for finding miraculous images. Stories of image discoveries fairly often involve animals such as sheep gathering daily around a bush, bulls pawing the earth, oxen kneeling in front of trees, or dogs sniffing at rabbit holes. In Spain, one image is said to have been dropped by an eagle.

Although the finder of the image is traditionally a shepherd, examination of the occupations described in shrine literature indicates that the term "country person" would be a better general description. The occupational variety is actually quite extensive. Images are said to have been found not only by shepherds who tended sheep, but also by cowherds, goatherds, and swineherds. Other finders have been described as common soldiers, military officers, sailors, ship captains, hermits, carters, merchants, and townspeople with a wide variety of occupations along with prosperous farmers, wine mak-

Figure 7-6 *A stained glass window in the shrine church at Josselin in Brittany, France, graphically conveys the story of a pilgrimage said to have been established because of the miraculous discovery of a long-lost image. According to tradition, during the ninth century a countryman found an old statue amid brambles in a church that had been destroyed by Viking raiders. A modern statue is now venerated, but fragments of a much older image, burned during the French Revolution, are kept at the shrine in a reliquary as if they were the fragments of a saint's remains.*

ers, woodcutters, miners, fishermen, and landless agricultural workers such as plowboys and reapers in hay meadows. Some images were supposedly found by nobles, often while hunting, and a few were found by priests and monks. People of all ages and both sexes have been identified as finders.

In spite of the demographic diversity represented in the 317 stories that describe the person who discovered the image, there are some general patterns. Images were found by males in 80 percent of the stories. Only 15 percent of the finders were girls and women, and the rest of the images were found by groups of people with both sexes represented. In 84 percent of the stories the finder was an adult. Of the adult finders, 88 percent were men, 7 percent were women, and the rest were mixed groups. In the relatively few cases of images found by children or young teenagers, 56 percent were found by boys, 38 percent by girls, and 6 percent by children of both sexes. Finders of images are very likely to be laypersons. Only 7 percent of the stories describe images found by priests, monks, hermits, or nuns. Finally, finders are usually members of the humbler classes. Seventy-seven percent were described as poor or as having humble occupations, 10 percent were from the middle ranks of society, and only 7 percent were kings, queens, or nobles. The typical finder, representing 56 percent of the cases, was a poor adult male, usually a countryman.

The found object story is generally thought of as particularly related to Medieval Spain. Indeed, this is the strongest time-space concentration of shrines with these stories. Sixteen percent of all dated cases are associated with Iberian shrines established during the High Middle Ages, a considerably higher proportion than for any other single time and place. However, an even greater number of such stories are told at twelfth- through fourteenth-century shrines outside Iberia, so the type can be thought of as generally Medieval rather than specifically Iberian. Slightly more than two-thirds of these stories are tòld at shrines established before 1529, but the stories remained fairly common through the eighteenth century. The greatest number of these formative stories are told at Iberian shrines, with 30 percent of the cases. Twenty-five percent are in Germanic lands, followed by Italy with 24 percent. In Italy, shrines with these stories are concentrated toward the south.

Apparitional Shrines

Accounts of visions resulting in the establishment of Christian pilgrimage shrines are at least as old as the second-century story of Christ's appearance to Saint Paul on the Appian Way near Rome in about A.D. 63, and as recent as reports that have drawn more than five million pilgrims and curiosity seekers to the village of Medjugorje, Yugoslavia, since a series of Marian apparitions began there in June 1981.[48] Both of these manifestations fall into the general category of apparitions, or that type of vision popularly conceptualized in the Roman Catholic tradition as an actual appearance of the Virgin Mary, Christ, or one of the saints to living individuals in specific localities. Although apparitions are usually beheld by only one or a few seers, they are, if reported, eminently social events. In Christian's words, "they attract immediate public attention and call for some sort of verification."[49]

Reports of apparitions, if believed, have considerable potential for generating pilgrimage shrines because the holy person who is assumed to have appeared on earth imbues the apparition site with a special, long-lasting aura of sanctity. Visions occurring in dreams are generally thought of as happening in the mental world of the visionary, but there is considerable conceptual overlap. Because of this we have included dream visions in the apparitional category in cases where the holy person "appeared" in the dream and the seer's account of his or her nocturnal vision was an important factor in the generation of the pilgrimage. Visions beheld by religious mystics are referred to as secondary visions by Christian, because "their social importance is secondary . . . to the sanctity of the seers."[50] Shrines established because of visions beheld by priests, monks, nuns, and pious hermits have been included in the apparitional category if the shrine is primarily dedicated to the holy person beheld, whereas those places dedicated primarily to the visionary have been categorized as significant sites.

Shrines with apparition stories that meet the criteria of the category are found throughout much of Western Europe, but are most common in Mediterranean peninsular countries. More than half of the shrines with apparition stories are in Italy, whereas Italy and Iberia combined account for over two-thirds of the cases (Table 7-12). Only 15 percent of the apparition shrines were found in French-speaking regions. It seems likely, therefore, that the historical-religious significance of a few, fairly recent French vision-related shrines has led to overemphasis on this part of Europe as a seedbed for apparitions. Apparitions per se have been less common as the basis for pilgrimage development in Germanic lands than in most other regions. In these areas, stories with a visionary element are often described as dreams rather than apparitions and frequently were not reported until after the pilgrimage had become established because of miracles or other events. A very famous apparitional shrine was established at Knock, Ireland, after visions were reported in 1879, and several of England's ancient apparitional shrines were reestablished as pilgrimage places in the nineteenth and twentieth centuries.

Apparitional shrines are usually dedicated to the holy person who appeared. This heavenly individual is most often the Virgin Mary, although a few shrines are related to apparitions of Christ, several of the saints, and the Archangel Michael. The cult object is usually an image, sometimes one that represents the apparitional event (Figure 7-7). Although females of various ages are more likely to have been seers of apparitions than they are to have been finders or donors of images, the majority of visionaries were males. Children are better represented, but there is relatively little difference between seers and image finders in terms of social status (compare tables 7-11 and 7-12).

Shrines established because of apparitions are relatively most prevalent

Table 7-12 *Characteristics of Shrines with Apparition Stories*

Regional Distribution	N	%	Time Period	N	%
Italian	181	52	Early Christian	10	3
French	52	15	Early Medieval	26	8
Iberian	66	19	High Medieval	54	17
German	40	12	Renaissance	83	26
British	5	1	Post-Reformation	106	34
Irish	3	1	Modern	36	11
Total	347	100	Total dated	315	99

Time/Space Distribution of Apparitions

Region	Early Christian	Early Medieval	High Medieval	Renaissance	Post-Reformation	Modern
Italian	2%	3%	7%	17%	19%	4%
French	1	2	2	2	4	4
Iberian	1	2	6	4	4	2
German	—	1	2	2	6	1
British/Irish	—	1	1	—	—	1

Devotional Subject	N	%	Devotional Object	N	%
Christ	7	2	Human remains	2	1
Mary	325	94	Other relics	1	‹1
Saints	15	4	Images	266	93
Total	347	100	Site only	17	6
			Total classified	286	100

Characteristics of 300 Visionaries

Males		Females		Males and Females	
Poor men	94	Poor women	31	Poor children	8
Poor boys	25	Poor girls	52	School children	1
Middle-class men	23	Middle-class women	12	Villagers	5
Noblemen	10	Noblewomen	2	Townspeople	7
Priests, monks	25	Nuns	5		

Table 7-12 (continued)

Sex		Age		Social Status	
Males	59%	Adults	71%	Poor or humble	72%
Females	37	Children and		Middle class	14
Both	4	adolescents	29	Nobles	4
				Religious	10

among those dating from the Renaissance, a period during which 18 percent of the surviving shrines have apparition stories. The proportional importance drops to 11 percent of the origin stories associated with Post-Reformation shrines, and declines to 9 percent of those related to shrines established since 1780 (Table 7-2). More than a third of the stories describing apparitions come from Italian shrines established between 1400 and 1779—a striking time-space concentration.

Types of Vision-Related Stories

A number of shrines with stories classified in categories other than apparitional include reference to some type of visionary experience. We, therefore, developed a supracategory of vision-related shrines that combines accounts of apparitions with stories related to dreams, appearing images, and visions beheld by saints to whom shrines are dedicated. These 524 vision-related shrines can be classified in several ways. Map 7-1 indicates the locations of four general types of vision stories.

In accounts of classic apparitions, the visionaries were not asleep, although, judging from modern reports, some probably were in trancelike states. If the story includes the discovery or acquisition of an image, as at Sainte-Anne-d'Auray, France, in the seventeenth century, the discovery or acquisition took place, or is said to have taken place, after the apparition was made public. Shrines with this type of story tend to be highly place-specific, the site for the shrine having been marked by the appearance of the holy person conceptualized to have been physically present on earth at that spot. These shrines, as illustrated by the solid dots on Map 7-1, are most numerous in Italy where they are especially concentrated in the central and northern parts of that country.

The shepherds' cycle variant, indicated by open circles and concentrated in

Figure 7-7 *The shrine image at Savona on Italy's Ligurian coast symbolizes an apparition reported by a humble man in 1536. Mary appeared alone and promised to intercede for humanity in exchange for prayer, penance, good works, and processions to the site of the vision. More apparitions have given rise to enduring pilgrimage shrines in Italy than in any other part of Western Europe.*

Spain and southern Italy, places emphasis on the discovery of an image. Either the image is said to have appeared, sometimes as if it were alive, or the holy person is described as appearing in order to tell the seer where to find the image. As these mostly legendary accounts are told, the vision is secondary to the discovery of the image. Traditionally, the shrine is thought to have been built where the image was found, often because it mysteriously returned to indicate the appropriate site after attempts were made to place it for veneration elsewhere. This type of story is essentially a "found object" account, differing from others primarily in the inclusion of a vision-related theme. In recent versions, as at Pompeii, Italy, where a much venerated painting was found lying neglected in an antique shop, the report or hint of a vision is used to support the miraculous qualities of the discovered image rather than the finding of the image being taken as proof of the reality of the apparition.

A third type of story, the dream vision, is represented by triangles indicating the location of the shrine site. In these cases, the visionary experience

Wondrous Events, Miracles, and Legends 271

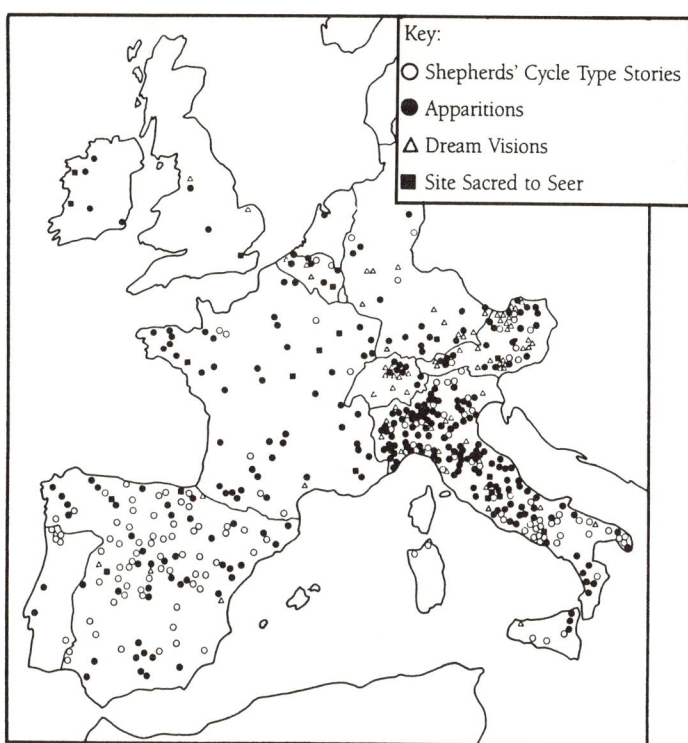

Map 7-1 *Shrines with Formative Stories Describing Visions*
Several different types of vision-related accounts have been responsible for the establishment of pilgrimage centers or have developed as legends to account for the formation of shrines. In the traditional shepherds' cycle type of story, especially prevalent at shrines of a Medieval date, the vision is said to have led directly to the finding of an image. Cases of this type of story are represented by an open circle. Triangles indicate shrines where the formative story involves a dream rather than a "waking" vision. Most cases date from the Renaissance and Post-Reformation periods, and they are concentrated in northern Italy and Germanic lands with scattered reports elsewhere. Squares indicate shrines dedicated to the visionary rather than the holy person who appeared in the vision. Closed circles represent events classified as apparitions per se in which the visionary was supposedly in a waking state and acceptance of the report does not appear to have been based on the mysterious discovery of an image. Although the most famous of the Modern apparitional shrines are in France, Portugal, Belgium, and Ireland, this type of vision-generated shrine is most common in Italy where many reports date from the Renaissance and Post-Reformation periods.

occurred while the seer was asleep and frequently involved instructions to travel, build a chapel, locate a lost image, or undertake some other activity. In some cases, the visionary fell asleep in a countryside location and was informed in the dream vision that the site was especially holy. More often, however, the shrine is located at a place specified in the dream rather than in the place where the dream occurred. A high proportion of these stories are told at shrines in Germanic lands.

The fourth category, the saints' visions, is composed of shrines established at places where religious mystics or founders of new orders experienced visions and ecstasies. These are usually dedicated primarily to the seer-saint rather than to the holy person or persons revealed in the vision. These shrines, indicated by squares on the map, are widely scattered throughout continental Europe.

Importance of Vision-Related Stories

Vision-related stories are particularly important as indicators of a popular religiosity that varies from place to place and changes through time. Over the past 2,000 years, there have been shifts in the regions where the largest numbers of shrine-formative visions have occurred, changes in the manner in which visions are said to have been manifest, and changes in the social characteristics of those visionaries whose experiences were accepted as authentic. As Christian suggested in his study of apparitions in Spain during the fifteenth and sixteenth centuries, "the changing faces of divine figures . . . leads us to changes in the societies that meet them."[51]

Following the same general line of thought, the Turners employed different types of vision-related stories as cases to illustrate their typology of stages in the historical development of Marian cultus. The shepherds' cycle type, in which an apparition is followed by the discovery of an image, represents the prototypical vision of the Turners' third, or Medieval, stage of shrine establishment. Vision-related stories illustrating these authors' fourth, or colonial stage, were drawn from Mexico. They conceptualized these as "shrines, which replaced, as it were, the shrines destroyed during the Reformation in Europe."[52] Resemblances between a few New World stories, such as the Mexican Guadalupe account, and the classic Medieval Iberian shepherds' cycle stories were stressed. Their model was based on, and perpetuates, general assumptions that Latin American pilgrimage developed from a syncretism of Medieval Iberian and Amerindian religious traditions.

The prototypical Marian apparition used by the Turners to illustrate a fifth, or modern, stage in the development of Christian pilgrimages has characteristics that distinguish it from the common Medieval type (Table 7-13). Specifically, Mary appears alone in the modern type. She delivers a message to the visionary calling for penance, appropriate actions to avoid pending catastrophe, or, as at Lourdes and Fátima, makes an announcement with politico-religious implications. No statue or painting is miraculously found to confirm the vision, although an image depicting the apparitional event may soon be created to serve as a devotional object. The seer is usually female. When the seers are boys and girls—as at La Salette, France; Fátima, Portugal; and Beauraing, Belgium—most messages are conveyed by a girl. The Turners interpreted this type of Marian apparition as a response to conditions of increasing secularism and rapid social change in nineteenth- and twentieth-century Europe, and viewed it as a manifestation of popular religion that spontaneously reemerged after nearly 300 years of relatively little pilgrimage formative activity in Western Europe.

The Turners' modern vision type is interpreted further as symbolizing a devotional "shift to Mary herself, as an autonomous figure who takes initiatives on behalf of mankind, often intervening in the midst of the economic and political crises characteristic of industrialized mass society."[53] Largely on the basis of this presumably new kind of vision, the Turners contended "that there is a significant difference between pilgrimages taken after the Industrial Revolution and all previous types."[54]

Two of the Turners' assumptions are invalid. First, as illustrated in Chapter 4, there was no general 300-year lull in shrine formation or pilgrimage activity in Europe between the sixteenth and eighteenth centuries. Second, all of their specifications for a postindustrial apparition type are met by documented accounts of visionary experiences that occurred in Italy and Spain during the fifteenth century. Apparitions of this type continued to generate new pilgrimages throughout the Catholic Reformation period. There was nothing new, or qualitatively different, about the French apparition reports from La Salette in 1846 or Lourdes in 1858. Such visions cannot, therefore, be interpreted as a response to social conditions beginning in the nineteenth century. The Turners' argument that a modern age in European pilgrimage expression emerged with a series of visions in which Mary appeared alone and delivered an apocalyptic message is probably valid, but only if it is understood that this post-Medieval response to increasing secularism, urbanization, and uncertainty in an age of rapid social change took place in fifteenth-century Italy and Spain rather than four centuries later in nineteenth-century France.

Table 7-13 *Characteristics of the Turners' Prototypical Medieval and Modern Visions*

Medieval	Modern
Subject of the vision is usually Mary.	Same
The seer is usually of humble station.	Same
A site feature often acquires sanctity.	Same
The seer is usually male.	The seer is usually female.
Mary appears with the Christ Child.	Mary appears alone.
An image is found.	No image is found.
No special message is given.	A special message is given.

Only a small minority of apparitional shrines, even among those established after 1800, meet all of the criteria for the Turners' modern vision type. A majority of stories, especially from shrines founded after about 1400, combine various prototypical "medieval" and "modern" elements in a variety of ways. In some cases, for example, Mary appeared alone but delivered no special message other than where to look for an image. Other visions combine her holding the Christ Child while delivering a doomsday warning, and no image is later discovered. The individual traits specified by the Turners as indicating a modern-type apparition appear quite early, although the unique combination of aloneness, message, and lack of image discovery can be traced back only to the fifteenth or possibly late fourteenth century. To facilitate the tracing of this and other variations through time in shrine origins related to visions, the following discussion of the type is presented by time periods.

Early Vision Shrines, Early Christian to 1099

Scattered throughout Europe are 56 active shrines where visions are said to have occurred prior to A.D. 1100. Most of these stories have mythical qualities, and few are documented in extant contemporary accounts. Several, however, provide a realistic time-place framework for the development of pilgrimages and are probably embellished versions of actual events. Some stories may be pious inventions of later times, perhaps generated to explain ancient pilgrimages of uncertain origins. Regardless of their exact origins, many of the old vision-related stories have been extremely important for centuries as sources for interpretation of themes occurring in more recent shrine-formative stories of the same general type.[55]

Visions were expected forms of religious experience in both the Jewish and pagan Greco-Roman traditions and probably were important for early Christians as well.[56] The description of the appearance of Christ to Saint Peter at the site of the "Domini Quo Vadis" church on the Appian Way outside Rome is clearly an apparition story. Here, according to the apocryphal *Acts of Peter*, written in Syria or Palestine in about 190, Christ appeared to the Apostle Peter who was fleeing persecution in Rome. Peter was told to return to the city and a martyr's death.

Possibly one of the earliest Marian apparition stories is part of the popular piety of Zaragoza, Spain, where it is said that the then still-living Mary appeared to James the Greater while he was on his legendary mission to convert Iberia. Other stories of early Marian appearances to holy men include visions beheld in the fourth century by Saint Ambrose of Milan at Varese, Italy; by Saint Maurilius at Saint-Florent-le-Vieil, France, in the fifth century; and by the archbishop Saint Ildephonsus at Toledo, Spain, in about 667. Another old apparition account, recorded in writing before the end of the eighth century, describes Mary's appearance in 708 or 709 to a swineherd, and shortly afterward to a bishop, at a place that became the site of England's Evesham Abbey.[57]

Tales of the visions of angelic birds and demons beheld by Saint Patrick while he was meditating for 40 days on the heights of Croagh Patrick in northwestern Ireland fall into the general category of ecstasies experienced by Christian mystics.[58] An early example of a dream vision comes from Rome where it is said that the great Basilica of Santa Maria Maggiore was established as the result of a vision to a patrician Roman couple in A.D. 352. An unusual snowfall outlined the shape the church was to take, thus resulting in the popular name, Saint Mary of the Snows. A South German story from Maria Thann has Mary appearing in a dream to a newly baptized couple converted by the missionary Celtic holy man, Saint Gall, in the seventh century. A later story from Tongre, Belgium, tells of a blinded knight's dream of an angel who told him to have servants search his garden. As a result, an image of the Virgin Mary holding the Christ Child was found, supposedly in about 1081.[59]

During early times, visions leading to the finding of saints' relics were common. Although many of these cults have faded, several shrines with these origin stories are still visited. At Sankt Trudpert in Germany's Black Forest region, a vision in about 642 seems to have led to the disinterment of the saint's body, which proved to be "incorrupt" or undecayed. It soon attracted pilgrims who have come ever since. In a Portuguese example, a monk in the late eighth century is said to have had visions of Saint Torcato, traditionally considered to have been a companion of Saint James the Greater. This vision supposedly led to the discovery of the incorrupt remains of Saint Torcato, whose body is believed to have been hidden to prevent desecration by Moorish invaders. The story is recounted at the saint's shrine in the small northern Portuguese town of São Torcato, which is the scene of a large annual pilgrimage festival.

In about 838, bones assumed to be those of Saint James the Greater were found a little over 100 miles north of the Portuguese shrine. In this case, the burial site was supposedly revealed by heavenly lights and celestial music rather than an appearance of the saint, but legend suggests that an apparition led to the acceptance of the relics as authentic. As the story goes, Don Ramiro I and a small group of Christian warriors were in danger of defeat by a stronger Moslem force at Clavijo in 844. The battle turned in their favor when a knight, mounted on a great horse, appeared on the field and began to push the Moors back. After the victory, it was assumed that the unknown champion had been none other than the Saint James whose relics had been discovered a few years earlier.

One of the oldest stories combining visionary experiences with the discovery of an image rather than a relic comes from Monte Sant'Angelo on the Gargano Peninsula in Italy's Puglia region. In about A.D. 491, the Archangel Saint Michael is said to have appeared here first to a farmer and then to a bishop. This story was the forerunner of many later accounts of the archangel's appearance, and it provides the general pattern for many Medieval shepherds' cycle legends of visions leading to the discovery of Marian images. At Monte Sant'Angelo, the visionary bishop was a native of Asia Minor where the cult of Saint Michael was already strongly implanted. It seems highly probable that some type of sacred manifestation occurred at the mountain-top grotto during the late fifth century. This Christianized pagan holy place soon began drawing large numbers of pilgrims, many bound for the Holy Land from distant parts of Europe. As the fame of the Italian shrine spread so too did the cultus of the archangel. In about 710, Saint Michael supposedly appeared to another bishop, a manifestation leading to the foundation of the great French abbey and shrine at Le Mont-Saint-Michel on the coast of Normandy.[60]

One of the oldest stories of an apparition leading to the discovery of an image of the Virgin Mary comes from Incoronata, not far from Monte Sant'Angelo. Here, according to a tradition that varies somewhat from one telling to another, Mary appeared in the branches of an oak tree to a nobleman while hunting, or to a peasant whose cattle knelt at its foot. According to tradition, the year was 1001 and the statue found in the tree was an eighth-century Byzantine image brought by refugees from Eastern iconoclasm. The current cult image, claimed to be the one discovered in the eleventh century, is a dark-skinned statue of Byzantine style with both hands raised in an ancient gesture of prayer. Another cult object at this shrine is a fair-haired, pink-skinned Madonna with Child of a stylistically much more recent type. Some devotional cards show the two images on different branches of the oak tree with the noble and humble seers and the oxen kneeling at its foot. According to the Incoronata story, Mary announced, "I am the Mother of God." In the context of eleventh-century Italy, this was not merely a statement of self-identification, but a theologically significant message of the same type as the beautiful lady's statement to Bernadette at Lourdes in nineteenth-century France that "I am the Immaculate Conception." Although Mary had been proclaimed *Theotokos*, or Mother of God, at the Council of Ephesus in Turkey in 431, debate about this near-deification of Christ's mother continued to rage for centuries, and indeed continues.[61]

Through the first millennium of the Christian Era at least to the mid-tenth century, visionaries were reported to be either adult males or groups of people such as married couples or the people of a community. The earliest shrine-formative story we found that described an adult laywoman as a seer comes from Capáccio in the mountains east of Paestum in Campagna. Local bishops seem to have promoted this vision story and created a shrine dedicated to Mary in about 967. No discovery of an image was mentioned in the story. Less than a century later, an image of Mary, thought to have been buried during the iconoclastic period, is said to have been found as a result of visions beheld by a pious woman in 1041 at Materdómini di Nocera, also in Campagna. Another story, told at a shrine near the mountain village of Fraine north of Brescia in northern Italy, describes an apparition in the first decade of the eleventh century. This account, possibly the earliest of numerous Italian stories of Mary appearing to a poor deaf-mute girl, does not mention the finding of an image. Instead, the apparition was accepted when the formerly mute girl spoke of her experience.[62]

Thus, from several widely separated places in tenth- and early eleventh-century Italy, there are instances of many of the characteristics that combined in later accounts of visions. There are female visionaries of humble status, apparitions that did not lead to the discovery of images, and, at Incoronata, a legend and iconography suggesting a vision in which the Virgin appears alone and delivers a theologically significant message. By the end of the eleventh century, variations on these themes seem to have been generating pilgrimages in the French-Hispanic borderlands and farther into Iberia behind the southward-moving Christian-Moslem confrontation zone. Shrine stories from Angosta, Las Fraguas, Sonsoles near Ávila, and other places in Spain are of the traditional shepherds' cycle type and include the motif of a shepherd's discovery of an image of Mary supposedly hidden during periods of Moslem control.[63]

Some of the greatest present-day shrines with formative stories attributed to early Medieval visions are of rather different types. For example, at Saint-Hubert, Belgium, pilgrims honor the eighth-century pagan nobleman who supposedly saw a crucifix, or possibly just a glowing cross, between the antlers of a stag. As a result of the vision, Saint Hubert converted to Christianity and became a missionary bishop, and later the patron of European hunters. The great Swiss shrine at Einsiedeln was raised on a site sanctified by an early hermit who is thought to have been greatly devoted to the Virgin Mary. The cultus grew vigorously after Christ appeared to the local bishop and informed the cleric that the site need not be further blessed because it was already sanctified, a theme that also appears in the much earlier visions at Monte Sant'Angelo. Another famous vision story comes from Walsingham, England, where Mary supposedly appeared to a pious gentlewoman in 1061 and asked her to build a replica of the Holy Family's Nazareth home in England's green East Anglia. At Gurk in Austria, the theme of Mary as comforter of women mourning their lost sons emerged in the story of the Virgin's appearance, sometime before 1045, to a noblewoman named Hemma who devoted her life to God after the murder of her two sons by rebellious miners and the death of her husband, Landgraf Wilhelm von Friesach, while returning from a pilgrimage to Rome undertaken as penance for his slaughter of the murderous rebels.[64]

Vision stories from shrines established during the first 1,100 years of the Christian epoch display considerable variety, but some tendencies are evident even during these early times, at least for those shrines that have survived as pilgrimage centers to the present. Christ, the Archangel Michael, and various other saints were more often the holy persons to appear than at later dates. As the stories are now told, however, Mary was seen in two-thirds of the 56 visions ascribed to the period. Adult males experienced slightly more than two-thirds of the 50 visions for which seers were described. Two seers were referred to as boys, and 8 visions were seen by mixed groups such as married couples or the people of a community. The visionary was described as a lone female in only six stories, or 12 percent of the cases. Two of the seers were women of noble birth; the others were described as a French shepherd girl, a poor deaf-mute Italian girl, and two mature Italian laywomen of unspecified social status. Up to A.D. 700, two-thirds of the visions were beheld by bishops, hermits, missionaries, or other religious, sometimes in combination with an adult male of humble status. After that date, however, 86 percent of the visions were beheld by laypersons.

In about one-third of the cases for the period, the visionaries were kings, nobles, or high-ranking churchmen such as bishops or abbots. Three visions combined persons of high and low status. Thirteen accounts, or about one-fourth, described people of humble origin. The social position of the remainder was mixed, unclear, or, in most cases, intermediate between high and low ranks. These seers included apostles and missionary saints, soldiers in battle, and various persons not described as poor or in humble occupations, nor as country people or villagers. In one case, supposedly occurring at Valverde north of Catania, Sicily, in 1040, the visionary was a bandit who reformed as a result. Although persons of humble status were not especially well represented as seers during the first 11 centuries of Christianity, this was changing. Among the 14 stories specifically dated to the eleventh century, only four visions were exclusively beheld by high-status seers. One was experienced by both a nobleman and a peasant, two by people of intermediate rank, including the Italian bandit, and eight by persons described as country folk, poor people, or persons with humble occupations such as shepherds or plowmen.

High Medieval Vision Shrines, 1100 to 1399

Vision stories, many of which were not recorded until later dates, are associated with 112 shrines established during the Middle Ages, a time when pilgrimage travel was a main channel for the exchange of ideas throughout Christendom. Of the stories from shrines that survived, slightly more than half perpetuate tales of the general shepherds' cycle type with emphasis on the vision as a prelude to the discovery of a miraculous holy object, usually an image of the Madonna and Child. Such stories are especially common in Iberia.

Social-psychological needs for literal symbols may be proposed as an explanation for the high proportion of vision stories from the period that were signified by the finding of images. The image-finding theme, however, should not be overemphasized. Nearly half of the vision stories told at pilgrimage centers established during the High Middle Ages do not include the theme of object discovery. Cult-formative visions could be proved in other ways, especially outside the Iberian peninsula. Francis of Assisi and other religious mystics, for example, did not have to find images to prove their visionary experiences. At least eight cult-formative visions in Italy were beheld by deaf-mutes who proceeded to speak, although in several of these cases an image was found to further confirm the epiphany.[65] In France and Belgium, where there are relatively few Medieval vision stories, a variety of signs could be accepted as proof of reported visions. A story from Mariastein, Switzerland, traditionally dated from the 1390s, tells of Mary appearing to catch and save a child who had fallen over the edge of a cliff. Salvation themes reappear in several later legends, especially in Italy and the Germanic lands.

Mary, usually holding the Christ Child, appeared in more than 90 percent of the visions reported at shrines dating from the High Middle Ages. In a vision of uncertain date at Trani in the Puglia region of Italy, Mary seems to have appeared alone; and in the thirteenth century near Florence, the young noblemen who founded the Servite order are said to have experienced a vision of Mary holding the dead Christ in her arms.

Of the 92 seers described in formative stories associated with High Medieval shrines, 74 were males. Ninety percent of these were adults. Of the 15 visions said to have been experienced exclusively by females, nearly three-fourths were seen by young, unmarried girls. Only two females, both Italian, were described as mature laywomen. More than half of the visionaries were described as poor or humble in station. Monks, priests, or nuns were the principal seers in 15 percent of the cases, and 13 percent of the visions reportedly were experienced by persons of noble birth. The remainder of the visions were attributed to groups representing a variety of social positions, or to persons of intermediate social status.

Renaissance Vision Shrines, 1400 to 1529

At least 108 vision shrines created during the 130 years between 1400 and 1529 continue to draw pilgrims. The average of 8 surviving vision shrines per decade is greater than the average of 4 per decade from the High Middle Ages, 5 per decade from the Catholic Reformation, and 2 per decade from 1800 to the present. About 55 percent of the Renaissance visions occurred in Italy, and 19 percent were reported from Spain. Many of the events are historically documented, and some of the records indicate that the shrine-formative accounts reflect experiences that happened to particular persons when, where, and in the way described.[66]

Renaissance visions in the aggregate differ substantially from those of earlier times. Only about 20 percent of the stories include the theme of a miraculously discovered image. In several of these cases, the vision was reported before the image was found. In other cases, the vision was experienced, or is said to have been experienced, many miles from the site where the image was eventually found. The story from Peña de Francia, Spain, for example, describes Mary's appearance to a Frenchman named Opida while he was in Paris. According to the tradition of this shrine, the seer set forth on a pilgrimage to Santiago de Compostela in about 1434 and on the way home was inspired to detour to a mountaintop south of Salamanca where he found a statue of the Virgin.[67]

In two fifteenth-century German stories, one from Marienbaum in the Lower Rhine and the other from Ottobeuren in Bavaria, sick persons dreamed they would be cured if they could find the place where they saw Mary in their dreams. In both cases, the seers found the place, discovered images of Mary attached to trees, and were cured. These stories are early examples of a type of dream vision that became more common in Germanic lands during the Catholic Reformation.

During the Renaissance, changes also occurred in the sex and social status of persons described as seers. The proportion of female seers nearly doubled to 30 percent. A majority of these were girls. Males still predominated, but several of the masculine seers were young boys. Visions beheld exclusively by adult males account for only 52 percent of the reports from this period. Two-thirds of the seers were of humble status, for an increasing emphasis on the poor and powerless as acceptable visionaries. The proportion of visions experienced by priests, monks, and nuns dropped to 6 percent, while only 4 percent of the Renaissance visionaries were of noble birth. The rise of a middle sector is indicated by the 14 percent of seers with essentially middle-class status. Most of the 11 percent not classified by social rank were probably also from the middle sectors of Renaissance society.

Apparitions not supported by image discoveries predate the Renaissance as do reports of Mary appearing without the Christ Child and of Mary giving an important message, but these three characteristics seem to have first combined in apparition accounts of the fifteenth century. Possibly the first shrine-formative apparition meeting all of the Turners' criteria for fully modern-type visions was experienced by a poor old woman on a hill above Vicenza, Italy, in 1426. Mary, who appeared alone, told the seer that Vicenza would be spared a plague if its people repented and built a church. No image was found, and the seer was not believed. Two years later, as a plague raged through the city, Mary appeared again to the same woman who said that the

Virgin traced the plan for a church on the ground with an olive branch and caused a spring to come forth. This time the seer was believed, the shrine of Monte Bérico was established, and the plague ended.[68]

A few years later, probably in 1432, a poor peasant woman, who suffered from the brutality of a cruel husband, experienced visions of Mary at Caravággio in Lombardy. The Virgin, who appeared alone, told the seer that Christ was angry. Unless people began to mend their ways and fast on Fridays, they would be punished. This vision was also signified by the appearance of a spring, as happened at Lourdes and several other nineteenth- and twentieth-century apparition sites.[69] More than one million pilgrims per year visit this northern Italian apparitional shrine. Poor males had similar visions at Saronno north of Milan in 1440 and at Motta di Livenza northeast of Venice in 1510. At least eight other Italian Renaissance apparitions were distinguished by two out of three of the Turners' criteria for a modern-type vision.

In Spain, the earliest documented modern-type vision seems to have been experienced by a young girl of humble status at Cubas in Old Castile in 1449. Although once fairly important, this shrine is now the focus of local devotion. Pilgrims still visit the sites of prototypically "modern" Spanish apparitions at El Miracle (1458), El Torn (1483), Escalona (1490), and Pinos (1507).[70] We found no examples of the genre in other parts of Europe prior to the sixteenth century.

Catholic Reformation Vision Shrines, 1530 to 1779

In the wake of the Protestant Reformation, shrines were destroyed and pilgrimages were banned in much of northwestern Europe; any visions that might have occurred did not generate shrines. Where Catholicism remained dominant, however, visions accounted for 153 new pilgrimage centers, although in Spain and probably in Hapsburg-controlled southern Italy, the Inquisition of the Catholic Reformation strongly discouraged reports of apparitions after about the mid-sixteenth century. Church authorities in those regions seem to have been more tolerant of visions that led to the discovery of images and of other events such as sudden cures by roadside crosses, weeping images of the Madonna, and bleeding statues of Christ on the Cross.

Several famous Catholic Reformation shrines outside of Spain and southern Italy have stories that combine visions with miraculous images that were found or otherwise obtained. In 1557, at Montallegro in the mountains above

Rapallo, Italy, a man of humble station saw Mary surrounded by angels. As the story goes, she announced, "I am the Mother of God." The seer was instructed to spread this message to the people. A spring came forth and the angels left a Greek-style icon of Mary's dormation, or "falling asleep," on a nearby rock. The themes of this vision combined the idea of Mary as Theotokos with the equally ancient tradition that she gently fell asleep and subsequently was assumed into Heaven. Both of these beliefs were under attack by Protestant reformers of the day.[71]

At Kevelaer, currently in West Germany, a traveling salesman saw Mary by a votive marker on a lonely place on the road. The year was 1641, and the Germanies were locked in the turmoil of the Thirty Years' War. Mary asked the man to build her a church. When the visionary arrived home, he found that the Virgin had appeared to his wife in a dream and had told the woman to buy a small paper picture of the statue of the Virgin venerated at Luxembourg that some soldiers had tried to sell her a few days earlier. The tiny devotional card was duly obtained and placed where it might receive veneration from passersby. Miracles followed, and Kevelaer became a rallying point for Roman Catholics of the Lower Rhine, as it still is.[72] Other Germanic stories report visions resulting in the finding of images hidden from Protestant iconoclasts.

Another extraordinarily significant shrine of the Catholic Reformation came into being in 1623 when a Breton peasant reported apparitions of Mary's mother, Saint Anne. The seer's experiences were accepted only after an old image was found in the ruins of an abandoned church several months after the apparitions began. This vision coincided with French colonization in eastern Canada and was a factor in the implantation of the devotions to Saint Anne that underlie so much of the religious life of Catholic Quebec. The Brittany shrine is visited by approximately 750,000 pilgrims annually from all over the French-speaking world. A subsidiary shrine at Sainte-Anne-de-Beaupré near Quebec City draws well over a million of the faithful each year, mostly from Canada and the United States.[73]

In northern Italy, and to a lesser extent elsewhere, apparitions unrelated to image discoveries generated numerous pilgrimage centers from the sixteenth to early eighteenth centuries. Prototypically modern-type Marian apparitions resulted in new Italian shrines at Savona in 1536, Arcoa in 1556, and Ribordone Canavese in 1619. A Swiss vision of the type initiated a shrine at Ziteil in 1580 and an account from Sant Aniol in Catalonia prompted the creation of a shrine there in 1618.

A curious combination of events was reported at Vinay, France, in 1656. A

Protestant man, whose wife was Catholic, was pruning a tree when it began to bleed from its "wounds." Then, Mary appeared alone to inform the man of his impending death. The seer converted to the Catholic faith and died shortly thereafter, as predicted. Apparitions that began at Le Laus in 1664 and continued for 50 years were also of an essentially modern type. Mary usually appeared alone, no image was ever found, and the seer delivered a continuous series of chiliastic messages.[74] Many other Catholic Reformation apparitions combined elements of the Medieval and modern-type visions in a variety of ways.

A number of visions took the form of dreams in which the visionary was told to search for a sacred place where he or she would be cured. In other cases, the dreamer was told to establish a chapel or votive marker at some designated spot, sometimes in fulfillment of a forgotten vow. Often the seer responded to instructions received in the dream by using personal funds to raise a chapel at the revealed site, by building a chapel with his own labor, or, if very poor, by simply attaching a picture to a tree. Pilgrimages to these sites began after miracles were reported. Usually the seer revealed his or her dream or other vision only after the pilgrims had begun coming. Visions of this type were most common in the Germanies, particularly Austria, possibly indicating a Germanic cultural predisposition to the dream vision as opposed to an apparition per se. However, because this type of vision was most common during the Catholic Reformation period when vision reports were viewed with rigorous skepticism in some parts of Europe and were sometimes brutally suppressed by the Inquisition in Spain, the dream-vision account may also be interpreted as a way for the seer to do what he or she believed the Virgin had requested and at the same time circumvent potential punishment from the authorities. A story from a seventeenth-century shrine at Heiligwasser in the Austrian Tirol is especially revealing. Here, in 1606, Mary is said to have appeared to two young boys and showed them where to find their lost cows. She asked that a chapel be erected by the spring where the cattle were found, but the boys were afraid to say anything about their experience. Many years later, in 1651, one of the seers built a chapel by the spring. After the man's mute child began to speak, the farmer told the story of his youthful vision.[75]

Although the Virgin Mary appeared in most Catholic Reformation visions, several cult-formative visions involved other holy persons, including Saint Anne in Brittany and Christ or the Christ Child in several other places. Perhaps the most important Christ-centered visions were experienced by a French nun at Paray-le-Monial between 1673 and 1690. These eventually led to the formation of the widespread cultus of the Sacred Heart of Christ. Paray-le-Monial has been a major center of pilgrimage since the seer's canonization in the nineteenth century. Similarly, the establishment of the Sacred Heart cultus in Spain originated with Christ's appearance to a priest at Valladolid in 1773.[76]

Adult males made a slight comeback as seers during the Catholic Reformation, accounting for 58 percent of the cases. Men and boys combined account for 62 percent of the visionaries, whereas women and girls make up 29 percent. The majority of these, however, were adult women. About 9 percent of the visions were beheld by priests, monks, and nuns. Three percent of the seers were nobles, and 56 percent were persons of humble status. The proportion of definitely middle-class seers rose to 23 percent, and many of the unclassified seers were probably of middle-rank social status.

Modern Vision Shrines, 1780 to 1980

During the nineteenth century a series of extremely influential, ecclesiastically accepted Marian apparitions occurred in France. These began with visions to a nun in a Paris convent at Rue-de-Bac in 1832, followed by reports from a boy and girl who were herding cattle at La Salette in the Alps near Gap. They reached a crescendo with the 1858 visions of Bernadette Soubirous at a grotto near Lourdes on the edge of the French Pyrenees. Other church-approved nineteenth- and twentieth-century Marian apparitional shrine centers include Pontmain, France; Banneux and Beauraing, Belgium; Knock, Ireland; and Fátima, Portugal.[77] Shrines at these places draw pilgrims from beyond the countries where they are found, and even beyond the boundaries of Western Europe. The fame and continued social importance of the Lourdes visions are attested to by the numerous secondary Lourdes shrines in other parts of Europe, the Americas, the Philippines, Africa, and India, as well as by the approximately 4.5 million pilgrims and tourists from all over the world who visit the French shrine each year. The 1917 Fátima apparitions and the cryptic messages delivered by one of the visionaries have been particularly influential in the development of popular piety in the twentieth century. Numerous secondary Fátima shrines are scattered around the world, and "Fátima Day" pilgrimages occur at many older Marian shrines on the thirteenth day of each month between May and October.

At a number of other places, apparitions led to the establishment of shrines that are ecclesiastically tolerated but not officially approved. French examples include Saint-Bauzille-de-la-Sylve where a winegrower saw Mary in 1873, Pellevoisin where a convent layworker experienced apparitions in 1876, and Kerizinen, Brittany, where a farmwife reported numerous visions between 1938 and 1965. A late-blooming shepherds' cycle vision occurred at Orans in 1803 when some young girls walking to church saw Mary in white, surrounded by angels in the branches of an oak tree by a spring. A small statue was found hidden in the tree branches.[78]

Austrians and Germans continued to have dream visions of various kinds, as well as occasional apparitions. At Dolina, Austria, a shrine developed after three shepherd children reported seeing Mary with the Christ Child in 1849; another came into being at Mettenbuch, Bavaria, after Mary appeared to a boy and four girls in 1876. Cultus is permitted and even encouraged at Pfaffenhofen, Bavaria, where a young woman encountered Mary in a woodland in 1946 while helping the local priest and his sister find a good site for the construction of a votive chapel promised by the priest during World War II.

Of the several shrine-formative apparitions in nineteenth- and twentieth-century Italy, probably the best known is at Tre Fontane near Rome where Mary appeared to a boy and his father in a cave that had been an early Christian place of worship. As a result of the visions, the father, a Seventh-Day Adventist, was converted and numerous cures have been reported.

In other cases—as at Collevalenza and San Vittorino, Italy; Braga, Portugal; and Schönstatt, West Germany—great modern shrines have developed without any need for ecclesiastical pronouncements on the possible validity of vision reports. In all of these cases, the visionary was a priest, monk, or nun, and apparently knew better than to make much of an issue of his or her mystical experiences. At such shrines, the vision is officially downplayed and generally referred to in shrine literature as "a moment of inspiration" or some other vague generalization. Of course, the pilgrims at some of these places talk constantly about the apparitions, often embellishing their tales with the kinds of details from which legends are made.[79]

Other reports of visions have been ecclesiastically disapproved, but have led to the development of major pilgrimages despite official attempts to stem the tide of devotees by such procedures as forbidding the celebration of Mass at the sites and prohibiting the erection of consecrated churches. Examples of such unaccepted, but nevertheless active, shrines are found at San Damiano near Piacenza, Italy; San Sebastián de Garabandal in northern Spain; and Heroldsbach in the West German Diocese of Bamberg. The messages delivered by the seers at several of these places can be interpreted as Marian denouncements of modern church policies. This, of course, reduces the likelihood of a more tolerant official attitude in the future and, at the same time, attracts conservative Catholics alarmed by the reforms of Vatican II.[80]

Of 47 nineteenth- and twentieth-century visions that have led to the formation of pilgrimage centers, whether approved or not, all but one were primarily Marian. The exception is Collevalenza, Italy, where pilgrim stories, although not shrine literature, tell of a special relationship between the Spanish nun who established the shrine in the 1950s and the Christ Child, who is said to have visited with her frequently and told her where to drill for water. The deep well, brought forth by modern drilling equipment at the nun's order, is considered highly curative. This shrine was the first place visited outside of Rome by Pope John Paul II after the attempt on his life in 1981. Only three stories involved the finding of images, and, except in Austria, apparitions per se were much more common than dream visions.

At least 14 of the Marian apparitions of the past two centuries are fully modern according to the Turners' criteria, at least if one allows for the appearance of angels in one or more of a series of visions, as at the disapproved shrines of Garabandal and San Damiano. Thus, although this type of vision was at least 400 years old by the time of the famous nineteenth-century French epiphanies at La Salette and Lourdes, it accounts for a higher proportion of modern visions than was the case during Renaissance and Catholic Reformation times. It is also interesting to note that, although the sites of visions giving rise to pilgrimages are rather evenly distributed across the subcontinent, all but two of the officially approved apparitional shrines are in France and the French-speaking region of Belgium.

Some Significant Aspects of Modern Visions

Perhaps the most striking difference between nineteenth- and twentieth-century visions and those of previous ages is a marked reversal in age and sex patterns as females and children emerged as the most common seers (tables 7-14, 7-15). Only 22 percent of the visions giving rise to pilgrimages during the past 200 years were beheld exclusively by males. Six of these seers were priests or monks, one was a boy, and one of the other three cult-formative visions involved an experience shared by a man and his young son. Sixty-three percent of the visionary experiences were exclusively female. Additionally, in the six cases of apparitions seen by boys and girls, the primary conveyors of the message were usually the girls, bringing the modern female predominance to 76 percent of the cases, and the female, child, and male-religious domination of the visionary experience to a near-monopolistic

Table 7-14 *Temporal Distribution of the Sex of Seers*

Time Period	Boys	Men	Total Males	Girls	Women	Total Females	Children	Mixed Group
Early Christian (N=19)	—	74%	74%	—	—	—	—	26%
Early Medieval (N=31)	6%	65	71	6%	13%	19%	—	10
High Medieval (N=92)	7	74	81	12	4	16	—	3
Renaissance (N=100)	12	52	64	17	13	30	1	5
Post-Reformation (N=144)	4	58	62	12	17	29	2	7
Modern (N=45)	2	20	22	27	36	63	13	2

Table 7-15 *Temporal Distribution of the Social Status of Seers*

	Social Status				
Time Period	Clerics	Nobles	Middle Class	Poor	Mixed or Unclassified
Early Christian	67%	5%	—	5%	23%
Early Medieval	14	32	—	46	7
High Medieval	15	13	3%	58	11
Renaissance	6	4	14	66	11
Post-Reformation	9	3	23	56	9
Modern	18	—	27	49	8

91 percent. This shift toward female and male-religious persons as the predominant seers marks a decided change from the past.

The modern emphasis on female seers might be viewed as the culmination of a trend that began with the Renaissance shift toward acceptance of visions beheld by girls and women, and it appears to reflect a change in social attitudes toward the reliability and importance of an ordinary female's testimony. Particularly important in this respect is the increasing number of married laywomen and widows of nonnoble status whose visions resulted in the founding of shrines after about 1400. If an increasing credibility assigned to female testimony were an adequate explanation in itself, however, only about half of the modern seers should be female. It seems likely that the marked nineteenth- and twentieth-century change in the frequency of female and child seers is related to a "feminization" of the Roman Catholic church in Europe, or a tendency for women in cooperation with priests and monks to keep the religion vital in an age where most men pursue predominantly secular objectives.

Despite an emphasis in the literature on poor peasant children, only half of the modern visions were beheld by persons of clearly poor or humble status. Over one-quarter were from the middle class, and 18 percent were priests, monks, or nuns, the highest percentage of religious seers since the turn of the twelfth century. These changes in the sex, age, and social status of seers whose visions were socially accepted provides some support for the Turners' thesis that the "postindustrial" age of pilgrimage is qualitatively different from cult formations in earlier times.

The Continuation of Shrine Establishment

The relative sparsity of modern vision shrines reflects the difficulties involved in establishing pilgrimages at sites of newly reported visions rather than any contemporary lack of visionary experiences. Two Belgian apparitions during the 1930s led to officially approved shrines. A few others reported since 1930 have gained ecclesiastical toleration, and some are visited by pilgrims in spite of clerical disapproval. Many apparition reports have failed to give rise to enduring pilgrimages, although most have attracted attention and drawn large crowds for a period of time.

In an analysis of 236 reports of apparitions that have occurred in Europe since 1931, Christian found a strong concentration of 112 cases between 1947 and 1954, for an average of about 14 vision reports per year.[81] Between 1955 and 1975, at least 59 apparitions attracted public attention. Forty-one percent of the reports since 1931 are from Italy, 16 percent from Spain, 12 percent from France, and 8 percent from West Germany. As Christian pointed out, these twentieth-century visions attracted attention because they fulfilled an age-old need for the specification of sacred places.[82] Many of these contemporary events have failed to prompt the establishment of enduring shrines, but others have become socially significant centers of religious activity. The apparition site at Medjugorje, Yugoslavia, for example, promises to become one of the major pilgrimage centers of the late twentieth century.

The dynamic process of identifying holy places continues. People believe they have seen holy persons. Objects, both found and acquired, are attributed with special religious significance. A seemingly wondrous thing happens, the faithful interpret it as evidence of divine intervention, and a fertile bed is laid for the growth of a new pilgrimage shrine.

eight

Location

and Environment

Shrines as Holy Places

Christian pilgrimage in continental Western Europe developed from a desire to be near holy persons who were believed to be especially present on earth in those places where their physical remains were entombed. As Peter Brown expresses this idea, the early pilgrims were "not merely going to a place; they were going to a place to meet a person."[1] Through time, the emphasis on relics was expanded to include images, but the basic idea of visiting a particular place in order to commune more intimately with a holy person remained essentially intact. This Christian emphasis on persons symbolized by objects was, however, superimposed on a much older tradition of pilgrimage to places that were holy in their own right, often because some natural feature such as a height, water source, or grotto was considered to have especially sacred power.

Early Christians on the Continent are thought to have avoided pagan holy places. Churchmen decried the ancient notion that natural site features were sacred, although the old traditions were never fully repressed. But in the Irish Celtic tradition, the ancient holy sites were accepted and Christianized from the beginning as fifth-century missionaries, including Saint Patrick, baptized holy wells and mountain heights in the name of the new religion. Gradually Continental resistance to old traditions of site sanctity were modified in a syncretism of Christian and pagan ideals. The factors leading to this synthesis were numerous. The eastward travels of Irish and British missionaries during the sixth through eighth centuries clearly played a role, as did the association of Syrian and Egyptian holy men with remote sites such as mountain heights, grottoes, and vast deserts. These holy hermits, venerated during their lifetimes, were usually buried at the places sanctified by their presence, and their tombs continued to draw pilgrims.[2] The intransigence of country people, who refused to give up pilgrimages to the places they had long considered holy, must also have been a factor, especially as missionaries spread the new religion both beyond the bonds of Roman influence and into the never fully Romanized backcountry regions of the former empire.

By at least the sixth century, Christian ideas about shrine location, which emphasized particular sites as holy through sanctification by the saints, converged on Romanized Western Europe from both east and west. Meanwhile, invasions and general chaos encouraged churchmen to remove the bones of the holy dead from their urban-edge tombs to the relative safety of the central city churches. This relocation of holy relics tended in continental Europe to urbanize pilgrimage and further detach it from specific place associations over the short run. Once the principal of holy object mobility was accepted, however, the object could, theoretically, be venerated anywhere. With the addition of miraculous images, any place could become a pilgrimage shrine given the proper set of circumstances.

As a result, shrine location in continental Europe can be conceptualized as evolving from efforts to find a resolution between two conflicting ideals concerning the proper location of cult objects. On the one hand, such objects should be venerated in a central place so as to bring the greatest good to the largest number of people. Traditionally, possession of a very miraculous object increased a city's importance, and even today may continue to generate income through pilgrimage and religious tourism. On the other hand, there are strong feelings that a holy object should be in a place of somewhat difficult access that is removed from the contamination of everyday life. Reports of apparitions generally include instructions on where the shrine should be built, and many votive and devotional shrines seem to have been built before or simultaneously with the acquisition of an image. But the problem of where to develop shrines remained, as it still does.[3]

In most cases the tension between the conflicting ideals of centrality and peripherality and/or remoteness has been resolved through compromise. As an example, literature from Brittany describing the establishment of a World War I memorial shrine pointed out that some of the founders felt the memorial should be built in the regional capital, whereas others felt it should be placed on top of the region's highest mountain. It was eventually decided that the city was too secular to be suitable, and that the mountaintop would be too difficult to reach and provided little in the way of space or facilities for large gatherings. After much deliberation, the preestablished shrine village of Sainte-Anne-d'Auray was chosen as the most suitable site. As a result, the war memorial is not really a separate shrine, but one of the several features that make up the religious complex of Brittany's greatest pilgrimage center.[4] In one way or another, similar compromises have been reached through the ages. About three-fourths of Europe's shrines are located in places that are neither highly central nor extremely remote.

Certain types of cult-formative legends, usually too fantastic to be taken seriously as reasons for specific shrine locations, make a great deal of sense if interpreted as folkways for explaining why shrines are sometimes found in places that seem "illogical" from a purely practical point of view. The model of economically rational human behavior in space did, after all, evolve as part of the European tradition. Some way needed to be found to express the reasons why "rational" human desires to build a shrine in or near a settlement were overwhelmed by manifestations of divine will indicating that the shrine should be more remote. The legends take various forms, but the basic theme is that people tried to establish veneration of an object in a village or town until a series of mysterious events convinced them that the shrine should be built in the countryside. In the most common version, an image that is "found" is taken to the discoverer's community, but mysteriously disappears only to reappear at the site where it was found. Usually this is said to happen three times, at which point the local people decide to build a church at the site where the image was found, even though the location may pose unusually difficult problems of construction and access. In another version, common in Austria and Bavaria, people begin building a church in the village, but a series of accidents injure or kill some workers. Subsequently, birds pick up bloody shingles in their beaks and fly with them to a remote mountain height, thus indicating that this is the proper site for the shrine church. Such stories are told by Austrian villagers today as straightforward explanations of why a pilgrimage church is located in a place of difficult access. Indeed, these stories are sometimes told rather apologetically with a shrug, indicating that it was not the fault of humans that the place is so hard to reach.

Occasionally, a shrine story indicates that human will prevailed. In one fascinating example from Sankt Kanzian, Austria, an image of Christ, which washed up on the bank of the Danube after a flood, is said to have been taken to the town church. True to form, it disappeared and was found again on the stream bank. In this case, however, the local priest sought advice from the abbot of a nearby monastery who said that the image should be carried to the parish church by 12 virgin girls dressed in white. According to tradition, this was done. The image stayed in the town church where it later became famous when it reportedly shed blood.

At present, the shrines of Europe are found in nearly every conceivable kind of place from city centers to remote country sites unreached by roads even in the late twentieth century (Figure 8-1). Shrine churches snuggle between shops on busy streets. They are found on mountaintops, on spires of rock, and inside dank caverns. They cling to the sides of sheer cliffs, nestle in narrow valleys, lie hidden in dense forests, and rise above grain fields on fertile plains. Some mark the sites of villages abandoned long ago and of ruined monasteries and castles. For each shrine located in a truly spectacular natural setting with sacred qualities attached to several natural site features, there are many others that draw pilgrims to nondescript places often marked by no special environmental features. Well over 2,000 shrines lie within villages, towns, and cities, and about 143 are found in cathedrals, which, because they are urban bishops' churches, represent the ultimate in ecclesiastical centrality. There is, however, a tendency for shrines to be somewhat peripheral to human settlements, either on the edge of town or some distance beyond.

Location Relative to Communities

Most shrines are associated with communities and are either located in these communities or near them. The locations of the 3,248 shrines for which relevant details were recorded suggest that only about 8 percent of modern Europe's shrines are located more than 10 kilometers by road or path from a settlement.[5] Some of these are monastic establishments with a resident population of religious. The other 92 percent are located in or within 10 kilometers of communities of various sizes. This is, to some extent, a function of population density because in many parts of Europe almost any place more than 10 kilometers from one settlement is within 10 kilometers of another. About 18 percent of the shrines are located in or near cities of 25,000 or more, and another 18 percent are related to large towns with populations of 5,000 to 24,000. Nearly one-quarter are associated with small towns of 1,000 to just under 5,000 people, and one-third are found in or near villages with fewer than 1,000 inhabitants.

Shrines vary in their spatial relationships to their communities. Some, like Notre-Dame de Paris and the shrine of the Three Kings in Cologne, are found in cathedrals that are located in the centers of large cities. Others are down-

Location and Environment 295

Figure 8-1 *At La Sainte-Baume in southern France, ancient buildings form the facade of a church in a cave where legend says Saint Mary Magdalene lived in penitence for 33 years. The forest on the talus slope at the foot of the cliff facing north is composed of a mix of tree species not found elsewhere in France south of the latitudes of Paris. This sacred grove, never touched by an ax, is now administered by the French Forestry Service. Pilgrims leave small stones along the forest path as they climb to the shrine church where water dripping from the dank walls is considered curative. On the heights above, a small chapel marks the spot where angels are said to have flown the saint for her evening meditations. In few other places have so many different types of environmental features been endowed with sacred qualities.*

town but not in cathedral churches, and many are scattered throughout the city, sometimes in affluent residential areas and sometimes in industrial districts and poor neighborhoods. Altogether, about 40 percent of the shrines are located within the built-up areas of their variously sized shrine communities, although not necessarily in the community's central district. Some of these pilgrimage centers were once on the edge of communities that have grown since the shrine was established. The Mariahilf shrine in the Koblenz suburb of Lutzel, for example, was originally established as a votive offering by a traveler who barely escaped being murdered by robbers in what was then a very lonely area. Today, the shrine is surrounded by an expanded urban zone and devotees hear the hum of traffic along the nearby freeway. About 13 percent of the shrines are currently located on the edge of town or within a kilometer of the community's outskirts (Figure 8-2). Nearly half are more than a kilometer from their settlements, although, as previously mentioned, relatively few are more than 10 kilometers from a community.

There is a definite relationship between the size of the shrine community and the probability that the shrine will be some distance from it. Of the shrines associated with cities, only 21 percent are located a kilometer or more from the edge of settlement, probably because modern cities have grown to or around most of the shrines originally on or near their edges. Shrines related to towns are more likely to be located a kilometer or more from the community edge. The proportion of shrines well outside the town is 43 percent for large towns and 42 percent for small towns. Of the shrines associated with villages, more than half are located a kilometer or more from the edge of the community (Figure 8-3).

In a modern age, road access is good for the majority of pilgrimage centers. Over 60 percent can be closely approached via major paved highways, although a short drive up an access road or the sometimes more difficult negotiation of city traffic is often necessary once the motor traveler leaves the highway. At some places, the visitor must walk the final route to the shrine, but this is usually an easy hike taking no more than 10 to 30 minutes. About one-third of the shrines require a journey of 15 kilometers or more on back roads after leaving a main highway. These back roads are usually paved but often narrow and, in mountainous country, winding to serpentine. As with shrines just off main highways, the visitor must sometimes travel the final stage of the journey on foot. Actual distance is a poor measure of the rigors of such approaches because some footpaths are easy walks while others involve precipitous climbs. In some cases, the distance from the nearest community

Location and Environment

Figure 8-2 An edge-of-settlement location presently characterizes about 13 percent of Europe's shrines. In many cases, as here at Saint Mary and Saint Valentine's church on the edge of Worms, West Germany, urban growth has reduced the distance between the shrine and the city. Many former urban-edge shrines have been engulfed by city expansion, while others, originally in the countryside, have formed the nucleus around which sizable communities have developed.

to the shrine is less than 10 kilometers by footpath, but considerably farther by a winding mountain road.

Several important shrines with difficult or nonexistent road access can be reached by cable car or cog railway as at Montallegro near Rapallo, Italy, and Nuria in the eastern Pyrenees of Spain. Some shrines, especially in Germanic lands, have restricted-use roads leading directly to the shrine church door. These are used to bring supplies to the shrine complex and to transport old, sick, or handicapped pilgrims who could not otherwise reach the holy place.

A substantial proportion of Europe's shrines can be closely approached by train, and modern pilgrims frequently cover a considerable portion of the distance from home to a distant shrine by air, particularly in the case of pilgrimage centers in or near major cities. At least two great shrine centers, at Lourdes, France, and Knock, Ireland, are served by international airports far

Figure 8-3 *A Portuguese romería center near Paredes de Viadores marks the gathering point for people of a district of small villages and dispersed rural residences. As in this case, more than half of the shrines predominantly associated with villages lie at least one kilometer from the edge of the nearest settlement. The pilgrims in the foreground are returning to the shrine church from a lonely hilltop where an apparition is said to have occurred long ago. The chapel was built in its present down-slope position in the nineteenth century to better accommodate the large numbers of devotees from the district and is somewhat closer to the paved road that now connects settlements than to the summit made sacred by the apparition.*

larger than would be warranted were it not for the pilgrim traffic. Only about 6 percent of the shrines are of truly difficult access, meaning that they can only be reached via a hike or climb taking an hour or more at a brisk pace.

The distance of shrines from major population centers provides another indicator of accessibility. Urban and urban-fringe shrines are usually easy to reach via public transportation. About 27 percent of the shrines sampled are either located in cities of at least 25,000 people or are within 10 kilometers of such settlements, often in an outlying town or suburb. Nearly half, or about 47 percent, are within 25 kilometers of a city, and 71 percent are within 50 kilometers of a large settlement. Distance to a city is of little importance if the shrine is visited only by people from the surrounding countryside. Many countryside shrines, however, draw pilgrims and other visitors from urban centers, and, in a modern age, a journey of 50 kilometers by car or bus on good roads represents less than an hour of driving time once one has gotten out of city traffic. Such shrines are thus within easy day-trip distance of sizable population concentrations.

Central versus Remote Shrines

Because shrines range from fully central to extremely remote, with most falling somewhere in between, it is useful to compare the characteristics of central and remote pilgrimage places. For this purpose, central shrines were defined as those located within the built-up area of a city with a population of 25,000 or more. Remote shrines were defined as those located more than 50 kilometers from a city and either associated with a village of fewer than 1,000 people or located 10 kilometers or more from a settlement of any size. Irish cases were excluded because of the divergent characteristics of Irish shrines in general and the fact that an unusually high proportion of that island's pilgrimage places qualified as "remote" by the above-mentioned specifications. Thus, the following discussion pertains only to Continental shrines.

Central shrines proved considerably more likely to be of major importance than remote shrines. Thirty-four percent of the central shrines draw large numbers of pilgrims from extensive catchment basins, as compared with 16 percent of the remote shrines. About 13 percent of the central shrines are in cathedrals as compared with none of the remote shrines. There was little difference in the proportions of shrines at monastic centers. Seventeen percent of the urban shrines and 15 percent of the remote shrines are located at convents or monasteries. Nonresident monks and friars, however, tend some of the remote shrines. These were not counted as monastic centers, so the connection between remote shrines and religious orders is greater than appears in the figures.

Differences in primary devotional subject focus are minor, although remote shrines are somewhat more likely to be dedicated to the Virgin Mary than are central shrines. Twenty-two percent of the urban shrines focus on a relic as compared with only 4 percent of the remote shrines. A saint's corporal relic is nearly six times as likely to be venerated in an urban shrine than at a shrine in the remote countryside. In addition, the urban relic shrines are often saints' tombs as contrasted with the fragmentary relics sometimes found at remote shrines. A relic of Christ's Passion is fifteen times more likely to be housed in a central city church than in a remote place, and relics of hair, cloth, or milk associated with the Virgin Mary are also far more likely to be located in central than remote places.

Even when Irish shrines are not included, 6 percent of the remote shrines have no cult object other than an environmental feature. This was true for 4 percent of the urban shrines. Images are by far the most prevalent type of cult object at remote shrines, but black or very dark images are twice as prevalent at central shrines. Byzantine icons, actually or reportedly brought from the Eastern Mediterranean, are also more likely to be venerated at urban shrines.

Obviously, the pull of centrality has been greatest in the case of very powerful cult objects. This pattern is confirmed by the varied frequencies of certain types of origin stories at shrines representing the extremes of the central-remote continuum. Central shrines are considerably more likely to have cult-formative stories involving the acquisition of holy objects, whereas stories of object discovery are more often associated with remote shrines. Urban shrines are somewhat more likely to be sites of special religious significance, usually involving the earthly activities or deaths and burials of saints, or to have come into being as purely devotional creations. Remote shrines have higher proportions of formation stories involving votive establishments and apparitions. Cult-formative miracles involving the bleeding or oozing of an object already at the site, however, are more common at central than remote shrines. Legends indicating that an object chose its place of veneration by returning to the place where it was found are twice as likely to be told at remote shrines. When all types of legends indicating divine intervention in the choice of shrine site are considered, remote shrines are about three times as likely to include such stories in their mystiques as urban shrines. This suggests a greater need to invoke heavenly powers in explaining the location of a remote shrine than is the case for a central shrine.

Urban shrines sometimes have sacred environmental features, as at Marseille, and Lyon where ancient Christian shrines top heights that have been considered sacred for several millennia. In general, however, remote shrines are more likely to have special connections to a feature of their sites. Fewer than 30 percent of the central shrines are marked by any special landscape feature with sacred connotations, as compared with about 56 percent of the remote shrines. The ratio of shrines with three or more different types of natural sacred site features is three to one in favor of the remote shrines.

Data on cult-formative periods suggest that higher-than-usual proportions of remote shrines in continental Europe date from Early Medieval and Post-Reformation times. Central shrines are relatively more likely to date from Early Christian, Renaissance, and Modern times. The proportions of central and remote shrines are the same for those established during the High Middle Ages. Nearly three times as many remote shrines appear to have been holy places in pre-Christian times than is the case for central shrines. Had the Irish cases been included, the relationship between remoteness and pre-Christian associations would have been considerably greater.

Contemporary Shrines at Pre-Christian Holy Sites

In a modern world, the idea of place sanctity reaching back through the millennia to times before Christianity spread throughout Europe has popular appeal. Whether the evidence is archaeological, historical, or largely speculative and based on traditional lore or wishful thinking, pre-Christian sanctity of place is generally seen as a positive value to be promoted rather than skimmed over or denied. Descriptions of such famous shrines as Italy's Monte Sant'Angelo, France's La Sainte-Baume, and Ireland's Croagh Patrick stress the ancient sanctity of their locations, and there is some speculation that the famous Massabielle Grotto at Lourdes was once sacred to pagans.

In this context, it is surprising how few of Europe's active shrines are likely to have been pilgrimage sites or religious centers in pre-Christian times. We found only 259 examples, making up little more than 4 percent of the shrines inventoried. At most of these places, archaeological or archival evidence supports the notion of pre-Christian sanctity. Other places are characterized by the survival of pagan festival dates that do not correspond closely with the usual dates of Christian celebration, by unusual customs that were common in pagan times but rarely survived as Christian traditions, and by other indirect evidence supporting assumptions of pre-Christian place sanctity. Claims for pre-Christian antiquity based only on the presence of venerated site features other than megalithic monuments or sanctified stones from pagan temples were not counted. Also excluded were the claims based on the supposition that if the place is holy now it must have been sacred long before.

The shrines most likely to be pre-Christian are scattered throughout Europe, although with an uneven distribution. Thirty percent are found in Germanic lands where they are especially concentrated in Austria. The French region claims 25 percent with a fairly even distribution; there are about the same number in the south as in the north. France has the highest proportion of presumably pre-Christian shrines found on the Continent. Ireland, with 15 percent of the 259 once-pagan holy places, has an unusually high proportion of its shrines at presumed pre-Christian sacred sites. These shrines are found in most parts of the island, although they tend to be concentrated in the west. Iberia, with many more shrines, also claims 15 percent of the pre-Christian holy sites, mostly located in the hills of northern Portugal and southern Galicia. Possibly the period of Islamic domination disassociated most shrines elsewhere in Iberia from any lingering tradition of pagan antiquity. Archaeological work might reveal a larger number of Iberian shrine sites with pre-Christian associations. Italy, with only 13 percent of the cases, represents something of a curiosity. Perhaps here, to a greater extent than elsewhere, early churchmen were successful in uprooting loyalty to the sacred sites of the pagans.

As a group, currently active shrines with a probable pre-Christian heritage of place sanctity have certain characteristics setting them apart from other shrines (Table 8-1). As might be expected, most of these shrines are of considerable antiquity as places of Christian pilgrimage. More than half seem to have become centers of Christian pilgrimage prior to the turn of the twelfth century, and more than three-quarters drew Christian pilgrims by the end of the High Middle Ages, or 1399. This antiquity helps explain the greater-than-usual proportions of saints as primary devotional subjects. As a consequence, the focus on female as opposed to male devotional subjects is less pronounced than at other shrines. Some of the originally pre-Christian shrines now dedicated to Mary are popularly thought to have been sites of pagan mother-goddess veneration, with most of these cases reported from France and Italy.

A fairly widespread misconception that many current shrines have pre-Christian associations probably relates to the tendency of such pilgrimage centers to be fairly important. Shrines with a probable pre-Christian heritage are twice as likely to be major centers of contemporary pilgrimage than is the case with other places of pilgrimage. They are more than three times as likely to be counted among the great shrines of modern Western European Christendom.

Twenty-three percent of the shrines with a certain or probable pre-Christian sanctity have no especially venerated relics or images. In addition, they are notable for their tendency to be associated with sacred site features. More than 80 percent are characterized by one or more sacred features of site as compared with about one-third of the other shrines. Neither figure takes into account the shrines for which information was too meager to make any judgment about the presence or absence of such site features. If a shrine now visited by pilgrims has three or more different types of sacred site features, such as a mountain cave by a curative spring or a sacred tree hanging over a holy well by a sacred stone, the probability is twelve to one that additional evidence proves or strongly suggests that the place was holy before the advent of Christianity in the region. There is a difference, however, between pre-Christian shrines and other environmentally based shrines in the types of site features most frequently sanctified. The pre-Christian shrines are considerably more likely to have holy water features or sacred stones than are other shrines with site features, and they are slightly more often found to be associated with caves. They are less often found on high places and considerably less likely to be associated with tree or grove cultus.

Environmental Site Features

The creation of national parks and nature reserves throughout Europe indicates an awareness of a symbiotic relationship between humans and the natural environment. Nature, often defined today in terms of natural ecosystems, is increasingly viewed as important in its own right. In addition, the idea that urban humanity needs to escape periodically into natural settings for inspiration and recreation is proclaimed in many languages. Some writers have argued that an ecological crisis is imminent due to a Judeo-Christian disdain for a nature for which pagans supposedly held greater respect.[6] Yet, as part of the Christian pilgrimage tradition, a sense of awe—even a veneration—of certain natural features has run as a thread through European thought and action for centuries. This theme is apparent in the numerous places of pilgrimage associated with such natural environmental features as heights, water, trees, stones, and caves. Much has been written about the presumed symbolism of various natural landscape features—the cave as earth's womb, water as the life force, the sacred tree connecting heaven and earth, and so forth. Our discussion is restricted to the patterns inherent in our data; it leaves interpretations of how our findings may fit into symbolic analysis to experts in the field.[7]

Between 33 and 42 percent of Europe's current shrines are associated with environmental features accorded a certain aura of sanctity. The more informa-

Table 8-1 *Characteristics of Shrines with Pre-Christian Associations as Holy Places (N = 259, or 4.2 Percent of Inventoried Shrines)*

Distribution by Region			
Region	Pre-Christian Associated Shrines	Percent of All Pre-Christian Associated Shrines	Percent of All Shrines in Each Region
Italian	34	13	3
French	65	25	6
Iberian	38	15	3
German	77	30	4
British	6	2	7
Irish	39	15	29
Total	259	100	

Devotional Subjects of Pre-Christian Associated Shrines			
Subject	Pre-Christian Associated Shrines N	%	Percent of All Shrines Devoted to Each Subject
Mary	133	51	3
Christ	11	4	2
Saints	108	42	7
No subject	7	3	7
Total	259	100	

Time Period of Christianization of 214 Dated Cases			
Time Period	Pre-Christian Associated Shrines N	%	Percent of All Shrines from Each Period
Early Christian	66	31	27
Early Medieval	50	23	12
High Medieval	47	22	5
Renaissance	14	7	2
Post-Reformation	25	12	2
Modern	12	6	4
Total	214	101	

Location and Environment 305

Table 8-1 (continued)

Frequency of Site Features at Pre-Christian Associated Shrines

Site Feature Frequency	Pre-Christian Associated Shrines N	%	Percent of All Shrines with Site Features
One or more	211	82	10
Two or more	96	37	24
Three or more	31	12	34
Four or more	9	3	82

Specific Site Features at Pre-Christian Associated Shrines

Site Feature	Presence at Pre-Christian Associated Shrines N	%	Percent of All Occurrences of Site Features at All Shrines
Height	89	29	9
Water	108	36	15
Tree	25	8	2
Stone	52	17	25
Cave	30	10	15
Total	304	100	

Types of Cult Objects at Pre-Christian Associated Shrines

Object	Presence at Pre-Christian Associated Shrines N	%	Percent of All Occurrences of All Objects at All Shrines
Image	154	70	4
Relic	17	8	4
No object	50	23	18
Total	221	101	

tion available on a shrine, the more likely it is that our inventory will include mention of a sacred site feature. Thus, while one-third of all shrines inventoried clearly have, or at least once had, such features, the proportion rises to 38 percent of the shrines assigned to periods of formation and 42 percent of those for which formative stories were recorded. Forty-eight percent of the major shrines have site feature associations, as compared with 36 percent of those minor shrines for which detailed information was obtained. Twenty percent of the 2,022 environmentally based shrines identified have two or more types of sacred site features, and 5 percent have three or more different kinds of features.

Of the several types of environmental features that tend to acquire special sanctity, the most common is height, followed by water. Trees, sites where miracle trees once grew, and sacred groves are the next most common as a general tree-focused category. Sacred stones and natural caves or grottoes are the least common types of site features considered in our analysis (Table 8-2). Heights and water features often stand alone as sacred aspects of environment, whereas a majority of caves and sacred stones are found in association with other features.

Christianization of environmental features revered by the pagans seems to have occurred, at least sporadically, in many parts of Europe. This phenomenon was soon transformed into processes whereby previously nonsacred environmental features were made especially holy in the Christian tradition. There is no need to speculate from legends or historical accounts as to how this process occurred. It is still happening. For example, in the early 1960s a sickly middle-aged woman living in the hamlet of San Damiano, near Piacenza in Italy's Po Valley, experienced a vision of the Virgin Mary. The apparition took place in or near a pear tree behind Mama Rosa's substantial stone farmstead. Although it was mid-winter, the pear tree was in full bloom. Cynical informants in Piacenza point out that pear and other fruit trees displayed unseasonably early blooms that year throughout the region, but this is not especially relevant from the viewpoint of a cult-formative tradition because only one such tree was simultaneously associated with an apparitional experience. Wondrous events have their own logic; perhaps all the other Po Valley pear trees bloomed in honor of the apparition tree. Any effort to suggest to believers in this manifestation that unusual weather conditions might be the best explanation for the early bloom could be countered with the argument that Heaven prepared the Po Valley for Mama Rosa's vision by making the winter unusually mild.

Near the pear tree was a backyard well. In her vision, Mama Rosa was

Table 8-2 Characteristics of Shrines with Sacred Environmental Site Features

Frequency of Site Features

Sacred Features per Shrine	Shrines with Features N	%
Four or more	11	›1
Three or more	91	5
Two or more	403	20
One or more	2,022	100

Representation of Site Feature Shrines in the Inventory

Shrine	Number	Percent of Inventory	Percent of Cases with Adequate Data
Shrines with site features	2,022	33	40
Shrines without site features	2,978	48	60
Subtotal	5,000	81	100
Cases with insufficient data	1,150	19	
Total	6,150	100	

Types of Site Features

Site Feature	Frequency of Occurrence	Percent of All Site Features	Percent of Environmentally Based Shrines with Features
Height	963	38	48
Water	712	28	35
Tree or grove	433	17	21
Stone	207	8	10
Cave or grotto	195	8	10
Total	2,510		

instructed to drink from this well, and the water proved curative. Soon the curious and the faithful flocked to the visionary's backyard in search of similar manifestations, and by 1980 an estimated 80,000 pilgrims were coming each year. The charismatic woman continued to have visions on a weekly basis. For nearly two decades, she stared at the sun as it hovered over the pear tree each Friday at noon, claiming to see the Virgin Mary, who was sometimes accompanied by rings of angels around the sun. The messages conveyed by Mama Rosa were mostly of a highly conservative nature, except for instructions that Mary wanted pilgrims to photograph the noonday sun in a search for visual revelations (Figure 8-4).

The official church position regarding the growing cultus was predictable. It was disapproved by the bishop of Piacenza. No church was to be built, and no Masses were to be offered at the site, although prayers and rosary devotions were tolerated if led by laypersons. Meanwhile, Mama Rosa sought support for acceptance of her visionary experiences by visiting Padre Pio, the stigmatized Capuchin priest who resided in the monastery at San Giovanni Rotondo hundreds of miles away in the Gargano Peninsula of southeastern Italy. According to an American priest at the monastery, Padre Pio commented that "the woman is seeing something, but it's not the Mother of God." The priest added, "The Mother of God has got better things to do than appear to that old woman every Friday at noon!" Nevertheless, literature from San Damiano implies that Padre Pio believed in Mama Rosa's visions, and a bronze statue of the holy man stands by the wall of the farmstead near the pear tree and the well.

When we visited San Damiano in October 1980 and in the spring of 1981, the tiny village boasted a shop that sold religious items, a well-stocked grocery and sundries store, and at least two small inns. The back walls of Mama Rosa's farmstead were covered with votive plaques in many languages, including several in Japanese. The well water had been piped to a long line of spigots above a trough where it was being collected in a variety of containers ranging from wine bottles to plastic jugs. Pilgrims chanted the rosary as they walked in groups along paths laid out in the backyard orchard. A sanctum, enclosed by a low wrought-iron fence, contained the miracle tree and a simple white statue of the Virgin Mary as a young woman. Around the pear tree were dozens of containers holding freshly cut roses. As the flowers wilted, they were taken from the fenced area by volunteer workers who carefully preserved the petals. These were dried and ground to make the base for a curative tea, which supposedly was most effective if brewed with water from the well. The carefully guarded tree was unscathed, and only the workers

Figure 8-4 At San Damiano, Italy, pilgrims photograph the sun each Friday at noon, hoping to record some of the signs that the visionary, Mama Rosa, claimed to see. Photos characterized by lens flare or circles around the sun are highly prized and are passed around among pilgrims traveling to shrines all over Europe. A tendency to accept Mama Rosa's unusual instructions to look at and photograph the noonday sun may be influenced by the famous "miracle of the sun" seen by large numbers of people at Fátima, Portugal, in 1917.

were allowed access to the fenced area. Women volunteers were required to wear modest dresses, as well as scarfs or other coverings on their heads, when they entered.

According to Italian newspaper accounts, Mama Rosa willed about $4 million to Pope John Paul II when she died in late 1981, but the bequest was rejected. We thought it unlikely that this officially unrecognized shrine would long survive the visionary's death; but when we returned in August 1983, a hospice had been established by a group of religious, and a small campground had been developed for the benefit of pilgrims with tents or caravans. Should this place enjoy long-term survival as a pilgrimage center, which is likely only if it eventually becomes acceptable within the context of mainstream Catholicism, devotional activities will undoubtedly continue to focus on the miraculous water and on the special pear tree, so long as it lives. When, in the course of events, the tree dies of natural causes, or is sacrificed so that a chapel can be erected on the apparition site, several things are possible. A new pear tree might be planted, ideally a descendant through seed or sprout from the original tree. An image of Mary might be carved from the tree's wood and replace the current white statue as the primary cult focus. If left natural, and the wood darkened with age, it could become a "dark image." Should the cultus become important enough to generate daughter shrines, perhaps the pear wood might yield several statues to be shipped to these new pilgrimage centers. If the tree should be sacrificed to make way for a chapel, it is possible that a piece of its wood might be enshrined in a reliquary within the chapel. All these things have happened before in the case of miracle trees.

Distribution of Environmentally Based Shrines

Shrines with sacred site features are found throughout those parts of Europe where pilgrimage thrives, and the greatest concentrations are in areas with many shrines. In Ireland, at least 90 percent of the pilgrimage places are characterized by venerated natural features, and here such features play an especially important role in the pilgrims' activities. Continental countries with the highest proportions of shrines with sacred site features are Austria, Italy, and France, in that order (Table 8-3).

There are some notable regional differences in predilections for particular types of sacred site features. Of the environmentally based shrines in Europe, 62 percent of those in Iberia, 52 percent in Italy, 46 percent in West Germany, and 45 percent in France are associated with height. In contrast, only 13 percent of the environmentally related shrines in Ireland have high place associations. Also in marked contrast, sacred water is found at most of the Irish and British shrines having site features, but, on the average, at only about one-third of the Continental shrines. The lowest proportion of environmentally based shrines with water features is found in the Italian region, where only about one-fifth of these shrines are related to water. Iberia also has a below-average proportion of environmentally based shrines with water features. That the two regions of Western Europe, which have, on the average, the driest climates, also have the lowest proportion of shrines with sacred water is something of an anomaly, suggesting that Christian veneration of water is not directly related to a shortage of water resources.

Location and Environment 311

Table 8-3 Regional Distribution of Site Features

Region	Shrines with Site Features		Distribution of Site Features among Shrines[a]									
			Height		Water		Tree		Stone		Cave	
	N	%[b]	N	%[c]	N	%[c]	N	%[c]	N	%[c]	N	%[c]
Italian	461	38	242	52	99	21	87	19	38	8	72	16
French	389	34	174	45	137	35	80	21	26	7	37	10
Iberian	346	26	213	62	103	30	58	17	25	7	49	14
German	681	32	311	46	249	37	189	28	56	8	31	5
Irish	121	90	16	13	104	86	14	12	60	50	4	3
British	24	28	7	29	20	83	5	21	2	8	2	8
Total	2,022	33[d]	963	48[e]	712	35[e]	433	21[e]	207	10[e]	195	10[e]

[a]Several shrines have multiple site features (see Table 8-2).
[b]Percentage of site feature shrines among all shrines of each region.
[c]Percentage of each region's site feature shrines having each feature.
[d]Percentage of all shrines that have one or more site features.
[e]Percentage of all site feature shrines that have the feature.

Tree and grove-related cultus is encountered at Germanic shrines considerably more often than elsewhere and is least common in Ireland. When a sacred tree is mentioned in regard to an Irish shrine, however, it is usually present at the site. Elsewhere, it is more likely that the association is with a place where there once was a sacred or miraculous tree. Stones are at least five times as likely to be found at Irish shrines than in any single Continental region, while caves are especially favored as site features in the Mediterranean peninsular regions, followed by France.

It is tempting to speculate about lingering shadows of varied pagan traditions. Areas with high proportions of water and stone cultus correspond roughly with regions where ancient Celtic traditions survived well into Christian times. Caves and heights, particularly important in pagan Greco-Roman religious orientations, are concentrated in the most fully Romanized parts of Europe. The temptation to make a connection between ancient Teutonic tree and grove cultus and the high frequencies of tree-related cultus in Germanic lands is difficult to resist, although neither time period data nor legends provide much support for the supposition.[8]

Another way of looking at these macro-regional variations is to point out that high frequencies of specific types of site features seem to reflect a relative abundance of particular features available to be sanctified. Thus, the cavern-dotted regions along the Mediterranean have more than a usual proportion of sacred caves. Predominantly mountainous and hilly regions, with a few exceptions such as Switzerland, have relatively high percentages of shrines on high places. Water-focused shrines are proportionately most common in well-watered areas, while cultus related to trees and groves is most frequently encountered in Germanic lands which have long had a high percentage of land under forest cover as compared with the rest of Europe. Sanctity attributed to stones, which in our inventory included megalithic monuments left by ancient peoples, is decidedly the most common in areas where there are many curious stones.

At a very high level of generalization, the pattern holds for all types of site features. It thus seems appropriate to argue that the more common a particular type of environmental feature is in a given region, the more likely it is that disproportionately large numbers of such features will be sanctified as compared with regions where the features in question are less abundant. If a connection between varied pagan traditions and frequencies of certain site features could be more firmly established, one might add that this "rule" has characterized the endowment of specific site features with holiness for a very long time.

The proposed model leaves ample room for the notion of a human propensity toward sanctification of an environmental feature that is considered to be unique. It may be that hills rising above areas that are generally flat, or caves in regions with few caverns, are more likely to have been considered holy than similar landscape features in areas where these are more common. Detailed information on specific numbers of distinct landforms throughout Europe would be necessary to test this hypothesis, which might best be attempted at the regional level. In addition, some quality of uniqueness of a particular hill, stone, or cave often seems to be part of the reason why a particular site feature was endowed with sanctity in a region where such features are common.

Formative Period and Environmental Features

As a general rule, the environmentally based shrines appear to be older than average (Table 8-4). Although the overall proportion of dated shrines with environmental associations is 38 percent, 63 percent of the surviving holy places established in Early Christian times have at least one venerated site feature, and 43 percent of these have two or more such features. Many of these shrines are in Ireland; but even on the Continent, the proportion of Early Christian shrines with site features is higher than average

Table 8-4 *Formative Periods of Environmentally Based Shrines*

Time Period	Datable Shrines with Site Features N	%[b]	Distribution of Site Features Among Shrines[a]									
			Height N	%[c]	Water N	%[c]	Tree N	%[c]	Stone N	%[c]	Cave N	%
Early Christian	157	63	48	31	97	62	23	15	69	44	11	7
Early Medieval	165	41	82	50	58	35	25	15	22	13	27	16
High Medieval	357	40	168	47	115	32	95	27	29	8	41	11
Renaissance	201	32	91	45	67	33	60	30	15	7	17	8
Post-Reformation	488	37	227	47	141	29	139	28	22	5	32	7
Modern	171	30	79	46	46	27	34	20	11	6	10	6

Temporal Distribution of Site Features among All Datable Shrines

Site Feature	Time Periods					
	Early Christian %[d]	Early Medieval %[d]	High Medieval %[d]	Renaissance %[d]	Post-Reformation %[d]	Modern %[d]
Height	19	20	19	15	17	14
Water	39	14	13	11	11	12
Tree	9	6	11	10	11	6
Stone	28	5	3	2	2	2
Cave	4	7	5	3	2	2

[a]Several shrines have multiple site features (see Table 8-2).
[b]Percentage of site feature shrines among all shrines founded in each time period.
[c]Percentage of each time period's site feature shrines having each feature.
[d]Percentages of all shrines in each time period having each site feature.

at 44 percent of the cases. About 40 percent of the shrines founded in Medieval times have sacred features of site. The proportion drops to 32 percent for Renaissance shrines, rises slightly to 37 percent during the Post-Reformation period, and drops to a low of 30 percent for pilgrimage centers established since 1779.

The data do not necessarily indicate a trend toward deemphasis of the sanctity of natural features. Shrines firmly rooted in environmentally based sanctity of place may have had greater potential longevity than others. If this is the case, higher proportions of shrines with sacred site features should be found among those that are older. This is probably the most logical explanation for the relatively large proportion of ancient Continental shrines that are associated with heights, water, caves, and stones, assuming that historians have correctly interpreted Early Christian attitudes toward pagan holy places as highly negative. The surviving ancient site feature shrines certainly indicate that a Christian aversion to places sacred to pagans was not universal on the Continent.

Water and stones are the site features most often found at environmentally based shrines that presumably became Christian pilgrimage centers prior to the turn of the eighth century, with 62 percent associated with water and 44 percent with stones. The 31 percent located on holy heights is low compared to later periods. Patterns of specific site feature emphasis shift considerably when shrines established between 700 and 1099 are considered. Half of the site feature oriented shrines from this period are on heights while the proportion with sacred water features drops to slightly over one-third. Sanctification of stones declines to 13 percent. Most interesting is the association of 16 percent of these shrines with caves or grottoes. This represents a higher proportion of shrines with this type of site feature than for the earlier or later periods and very likely is related to a propensity for holy hermits to retreat to caves and grottoes during this period.

Environmentally based shrines dating from the High Medieval period show patterns of individual site feature focus that resemble those found at shrines of later periods. Most interesting is the increase in the number of shrine stories indicating tree cultus from 15 percent for shrines of earlier times to 27 percent. Tree associations continue to rise among the environmentally based shrines of later periods, reaching a high point of 30 percent of Renaissance shrines but declining to 20 percent in Modern times.

The same general pattern is obvious when the percentage of different site features found at shrines from each period is calculated. Shrines dating from the Post-Reformation period have close to the same proportions of different types of site features as those dating from the Renaissance and High Medieval periods. Those established after 1780, which are somewhat less likely to have environmental associations than those from earlier periods, show a decrease in the tendency to sanctify trees.

Environmentally Based Shrines and Subjects of Devotion

Shrines dedicated to Mary and the saints are almost equally likely to have sacred environmental features. These are found at 34 percent of the Marian shrines and 33 percent of the saints' shrines. Less than one-quarter of the shrines that focus primarily on Christ are characterized by a sacred environmental feature. Because most shrines could be classified by devotional subject, the actual proportion of site feature associations with each category of holy personage is probably somewhat higher.

The associations between subjects of devotion and an emphasis on particular site features vary considerably (Table 8-5). The relatively small proportions of Christ-centered shrines with site feature associations are on high places 60 percent of the time. Environmentally based Marian shrines are less likely to be on high places than are those dedicated to Christ, but considerably more likely to be on heights than those dedicated to the saints. In contrast, saints' shrines are much more often related to sacred water features than are shrines dedicated to either Mary or Christ. Tree cultus appears to be especially Marian. Over one-quarter of the Marian shrines with one or more environmental associations have stories related to miraculous trees or groves, as compared with 16 percent of the shrines where Christ is the primary devotional subject and only 12 percent of the saints' shrines. Associations between Mary and trees are usually tree-specific, and the particular plant has rarely survived—often, if the past can be judged from the present, because it was rapidly reduced to splinters by eager pilgrims. In these cases, unless there is some other type of site feature, the shrine can be considered environmentally based only in the sense that it is said to have been built on the site where there once was, or supposedly was, a very special tree. In contrast, stories from saints' shrines associated with trees and groves tend to place less emphasis on any particular tree and are more often characterized by an existing tree, its descendant, or a forest or grove that is considered holy.

Saints' shrines are more than twice as likely to have sacred stones than are Marian shrines, largely reflecting a strong Irish emphasis on both saints and stones. In actual numbers of cases, there are sacred stones at a few more Marian shrines than at shrines now dedicated to saints. Natural caves and grottoes are found at the environmentally based shrines of Mary, Christ, and the saints in near-equal proportions, although with more than twice as many at Marian shrines than at the smaller number of saints' shrines. A considerable number of the Marian shrines connected to grottoes are places where the

Table 8-5 *Devotional Subject Focus of Environmentally Based Shrines*

Subject	Shrines with Site Features N	%[b]	Distribution of Site Features among Shrines[a]									
			Height N	%[c]	Water N	%[c]	Tree N	%[c]	Stone N	%[c]	Cave N	%[c]
Mary	1,370	34	675	50	398	29	354	26	98	7	127	9
Christ	99	22	59	60	27	27	16	16	8	8	8	8
Saints	526	33	219	42	272	52	63	12	96	18	60	10
No subject	23	23	10	43	15	65	—		5	22	—	
Total	2,022	33	963	48	712	28	433	21	207	10	195	10

Distribution of Site Features Among Devotional Subject Shrines

Subject	Height	Water	Tree	Stone	Cave
Mary	17%	10%	9%	2%	3%
Christ	13	6	4	2	2
Saints	14	17	4	6	4

[a] Several shrines have multiple site features (see Table 8-2).
[b] Percentage of site feature shrines among all shrines with each subject focus.
[c] Percentage of each subject's devotional shrines having each site feature.

cult-formative story credits the rise of Marian devotions at the site because the cave was supposedly the residence of a holy hermit. Some of these stories suggest that the hermit's devotion to the Virgin inspired people in the area to seek her aid at the grotto. Others refer to the discovery of an image, presumed to be the hermit's prized devotional object.

Another way of examining the data is to consider the proportions of different types of site features at all shrines dedicated to different holy persons rather than just those with environmental features. These figures indicate that Marian shrines, in general, are more likely to be on high places than those dedicated to Christ or the saints and are more than twice as likely to be associated with a tree mystique. Shrines where saints are the devotional subjects are the most likely to have cultus focusing on water or stones and slightly more likely to have sacred caves or grottoes. If Irish cases were excluded, the pattern would shift toward a somewhat greater resemblance between Marian shrines and saints' shrines in the proportions of various types of site features; but even when Continental shrines alone are considered, those devoted to the saints still are most likely to have water, stones, and caves.

Location and Environment 317

These are the same types of site features more frequently found at pre-Christian holy places than at other shrines.

Site Features and Shrine-Formative Stories

Forty-two percent of the shrines for which origin stories were recorded have environmental site feature associations. The degree and type of focus vary considerably with the type of story (Table 8-6). Sixty percent of the shrines where cultus is said to have begun with the discovery of a relic or image have site feature associations with a special emphasis on trees. Indeed, although shrines with found object stories make up only 18 percent of the cases, they account for 40 percent of the trees and groves found at shrines with origin stories. Shrines with found object stories are also more likely to be associated with caves or grottoes than those with other types of formative accounts.

Shrines at significant sites and those with accounts of apparitions are also well above average in their focus on site features, at 49 percent and 48 percent respectively. Apparitional shrines are more likely to be associated with heights and trees, whereas significant site shrines are more commonly marked by water, stones, and caves. Votive and devotional shrines have a greater-than-usual propensity to be located on high places. They are considerably less likely to be associated with other types of site features than are shrines with most other kinds of stories. Thirty-six percent of the shrines with formative stories classified as spontaneous miracles have site feature associations. Water, often directly involved in the miracle account, is the most frequently encountered site feature at these shrines, although nearly as many are associated with heights and trees.

Shrines with stories of holy object acquisition are the least likely to have any kind of sanctity attached to an environmental feature. When there is such an association it is usually a high place location, and the height generally gains its sanctity from the fact that the object is there enshrined.

The above generalizations obscure the fact that there are several different kinds of holy heights, waters, trees, stones, and caves, each with particular kinds of significance to modern pilgrims. These variations within each general category of site feature type are considered in the following sections.

Table 8-6 *Origin Stories of Environmentally Based Shrines*

Type of Origin Story	Origin Story Shrines with Site Features		Distribution of Site Features among Shrines								
			Height		Water		Tree		Stone		Cave	
	N	%	N	%	N	%	N	%	N	%	N	%
Significant site (N=542)	266	49	94	35	136	51	41	15	72	27	43	16
Ex-voto (N=600)	219	37	118	54	63	29	45	21	11	5	12	5
Devotional (N=161)	65	40	35	54	10	15	9	14	2	3	5	8
Miracle (N=459)	166	36	66	40	67	40	59	36	16	10	7	4
Acquired object (N=454)	104	23	70	67	26	25	12	12	7	7	7	7
Found object (N=563)	338	60	102	30	107	32	148	44	30	9	52	15
Apparitional (N=347)	167	48	84	50	63	38	56	34	18	11	19	11

Types of Holy High Places

Heights are the landscape feature most commonly associated with pilgrimage shrines. These range from dramatic mountains to low hills in areas of gentle relief. There is no single type of high place location with sacral connotations. Some shrines are true high point holy places crowning the summit of the highest elevation in the visible landscape, as at Sion, France; Monte Sant'Angelo, Italy; or Peña de Francia, Spain. Isolated hills or mountains are especially favored sites for high point shrine location. Other shrines, on or near summits, are adjacent to much higher mountains. At Locherboden near Stams, Austria, for example, the shrine church rises above a cavern on a range of alpine foothills, but is overshadowed by much higher mountains beyond (Figure 8-5). Abrupt rock spikes, which tend to be dramatic features in the landscape, are fairly often endowed with special sanctity, especially if they loom over a settlement.

Shrines are seldom found on summits rising more than 3,000 feet above adjacent lowlands, and the vertical relief between high shrines and lower settlements is usually much less. Sacred heights in a countryside with gentle

Location and Environment 319

Figure 8-5 *The shrine church of Maria Locherboden rises near the crest of a line of foothills in the Austrian Tirol. The exact site of this church was determined by the location of a cave just below the church where a votive image became associated with miracles in the eighteenth century.*

relief generally rise only a few hundred feet above the surrounding landscape. Extremely high, rugged mountain peaks, such as the Zugspitze in the Bavarian Alps, may be topped by crosses, but have not been developed as shrine sites. This may reflect a certain practicality. Until the development of cable-car technology, Europe's highest peaks were essentially unreachable except by skilled mountaineers. The development of technical climbing and sophisticated mountaineering is of fairly recent origin, although pilgrims have long taken risks in approaching precipitous holy places.

A majority of high place shrines are located on slopes rather than summits. Often the sanctuary is about one-third the way to the top of the rise, particularly in areas with high vertical relief. Other shrines are on mountain spurs extending outward into the lowlands from higher ridges and summits. Many slope and ridge shrines hover protectively above valley settlements, their high place symbolism related more toward guardianship of the faithful below than a reach for the heavens. Indeed, shrines are often positioned in much the same kinds of sites traditionally chosen for building castles and watchtowers, and a substantial number are located at the sites of fortified high places ranging from ancient Celtic hill forts to Medieval castle ruins. Some were castle chapels that became places of pilgrimage as the result of a past event often involving salvation from enemy attack. Shrine position part way up a slope may also be dictated by the presence of some other site feature. Forty-four percent of the shrines with sacred grottoes, for example, are located on heights, as are 27 percent of the sacred stones and 18 percent of the holy water features. These include a number of summit springs that are regarded as especially marvelous.

Some pilgrimage centers are more appropriately thought of as high elevation rather than high place shrines. La Salette in France, Oropa in Italy, and Nuria in Spain are examples of famous sanctuaries located high in the mountains above zones of regular human habitation. The main structures, however, are set on terraces or in protected valleys shadowed by higher peaks. Remoteness from settlement appears to be an important symbolism attached to these high holy places.

At many high place shrines, the height seems to acquire its sanctity from a combination with another site feature or simply from the presence of the shrine. In such cases, the height is sacred only in a very general way. There are also, however, holy mountains sacred in and of themselves. These include Ireland's Croagh Patrick (Figure 8-6), the Bavarian hill covered with the structures of Kloster Andechs, and the sacred hill above Guimarães, Portugal.

One of the most interesting cults related to high places is a kind of ancient, sacral "peak-bagging" celebrated as the Four Mountain pilgrimage in southern Austria. Pilgrims must complete the full circuit of a climb to chapels topping the heights of four steep hills within a 24-hour period, beginning in the dark of night and ending at midnight the next evening. The distance that must be covered between the hills is considerable, so the effort is something of an athletic feat. The pilgrimage is thought to have pre-Christian origins, and, according to tradition, the year in which no pilgrim accomplishes the task on the specified date will mark the end of the world.[9]

The sanctity of high places is complex and multivariate, apparently differing from shrine to shrine and probably, in the aggregate, from region to region. The mystiques that appear to be most important at present include the comfort of feeling guarded by a sacred persona looking down from a specific place above, the sense of journey beyond the mundane world gained

Location and Environment 321

Figure 8-6 *The often-clouded heights of Croagh Patrick, Ireland, are thought to have been sacred to the pagan Celts. The entire mountain is considered holy in the Christian tradition in honor of Saint Patrick's legendary sojourn on its summit.*

by climbing to the shrine's heights, and the feeling of exhilaration, perhaps related to a sense of mastery and control, gained by the view out from the high place. In the case of district shrines, the pilgrim's visual experience on the high place during times of celebration probably reinforces the sense of being protected during ordinary days when the devotee looks up at the shrine church and remembers the scope of the view. For some pilgrims, the exertions of the climb take on a penitential dimension, especially in regions where vows to walk barefoot or climb on one's knees are still customary.

Sacred Water Features

Shrines with sacred water features are most concentrated in Austria, Brittany, and Ireland. Elsewhere the distribution of recorded cases is scattered. Over 90 percent of the sacred waters at shrines are water sources, either springs or wells (Figure 8-7). At many shrines, the water flows from spigots and it is not always possible to find out whether the water was originally a "spring" in the hydrological sense of water spouting forth from the

Figure 8-7 A small holy well at Our Lady's Island, County Wexford, Ireland, is embellished with a stone housing, flowers, a small statue of the Virgin, and the usual drinking cup. Most Irish "holy wells" are springs, which seem to be considerably more common as sacred site features than wells that have been dug or drilled. Taken together, wells and springs, or water sources, make up about 90 percent of the sacred water features at European shrines.

ground or a "well," technically meaning a hole dug to reach an aquifer. Most of the so-called Irish holy wells are actually springs. Throughout Europe, springs seem to predominate, but in some cases the sources of holy waters are technically wells, as at Collevalenza, Italy, where thermal water from a deep well drilled with modern equipment is considered to have curative properties.

It is not unusual for a shrine church to be built directly over a water source. At Wemding in Bavaria, for example, pilgrims drink from a miraculous fountain inside the Maria Brunnlein shrine church. Elsewhere, as at Maria Martental in West Germany's Eifel region near Cochem, a spring flows from beneath the church and winds down the narrow valley as a tiny rivulet. Pilgrimage may have been more strongly concentrated on water in the past than at present, because a number of shrine stories refer to a holy well or spring that has either dried up or is no longer a focus of pilgrim activity.

Occasionally, excavations have revealed water lying close below the ground surface under pilgrimage churches, providing support for legends suggesting that the site was originally marked by a sacred water source.

Sacred waters are used in numerous ways, mostly related to a search for cures. They may be drunk; used to wash sores, rashes, or injuries; or bathed in ritually as at Lourdes. Sacred water is often taken home, sometimes in large quantities, for future use and for the benefit of sick relatives or friends (Figure 8-8). Although the water at many shrines is regarded as generally curative, there is a particularly strong connection between sacred springs and the treatment of eye ailments. About 10 percent of the water sources are referred to as "eye wells," or recommended for eye problems, and nearly three-fourths of the shrines where eye cures are mentioned have sacred waters.[10]

Although shrines are often found on river banks, rivers are not generally considered sacred in the European tradition. Even the sources of such major rivers as the Rhine, the Rhône, and the Danube are not, at present, marked by centers of pilgrimage. The primary sources of a few minor rivers, such as the Reus in Spain, are sites of pilgrimage, and a few small streams are thought to have sacred qualities at specific spots along their banks. For example, there is a legend that the stream at the Marian shrine near Hart im Zillertal, Austria, was sanctified when Mary washed the Christ Child's diapers at the spot during the flight to Egypt. Similarly, water dipped from the river near Cuenca, Spain, at the site of a twelfth-century holy man's hermitage is known as the water of Saint Julian and is considered sacred. The same water apparently has no special qualities downstream, even where it flows past urban Cuenca's Marian shrine church.[11] A few shrines at river confluences seem to give a special quality to a meeting of the waters, and these, along with a few of the river bank shrines, sometimes have formative stories involving images that floated ashore. Despite these occasional associations between rivers and sanctity, European water cultus is clearly different from that of Hindu India where sacred rivers provide a principal focus for place sanctity.

Ireland has several holy lakes and lake islands, including the famous Lough Derg in County Donegal, and there are a few holy lakes in northern Italy and Austria. Elsewhere, however, lakes are rarely considered sacred. Sea and lake islands are most often regarded as sacred in the Irish and British traditions. Sea water is sacred in a few specific places, usually at particular times of the year. Ireland is noted for several spots where water in tide pools is considered especially curative, and there used to be such places in Scotland. At Playa de Lanzada on Spain's Galician coast, pilgrims wade into the water on the early morning of Saint John's Day to receive the "nine waves,"

Figure 8-8 *Pilgrims at Collevalenza, Italy, fill large containers with water pumped from a deep well that was drilled in the 1960s as the result of a Spanish nun's visionary experiences. The ancient and widespread custom of taking home water from shrines offers a means of distributing the curative efficacy of the shrine to the sick at home as well as maintaining a reserve supply against future personal needs. In some places, local people still collect water from shrine springs or wells to use for drinking water during periods when the regular village water sources are most likely to be contaminated.*

and at several places on the Mediterranean coast, including France's Saintes-Maries-de-la-Mer, images are carried into the sea in a Christianized version of an ancient Mediterranean ritual. Water that collects in stone hollows is thought to have especially curative properties at a number of shrines, particularly in Ireland and Austria (Figure 8-9).

Sacred Trees and Groves

Reports of cultus involving trees, groves, or forests, although proportionally most common at shrines in Germanic regions, are broadly distributed. Nearly three-fourths of the cases involve stories related to individual trees (Table 8-7). Occasionally, as at Tosters, Austria, a very old tree standing near the shrine church is considered to be the original "miracle" tree. Elsewhere, the venerated tree of the present is said to be a descendant of

Location and Environment 325

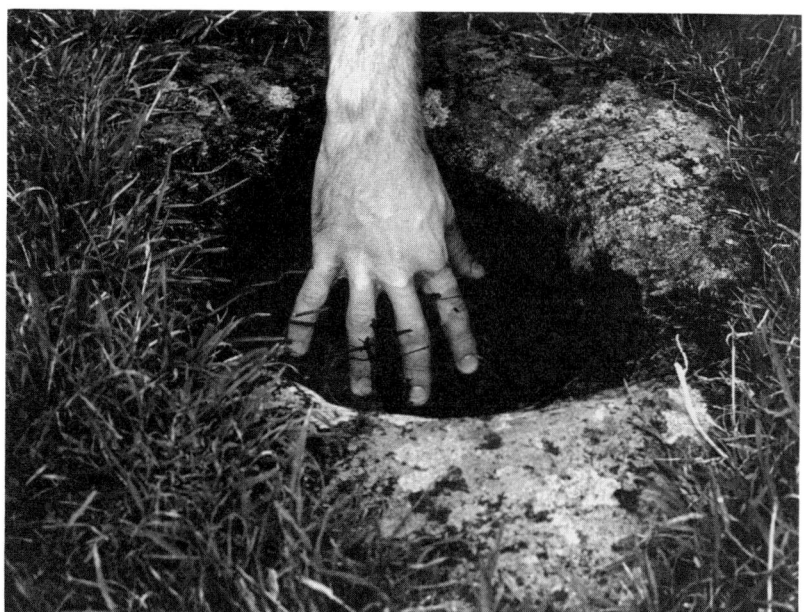

Figure 8-9 *The water that collects in this bowl-shaped stone at the Celtic monastic site of Clonmacnois, Ireland, is believed to cure warts. The stone appears to be an old mortar, and, due to its location near a structure that may once have served as an infirmary, may have been used to grind medicinal herbs. Special curative qualities are often attributed to water that fills hollows in sacred stones.*

an older sacred tree, especially in Ireland where the regeneration of new trees, particularly thorn trees, from the roots of older trees is an especially important part of tree-cultus mystique. The majority of shrines classified as having cultic associations with individual trees, however, are merely sites on or near which there is said to have once been a miraculous tree. What appears to be one of the oldest of the tree-related stories involves the theme of the sacred tree springing from a staff planted in the ground by an early saint. Such stories have been repeated at least as recently as the late seventeenth century. From a shrine near Celles, France, for example, comes a story of a local man whose claims to have seen the Virgin Mary were believed when he followed the Virgin's instructions and stuck his spade handle in the ground. According to tradition, the handle took root and sprouted three leaves.

The most common stories from tree-related shrines involve the finding of images in trees, apparitions associated with trees, and, particularly from Ger-

Table 8-7 *Variations among Tree and Grove Cultus and Types of Trees*

Category of Shrines	Number	Percent
Site is in a large grove or forest, which is part of the mystique of the shrine	116	27
Shrine story has an image found in a tree, originally venerated in a tree, or a tree-related apparition	264	61
Other wondrous events reported involving trees	35	8
Other cases where old trees on site are incorporated into shrine ritual	17	4
Totals	433	100

Type of Trees	Number	Percent
Oaks—All types	99	36
Thorns—Hawthorns most often named	26	9
Needleleaf evergreens—mostly firs and pines	24	9
Birch, Alder, Beech	15	5
Olives	14	5
Lindens	12	4
Elms	11	4
Chestnuts	9	3
Pears	7	3
Other trees mentioned up to five times each (apple, holly, fig, lime, pomegranate, larch, laurel maple, mulberry, willow, elder, poplar, yew, almond)	59	21
Total trees mentioned by type	276	99

manic regions, stories of images attached to trees or placed in tree hollows that eventually proved to have miraculous qualities (Figure 8-10). In stories of this kind, most of which come from shrines established since the fifteenth century, the tree acquires its miraculous attributes from association with the image or apparition. Often such trees, in those cases where there really was a tree rather than merely a legend about a tree, fail to survive the discovery of their miraculous qualities for very long. As is presently occurring at the 1960s' Marian apparitional shrine of San Sebastián de Garabandal, Spain, "miracle" trees are often killed by pilgrims collecting talismans.

Occasionally, a tree associated with a wondrous event survives long enough to become considered so sacred that stripping it of its bark, leaves, and other parts was, and is, considered a desecration that could bring misfortune upon the talisman seeker. This is especially likely to be the case if the tree is

Location and Environment 327

Figure 8-10 *Some shrines are associated with sacred groves or individual living trees, as at the Marian shrine of Sion in France's Lorraine region where pilgrims pay their respects to this image of Saint Marguerite of Lorraine displayed in a hollow tree. Much smaller statues in tiny hollows of thriving trees are fairly common and suggest that stories of woodcutters finding images inside felled trees are not improbable. Most tree cultus in Europe is related to the memory of trees in which the Virgin Mary is said to have appeared or on which an image is reported to have been found. Although trees associated with such wondrous events rarely long survive the discovery of their miraculous qualities, they still give the shrine a tie to a specific place originally marked by an environmental feature.*

reported to have done something unusual such as blooming out of season, putting forth new growth after a fire, or otherwise asserting its floral individuality. Even when protected, of course, trees have finite life spans. Forests, in contrast, can perpetuate themselves indefinitely unless destroyed by natural events, such as fire, or by human action. A considerable number of shrines with stories of tree-related miracles are located in wooded areas that provide an aura of forest mystique to the holy place and its pilgrimage.

In about 27 percent of the cases of tree cultus, the focus is on a grove, woodland, or forest rather than an individual tree, living or dead. Occasionally, as at La Sainte-Baume in southern France along with Camáldoli, Gréccio, and several other places associated with Medieval Italian saints, the forest is considered sacred in its own right, usually as a result of having been consecrated by a Christian saint. More often, the forest is attributed with a rather generalized aura of holiness stemming from the location of the shrine within it or beside it. The approach through the trees, or prayerful walks on woodland paths near the shrine, give the pilgrimage a special flavor, now often related to a respect for nature cast in the framework of ecological awareness. It is interesting to note that a number of sacred European forests are currently protected by national forestry services.

Irish shrines are the most likely to focus on groups of plants as opposed to individual trees, but the stands are often very small, perhaps a thicket of thorn trees by a spring-fed stream or a grove of oaks by a holy well. On the Continent, the highest proportions of generalized forest-grove cults as compared with tree-specific cults are in Italy (31 percent), France (30 percent), and West Germany (28 percent). The lowest proportions are in Spain (17 percent) and Austria (17 percent). Austria, of course, is a much more forested country than Spain and has a greater proportion of its shrines in wooded settings. What the two countries seem to share is a strong propensity to credit individual trees with special sanctity.

The particular trees or groves of trees to which sacred qualities have been attributed include a large number of types ranging from domesticated orchard varieties to wild trees of the forests. Of the shrines for which wondrous trees were identified by type, oaks predominate, comprising 99 of the 276 cases of named trees. No other single genus has anything close to so many reports of miraculous qualities. The French region leads with accounts of wondrous oaks with 34 percent of the cases, followed by Germanic Europe with 25 percent, and Italy with 19 percent. South of Scandinavia all European countries have stories involving sacred oaks. There are, of course, many oaks in Europe, as has been the case since climatic changes occurred toward the end of the Pleistocene, and this may partly account for the frequency with which the genus has been associated with wondrous events. Oaks seem to be preferred, however, even when other types of trees are present or even predominate. At Klein-Krötzenburg near Aschaffenburg, West Germany, for example, the shrine formation story indicates that two seventeenth-century shepherds saw lights and heard music in a beech grove for three nights in a row and heard a voice saying, "This is a holy place." On the fourth night one of the shepherds had a vision of a hollow oak tree, and, when he located the tree, found a low relief pietà in the hollow. The idea of a Christianized version of ancient cultus centered on oaks is certainly plausible.[12]

Reports of sacred thorn trees are also widespread, but only 26 references were found and these rarely mentioned the plant as anything other than a thorn. Hawthorn and dog rose trees were occasionally specified in France. Conifers account for 9 percent of the named trees, consisting of 15 firs, mostly in West Germany and Austria, and 9 widely scattered pines. Olives were referred to as miracle-related trees in 14 reports, all from the environmentally appropriate areas of Iberia and Italy. Lindens were mentioned in 12 cases, all from Germanic regions, and chestnuts in 9 cases, all Italian. Of the orchard trees, pears seem to have the greatest propensity to acquire miraculous qualities. Three reports were from Italy, 3 from West Germany, and 1 from Austria. In a story from Maria Birnbaum near Sielenbach, West Germany, the pear motif is intertwined with that of the oak. Supposedly a Marian image placed in a hollow oak during the early seventeenth century was removed and thrown away by Swedish soldiers during the Thirty Years' War. It was later found by a shepherd who placed it in a hollow pear tree. Then, in about 1659, an Austrian woman is said to have dreamed that she and her son would be cured if she could find an image of Mary in a pear tree. After searching all over Bavaria, she finally found the dream image at the place where the Maria Birnbaum shrine developed.

In addition to trees and groves, there are many other kinds of plant associations. Shrine-formative stories refer to brambles, rushes, grape vines, rosemary bushes, and various types of flowers, especially roses and lilies. Pilgrims bring plants of many kinds as offerings and, at some shrines, make a particular point of leaving with certain kinds of plants. The tendency to reduce miraculous trees to splinters has already been mentioned. Detailed studies of these relationships by scholars trained in the techniques of ethnobotany would make an interesting contribution to knowledge.[13]

Sacred Stones

Shrines with cultic rocks or stones are most numerous in Ireland and Austria and are distributed throughout these countries. Most of the few German examples are located toward the south near Austria. In Italy, stone cultus is most common in the central and southern parts of the peninsula far from the Austrian focal area. An Austrian type of stone cultus is found in Italy's Germanic northeastern region. Southern Italian stone cults focus on rocks associated with the discovery of images, including some that were found painted on stones. Stone cultus in Iberia appears to be a central-to-northern phenomenon. The French cases are concentrated in the Breton peninsula, along the Mediterranean, and in the western part of the Massif Central.

There are several different types of stone cultus. The most common, making up 36 percent of the examples recorded, are rocks with indentations. These are often referred to as "trace" stones, and the dents are usually explained as marks, or traces, left by a holy being during his or her reported wanderings through the area or by a heavenly person touching earth in apparitional form. Water from these hollows is considered especially sacred. The indentations, depending on their size and placement, are variously referred to as footprints, knee prints, or places where the saint sat or lay. The Irish discriminate between saints' chairs and beds and refer to stones with rounded hollows as "bullauns." In Austria, a distinction is often made between trace stones and bowl stones, the latter having a fairly large, rounded hollow generally filled with water and often explained "folkloricly" as places used by the Virgin Mary to bathe the infant Jesus during the Holy Family's fantastic journey from Bethlehem to Egypt via Austria. Most of these tales seem to date from about the seventeenth century when "Holy Family" cultus was important in southern Germanic lands. It would be interesting to attempt to trace the older stories such tales may have replaced.[14]

Although some of the indented stones are purely natural features, many are man-modified. These include old mortars where grain or medicinal herbs were ground. Others are graves cut into stone slabs, once covered over but long ago exposed to the elements as body-sized notches in the rocks. Trace stones are particularly common in Austria and other southern Germanic areas where they make up 55 percent of the recorded cases of cultic stones. Irish shrines often have several different kinds of cultic stones, and most with any kind of stone cultus have one or several types of trace stones. The only other area with more than a very small percentage of trace stones is Italy, with 22 percent of its stones so categorized. These are mostly found toward the center and north of the peninsula and represent a different tradition from that reflected by the image-related stones toward the south.

Christianized megalithic monuments make up 11 percent of the stones classified as sacred. Included are dolmens, isolated menhirs, stone circles, and other large stones placed by Europeans of approximately the third and second millennia B.C. It is generally assumed that religious concerns motivated the original creators of these man-modified, stone-embellished landscapes. Certainly, the stones were considered sacred by later peoples long before the Christian Era. French shrines, especially those in Brittany, have the largest proportion (27 percent) of sacred stones that are Christianized megaliths of various kinds. Ireland has the largest number of shrines with these types of stones and the second highest proportion. A few Christianized dolmens are reported from northwestern Iberia, and two curious standing stones are mentioned from Germanic Europe.

A varied assortment of curious, but presumably natural, rock features accounts for 18 percent of the reported cases of stone cultus. These show no special regional concentrations, suggesting that a strange-looking natural stone feature is about as likely to be credited with sanctity in one place as another. A variation on this theme is cultus related to small rocks. Sometimes these are pebbles picked up at the site or brought from other places and piled up as cairns.[15] In other places, certain types of small rocks found near the shrine are considered especially sacred and are taken home by pilgrims as talismans, good luck charms, or souvenirs. For example, beach pebbles with holes all the way through them are considered special when collected on the beaches of Holy Island off England's Northumbrian coast. Known as "Saint Cuthbert's beads," these pebbles are hard enough to find to make them special but plentiful enough to make the search worthwhile. In another example, rocks in the area around the shrine of Nuestra Señora de Inodejo near Las Fraguas in Old Castile contain fossils of sea creatures, some of which look like fossilized sand dollars. These are called the "Little Rocks of the Virgin" and are considered to have miraculous qualities. According to the local priest, one such rock has been recently associated with a cure.

A different kind of stone cultus, making up 14 percent of the cases, involves rocks that are thought to resemble a holy person (Figure 8-11) or that were associated with the discovery of an image—often because the miraculous image was reportedly found painted on the stone, cut into its surface, or carved out in low relief. In other stories, the image was described as having been found "in" the stone. Sometimes this means that the image was found in

Figure 8-11 *At the mountaintop shrine of Peña de Francia, Spain, a monk demonstrates the resemblance of a curious stone to the head and shoulders of a woman. According to tradition, this stone is considered a "natural" image of the Virgin Mary.*

a hollow or notch in the stone. In other cases, the "image" seems to have been a curious mineralized marking or quartzite deposit found inside a broken stone.[16] Stories relating stones to images have a strong spatial concentration in Mediterranean peninsular areas, accounting for 47 percent of the Italian cases and 39 percent of the Iberian examples of shrines with a stone cultus. This type of stone cultus is fairly common in Latin America, but it is rarely found in Europe north of the Mediterranean peninsulas.

Sixteen percent of the cultic stones are ruins of Roman temples, long-abandoned Christian structures, and, in Ireland, Celtic crosses. Shrine churches in and of themselves do not seem to be thought of as cult objects in the European tradition, but the ruins of such churches may, over time, acquire these qualities, with some tendency toward emphasis on stone ruins—the most likely to survive for long periods in the European climate. In Ireland, some of the hidden Mass Rocks of penal times have become focal points for district pilgrimages.

Sacred Caves and Grottoes

Shrines where sanctity is attached to caves and grottoes are most numerous in southern Europe. Most of those counted are natural landscape features, although we also included places where pilgrims are attracted to caves hollowed out in soft rock by holy hermits of long-past generations, such as those found at the Sacred Savior shrine near Schwäbisch-Gmünd, West Germany. Other man-made features with a cavelike mystique include the crypts or cellars of ruined churches or castles that appear to have begun attracting pilgrims after the superstructures above these foundation excavations crumbled. Churches were sometimes built over caverns; and, in these cases, the crypt of a pilgrimage church is a natural, although much man-modified, feature. At present, Europe's most famous sacred grotto is at Lourdes (Figure 8-12). Artificial grottoes commemorating the grotto of the Lourdes apparitions are virtually ubiquitous in many parts of predominantly Catholic regions. They are found at ordinary parish churches and numerous countryside chapels, by roadsides, and in the yards of private homes. The numerous Lourdes replicas were not included in our count of cave-related shrines except in the few cases where a natural cave or grotto has been converted into a particular devotional point as a subsidiary Lourdes shrine.

As is the case at Lourdes, few of Europe's sacred "caves" are very deep. A physical geographer would probably classify most of the natural features we have seen as shrine focal points as rock shelters rather than caves or caverns.

Figure 8-12 *Europe's most famous pilgrimage grotto is at Lourdes, France, where millions of pilgrims gather each year in the place made sacred by Saint Bernadette's visions of the Virgin Mary.*

Several are marked by very open entrances, as at Covadonga in northern Spain where Don Pelayo is said to have prayed in 718 after launching the first successful Christian counterattack against the Moslem invaders. Others, as at La Sainte-Baume, are fronted with man-made facades through which the pilgrim must pass to reach a church that is literally in a cave. Even when the cave extends, chamber after chamber, deep into the earth, the focal point for Christian cultus is usually the cavern's upper reaches, particularly the front chamber where one has the initial experience of leaving a world open to the sky. Only at Monte Sant'Angelo on Italy's Gargano Peninsula did we have an impression of moving very deeply into a cavern before encountering its most sacred point. Even there, it is a short distance compared to the explorative depths usually promoted by modern tours of deep caverns. The caves noted for Paleolithic art, several of which we visited years ago before they were closed to the public, involve journeys far deeper into the earth than is the case at most of Europe's cave-focused pilgrimage shrines.

Shrine stories suggest that many of today's sacred caves were places where holy hermits once lived. It is generally accepted that actual human residence, as opposed to ancient cultic practices and modern cavern explorations, has always been primarily in rock shelters, the front chambers of deeper caverns, or shelters burrowed into the earth by human beings. For the most part, then, modern Christian "cave" cultus is largely a grotto or rock shelter cultus, presumably more closely related to a need for shelter extrapolated symbolically into an idea of the sheltering earth than a mystique of penetration into the mysterious bowels of the earth.

Cultus Relating to Abandoned Villages and Churches

There seems to be a special mystique associated with places where people once lived and worshiped, but which were later abandoned for various reasons. Thus, many of the sacred caves were once the homes of saintly hermits, and the stones of ancient religious structures, pagan as well as Christian, sometimes acquire cultic status. Other shrines have been built at the sites of abandoned villages. Notre-Dame de Altbronn in Alsace, for example, is said to have been established in 1397 by order of the local bishop at the site of an eighth-century village that had been depopulated during the Black Death in 1348. A story from the Maria Egg shrine near Peiting, West Germany, tells of a seventeenth-century dream that led the seer to a site where he found an abandoned cemetery full of the bones of people who presumably had died in the mid-fourteenth-century epidemic of bubonic plague.

Stories involving the discovery of miraculous images sometimes specify the location as the site of an abandoned village, chapel, or monastery—fairly likely places for images to be found, one would suppose. One story, from the shrine of Nuestra Señora de Codes in Spain's Navarre Province, begins with the description of a monastery located at the site from the tenth through thirteenth centuries. A village seems to have remained for a time after the monastery was abandoned; after 1310, however, the village is no longer mentioned in old records, so the population presumably died out or moved elsewhere. Sometime later an image of Mary, of thirteenth-century date, is said to have been found in a chapel hidden in an undergrowth of thorn bushes.[17]

A substantial proportion of Irish and British shrines are marked by the ruins of former pilgrimage churches and monastic establishments destroyed during the Reformation, and in many parts of Europe shrines have developed or become revitalized at the sites of monasteries forced to close during the eighteenth and nineteenth centuries. At Lich north of Frankfurt, West Germany, for example, the Cistercian monastery of Kloster Arnsburg fell into ruins after its closure in 1803. Although not formerly a pilgrimage site, the monastic ruins now attract refugees from Hungary, the Sudetenland, and other Communist areas. These pilgrims gather every other year in a memorial garden by the ruins where they hear Mass in the open air and pray for friends, relatives, and their departed ancestors whose tombs lie in their lost homelands.[18]

Holy Places in a Modern Age

There is no universal rule for the most suitable kind of holy place in modern European Christendom. Although locations peripheral to the mainstreams of urban commerce seem to be valued in a general way, several of the most important pilgrimage goals have long been located in the midst of large cities with no apparent loss of sanctity. New urban shrines have developed within the past few decades. Remoteness gives an aura of special mystique to certain shrines; but in a modern age, few European pilgrimage places are very remote from human settlements in terms of either distance from cities or difficulty of access. In the mountainous regions of Catholic Austria, large-scale map plotting shows lines of shrines that follow the main transportation routes through the glacially carved valleys. Many of these are located on foothills or alpine slopes, but they are seldom far from the routes of modern highways, very rarely on the summits of the higher ridges, and never on the highest peaks. The virtually uninhabited mountainous regions of this country are as devoid of shrines as of people. Elsewhere in Europe, the pattern is similar, although harder to see due to less dramatic terrain or variations introduced by such cultural complexities as strong Protestant influences or highly secularized populations in some subregions. In general, shrines may not be proportionally concentrated in the areas where there are the most people, but they are rarely far from places where there are either a fair number of humans in residence or in transit from one place to another.

Centrality, in the form of an urban location, is especially valued in the case of certain kinds of very powerful holy objects. This is particularly true when the object was acquired from another place and has no intrinsic connection with the countryside of the region where it is kept for veneration. In such cases, sacred features of site may be more or less incidental, and indeed are infrequently found at shrines with acquired holy objects. In other cases, the urban shrine is associated with a special event in the life of a saint, a report of a weeping, bleeding, or crying image, or some other manifestation of divinity reported to have happened in the city.

The fairly common connection between ex-voto and devotional shrines and heights overlooking a community or a series of settlements suggests a preference for a slightly distant location that people can look up toward and feel protected. Stories indicating that people deliberately chose the site for the pilgrimage church or chapel often reflect the ideal of a shrine that is neither too close to the mainstream of urban influences nor too remote to be reached with practicality. Some of these stories connect locational decisions with an event—the height where people fled to escape enemy attack, the chapel where they prayed for the end of a plague, or the first spot on the coast sighted by fog-bound sailors.

Connections between a shrine's location and sacred environmental associations are often specified in formative stories describing the discovery of objects. Many of these stories are legends, but they make sense as attempts to explain the remoteness of shrines in terms of an "event" that indicated divine instructions as to where the shrine should be established.

The event theme appears repeatedly in Christian pilgrimage lore.[19] A place often becomes especially holy because it is believed to have been touched by divinity, usually as manifest by events related to holy persons during their lifetimes or as a result of their heavenly intervention. In accounts of apparitions, the holy person is thought of as actually coming to earth, often primarily to indicate where a shrine should be established. Such events presumably have occurred in all kinds of places and have happened to all kinds of people for centuries, as they still do. Whether or not the "event" reported is believed to indicate a manifestation of divine will, and becomes a place of enduring pilgrimage, is related to a subsequent interplay of numerous factors—political, economic, and social-psychological. The charisma, believability, and influence of personalities are involved and are highly apparent in many of the more recent shrine-formative stories.

The event theme also helps explain why there can be no single rule for the most appropriate shrine location. If a place is marked as especially sacred through a manifestation of divinity, interpreted as an event, and if, as in the modern Christian tradition, it is assumed that divinity is everywhere present, or at least potentially present, then shrines should, indeed must, be found in all kinds of places. To carry the logic of divine omnipresence one step farther, as the Protestants did in the sixteenth century, there can be no especially holy places, because God is everywhere, equally, in the hearts of the just. Pilgrimage loses any earthbound, geographical focus and becomes a metaphor for the journey through life toward a heavenly goal.[20]

This logic has a certain intellectual elegance, but it strips the earth of sanctity and leaves us no place truly sacred to go during our earthly sojourn. Perhaps this is an unacceptable condition for ordinary humans, so in Anglo-America we substitute national parks and officially designated wilderness areas where we can venerate the mystique of nature in socially acceptable ways on heights, beside and in water, among trees and stones, and deep in caverns. We attend campfire sessions on ecology conducted by park and forest service employees appropriately dressed in special clothing that symbolizes their credentials for interpreting such things. We prepare lavish celebrations in tribute to an image symbolizing the welcoming mother figure known as the Statue of Liberty. And we leave offerings by the hundreds of thousands at a black wall inscribed with the names of our dead of the Vietnam War.[21]

Thus, the urge to identify certain places and things as especially significant, indeed sacred, seems a deeply rooted human need, as is the desire to go as pilgrims to such places. Catholic Europe has retained this understanding.

Notes

Chapter One

1. The basis for visitation estimates is discussed in Chapter 2 and summarized in Table 2-1.

2. This phenomenon is considered from an ecclesiastical point of view by Lefèuvre, "Religious Tourism and Pilgrimage."

3. Daniel, "Megalithic Monuments."

4. Insights into pre-Christian pilgrimage in Europe are found in numerous works including Davidson, *Gods and Myths*; Delcourt, *Sanctuaries de la Grèce*; Fowler, *Roman Festivals*; Grimm, *Teutonic Mythology*; MacNeill, *Festival of Laghnasa*; Ogilvie, *Romans and Their Gods*; Rouse, *Greek Votive Offerings*; and Scullard, *Festivals and Ceremonies*.

5. See Brown, *Cult of the Saints*, and his various discussions in *Society and the Holy*. For early pilgrimage in the Eastern Mediterranean see Kitzinger, "Cult of Images"; for Holy Land pilgrimages during the later Roman period see Hunt, *Holy Land Pilgrimage*; and for the period between 500 and 800 see Jenkins, "Christian Pilgrimages."

6. See Chapter 4 for discussion.

7. English-language scholars dealing with Christian pilgrimage in Europe have tended to concentrate on the Medieval tradition. Examples of this literature include Cohen, "In the Name of God and Profit"; Finucane, *Miracles and Pilgrims*; Geary, "The Saint and the Shrine"; Guilford, *Travellers and Travelling in the Middle Ages*; Hall, *English Medieval Pilgrimage*; Heath, *Pilgrim Life in the Middle Ages*; Hell and Hell, *Great Pilgrimage of the Middle Ages*; Howard, *Writers and Pilgrims*; Jusserand, *English Wayfaring Life*; Kendall, *Medieval Pilgrims*; King, "England's Nazareth"; Layton, *The Way of Saint James*; Mullins, *The Pilgrimage to Santiago*; Newton, *Travel and Travelers of the Middle Ages*; Sumption, *Pilgrimage*; Thomson, *Medieval Pilgrimages*; and Williamson, "Medieval English Pilgrims."

8. Relationships between pilgrimage and other dimensions of society in the Germanies during Late Medieval and Reformation times have been examined by Rothkrug, "Popular Religion" and "Religious Practices." Two important works on Late Medieval and Early Modern pilgrimages in Spain are Christian's *Local Religion* and *Religious Apparitions*. The sociopolitical importance of pilgrimage in nineteenth-century France has been discussed by Kselman, "Miracles and Prophecies." Harvey's "Monument and

Myth" examines the cult of Sacré-Cœur in Paris from a political-geographical perspective.

A greater amount of historical research on Christian pilgrimages from all time periods has been undertaken by Continental scholars than is available in English. For an introduction to the literature on historical topics of current concern see articles in Kriss-Rettenbeck and Mohler, *Wallfahrt kennt keine Grenzen*, especially Chorherr's "Bibliographie," and the articles on pilgrimages in different time periods in Chelini and Branthomme, *Les chemins de Dieu*.

9. Pioneering English-language studies related to contemporary European pilgrimage were produced by anthropologist Victor Turner as a result of his interest in the symbolic nature of Christian pilgrimage. See Turner, "The Center Out There" and *Dramas, Fields and Metaphors*; Turner and Turner, *Image and Pilgrimage*. Christian's *Person and God* also deserves mention as an important pioneering effort. This book is the best study in English of the range of contemporary pilgrimage activities within a small European area.

Classic works on the geography of religions such as Deffontaines, *Geographie et religions*, and Sopher, *Geography of Religions*, mention contemporary European pilgrimages, but only a few major shrines are given as examples. Geographically oriented studies of Christian pilgrimage outside Europe include articles by Nolan, "The Mexican Pilgrimage Tradition," and Gurgel, "Travel Patterns of Canadian Visitors to the Mormon Culture Hearth." Most geographical studies have focused on non-Christian traditions, especially those of Hindu India, the Islamic pilgrimage to Mecca, and Buddhist shrines in Japan. Some of the more important analytical works include Bhardwaj, *Hindu Places of Pilgrimage*; Caplan, "Pilgrims and Priests"; Shair, "Muslim Pilgrimage Circulation;" Sopher, "Pilgrimage Circulation in Gujarat"; Stoddard, "Hindu Holy Sites"; and Tanaka's work on Buddhist pilgrimage, "Pilgrim Places." A book of readings, *Sacred Places, Sacred Spaces*, is being compiled by Stoddard and Morinis. Although mostly oriented toward non-Christian pilgrimage, it will contain an article by Nolan on "Regional Variations in Western European Pilgrimage Traditions."

As is the case with geographers, anthropologists publishing in English have tended to focus on non-Christian pilgrimage traditions, but have done relatively more work on Christian pilgrimage in Latin America. Examples include studies by Crumrine, "Three Coastal Peruvian Pilgrimages" and "Peruvian Pilgrimage," and Gross, "Ritual and Conformity." A much broader body of information on Latin American pilgrimage will become available with the publication of Crumrine and Morinis, *La Peregrinación: The Pilgrimáge in Latin America*. This volume includes papers by scholars representing several disciplines. Nolan's article on "The European Roots of Latin American Pilgrimage" represents a preliminary attempt to interpret the similarities and differences of Christian pilgrimage as expressed on opposite sides of the Atlantic.

Within the past few years there has been a strong surge of interest in contemporary European pilgrimage and related aspects of popular piety among Continental scholars writing in languages other than English. An important anthropological interpretation is Dupront's recent *Du Sacré*. Also see Kriss-Rettenbeck and Mohler, *Wallfahrt kennt keine Grenzen*, and Kolb's *Marien-Gnadenbilder* and *Vom Heiligen Blut*. However, the majority of works so far published by European authors are historical, philosophical, or theological in orientation, and/or consist of geographically limited investigations such as studies of individual pilgrimage centers, of regional shrines, or of shrines within a given country.

References to the various compendia used as sources for developing our inventory are given in n. 12 below.

10. Turner and Turner, *Image and Pilgrimage*, p.19.

11. Ibid., p. 132.

12. The inventory was developed largely between 1975 and 1983. In addition to information from diocesan offices and publications described here, we acquired substantial amounts of information on specific shrines through correspondence with shrine administrators and by means of on-site visits. Much of this information consists of letters, filled-in questionnaires, anonymous undated pamphlets, post cards, devotional cards, observational field notes, and similar materials that are impractical to cite. Books, booklets, and other published materials on individual shrines are referred to where appropriate throughout the text and are listed in the bibliography.

General Works—Books and articles of varying quality and levels of scholarship were used to develop preliminary shrine lists. These included Aradi, *Shrines of Our Lady*; Beevers, *The Sun Her Mantle*; Cartwright, *Catholic Shrines of Europe*; Dorcy, *Shrines of Our Lady*; Gillett, *Famous Shrines of Our Lady* and "Shrines"; Kolb, *Grosse Wallfahrten*, *Marien-Gnadenbilder*, and *Vom Heiligen Blut*; McNaspy, *Guide to Christian Europe*; Madden, *Religious Guide to Europe*; Perowne, *Holy Places of Christendom*; and Spicer, *Festivals of Western Europe*. With the exception of the works by Kolb, which reflect Germanic orientations, these compendia tend to repeat much of the same information on more or less the same set of important shrines. W. J. Walsh, *Apparitions and Shrines of Heaven's Bright Queen*, provides an interesting early twentieth-century description of selected Marian apparitional shrines from an English point of view.

Austria—The most comprehensive source found for twentieth-century Austria was a five-volume work by Gugitz, *Österreichs Gnadenstätten*. This was supplemented with a more recent three-volume work on Marian pilgrimages by Fischer and Stoll, *Kleines Handbuch*, and Plechl, *Wallfahrtsstätten in Niederösterreich*. The Austrian National Tourist Office and the Austrian Institute in New York City provided annotated copies of tourist-oriented literature that was helpful in the initial phases of the study. Of the nine Austrian diocesan offices for which addresses were listed in the 1978 edition of the Vatican's *Annuario pontificio*, eight responded with shrine lists. Places marked as pilgrimage churches on the l975–76 Freytag-Berndt *Auto Atlas Österreich* are described in the above sources. We visited 116 Austrian shrines, mostly in 1978 and 1981.

Belgium and Luxembourg—The basic work used to identify Marian shrines in Belgium was Staercke, *Notre-Dame des Belges*. To find saints' shrines and identify other Marian shrines, we used La Barthe and Renoy, *Het grote feestenboek*; Belgian National

Tourist Office, *Belgium: Festivals and Folklore*; and Vrancken, "Les pèlerinages en Belgique." Reume, *Les Vierges miraculeuses*, provides a nineteenth-century viewpoint. Of the eight Belgian diocesan offices, four responded to queries. The bishop of Luxembourg sent a list of shrines in that small country. We visited a total of 17 shrines in Belgium and Luxembourg at various times in 1976, 1980, and 1982. We also were present at the dancing pilgrimage at Echternach, Luxembourg, in 1965, and the fall festival in honor of the hunter patron, Saint Hubert, at Saint-Hubert, Belgium, in 1983.

France—Sources for the French inventory included Couturier de Chefdubois, *Mille pèlerinages de Notre-Dame*, and other books describing shrines throughout France by Antier, *Le pèlerinage retrouvé*, and Ladame, *Notre-Dame de toute la France*. Regional studies used for the inventory included Duret, *Fêtes de Haute Provence*; Jean-Haffen, *Les fontaines bretonnes*; Knittel, "Les pèlerinages du Bas-Rhin"; Navatte, *Les saints guérisseurs bretons*; and Strappazzon, "Pèlerinages en pays D'Aude." Also used were *Le Guide religieux* for Alsace and "Les pèlerinages du Haut-Rhin." Fifty-nine of the 90 French dioceses responded with lists, and most of the 119 shrine administrators listed in a 1978 issue of *Missi* as members of an association of Recteurs de Sanctuaries de France replied to requests for information. Useful for identification of saints' shrines, in a country where most published compendia deal with Marian shrines, was France's Institut Géographique National, "Pèlerinages et fêtes religieuses," keyed to symbols on the *Carte touristique* series. Also useful in locating shrines was the Recta-Foldex *Carte index*, which accompanies a 15-map series. These maps also include symbols for numerous unnamed shrines. We tried to find eight unnamed sites that were not included in other sources. Three proved to be active, although of minor importance; two were ruins, one a parish church with no apparent history of recent visitation; and the others could not be found.

An event list sent by the French National Tourist Office in 1976 also proved useful for identifying saints' shrines, as did a lengthy descriptive list of events in a 1969 publication by the Automobile Association of Great Britain. Drochon's classic nineteenth-century compendium of Marian shrines, *Histoire illustrée des pèlerinages français*, was used to supplement information on shrine inventories from more recent sources. Most of our visits to 195 French pilgrimage sites took place at various times during 1978, 1980, 1981, and 1983.

Germany (Federal Republic)—Our initial source for West Germany was a short article by Mockenhaubt, "Pèlerinages des catholiques allemands." A more comprehensive description of 129 major West German shrines was subsequently found in Läpple, *Deutschland, deine Wallfahrtsorte*. Responses from all but one of the 21 West German diocesan offices yielded long lists of shrines, often with summary descriptions. Individual shrine administrators also responded well to inquiries. Anonymously authored handbooks that included detailed shrine lists were provided by the Freiburg, Munich, and Speyer dioceses. The Diocese of Trier provided a copy of a similar, but more abbreviated, publication. Other regional studies used were Dorn, *Die Wallfahrten des*

Bistums Augsburg; Gegenfürtner, *Gottesmutter im Bistum Regensburg*; Hahn, *Siedlungs- und wirtschaftsgeographische*; Rosenegger and Bartl, *Wallfahrten im Bayerischen Oberland* and *Wallfahrten in und um München*; Rosenegger and Molodovsky, *Wallfahrten zwischen Inn und Salzach*; and Schaffer and Peda, *Wallfahrten im Passauerland*.

An especially strong Marian emphasis in our analysis of southwestern Bavarian shrines in the Regensburg and Passau dioceses led us to suspect a bias in the data for that region. Inspection of records indicated that almost all information on shrines in the large Diocese of Regensburg had been derived from a photocopy of Gegenfürtner's survey of Marian shrines, the only material sent by the diocesan office in response to our 1977 query. During a visit to Bavaria in late 1984, we obtained copies of compendia by Mäder, *Wallfahrten im Bistum Passau*, and Utz, *Wallfahrten im Bistum Regensburg*. As we suspected, there were far more active shrines dedicated to Christ and the saints in these dioceses—especially Regensburg—than were included in our original inventory. This information was added to computer printouts and manually recorded on computer-generated maps.

The 118 West German shrines we have visited include the few pilgrimage churches that are indicated on the maps in the ADAC *Generalatlas* but not inventoried from other sources. Information on these shrines was obtained on site. Most of our field work in West Germany took place during 1976, 1980, and 1981. A few additional shrines were visited in 1982, 1983, and 1984.

Great Britain and Ireland—We inventoried shrines described as active by Adair, *The Pilgrim's Way*; Gillett, *Shrines of Our Lady in England and Wales*; Hole, *English Shrines and Sanctuaries*; Logan, *Holy Wells of Ireland*; MacNeill, *Festival of Laghnasa*; and Pochin-Mould, *Irish Pilgrimage*. Places listed by Dowse, *Shrines of England* and *Shrines of Scotland*, were inventoried if a formalized pilgrimage of apparent ecumenical and/or Anglo-Catholic interest was described. A few additional Irish shrines mapped in Walther, "Wallfahrten im Westen Irlands," were added to the inventory in 1985.

Thirteen of the 26 diocesan offices in the Republic of Ireland and in Northern Ireland sent information, as did 19 of the 26 dioceses in England, Wales, and Scotland. Local inquiries were especially important in expanding the list of minor Irish shrines. We visited 30 places of pilgrimage in the Republic of Ireland in 1979, and 34 shrines in England, Scotland, and Wales in 1982.

Italy—The most comprehensive description of Marian shrines in Italy is the lavishly illustrated *I mille santuari* compiled by Vinciotti. Other sources for Italy are Colangeli, *Le feste dell'anno*; Gabrielli, *Saints and Shrines*; Kriss and Kriss-Heinrich, *Peregrinatio Neohellenika*; Labanchi, *Holy Year Rome 1975*; Pinto, *Pilgrim's Guide to Rome*; Rombi, *I segreti*; and Salvini, *Cento santuari Mariani*. Fifty-nine of the 250 Italian diocesan offices sent information on shrines. We primarily field-checked Italian shrines during 1976, 1978, and 1981, but visited a few others in 1982 and 1983 for a total of 120.

Netherlands—Sources for the Netherlands inventory included information sent by four of the five diocesan offices. Most additional information came from Dutch shrine administrators who responded to letters of inquiry. A few additional places of pilgrimage were identified by means of local inquiries, but we visited only four Dutch shrines—one in 1978, two in 1981, and another in 1983. Pilgrimage centers in the Netherlands may be underrepresented in this study.

Portugal—The foundation of our information on Portuguese shrines is based on field checking and materials provided by the Portuguese National Tourist Office, including mimeographed "Tourist Calendars" for 1976 and 1983 (Portugal, untitled lists). Of most value were 1980–81 monthly lists, with descriptions of events for all months but February and November, plus an overview of the most important events for all of 1980. Each event was described in considerable detail and classified as a pilgrimage, *romería*, *festa*, fair, or exhibition. These mimeographed materials were prepared for distribution to regional tourism offices by the Direccion General de Turismo, Sector de Animação, and were found in the files of the regional office in Viseu, Portugal, in late June 1981. Important additional insights were provided by Sanchis, "Portuguese 'Romarías'." A small book by Silva Barros, *Four Altars to the Virgin*, provides photographs and brief descriptions of the famous sanctuaries at Fátima, Batalha, Alcobaca, and Nazaré. We visited a total of 42 Portuguese sites during the summers of 1981 and 1983. Of the 16 diocesan offices in mainland Portugal, 2 sent lists of shrines.

Scandinavia—Information was obtained from diocesan offices in Copenhagen, Stockholm, Oslo, and Helsinki. In 1983 we visited two shrines in Denmark and one in Sweden.

Spain—Numerous Marian shrines in Spain are mentioned or described by Manfredi, *Santuarios de la Virgen*. Christian's "De los santos a María" contains a useful list of several hundred shrines and a map showing their locations. Also important is a series of individually authored articles on sanctuaries in the 1978 *Diccionario de historia eclesiástica de España* by the Consejo Superior de Investigaciones Científicas. We also used festival listings and descriptions with information on pilgrimages and romerías, including Epton's *Spanish Fiestas*; a descriptive list in a 1964 edition of *España turística*; a list of important and/or colorful events provided by Spain's Ministerio de Transportes, Turismo y Comunicaciones in 1976, and that agency's *Feasts and Festivals: Spain*; and Sánchez, *Guía de fiestas populares de España*. "Romerías gallegas" in Costa Clavell, *Bandolerismo, romerías y jergas gallegas*, provides information on several Galician sites, whereas Montes Bardo, *Iconographia de Nuestra Señora de Guadalupe*, mentions a few Extremaduran pilgrimages not described in other literature. Twenty-three of Spain's 59 diocesan offices responded to requests for information.

Our first observations of Spanish pilgrimage took place in 1965 when we attended the Holy Year celebrations at Santiago de Compostela. We revisited Santiago and checked 133 other Spanish shrines at various times during 1980, 1981, and 1983, when we spent most of the summer in Spain. Several of these were found by making local inquiries and by seeking out some of the places marked by the symbols for isolated churches, hermitages, and monasteries on two road atlases, Editorial Everest, *Mapa Everest*, and Spain, *España: Mapa oficial*.

Switzerland—The most comprehensive compendium is Henggeler, *Helvetia Sancta*. Other publications used to develop the Swiss inventory were Lüstenberger, *Wallfahrtsorte in der Schweiz*, and Lüthold-Minder, *Helvetia Mariana*. Four out of five diocesan offices sent information. We visited a few Swiss pilgrimage places in 1980–81 and more in 1982, for a total of 35.

13. The lack of a Vatican list of shrines was noted in a letter of April 10, 1976 from Monsignor Coppa. Extensive materials concerning shrines and pilgrimages exist in the Vatican archives and are accessible to scholars. However, as explained by Archivist Monsignor Charles Burns, the proper documents can be located only if the researcher can specify both the location of the shrine and the time period, or periods, during which correspondence or other documents concerning the place might have reached the Vatican. Because the Vatican Library is primarily a manuscript collection, it does not maintain an up-to-date collection of publications related to shrines and pilgrimages. Most of the materials on pilgrimage, including a fairly comprehensive collection of English translations of early Holy Land pilgrimage accounts, came to the library as donations from private collections. The Pontifical Commission on the Pastoral Care of Migrants and Tourists, established in 1971, corresponds with numerous shrine administrators but maintains no master shrine list.

14. Christian, "De los santos a María," p. 87.

15. British holy wells that are currently the scene of Catholic and/or Anglo-Catholic pilgrimage are included in the inventory. At least 38 "wishing wells," sometimes locally referred to as "holy wells" or "saints wells," are still visited by people in country districts of England, Scotland, and Wales for quasi-religious reasons, including quests for cures. At least 4 stone circles and natural rock formations are visited for similar reasons. After inspecting 4 of these wells and 1 curious stone in 1982, we decided not to include such places in our shrine inventory because the local people did not seem to regard the visits as pilgrimages. However, the resemblances between these British sacred and/or magic places and the holy wells of Roman Catholic Ireland, Brittany, and parts of Austria are striking and merit further study. For additional information see Muir, *Riddles in the British Landscape* and Coxe, *Haunted Britain*.

16. Apparitions and other events perceived to be miraculous of the type that may lead to pilgrimage cult formation rarely have received much initial ecclesiastical encouragement in twentieth-century Europe. As a result, information on pilgrimage activity at nonapproved sites is seldom acquired via the fairly conventional sources from which we have drawn much of our data. An indication of the scope of potential cult-formative events in recent times is provided in a work by Billet et al., *Vraies et fausses apparitions*, which lists 232 claims of apparitions and other miraculous manifestations occurring since 1928, of which 176 took place in Western Europe. William Christian, however, points out that the list is far from complete even for Europe (personal correspondence). Only some of the reports listed by Billet have generated pilgrimage activities lasting for any length of time.

17. A summary of the preliminary analysis that revealed the persistent pattern is

contained in Nolan, "Spatial and Temporal Aspects of Contemporary Western European Pilgrimage."

Chapter Two

1. Turner and Turner, *Image and Pilgrimage*, p. 6.
2. Christian, "De los santos a María," p. 87.
3. This usage has been noted for Spain by Christian, ibid.
4. Jacobs, *Horizon Book of Great Cathedrals*.
5. Christian, *Local Religion*, pp. 63–66.
6. Perez Lopez, *Cathedral of Burgos*, p. 29. Christian, "De los santos a María," pp. 94–95, categorizes the Christ of Burgos as a cult object that was far more important in the past than at present.
7. Pilgrimages imposed as judicial sentences are described by Sigal, "Les différents types de pèlerinage," pp. 80–82.
8. Bhardwaj, *Hindu Places of Pilgrimage*, p. 97.
9. The most elaborate ranking systems have been developed by scholars working with the shrines in a single country. Bhardwaj, *Hindu Places of Pilgrimage*, p. 46, uses (1) Pan-Hindu, (2) supraregional, (3) regional, (4a) subregional-high, (4b) subregional-low, and (5) local. Christian, "De los santos a María," pp. 93–94, categorizes Spanish shrines as (1) national, (2) regional, (3) provincial—radius of 9–12 communities, (4) one-half of a province—radius of 6–9 communities, (5) one-quarter of a province—radius of 4–6 communities, (6) surrounding communities, district—radius of 2–4 communities, (7) 4–6 communities, and (+) once important shrines no longer of importance even at the district level. Turner and Turner, *Image and Pilgrimage*, p. 239, propose that Christian pilgrimages can be stratified into four major levels: (1) international, (2) national, (3) regional, (4) intervillage. European writers use similar classifications. Shrine lists sent from diocesan offices often expressed levels of importance in terms of the diocesan unit, such as "one of the most important shrines in the diocese," "visited from throughout the diocese," or "visited from three adjacent dioceses."
10. See n. 9 above for Christian's ranking system.
11. *Notre-Dame de Sion*, p. 184.
12. It should be emphasized that visitation counts at shrines, as at national parks, state borders, or theme parks, do not measure numbers of individual people. Some individuals may visit the place in question several times during a single year and be counted each time. Also, during a single trip, an individual may visit many places of a similar type, such as shrines or national parks, and be counted at each place. Thus, an estimate of 100 million pilgrim visitations at European shrines does not imply an equal number of individuals making a pilgrimage. For a discussion of the problems

of conducting visitation counts and extrapolating from such counts to numbers of individual visitors see Lundberg, *The Tourist Business*, and Smith, *Recreation Geography*.

13. Bhardwaj, *Hindu Places of Pilgrimage*, pp. 82–93.

14. Gugitz, *Österreichs Gnadenstätten*; Henggeler, *Helvetia Sancta*.

15. The figure for the United States is based on an inventory of shrines that we undertook during 1984 and 1985. No results of this study have, as yet, been published.

16. Information on Scandinavian shrines comes from letters sent from the dioceses of Copenhagen, Stockholm, Oslo, and Helsinki in 1978.

Chapter Three

1. Baumer, "Gestalt und Sinn," p. 22. Another recent discussion of the meaning of pilgrimage in the Christian tradition is found in Kriss-Rettenbeck, Kriss-Rettenbeck, and Illich, "Homo Viator." These authors suggest a cultural continuity of the theme of "man as a wayfarer and stranger in this world" as a means for interpreting Christian pilgrimage. However, they also point out that Christian pilgrimage is a complex historical phenomenon that must be considered in cultural context, adding that "its nature and content [cannot] be circumscribed precisely or described in terms of an absolutely binding definition." p. 22.

2. Turner and Turner, *Image and Pilgrimage*, p. 7.

3. There is an extensive literature on early pilgrim journeys to the Holy Land written after Christianity became the accepted religion of the Roman Empire in the fourth century. For a list of original sources see Chorherr, "Bibliographie," and for discussion see Hunt, *Holy Land Pilgrimage*. Earlier pilgrimages presumably occurred.

4. Lefèuvre, "Religious Tourism and Pilgrimage," p. 81.

5. Ibid., p. 86.

6. The French list was taken from the Automobile Association, *AA Road Guide to France*. The Spanish list was taken from Spanish tourist promotional literature for 1980 in English and 1982, *Fiestas y festivales*. The West German data were derived from a photocopied list of events provided by that country's national tourist office in 1977. Only those West German events held on a regular annual basis were counted, thus excluding many conventions and expositions of a purely secular nature.

7. The events were described in McGahey, *Playboy's Guide*. In spite of its somewhat misleading title, this book provides a good overview of Europe's better publicized festivals and special events. In the author's words, "Included are folklore events, historical commemorations, wine and beer festivals, music and performing arts festivals, royal ceremonies, religious processions, sports and athletic competitions, and numerous other festive occasions." pp. 9–10. The listing was compiled over a ten-year period

from the author's personal experience; from consultation with local, regional, and national tourism agencies; and from conversations with Europeans.

8. During a 1979 interview the parish priest responsible for the Croagh Patrick pilgrimage pointed out that most of the dangers and "abuses" connected with the traditional nighttime mountain climb had been corrected by transforming the arduous ascent into a "family-type" day climb.

9. Greenwood, "Culture by the Pound."

10. This analysis of seasonality is based on 4,268 dates of pilgrimage to 3,125 shrines. Only the most important dates, up to three per shrine, were considered. One annual date was recorded for 2,235 shrines, two major dates for 637 shrines, and three dates for 253 shrines. Pilgrimage centers placing equal emphasis on four or more events in different months were not included in the count, and no two dates within the same month were recorded for any of the shrines. The resulting patterns represent only an approximation.

11. Lumiansky, *The Canterbury Tales*.

12. Several informants in Ireland and Scotland mentioned this characteristic of holy and "wishing well" water.

13. The problem is not new. Sumption, *Pilgrimage*, p. 234, mentions serious food shortages during major pilgrimages in the past.

14. Calculations are based on the number of times Easter has occurred or will occur on different dates during the 248 years between 1753 and 2000.

15. See Chapter 8, n. 5, for a discussion of town size.

16. This summary of the Roman Catholic liturgical year is based on Van Doren, "Liturgical Year in the Roman Rite."

17. The data for interpretation of pilgrimage seasonality in Latin America are based on 672 dates of pilgrimage to the shrines that we have so far identified in this part of the world. A major monthly reversal of pilgrimage dates to fit the warm season in southern South America should not be expected because the more densely populated parts of the region lie closer to the equator than do most parts of Europe and do not experience extremely severe winters.

18. Logan, *Holy Wells of Ireland*, p. 35. Also see MacNeill, *Festival of Laghnasa*.

19. Rouillard, "Marian Feasts," p. 211; McIver, "Visitation of Mary," p. 721. Two of the four ancient feast days of the Virgin Mary, which spread from the Eastern Mediterranean to Italy in the seventh century, seem to have diffused rather rapidly through Western Christendom. These were the feasts of the Purification on February 2 and the Annunciation on March 25. Neither appears to have become important as an occasion for visiting Marian shrines. The other two ancient Marian feasts—of the Assumption on August 15 and the Nativity on September 8—spread much more slowly toward the northwest, becoming established as times of celebration beyond Mediterranean lands more or less simultaneously with the twelfth-century rise of Marian devotions and the development of numerous Marian shrines. These occasions did become established as important times for pilgrimage, as they still are.

20. The striking covariation between zones where the wheat harvest does not begin until August or later and the establishment of Protestantism would seem, at first glance, to be merely a curiosity. There may, however, be an ecological dimension to the Protestant rejection of Marian devotions and pilgrimages. The late summer Marian pilgrimage dates that spread northwestward during the Middle Ages were well suited to pilgrimage expression in Mediterranean lands, but were potentially disfunctional toward the north. Data presented in Broekhuizen, *Atlas of Cereal Growing*, indicate that the wheat harvest begins in June throughout much of Iberia and Italy, and by mid-July in a zone extending from southern France through northern Italy. In most of France, the harvest begins in late July. The zones where the harvest season begins in early August include Flanders, the Low Countries, southern West Germany, and much of Austria. In central and northern West Germany, the British Isles, and southern Scandinavia, the wheat harvest does not begin until mid-August or later.

During the Middle Ages, and indeed until the fairly recent mechanization of European agriculture, the harvest took much longer to accomplish and required major inputs of human labor. In addition, a pilgrimage to a regional shrine drawing devotees from a radius of 40 to 60 miles would have required at least a week's time for people in the outlying districts. It is difficult to see how pilgrimage dates poorly suited to the northern agricultural cycle became established, although serious outbreaks of ergotism in the early through mid-twelfth century may have been a factor. The disease is caused by eating fungus-infected rye, so presumably the condition became apparent in late summer or early fall as the first of a infected rye harvest was being consumed. According to Sumption, *Pilgrimage*, p. 75, pilgrims seeking relief from this condition converged in large numbers on the emergent Marian shrines of the period, perhaps helping confirm the late summer pilgrimage dates to Marian shrines.

As time went on, these late summer dates became increasingly out-of-step with the labor needs of the northern agricultural cycle because the Julian calendar was becoming desynchronized from the solar year at the rate of 11 minutes and 14 seconds per year. When the Gregorian calendar was adopted by the Roman Catholic world in 1582, dates were pushed forward by 10 days in order to adjust the new calendar to the solar year. Thus, by the sixteenth century, the date of August 15 was falling on about August 5, and the September 8 holy day was occurring in late August in terms of plant growth. Throughout Germanic lands and in parts of northern France, the celebrations of "Our Lady's 30 days" between the Assumption and Nativity coincided with the grain harvest.

The adoption of an ecologically unsound behavioral pattern often takes years, or even centuries, to become clearly maladaptive because the increments by which its disfunctionality become apparent are small. By that time, it may be intrinsically built into the cultural system and difficult to change without major social upheaval. Late summer pilgrimages in the north may not have represented a serious problem during the twelfth century. Marian pilgrimages probably were not yet making serious inroads into the more evenly distributed seasonality of pilgrimage to saints' shrines, and mass pilgrimages involving the travel of large proportions of the population beyond their immediate areas of residence, and work was still in its infancy. From the mid-thirteenth century on, however, the late summer Marian pilgrimage times became increasingly disfunctional in the north as the solar and calendar years continued to grow apart and as increasing numbers of people made pilgrimages to more distant shrines. After the mid-fourteenth-century Black Death, there were severe labor shortages, some of the older saints lost popularity, and mass pilgrimages to Marian shrines reached even greater heights.

It, therefore, seems possible that the interference of late summer pilgrimages with labor demands of the harvest season in northern Europe was, at least indirectly, related to the rise of the Protestant work ethic and the rejection of both pilgrimage and Marian devotions. Northerly areas, such as the Lower Rhine, where the Roman Catholic faith remained important, developed a Post-Reformation seasonality of pilgrimage that has emphasized a minor July Marian holy day in contrast to the more usual August concentration of activity. September, however, remains the most important month of pilgrimage in these regions, and the above arguments should be viewed as suggestive rather than definitive. Further research along these lines might yield some interesting results. The possibility of an ecological dimension to the Protestant rejection of pilgrimage was discussed in more detail in Mary Lee Nolan, "A Time to Make Pilgrimage: Seasonality of Religious Travel in Europe" (paper presented at the Annual Meeting of the Association of American Geographers, Philadelphia, April 1979).

21. Turner and Turner, *Image and Pilgrimage*, p. 240. Also see Christian, *Person and God*.

22. See Bruckner, "Fusswallfahrt," for a discussion of the increasing popularity of foot pilgrimage in West Germany. Perche, *Sur les routes*, provides a guide to 40 of the old pilgrim routes of France.

23. For introductory discussions of transportation theory see Taaffe and Gauthier, *Geography of Transportation*, and various papers in Hurst, *Transportation Geography*. Summary discussions of literature related to recreational travel are found in Smith, *Recreation Geography*.

24. Logan, *Holy Wells of Ireland*, devotes a chapter to votive offerings in Ireland; Sanchis, "Portuguese 'romarías'," describes some of the votives left at pilgrimage centers in Portugal. In general, however, very little has been written in English about votives at Christian shrines. Wilson, "Annotated Bibliography," pp. 350–52, provides an introduction to a small amount of the extensive literature in other languages. For an introduction and additional references, Cousin, *Ex-voto de Provence*, and Cazes, *Ex-voto du Roussillon*, are useful for France. German votives are described by Kriss-Rettenbeck, *Bilder und Zeichen* and *Ex-voto, Zeichen, Bild*, and by Scharfe, Schenda, and Schwedt, *Volksfrömmigkeit-Bildzeugnisse*. Selhofer, *Votivtafelkapelle*, and Goebeler and Schulten, *Ex Voto Weihgaben*, provide insights into individual shrine collections. Some of the numerous studies of Italian votives are Ciarrochi and Mori, *Le tavolette votive*; Tempera, *Gli ex-voto*; and Toschi and Pennia, *Le tavolette votive*. Also see Toschi,

Bibliografia. Carrara, *Bocche parlanti*, provides an illustrated account of the vast collection at Montenero; and Bagnaia, *Museo della basilica*, describes the important collection at the shrine of the Madonna della Quércia in Viterbo. For Spain, see Rodríguez and Vazquez, *Exvotos de Andalucía*. A detailed early twentieth-century study by Rouse, *Greek Votive Offerings*, indicates the antiquity of nearly all types of votives currently left at European shrines.

25. Technically, a votive offering is a voluntary gift, and the spirit of the offering as freely given is maintained. Places to leave offerings are provided in pilgrimage churches, but donations are not required as a condition for visiting Catholic shrines. A few shrine churches, mostly among those visited by large numbers of tourists, charge small sums for visiting attached religious museums or treasuries or for climbing a bell tower to enjoy the view. Occasionally, there may be a parking fee at large, heavily visited shrines, but, in the few cases we observed, the parking lots appeared to be adjacent to rather than on shrine grounds. A charge for admission to enter the sanctuary is virtually unheard of at the Roman Catholic shrines of Europe. Among the hundreds of shrines we visited, we found only one apparent exception. At a shrine near Vienna, during the height of the August tourist season, tour directors—including directors of religiously oriented tours—were paying a per-head sum for the groups they were herding through the sanctuary. At the famous Anglican cathedrals of England there was usually either an admission charge or a posted request for an entry contribution of a specified amount that was diligently collected by persons posted at the entry.

26. Sanchis, "Portuguese 'Romarías'," p. 277, discusses ritual gifts devoted to particular saints, such as eggs for Saint Benedict, black chickens for Saint Bartholomew, and pigeons and rabbits for Saint Lucy. He also discusses the buying of foodstuffs and wine in shops to be presented as gifts (p. 272) and auctions (p. 278). We have made similar observations in Portugal.

27. Marnham, *Lourdes*, provides an interesting discussion of volunteer work at a famous modern shrine.

28. Logan, *Holy Wells of Ireland*, p. 116, mentions that red was once the preferred color for rags at some Irish wells, possibly because the color was used for magical purposes and was believed to resist evil spirits. At the rag wells we have seen there was no special color evident, although all the rags tend to turn gray as they weather.

29. Cousin, *Ex-voto de Provence*, p. 21. Cazes, *Ex-voto du Roussillon*, p. 30, suggests that the painted votive was promoted by mendicant friars in the fourteenth and fifteenth centuries and benefited from the development of a technique for using oil paints on votive tablets.

30. The similarity between the small offerings among the marble plaques that line shrine walls in Europe and the tokens left by thousands of people at the monument to the dead of the Vietnam War in Washington, D.C., is striking.

31. Rouse, *Greek Votive Offerings*.

32. See Weitzmann, *The Icon*, plate 5, for a fresco from the funerary church of Felix

and Adauctus in the catacombs of Rome showing the Virgin Mary with the Christ Child enthroned and flanked by saints with the Widow Turtura, mother of the donor, in the foreground. A marble inscription dates the fresco to 528.

33. Cousin, *Ex-voto de Provence*, pp. 9–39.

34. Painted ex-voto displays are most common at Italian shrines. In addition to Madonna della Quércia near Viterbo and Santa Maria del Monte at Cesena, there are outstanding votive collections at Madonna della Guárdia near Genoa, Montenero near Livorno, Pietralba in Trentino-Adige, Incoronata near Foggia, the Convento San.Matteo on the Gargano Peninsula, Madonna dell'Arco near Naples, and numerous other places. Small Italian shrines in out-of-the-way places sometimes have fascinating painted votives dating from the fifteenth and sixteenth centuries.

French shrines with painted votive collections are most common in the provinces bordering the Mediterranean, in the eastern Pyrenees, and in Alsace where Notre-Dame de Theirenbach has a particularly interesting collection.

Many Swiss, Austrian, and southern West German shrines display a few painted votives. Some of the larger collections are at Altötting and Erding in Bavaria, and at Maria Plain, Maria Lavant, and Maria Kirchental in Austria. The shrine of Saint Francis Xavier near Morschach, Switzerland, has an outstanding collection related to that saint. Iberian shrines tend to have a mix of many different kinds of votive offerings. Many have at least a few of the painted votives.

Chapter Four

1. Turner and Turner, *Image and Pilgrimage*, p. 19.
2. Ibid., p. 21.
3. Sumption, *Pilgrimage*, p. 279.
4. The ephemeral nature of many pilgrimage places has been discussed by several scholars including Christian, *Local Religion*, and Sumption, *Pilgrimage*. Reasons for the decline and eventual oblivion, or current dormancy, of some places of pilgrimage after short or long periods of visitation are numerous. Among these are the fickleness of pilgrims searching for the most recent places of miracles; the lack of ecclesiastical promotion or ecclesiastical bans; iconoclastic outbursts leading to the physical destruction of the shrine center, its records, and its holy objects; the transfer of an especially venerated object to another place; and the inertia related to a new generation's lack of identification with the events making the place initially sacred.
5. Aspects of the early Celtic pilgrimage tradition that distinguish it from Continental pilgrimages are mentioned by Evans, *Irish Folk Ways*; Nolan, "Irish Pilgrimage"; and Wagner, "Tradition der Askese." Ashe, *The Discovery of King Arthur*, pp. 132–33, suggests that Celtic Christianity was more receptive to the incorporation of pagan ideas because the peoples of Britain and Ireland "had not been subjected to the same

pressures as Christians on the Continent," where a long history of Christian persecution by pagans had led to a view of "paganism as diabolic."

6. Gabrielli, *Saints and Shrines*, p. 112, and the entry under "Cathal" in Delaney, *Dictionary of Saints*, p. 137. This Celtic saint who served as a missionary bishop in southern Italy is also known as Cataldus, Cataldo, and Catald.

7. According to Almagro, *Guia de Mérida*, pp. 104–6, the Basilica of Santa Eulalia was built during the fourth through sixth centuries and survived until the Almoravide invasion of the twelfth century. One set of legends claims that the saint's relics were taken to Oviedo by King Silo of Asturias in about 783. However, documents from the ninth and fourteenth centuries refer to the conservation of the saint's body in Mérida, although the location of the tomb is presently unknown. Given the seemingly infinite divisibility of human remains, it is possible that Oviedo and Mérida have equally good claims to some of Santa Eulalia's relics. For additional information on Santa Eulalia and other saints' cults in Early Christian Spain see García Rodríguez, "El culto de los santos."

The thirteenth-century Gothic image of La Virgen del Sagrario venerated in the cathedral at Toledo is much too recent to be directly associated with the Marian piety of the seventh-century bishop San Ildefonso as was believed in the sixteenth century, according to Gomez-Menor, "Virgen del Sagrario," p. 2337. However, as pointed out by Collins, *Early Medieval Spain*, p. 77, Bishop Ildefonso's treatise *On the Perpetual Virginity of the Blessed Virgin Mary* was the "first great outburst of Marian devotion in the Spanish Church" and may have been partly responsible for the further spread of Marian devotions in the West during the seventh century and afterward. Certainly, Toledo has been associated with Marian cultus for a very long time, and Moslem rulers there seem to have been fairly tolerant of Christian devotions.

8. For a discussion of attempts to date the famous Zaragoza cultus see Gomez, "Virgen del Pilar," pp. 2316–17. This Roman city had a Christian bishop by the third century and was a center for the cultus of the Ebro valley recluse, Saint Aemilian, by the seventh century. See Collins, *Early Medieval Spain*, p. 81.

9. For descriptions of these shrines see Vinciotti, *I mille santuari*. Although few of the Italian cult images said to have been brought from the East are currently thought to predate the eighth century, and most appear to be of much more recent vintage, this does not disprove the basic idea of a flow of venerated icons from east to west during the Byzantine iconoclastic period. Judging from what people tend to do, including Spanish Civil War refugees, Cubans escaping to Miami in the wake of Castro's imposition of a Communist ideology, and countless other well-documented modern examples, stories suggesting that refugees from Byzantine iconoclasm carried with them their most sacred images are so plausible that no extant shrine icon of a demonstrably correct date is necessary as proof. As will be discussed in more detail in Chapter 5, cult objects at shrines are often subject to extreme modification as styles change, and at some shrines the currently venerated image is a reliquary for tiny

fragments of a much older one. For a discussion of copies of images conceptualized as if they were the originals see Kolb, *Marien-Gnadenbilder*, pp. 44–46. It should also be pointed out that the age of a particular cult object is frequently of no special value in determining when the shrine came into being, even when the pilgrimage formation story describes the cultus as developing around the discovery or acquisition of an image. In modern Spain, for example, at least 36 very old cult images were destroyed during the Spanish Civil War (1936–39) and have been replaced. Some replacements are copies from old photographs of the original images, while others, stylistically new, contain fragments of the older cult objects.

10. Lazzarini, *Il Volto Santo di Lucca*.

11. The idea that the fifteenth-century appearance of ex-voto paintings is related to the beginnings of a modern form of individualized piety is developed and illustrated by Cousin, *Ex-voto de Provence*, pp. 15–17.

12. See Chapter 7 for a discussion of these characteristics and the evolution of modern-type Marian pilgrimages.

13. The importance of the Catholic Reformation and the points of origin for missionaries to the Hispanic New World are particularly important due to a tendency of many Latin Americanists to attribute aspects of Latin American pilgrimage, which do not appear to be characteristically Medieval Iberian, to an American input into the syncretism of Old and New World belief patterns. Although a syncretism undoubtedly occurred, many distinctive features of Latin American pilgrimage, such as an emphasis on shrines devoted to Christ and certain types of miracle stories, were more pronounced in Europe during Catholic Reformation times than during the Medieval period and some traits seem to be more strongly rooted in Germanic than Iberian traditions. The possibility of the diffusion of Christianized Amerindian ideas from the New World to Europe should not be dismissed out-of-hand, although we have no firm evidence of this. Further discussion of the problem will appear in Nolan, "The European Roots."

14. Some recent Marian apparition sites have generated a substantial amount of literature, much of which is apocalyptic in tone. Especially see Gabriel, *San Damiano*, and Speckbacher, *Garabandal*. A recent English account of the Garabandal apparitions is Gonzales and Daley, *Miracle at Garabandal*. For Heroldsbach, Germany, see Altgott, *Heroldsbach*. Although outside our study area, apparitions in Medjugorje, Yugoslavia, in the early 1980s have attracted considerable attention throughout Europe and in the United States as well. These visions are described by Ljubic, *Erscheinungen der Gottesmutter*, and Laurentin and Rupcic, *Is the Virgin Mary Appearing?* Laurentin, *Pèlerinages, sanctuaires, apparitions*, provides a brief discussion of several recent apparition sites.

15. For a Marxist interpretation of the cult of Sacré Cœur in Paris by a geographer see Harvey, "Monument and Myth." For the Sacred Heart shrine on Cerro de los Ángeles near Madrid, see Anibarro Espeso, *Estampas del Cerro*.

16. For information on the lives of these persons see Johnson, *Addict for Christ*, about Matt Talbot; Villaviciosa, *El siervo de Dios*, for Fray Leopoldo de Alpandeire;

Koerbling, *Father Rupert Mayer*; Di Flumeri, *Padre Pio of Pietrelcina*; Mischitelli, *Remembering Padre Pio*; and Sullivan, *Journey of Love*, about Pope John XXIII.

17. Ketchum, *The Renaissance*, p. 7.

18. Kselman, "Miracles and Prophecies," is especially useful for interpreting pilgrimage formations in nineteenth-century France.

19. Pötzl, "Santa-Casa-Kult," p. 382.

20. Hartinger, "Mariahilf ob Passau," pp. 290, 299.

21. The names of these priests are listed on a plaque inside the Holywell church, and the inn can still be visited. Also see Charles-Edwards, *Saint Winefride*, and David, *St. Winefride's Well*.

22. Places where Masses have been said in unbroken sequence since the Middle Ages or earlier include St. Mawgan, Cornwall, and Hazelwood Castle near Tadcaster, Yorkshire. The Lady Chapel near Osmotherly located on a wooded hill above Mount Grace Priory is an example of an obscure place that became a secret shrine during the sixteenth century. Devotions were encouraged by Franciscans living under cover in the nearby village. At Welsh Newton, Wales, the grave of John Kemble, a priest executed in 1677, is said to have drawn covert pilgrimages since that time. And at Aston-in-Makersfield, the hand of Saint Edmund Arrowsmith has been venerated since he was hanged, drawn, and quartered in 1628; he was one of the 88 English "Martyrs of the Reformation" canonized in 1970. For more information on these English Reformation saints as presented by their devotees, see Caraman, *Saint Cuthbert Mayne*; Dempsey, *Richard Gwyn*; McGoldrick, *Saint Margaret Clitherow*; Murphy, *Blessed Richard Gwyn*; Quinn, *Cavalier of Christ*; Ripley, *Holy Hand* and *Saint Edmund Arrowsmith*; Walsh, *Forty Martyrs of England and Wales*; Whitfield, *Saint John Southworth*; and a booklet by the nuns of Tyburn Convent, *They Died at Tyburn*.

23. Field work in 1982 indicated that, except for a few places such as Canterbury Cathedral, there is relatively little actual overlap between places visited by Roman Catholic and Anglo-Catholic pilgrims. At Walsingham, for example, there are two separate shrines. One in town is maintained by the Anglican church and the other, at the Slipper Chapel a mile from town, by the Roman Catholic church. Of the two, the Anglican shrine—with its holy well, its numerous Catholic saints' statues, and its votives—is the most overtly Catholic in appearance, a phenomenon sometimes confusing to pilgrims of both religious persuasions. To further complicate matters, the actual site of the great Medieval shrine and the ruins of its monastic establishment are in private hands, as has been the case since the Reformation. An admission is charged for entry onto these grounds. For additional discussion of modern relationships between the two shrines see King, "England's Nazareth." Connelly's *Walsingham Is for Today*, *Walsingham Pilgrim Book*, and *The Slipper Chapel* represent a Roman Catholic point of view. For the story of the Anglican shrine see Guardians of the Shrine, *The Meaning of Walsingham* and *Walsingham: England's Nazareth*.

24. See Nolan, "Irish Pilgrimage." Walther, "Wallfahrten," has documented recent changes in pilgrimage in counties Galway and Mayo. She found a strong tendency

toward concentration of pilgrim activity at a relatively small number of important shrines and a replacement of many old worship patterns, such as "making the rounds" by walking around sacred site features, with recitations of the rosary and assistance at Mass.

25. Turner and Turner, *Image and Pilgrimage*, p. 49
26. Ibid., pp. 18–19.
27. Ibid., pp. 162–63
28. Ibid., p. 203.
29. Ibid., p. 38.
30. For transcripts of records from ecclesiastical investigations of Spanish apparition reports see Christian, *Religious Apparitions*.
31. Christian, *Local Religion*, comments on the decline of some seventeenth-century Spanish shrines, especially those dedicated to Christ.

Chapter Five

1. Detailed analysis of male and female principles and symbols of divinity in the Christian tradition is beyond the scope of this study. For an introduction to the extensive literature related to this topic see Eliade, *Patterns*, *Images and Symbols*, and *The Sacred and the Profane*; Neumann, *Great Mother*; Warner, *Alone of All Her Sex*; Sharbrough, "Cult of the Mother"; and, for an American priest's interpretation, Greeley, *The Mary Myth*.
2. The story of the Le Dorat ostensions is told by Schneider, *Saint Israël*.
3. Sanchis, "Portuguese 'Romarías'," p. 264. Sanchis identified 14 romería centers dedicated to the Holy Spirit, whereas we only located 5. In addition, his figures on orientation toward other subjects are somewhat different from ours; 46 rather than 52 percent Marian, 38 rather than 39 percent oriented toward saints, and 15 percent rather than 9 percent centered on Christ if Holy Spirit shrines are combined with Christ-centered shrines. These variations are probably related to a difference in definitions of what was to be studied. Sanchis apparently did not consider pilgrimage centers such as Fátima and Samiero near Braga that are not settings for romerías per se and are devoted to the Virgin Mary, but did include events—such as the celebration in honor of the Holy Spirit at Tomar—that we did not count on the assumption that they were a better fit with a category of religious festivals than pilgrimages. He mentions that "some of the festivals which we shall be discussing, . . . are called romarías only by extension of the term." p. 261.
4. See Sharbrough, "Cult of the Mother."
5. Berthou, *Saint-Hervé*.
6. Gugitz, *Österreichs Gnadenstätten*, 2:188–95.
7. Past pilgrimages to living persons in the Christian tradition are discussed by Brown, "Rise and Function" and "Town, Village and Holy Man"; Geary, "The Saint and

the Shrine"; and Kotting, "Wallfahrten." For recent holy men see Christian, "Holy People."

8. Descriptions of saints have been drawn from several sources including Attwater, *Penguin Dictionary*; Delaney, *Dictionary of Saints*; Thurston and Attwater, *Butler's Lives*; articles on individual saints in *The New Catholic Encyclopedia*; and information relevant to individual saints' shrines in compendia and obtained directly from shrine administrators. Additional references are cited in the text.

9. The discovery at Apt is described by Barruol, *Sainte-Anne d'Apt*. For the Saint Anne cultus in the Germanies see Fastner, *Oh, heilige Mutter Anna*.

10. The face of the old image can be seen through the glass front of its reliquary in the base of the current gilt statue of Saint Anne with the child Mary. See photographs in Danigo, *Saint-Anne D'Auray*.

11. Herwaarden, "St. James in Spain," p. 235, argues that the legend of the apostle in Spain "may possibly be based on falsehood, but has obtained more real power thereby than ever could have been provided by truth. Proof that Saint James the Greater is not buried in Spain would not deter a single pilgrim."

12. For an interpretation of the cultus of Saint Michael as a popular, spiritual devotion see Delaruelle, *La Piété populaire*, pp. 389–400.

13. For an interesting account of this cultus see Warner, *Alone of All Her Sex*, pp. 224–35. The controversy between Saint-Maximin and Vézelay is discussed by Sumption, *Pilgrimage*, pp. 37–38. For a more comphrensive treatment see Saxer, *Le culte de Marie-Madeleine*.

14. The story of Saint George and the Dragon is related to early combat myths in Fontenrose, *Python*, app. 4.

15. Relics of this Italian saint are venerated as far from Europe as the Caribbean island of Saint Lucia.

16. A description of automobile pilgrimages beginning in 1912 to a French shrine dedicated to the legendary giant is found in Brandicourt, *Saint-Christophe*.

17. For a recent discussion see C. W. Jones, *Saint Nicholas*. Mâle, *Religious Art in France: The Thirteenth Century*, pp. 327–32, discusses the Medieval pilgrimage to Bari.

18. As an introduction to the extensive literature related to Saint Patrick see Hanson, *Saint Patrick*.

19. Sanchis, "Portuguese 'Romarías'," pp. 267, provides an interesting discussion of the relationships between São Bento and his devotees. The saint is considered especially strict in demanding payment of vows and likely to be vindictive when promises are not fulfilled.

20. See Rothkrug, "Popular Religion," pp. 30–31, for a discussion of this type of pilgrimage.

21. Gugitz, *Österreichs Gnadenstätten*, 4:105–7.

22. A detailed study of the spread of Saint Wendel's cultus is provided by Selzer, *St. Wendelin*.

23. A bibliography of works related to this cultus is provided by Dunninger, "Four-

teen Holy Helpers," 5:1045–46. For a series of historical and folkloric studies see Schreiber, *Die vierzehn Nothelfer*.

24. Delaney, *Dictionary of Saints*.

25. L. White, "Historical Roots." For descriptions of Franciscan shrines near Gréccio see Di Pietri, *Sulle orme di San Francesco*.

26. Christian, *Religious Apparitions*, p. 99, mentions the sixteenth-century transfer of emphasis from Saint Anthony Abbot to Saint Anthony of Padua in Spain.

27. For an account of the spread of Saint Roch's cultus see Telfer, *The Treasure of São Roque*.

28. Christian, *Local Religion*, chapters 6, 7.

29. There are two basic schools of thought concerning the antiquity of Marian pilgrimage in Western Europe. Scholars trained in the cannons of a secularly oriented, critical history, and relying primarily on "proven" documentary evidence, emphasize the late blooming of Marian cultus in the West. Religiously oriented scholars—along with anthropologists, folklorists, and some social historians—are more inclined to accept oral traditions, legends, archaeological findings, and combinations of evidence that have strong plausibility, because they relate to common patterns of human behavior, as indicators of very ancient Marian devotions in Western Europe.

A rather different reason for probable early Marian shrines in some parts of Western Europe lies in the fact that much of Italy and the southeastern coast of Spain were under Byzantine control during various periods before the turn of the eighth century, or before the rise of iconoclasm in the East. The Byzantine order for the destruction of images was never fully enforced in Byzantine-controlled Early Medieval Italy. There is no real doubt about Marian pilgrimage by the sixth and seventh centuries in the Byzantine East. See Kitzinger, "Cult of Images," and Grabar, *Christian Iconography*.

Sumption, *Pilgrimage*, and Rothkrug, "Religious Practices," represent the document-based historical approach. These scholars doubt that Marian pilgrimage shrines existed in the West prior to the ninth or tenth centuries because they can find no acceptable documentary evidence for such cultus. Claims made by individual shrines on the basis of folklore and oral traditions are generally dismissed because it can be demonstrated that some such claims are based on pious "inventions" by Medieval monks. These scholars, who consider Western Marian cultus to have been very minor through the tenth and eleventh centuries, also stress the twelfth-century rise of the Medieval "Cult of the Virgin." Obviously this particular form of Marian cultus did not exist before the eleventh or twelfth centuries in the West, or anyplace else, because it was a Medieval creation. Similarly, the King Arthur of Medieval romance and chivalry did not exist before the creation of appropriate legends in the twelfth century, although there almost certainly was a sixth-century Roman-Briton ruler named Arthur who served as an appropriate model for the later legends as recently demonstrated by Ashe, *Discovery of King Arthur*.

In contrast to the documentary historical school of thought, Sharbrough, "Cult of the Mother," has presented considerable evidence to support the argument that lack of evidence does not indicate a dying out of mother goddess veneration in the Early Christian West and suggests that ancient female qualities of divinity were early attributed to Christ's mother. The lack of documentation is, at best, negative evidence and is especially problematic as proof for the nonexistence of popular beliefs in a poorly documented period when many people were illiterate. Geary, "Ninth-Century Relic Trade," p. 8, points out that the only written sources for eighth- and ninth-century religious practices and beliefs in Western Europe are Latin texts written by the clergy or by educated members of the aristocracy, and that these elites "lived a world apart" from the common people. In Geary's words, "direct evidence from the 'people' is entirely lacking," and the only insights from the written record come in the form of polemics about what the people should ideally be doing or should not be doing. One of the things they were doing, in disregard for church teaching, was worshiping at pagan holy places.

There is little question about the continuity of graphic and other symbolism from pagan mother goddesses to the explosive twelfth-century rise of the "Cult of the Virgin" in the West. (See Grabar, *Christian Iconography*, for illustrations.) It seems most unlikely that Western Europeans entirely gave up their mother goddess devotions for several centuries only to rediscover such a focus through adoption of ideas diffusing from the East. Indeed, one of the best arguments for the great antiquity of some form of Marian devotions in Western Europe is the rapidity with which the Medieval "Cult of the Virgin" caught hold of popular imagination all over Europe. There must have been a predisposition toward such a devotion. Perhaps it represents a sudden surfacing of a poorly documented process by which Europe's ancient mother goddesses were allowed to live on in tolerated, if not promoted, "Christianized" folk traditions centered on Christ's mother.

30. See plates in Lasko, *Ars Sacra*, and an illustrated discussion in Beckwith, *Early Medieval Art*, pp. 149–51.

31. Rothkrug, "Popular Religion" and "Religious Practices"; Kolb, *Vom Heiligen Blut*.

32. See Christian, *Person and God*, pp. 181–82, and Turner and Turner, *Image and Pilgrimage*, p. 207, for discussion of the role of saints as local "territorial demideities."

33. Bhardwaj, *Hindu Places of Pilgrimage*, p. 92, reports a more frequent emphasis on female goddesses at local Hindu pilgrimage centers than is the case at shrines of greater importance levels. If anything, the reverse is true in Europe, where there is some emphasis on saints, mostly male, at the levels of local festivals and chapel dedications. However, most saint-oriented local devotions do not fall into the categories of behavior that Europeans tend to think of as pilgrimages, and the emphasis on saints as a type of holy person is largely masculine-oriented merely because most people who have come to be considered saints in Western Europe were men.

Chapter Six

1. Dünninger, "Wahres Abbild," p. 281, discusses the translation of visionary experiences into the visual form of pictures or statues.

2. The word "miraculous" in its various translations has not meant the same thing to all peoples at all times. A study by Finucane, *Miracles and Pilgrims*, is useful for insights into the concept of the miraculous for English men and women of Medieval times. Also see Ward, *Miracles and the Medieval Mind*. Two definitions for the word "miracle" are given in the *American Heritage Dictionary of the English Language* (Boston: American Heritage Publishing Co., 1969): (1) "An event that appears unexplainable by the laws of nature and so is held to be supernatural in origin or an act of God," and (2) "A person, thing, or event that excites admiring awe." The word "miracle" comes to English from Old French and ultimately from the Latin word *mirari* meaning "to wonder at." Many wondrous events that give rise to pilgrimages or subsequently occur at shrines can be explained without reference to the supernatural as this is understood by people of the late twentieth century. Of course, to the faithful, possible alternative explanations are no proof that God did not have a hand in producing wondrous or strongly desired results.

3. Christian, "De los santos a María," p. 87.

4. Dünninger, "Wahres Abbild," p. 283.

5. Bagnaia, *Santuario Madonna della Quércia*.

6. Some churchmen seem to prefer this idea. Letters of inquiry sent to Roman Catholic bishops throughout the world in 1984 and 1985 have elicited a few responses from North America, Australia, New Zealand, and parts of formerly British Africa informing us that all churches in a particular diocese are equally sacred, or that the peoples' true pilgrimage is regular attendance at Mass. This type of comment, however, was usually followed by a statement to the effect that the diocese has no shrines such as those found in Europe.

7. Rothkrug, "Religious Practices," p. 7. The following discussion of the origins and evolution of pilgrimage related to saints' relics also draws from Brown, *Cult of the Saints* and "Relics and Social Status"; Geary, *Furta Sacra* and "Ninth-Century Relic Trade"; Sumption, *Pilgrimage*; and articles in Wilson, *Saints and Their Cults*. These works contain extensive bibliographical references. See especially Wilson, "Annotated Bibliography."

8. Theodoret of Cyrus quoted by Sumption, *Pilgrimage*, p. 28.

9. See Geary, *Furta Sacra* and "Ninth-Century Relic Trade."

10. Rothkrug, "Religious Practices," p. 6, writes: "The 'noble' parts of the saint were placed in a portable *capsa*, like martyr relics. On feast days, the capsa appeared on the altar; at other times it was concealed near the altar. In periods of epidemic or other public disaster, the people carried the capsa in processions. Meanwhile the less 'noble' parts of the saint remained in the original casket."

11. Mâle, *Religious Art in France: The Twelfth Century*, p. 4, and Sumption, *Pilgrim-*

age, p. 51, mention statue reliquaries in tenth-century southern France. Lasko, *Ars Sacra*, p. 104, points out that "representational" reliquaries were in use by the ninth century and that "a head-reliquary of St. Mauritius is known to have been given to Vienne Cathedral by King Boso of Provence" who died in 887. Reliquary busts are still much used in southern France, although most now found in churches and museums were created between the fifteenth and eighteenth centuries, according to an exhibition guidebook from Villefranche de Conflent, *Reliquaries*.

12. Sumption, *Pilgrimage*, p. 51, and Lasko, *Ars Sacra*, p. 105. Also see Lasko for a discussion and illustration of the tenth-century golden Virgin of Essen, West Germany, and Wilson's "Introduction" to *Saints and Their Cults*, p. 5, for further speculation on the evolution of statue veneration from reliquary images. Forsyth, *The Throne of Wisdom*, provides a detailed discussion of the development of Romanesque seated Madonnas.

13. Grabar, *Christian Iconography*, pp. 27–28, argues that the earliest Christian art may have been inspired by Jewish religious art and perhaps further encouraged by the spread of Manicheism, a new Persian religion that spread westward in the mid-third century and used images as propaganda for conversion. Also see du Bourguet, *Early Christian Painting*, pp. 1–14, and Gerhard, *World of Icons*, pp. 9–55. Possibly the oldest representation of the Madonna and Child, in the Catacomb of Priscilla, Rome, is discussed by Testini, *The Christian Catacombs*.

14. Epiphanius is quoted by Kitzinger, "Cult of Images," p. 93. We have drawn on Kitzinger's study for our discussion of image veneration in Early Christian times along with Beckwith, *Early Christian and Byzantine Art*; Grabar, *Christian Iconography*; and Brown, "A Dark Age Crisis." Brown, p. 277, points to the importance of Byzantine travelers through the cities of the Mediterranean world as agents for the westward diffusion of icon veneration in the sixth century. Our comments on early Marian image veneration in Byzantine-controlled or influenced Italy are largely drawn from shrine-specific literature and Vinciotti, *I mille santuari*. For relics and paintings of the Virgin brought to Northumbria, England, from Rome by Benedict Biscop in about 675 see Oakeshott, *Classical Inspiration*, p. 28.

15. Weitzmann, *The Icon*, p. 50.

16. Kolb, *Marien-Gnadenbilder*, p. 44. Also see Beckwith, *Early Christian and Byzantine Art*, p. 29.

17. Kolb, *Marien-Gnadenbilder*, p. 46.

18. For the rise of Christ-centered iconography see Grabar, *Christian Iconography*, pp. 71–75; du Bourguet, *Early Christian Painting*, pp. 15–17; and Beckwith, *Early Christian and Byzantine Art*, pp. 37–38. Beckwith mentioned that Eusebius of Caesarea wrote disapprovingly of painted icons of Christ that were widespread by the early fourth century. Also see Beckwith, *The Art of Constantinople*, p. 55, for discussion of a link between images and relics such as pieces of the True Cross.

19. These examples are from Kitzinger, "Cult of Images," pp. 101, 132.

20. A short version of the Avenum story was related in a 1981 letter from Abbe

Jacque Leroy, rector of Notre-Dame des Miracles in Orléans, and also told in Guillaume, "Notre-Dame des Miracles." A detailed discussion by Leroy, *La tradition vivante de Notre-Dame*, pp. 6–7, cites the first long account of the miracle of the arrow during the Norman Invasion as written in 1221 by Vincent de Beauvais in *Miroir Historique*, but mention of a growing devotion to the Virgin of the Miracles, encouraged by bishops and kings of France, was recorded in the tenth and eleventh centuries. Images were venerated in Syria by the late fifth century, so an example could have been part of the baggage of Syrian immigrants to France at that time. According to Kitzinger, "Cult of Images," pp. 103, 111–12, citizens of Edessa were saved from the Persian siege of 544 by a picture of Christ, and similar stories dating to the sixth century come from other eastern Mediterranean places.

21. Villette, "Que savons-nous de la Vierge," represents the continued speculation about the origins of the Chartres cultus in shrine literature.

22. The Longpont-sur-Orge story is told in a pamphlet available at the shrine. For Saint Germain see Kolb, *Marien-Gnadenbilder*, p. 34, and for Baud see Drochon, *Histoire illustrée des pèlerinages français*, p. 227, and Jean-Haffen, *Les fontaines bretonnes*, p. 72. Bardout, *La paille*, p. 15, illustrates a seated Gallo-Roman mother goddess from Alsace.

23. Recounted by Beckwith, *Early Medieval Art*, p. 29. Mâle, *Religious Art in France: The Twelfth Century*, p. 289, mentions that many mother goddess figures were transformed into Christian images of the Virgin Mary and suggests that the ancient image of the Virgin at Le Puy may have been a statue of the Egyptian Isis. Also see Forsyth, *The Throne of Wisdom*.

24. Many of the Spanish tales about mysteriously found images may have been made up after a pilgrimage began to explain the image's miraculous qualities. Some images, however, probably were found, which does not mean that these were hidden or lost during Moslem invasions. See Christian, *Local Religion*, pp. 89–90. For a discussion of Catalonian images about which such tales are told see Manfredi, *Santuarios de la Virgen*, pp. 183–88. For mention of Early Christian art in Spain see Beckwith, *Early Christian and Byzantine Art*, p. 13. García Rodríguez, "El culto de los santos," pp. 126–28, points out that although several Spanish basilicas and cathedrals had been dedicated to Mary by the seventh century, images of the Virgin, which can be interpreted as having received cultus, are not known for Spain before the Moslem invasions. Carvings at the hermitage of Quintanilla de las Vinas might represent Christ and Mary, and a figure on the tomb of Santa Engracia at Zaragoza has been interpreted as a representation of the Assumption, but it could have other meanings. On the other hand, García Rodríguez, p. 370, writing of saints, states: "True images of this period have not been found, but this does not allow us to conclude they did not exist." There are references in old documents to a few images of saints venerated during Visigothic times. García Rodríguez, pp. 387–417, also details evidence of extensive contacts between Visigothic Spain and North Africa, Italy, and the Eastern Mediterranean. As at Orléans, there appear to have been settlements of Eastern merchants and professionals

in Spanish cities, and southeastern Spain was under direct Byzantine control for a period of 70 years in the sixth century. Also see Collins, *Early Medieval Spain*.

25. German culture may have been particularly receptive to the suffering Christ as an object of pilgrimage cultus. Whereas Western iconography typically featured a triumphant Christ on the Cross prior to the thirteenth century, Byzantine-influenced portrayals of a spear-pierced Christ with head bowed forward were fairly common motifs in ninth-century Carolingian ivory carvings now found in northern West German and French museums and in church treasuries. Most remarkable is a crucifix engraved on the late tenth-century Lothar Cross kept in the Palace Chapel at Aachen, West Germany. There is no ambivalence in the symbolism. Christ slumps on the Cross, head down, with blood pouring from wounds in his hands, feet, and sides. Representations of the Crucifixion scene with a woman holding a chalice to catch blood gushing from the Savior's wounded side appeared in Germany by the twelfth century. Examples of such images can be see in in Lasko, *Ars Sacra*, plates 29, 31, 33, 61, 76, 107, 181, 221, 222, and fig. 3, p. 100, and in Beckwith, *Early Medieval Art*, pp. 149–51.

An early transfer of sanctity from relics to images seems to have been especially common in Bavaria where, according to Rothkrug, "Religious Practices," p. 86, to "have an image of the suffering Christ work miracles alongside other prodigies performed by the bleeding Host and relics from the passion was manifestly to intensify the impression that Jesus physically re-enacted His martyrdom at the site of the shrine."

26. These places are drawn from a survey of shrines in North America which we began in 1984.

27. See Wierermüller, *Heilige Walburga*. Cruz provides popularized discussions of several of these shrines in *The Incorruptibles* and *Relics*.

28. According to an old legend recounted by Warner, *Alone of All Her Sex*, pp. 86–87, the fifth-century Byzantine Empress Pulcheria asked the patriarch of Jerusalem to send her Mary's body so that it could be venerated in the imperial chapel in Constantinople. The request was refused on the grounds that the Virgin's body had vanished and the empress had to be satisfied with Mary's veil and sash. Pilgrims began to mention Mary's empty tomb near Jerusalem in seventh-century accounts. This church-enclosed tomb is still a place of pilgrimage as is Ephesus (modern Turkey), which also claims to be the site of the Virgin's empty tomb.

29. A letter from a priest at the Basilica of Notre-Dame in Évron, Department of Mayenne, France, mentioned that modern pilgrims still venerate a rock from the Bethlehem Milk Grotto brought by a pilgrim who returned from the Holy Land in about 648.

30. See Kolb, *Vom Heiligen Blut*.

31. Rothkrug, "Popular Religion," p. 36.

32. See Rothkrug, "Popular Religion" and "Religious Practices." Kolb, *Vom Heiligen Blut*, p. 6, distinguishes between five types of Holy Blood shrines. These are focused

on (1) blood from the Crucifixion, brought to Europe from the Holy Land; (2) blood from injured statues or paintings; (3) bleeding Hosts, involving events occurring during the Mass, or the abuse of a Host presumed to have been consecrated prior to its desecration; (4) Eucharistic wine turned into blood, which usually stains altar cloths; and (5) the bleeding Savior in the form of an image showing Christ bleeding profusely from many wounds.

33. Details of the story are given by Brückner, *Die Wallfahrt Walldürn*, and Gramlich, *250 Jahre Wallfahrtskirche*.

34. Several observers have noted that cult objects frequently have little artistic merit. An exception to the rule is sometimes noted in shrine literature, as for example Wellnhofer, *Ettal*, p. 23, who states, "Ettal is a rare case of a miraculous image being at the same time a valuable work of art." The thirteen-inch high Carrara marble statue of the Madonna and Child venerated at this South German shrine is thought to be the work of either Giovanni Pisano (d. 1328) or Tino di Camaino (d. 1337). In contrast, as pointed out by Kolb, *Marien-Gnadenbilder*, p. 107, many of the most famous representations of Mary have never acquired any special spiritual significance. As examples of famous works of art that have never been cult objects, Kolb mentions the *Sistine Madonna* by Raphael, the *Stuppacher Madonna* by Grunewald, and Michelangelo's famous *Pietà*. Copies of Michelangelo's work approach the status of cult objects, however, at some North American shrines—for example, at the Servite-maintained Grotto of the Sorrowful Mother in Portland, Oregon. On very rare occasions an image acquires special qualities because it is by a well-known artist. This occurred at Ostrach, Bavaria, where a painting of Mary and the Child that had hung in a damp chapel for centuries was taken down in 1935 and found to be by Hans Holbein the Elder. This discovery triggered a modest pilgrimage. See Dorn, *Die Wallfahrten des Bistums Augsburg*, pp. 135–36.

35. Image placement within Parisian churches has been considered by Wilson, "Cults of Saints." He found that saints' images and those of Christ were more often on the right than the left side of the churches. Images of the Virgin Mary were predominantly central or on the left, but there was no inevitable placement, only general tendencies.

36. For a geographer's study of devotions based on a movable object in the Jewish tradition see Maier, "Torah as Moveable Territory," pp. 18–23.

37. See Grosse Boymann and Grosse Boymann, *Basilica in Kevelaer*, and Oomen, *Kevelaer*. Material on Neviges comes from interviews.

38. According to Hartinger, "Mariahilf ob Passau," the pilgrimage church of Mariahilf was established at Passau, Bavaria, as the result of a series of visions in the early seventeenth century, and a copy of Cranach's painting was set up for veneration. As the popularity of this cultus spread through southern Germanic lands, more than 500 secondary shrines were established and developed into pilgrimage centers of greater-than-local significance. Also see Drunkenpolz, *Mariahilf ob Passau*. Emphasis on two-dimensional cult images is even more pronounced in Poland than in Italy and the

Germanic lands. Out of 126 Marian cult images illustrated in a book compiled by a Polish convent, Siostr Niepokalanek, *Z Dawna Polski*, 76 percent are characterized by flat surfaces.

39. The lack of two-dimensional pilgrimage cult images in France and Spain does not appear to have anything to do with a particular emphasis on sculpture as opposed to painting as an art form, even when religious subjects are involved, because both countries have important traditions of painting.

40. Weitzmann, *The Icon*, p. 9. In his "Introduction," p. 3, Weitzmann points out that "in late antiquity a more spiritual concept of deity developed, and the statue in the round gradually went out of fashion, to be replaced first by rather flat relief sculpture and then by painting. This tendency is most noticeable in the mystery religions, in which a transcendental outlook found more appropriate expression for the Deity in the dematerialized rendering of the human body." The process appears to have characterized the cults of both Mithras and Isis.

41. Most studies of symbolism in Christian art are based on museum and church collections and make no attempt to distinguish between cult images venerated at shrines and images in general. Kolb's *Marien-Gnadenbilder* is an exception.

42. Mâle, *Religious Art in France: The Thirteenth Century*, pp. 281–92, discusses Medieval artists' efforts to portray saints in a way that people could easily distinguish between them. He observes that some of the visual symbols placed in saints' hands derived from their patronage of specific craft guilds rather than episodes in their lives (pp. 291–92).

43. See Lasko, *Ars Sacra*.

44. See Satzger, *Wies Church*. Another well-known image of Christ chained to a pillar is found at Bihlafingen, West Germany. See Konrad, *Bihlafingen bei Laupheim*.

45. Recent literature concerning the Shroud of Turin is extensive, especially as it concerns the 1978 exhibition and the related scientific investigations, the results of some of which appear in Heller, *Report on the Shroud*. The official interpretation is Matteotti, *La santa sindone*. Variations in depictions of Christ through the centuries are illustrated in Thomas, *The Face of Christ*.

46. The Christ Child cultus is especially common in Peru and Bolivia.

47. The history of the Agreda pilgrimage is detailed by Peña García, *Agreda*. The statue in the photograph is a processional image.

48. Weitzmann, *The Icon*, pp. 62–63.

49. Warner, *Alone of All Her Sex*, provides a discussion on this theme in a chapter on "The Milk of Paradise."

50. For discussions of the symbolism of Mary with Christ in her womb, and as the merciful Mother holding her cloak over humanity, see Warner, *Alone of All Her Sex*, chapters 3, 21.

51. The early fifteenth-century image of Maria im Moos venerated at Halfing shows Mary holding an infant of about six to eight months represented in the proportional size of a three- or four-year-old child. See Bomhard, *Halfing/ Oberbayern*. A similar

image in German Swabia is illustrated in Stadelmaier, *Wallfahrtskirche*.

52. Sharbrough, "Cult of the Mother."
53. Warner, *Alone of All Her Sex*, pp. 206–9.
54. Rothkrug, "Popular Religion," pp. 73–74. At Donauwörth, West Germany, where documents related to the acquisition of Cross particles date from 1094, most of the votive paintings show a pietà, thus suggesting a special relationship to Mary. See Auer, *Heilig Kreuz Donauwörth*.
55. Kolb, *Marien-Gnadenbilder*, pp. 75–76.
56. See *Cenni storici* for Montallegro.
57. Shrine-specific literature for some of the more important pilgrimage centers where dark images are venerated includes Albareda, *Historia de Montserrat*; Alders, *Das Gnadenbild*; Angerhausen, *Die schwarze Muttergottes*; Bascher, *La Vierge noire de Paris*; Boix, *What Is Montserrat*; Espinel, *Peña de Francia*; Ferrer, *Notre-Dame de Font-Romeu*; Godin, *Rocamadour*; *Het zwarte Christusbeeld*; *Histoire de Notre-Dame de Délivrance*; Hoedl, *Altötting*; Hohmann, *Xanten-Marienbaum*; Lazzarini, *Il Volto Santo di Lucca*; MacGowan, *An Illustrated History*; Montaigu, *Rocamadour ou la pierre*; Raeber, *The Abbey of Einsiedeln*; Rocacher, *Rocamadour*; Rudel, *Le Folgoët*; Ruelle, *Notre-Dame du Chêne*; Trompetto, *Storia del santuario di Oropa*; Wiebel-Fanderl, "Die Verehrung der Altöttinger"; and Wimet, *Notre-Dame of Boulogne-sur-Mer*.
58. Warner, *Alone of All Her Sex*, p. 275.
59. Turner and Turner, *Image and Pilgrimage*, p. 75. See Mâle, *Religious Art in France: The Thirteenth Century*, p. 235, for a discussion of the application of metaphors in the Song of Songs to Mary in the sermons of Saint Bernard. Mâle, however, does not mention the dark-but-beautiful theme.
60. The idea that dark images of the Virgin Mary represent a Christian syncretism with dark mother goddesses has been developed by Moss and Cappannari, "In Quest of the Black Virgin," and Saillens, *Nos Vierges noires*. Also see Huynen, *L'Énigme des Vierges noires*, for claims of a relationship between darkness and special mystic powers. Begg, *The Cult*, provides an interesting gazetteer and imaginatively relates Black Virgins to mother goddesses, Gnosticism, Catharism, twelfth-century troubadours, the Merovingian Dynasty, and the Prieuré de Sion. Christian, "Devotion to Dark Images," finds no evidence for a pilgrim's conception of darkness as having any relationship to special powers; he also points out that many of the Catalonian images described as dark by Camos in the seventeenth century have been restored or replaced as light-skinned since that time.
61. For the spread of the Loreto cultus northward into the Germanies see Pötzl, "Santa-Casa-Kult." The Holy House was usually replicated, although such shrines nearly always have a cult image as well. Two fairly important subsidiary German Loreto cults with very black images are described by Beicht, *200 Jahre Pfarr- und Wallfahrtskirche*, and Plenker, *St. Maria in der Kupfergasse*.
62. Mâle, *Religious Art in France: The Twelfth Century*, p. 289.
63. Christian, personal communication.

64. For a detailed account of the Lucca cultus see Lazzarini, *Il Volto Santo di Lucca*. The Pan-European importance of the pilgrimage is discussed by Mâle, *Religious Art in France: The Twelfth Century*, pp. 253–57.

65. The idea that pilgrims may not pay much attention to the color of an image is developed by Christian, "Devotion to Dark Images."

66. This version of the story comes from signs and pamphlets found at this Valencian shrine in 1980 and 1983. Also see Diez, "Puig."

67. Photographs and description of these events are contained in Anibarro Espeso, *Estampas del Cerro*. A sermon by Alvarez Gallego, *Santuario Nacional*, provides information on the early years of the Sacred Heart cultus in Spain centered in Valladolid.

68. See Delarue, *Notre-Dame des Lumières*. Several shrines have more than one cult image. West German shrines at Gernsheim and Arnstein are among those with both a miraculous pietà and a miraculous Madonna and Child.

69. See Holstein, *Notre-Dame de Dusenbach*.

70. Several shrine booklets from places where the image is no longer vested show old prints portraying an elaborately garbed figure. For example, a pietà dating from 1370 venerated at Telgte, West Germany, is currently displayed with no embellishments and is of a natural dark wood. Votive cards from 1754 and 1850, however, show the image as light-skinned, elaborately vested, and decorated with ex-voto offerings. See Engelmeier, *Propsteikirche St. Clemens*. Very little seems to be known about the origins of image vestments, although the Turners suspect a Spanish origin. Moroccan brides still wear garments very similar to those found on vested Andalucian images such as the Virgen de la Cabeza when they stand on platforms to receive gifts on the third day of their weddings, as indicated by footage in a television documentary entitled "Women of Marrakech," broadcast in Oregon by the Public Broadcasting System during the winter of 1983. The resemblance in costume may only reflect a common source during the same time period in an Iberian region shared by Christians and Moslems, but the similarity does suggest a lead for further research. Also, the custom of dressing shrine images in cloth garments may be very old in the Mediterranean world. Rouse, *Greek Votive Offerings*, p. 354, mentions garments given to images as votives in Classical Greece.

71. For the Arroyo de San Servan example see Montes Bardo, *Iconografía de Nuestra Señora de Guadalupe*, pp. 101–2. Apparently, devotees of this image were unaware that it served as a reliquary for an earlier image until a recent restoration indicated this fact. The other examples are from Angely, *Notre-Dame de Bon-Encontre*, pp. 13–14, 45, and Moisan, *Basilique Notre-Dame du Roncier*.

Chapter Seven

1. Turner and Turner, *Image and Pilgrimage*, p. 110, pointed out that one can study "beliefs and myths as legitimate data in themselves." For an examination of the relationships between shrine legends and events that are described in documentary records see Christian, *Local Religion* and *Religious Apparitions*. Even fully documented shrine-formative events often have a quality that seems mythical to skeptics in that shrine stories are generally supposed to provide evidence for divine intervention.

2. This story is told in Consejo Superior de Investigaciones Científicas, "Santuarios," p. 2254. Recent details were contained in a letter from the diocesan office at Segorbe-Castellon in 1978. Many of the stories mentioned in this chapter were collected or expanded by correspondence or interviews at shrines, or are told in anonymously authored, undated booklets. For the most part, only published sources are cited here and do not, in all cases, contain all information on file concerning each story.

3. In cases where formative stories contained elements representative of more than one formative type, the assignment to specific categories followed certain rules that should be mentioned at this point. Any shrine specifically related to real or legendary events in the life of a saint was classified as a significant site except for those cases in which cultus was clearly generated by a much later discovery or acquisition of the saint's relics. Shrines not related to the birthplaces, death places, or earthly activities of saints were assigned to this category only when they were clearly at places of ancient religious importance and had no other story explaining the reason for their establishment.

Ex-voto shrines were usually easy to classify due to the generally matter-of-fact nature of such accounts. The most frequent overlap was with spontaneous miracle shrines. In cases where the cult-triggering events involved cures, those places at which the recovered individual or a member of his or her family built the initial votive chapel or church were counted as ex-voto shrines. Those where a shrine structure was sponsored by someone other than the initially cured person after several cures and/or other marvels had accumulated among pilgrims attracted to the place by miracle reports were counted as miracle shrines. To some extent, the miracle category is residual in that it is made up of places where no image was found or had recently been acquired. In cases where salvation from war, plague, or other hazard coincided with such miracles as weeping Madonnas, the miracle was given classificatory precedence over the votive element in the story.

The acquired object category was used whenever the origin of cultus was said to be contemporaneous with the arrival of an image or relic from some reasonably distant place. The major overlap is with the found object category, as, for example, when a ship was wrecked and an image that was being transported was cast up on a beach and soon discovered by the local people. As a general rule, we counted such events as examples of acquired image stories if the object was said to have been found right away. If stories suggested that the object had been en situ for a long period of time before it was found, as for example at Santiago de Compostela, Spain, the shrine was placed in the found object category even though the object had originally come from afar.

Found object shrines also tend to overlap with apparitional shrines, especially in early accounts of visions. If the legend referred to an image that "appeared," often behaving as if it were alive, the story was placed in the found object category. If the vision preceded the finding, and especially when the discovery occurred after the vision had been reported, the place was counted as an apparitional shrine. Some stories stressed miracles of the acquisition of holy objects, but included references to dream visions reported after pilgrims began arriving at the site. These shrines were classified as miracle or acquired object shrines rather than apparitional shrines. In the final section of this chapter, however, all stories with a visionary element are examined as a class.

4. Turner and Turner, *Image and Pilgrimage*, pp. 17–18.

5. Ibid., p. 18.

6. Keiser, *Der Kaltenbrunnen* and *Wallfahrtsort*.

7. Henggeler, *Helvetia Sancta*, p. 212.

8. An early version of this story appears in Konas, *Märterle*.

9. According to Stephenson, *Walsingham Way*, p. 42, the region around the English shrine at Walsingham was especially devastated by the Black Death of 1348–49 possibly as the result of large numbers of pilgrims in the area.

10. For useful examples of the rich geographical literature on the human response to environmental hazards and sociological studies of behavior during and after disasters see Burton, Kates, and White, *Environment as Hazard*; G. F. White, *Natural Hazards*; Haas, Kates, and Bowden, *Reconstruction following Disaster*; and Baker and Chapman, *Man and Society*. Case studies indicating the functional role of religious beliefs and activities in the aftermath of disaster include works by Davis, "The Role of the Russian Orthodox Church," and Nolan, *Research on Disaster*. Part of the explanation for the efficacy of pilgrimage as a response to disaster is suggested by Perluter and Monty, "The Importance of Perceived Control." These authors found that a sense of control, whether real or not, seemed to increase the functional viability of experimental animals.

11. The story recounted here is told on a plaque in the Tulle Cathedral.

12. The Aire story comes from *Notre-Dame de Panetière*. Additional details on the Telgte story are found in Angerhausen, *Die schwarze Muttergottes*, and Engemann, *Propsteikirche*. For Kaiserslautern see Minoritenkloster, *50 Jahre*.

13. Schnell, *Votiv- und Wallfahrtskirche*.

14. Vinciotti, *I mille santuari*, p. 810.

15. Staercke, *Notre-Dame des Belges*, p. 70.

16. These Austrian stories are recounted by Gugitz, *Österreichs Gnadenstätten*.

17. Floc'h, *Perros-Guirec*, contains photographs of the sailors' votive offerings.

18. The Sannazzaro story is in Vinciotti, *I mille santuari*, p. 73; the Zafferana story is

from Colangeli, *Le feste dell'anno*, p. 243; and details of the Brouilly story written only a few years after the event are in Drochon, *Histoire illustrée des pèlerinages français*, p. 1020.

19. The Hötting story is told by Fischer and Stoll, *Kleines Handbuch*, 2:76, and the Kirchberg story by Gugitz, *Österreichs Gnadenstätten*.

20. Fischer and Stoll, *Kleines Handbuch*, 3:72–73.

21. During the fall and early winter of 1980–81 we lived just below the Kaulbach chapel, and sometimes it seemed as if the Catholic pilgrimage chapel and the Lutheran parish church were engaged in a duel of bells.

22. Gabrielli, *Saints and Shrines*, p. 13; Vinciotti, *I mille santuari*, p. 39.

23. Shrine literature at Pontchâteau specifically mentions the apparitional tradition, but points out that the vision was never "officially" recognized. Leite, *História do Sameiro*, provides a detailed history of the Portuguese shrine.

24. At the San Vittorino shrine, many people, including the young Americans who have become members of the community, talk about the apparition. Brother Gino Burresi, O.M.V., received the stigmata on the day Padre Pio died and provides a good example of a modern version of the holy man venerated in life. For the antiquity of such traditions in the Christian context see Brown, "Rise and Function."

25. Our account of the Treviglio story follows Gabrielli, *Saints and Shrines*. A plaque on the side of a church in this Po Valley town marks the spot where the image reportedly shed tears and blood. The most elaborate version we found of the story from Bar-le-Duc comes from Drochon, *Histoire illustrée des pèlerinages français*, p. 1200. The shouting statue, or a later copy of it, was destroyed during the French Revolution, but a few pieces are said to have been saved and incorporated into a new image that was moved to the church of Notre-Dame. This town has several other Marian images that are considered miraculous, some of which seem to have changed their names several times, perhaps as a result of major restorations or replacements.

26. See Vinciotti, *I mille santuari*, pp. 40–41, for the Re story. The Bergatreute story is told in a shrine booklet, Unglert, *Neun-Tage-Gebet*. The photograph of the currently venerated Re image reproduced in *I mille santuari* does not look very much like the image venerated at the West German shrine. A fascinating account of the Madonna dell'Arco pilgrimage, its origins and current significance, is given by Tentori, "An Italian Religious Feast."

27. The Siracusa story is retold in numerous general works on the shrines of Europe because this particular manifestation quickly received official support.

28. Henggeler, *Helvetia Sancta*, p. 25, and Lüthold-Minder, *Helvetia Mariana*, p. 206, recount the Bourgillon story.

29. Henggeler, *Helvetia Sancta*, p. 180.

30. Rosenegger and Bartl, *Wallfahrten in und um München*, p. 18; Friedel, *Maria Eich*.

31. Marnham, *Lourdes*, is useful for a description of the social dynamics of cures at modern shrines. Although our study does not probe deeply into the social-psychological dimensions of pilgrimage and deliberately avoids theological implications, it is a

matter of record that some quite unusual cures coincide with pilgrimages or vows to make pilgrimages and that a lot of sick or handicapped people and/or those who love them feel better as a result of pilgrimages.

32. The Truns story is told by Fry, *Nossa Donna*. See Dorn, *Die Wallfahrten*, pp. 65–66, for the Kempten story.

33. Fahrmann, *Führer*, on Xanten.

34. For details on the Seligenstadt shrine see Effelborn, *Die Übertragung*.

35. For an overview of the peregrinations of Holy Blood relics see Kolb, *Vom Heiligen Blut*.

36. The Trápani story is told by Monaco, *Notizie storiche*; the Nettuno story by Amodei, *El Santuario di Nettuno*, and Cempanari and Amodei, *Il Santuario*; and the Chiávari story by Rombi, *I segreti*.

37. See Bernhard, *Kirchwald*, for the story as told by the Franciscan hermit who was tending the shrine when we visited in 1981.

38. For details on such stories see Geary, *Furta Sacra*.

39. There are obvious resemblances between many of the stories of images arriving mysteriously by water and the stories of shrines that developed because images were found under mysterious circumstances. Of the 70 stories that included the motif of object arrival by water, 20 were classified as stories of image finding rather than image acquisition because the tale stressed the circumstances under which the object was found and the water arrival element was merely an explanation of how it must have come to be where it was discovered. For Mariaort see Utz, *Wallfahrten*, pp. 140–41.

40. Large numbers of holy images were shipped from Iberia to the Americas during the colonial period, and many were then carried overland by mule train to inland destinations—usually the major Hispanic cities. Stories of images mysteriously brought by animals, as well as by ships that refuse to leave harbor until the image is taken ashore, are typically told at Latin American shrines that obtained images said to have been bound for some other, usually more important, place.

41. Toor, *Festivals*, pp. 130–31.

42. In March 1981, we discussed the implications of the formation story and the pilgrimage with a resident Augustinian monk in Genazzano. He attributed the widespread popularity of the cultus to vigorous promotion by Augustinians, and, indeed, many widespread pilgrimage devotions have been promoted by religious orders.

43. An account of the northward spread of the Loreto cultus in the form of a large number of subsidiary shrines is provided by Pötzl, "Santa-Casa-Kult." For an account of the 1920 papal proclamation of the Virgin of Loreto as patroness of aviators see Grimaldi, "La Madonna di Loreto."

44. The shrine image at Chipiona is one of the curious Black Madonnas holding a white Christ Child.

45. Christian, *Local Religion*, p. 89.

46. Drochon, *Histoire illustrée des pèlerinages français*, p. 1187, gives the traditional story of the discovery of the image of Notre-Dame de Bon-Secours at Saint-Avold.

Reference to the probable "plant" of the image by Benedictine monks is contained in a leaflet distributed at the shrine.

47. The story of the body floating down the river comes from Steinheim am Main, West Germany, and is said to have occurred in 1309.

48. The Medjugorje visions began on June 24, 1981, near a village about 18 miles from Mostar in Yugoslavia's culturally varied Herzegovina region—an area where Roman Catholics, Eastern Orthodox Christians, Moslems, and atheistic Marxists coexist. Here, the sociopolitical implications of Mary's appearance in a Marxist country, along with the demeanor and testimonies of the six young Catholic visionaries, have made a favorable impression on a number of influential Western European churchmen. As of 1984 the visions were still occurring and the local bishop had reserved judgment in this politically explosive situation. See Laurentin and Rupcic, *Is the Virgin Mary Appearing?* and Ljubic, *Erscheinungen der Gottesmutter*. Large numbers of pilgrims were traveling to the shrine from the United States by 1988, and articles in newspapers and popular magazines concerning apparitions were including Medjugorje with Lourdes, Fátima, and Knock.

49. Christian, *Religious Apparitions*, p. 4.

50. Ibid., p. 5. Apparitions as socially significant phenomena have recently attracted the attention of several other scholars. Kselman, "Miracles and Prophecies," examined nineteenth-century French reports of visions and shrines generated by these events from the perspective of gaining insights into the complex interactions between political, economic, secularizing, and religious dynamics in that place and time. Sociologist Carroll, "Visions of the Virgin Mary" and "The Virgin Mary at La Salette and Lourdes," explores some of the psychological and social-psychological dimensions of socially significant visionary experiences. As will be discussed in the next section of this chapter, Turner and Turner, *Image and Pilgrimage*, used two types of Marian apparitions as models for examining change in religious orientations. For studies of apparitions by churchmen concerned with how to identify a "true" apparitional experience see Staehlin, *Apariciones*, and Billet et al., *Vraies et fausses apparitions*. A shorter discussion is found in Laurentin's *Pèlerinages, sanctuaires, apparitions*. It should be pointed out that even when an apparition is officially accepted and an ecclesiastically supported pilgrimage shrine developed, no Roman Catholic is required to believe that the apparition "really" occurred in the sense of the Virgin or any other holy person actually appearing on earth. Official approval in a modern day merely indicates that the local bishop finds that nothing associated with the vision is contrary to faith or morals, and that sufficient evidence of the vision's supernatural reality exists to justify belief.

51. Christian, *Religious Apparitions*, p. 4.

52. Turner and Turner, *Image and Pilgrimage*, pp. 162–63. We are particularly aware of the assumptions built into the literature on Latin American pilgrimage because, in the early 1970s, our interpretations were much the same as the Turners, although we

were working independently. In Nolan, "Mexican Pilgrimage Tradition," Mexican pilgrimage was summarized as a syncretism of Spanish Medieval and Amerindian traditions. This assumption pervades the literature to the extent that it deals with the transatlantic diffusion of Christianity. Although it is generally understood by Latin Americanists that the sixteenth- through eighteenth-century explorers and colonizers of the Hispanic New World were very much men of their day and were, for the most part, introducing or attempting to introduce the very latest ideas of their times, the missionaries, for some curious reason, seem to be thought of as representatives of Iberian medievalism. This notion prevails despite the fact that it is fairly well understood that major reinterpretations of religious belief systems had occurred during the Renaissance, even in lands that remained Roman Catholic after the Protestant Reformation, and that still further reinterpretations took place in these lands as a result of the Catholic Reformation. In addition, a considerable number of the Catholic missionaries on the expanding frontiers of the Spanish colonies were not native Iberians and could hardly be expected, for that reason alone, to be transmitters of Medieval Iberian ideas about pilgrimage. The issue is important for the development of better interpretations of the evolution of Latin American pilgrimage traditions.

53. Turner and Turner, *Image and Pilgrimage*, p. 203.

54. Ibid., p. 38. These authors view modern pilgrimage, and especially the modern-type Marian apparition, as "a 'metasocial commentary' on the troubles of this epoch of wars and revolutions with its increasing signs of industrial damage to the natural environment."

55. Christian, *Local Religion* and *Religious Apparitions*, provides a good discussion of the building of new shrine-formative stories on older stories in wide circulation.

56. Fox, *Pagans and Christians*, provides an extensive discussion of pagan and early Christian visionary expectations and experiences.

57. The actual age of Marian cultus in Zaragoza is unknown. The city was a pilgrimage center by the late sixth century, but in those days the officially promoted cultus appears to have centered on Saint Aemilian. See Collins, *Early Medieval Spain*, p. 71. Some historians think that shrine stories describing very early Marian visions are suspect because Marian pilgrimage in the West seems to be of a fairly late date, at least in written records. However, there seems little doubt that the seventh-century Spanish bishop, Ildephonsus of Toledo, could have had, and probably did have visions of the Virgin Mary. As presented by Collins, ibid., p. 76, the bishop's best known work, *On the Perpetual Virginity of the Blessed Virgin Mary*, begins: "O, My Lady, my Queen, my Ruler, Mother of my Lord, Handmaiden of your Son, Bearer of the Creator of the World, I beg you, I pray you, I beseech you, that I may have the spirit of your Lord, that I may have the spirit of your Son, that I may have the spirit of my Redeemer, that I may truly and worthily know you, that I may truly and worthily say things about you that ought to be said." Ildephonsus, of course, was extremely important as a promoter of Marian devotions in the early Spanish church.

The Evesham story appears to have been written down during the eighth century. See Christian, *Religious Apparitions*, p. 36. For a detailed early twentieth-century version see W. J. Walsh, *Apparitions and Shrines of Heaven's Bright Queen*, pp. 209–17.

58. For Irish legends, including vision stories, see Pochin-Mould, *Irish Pilgrimage*.

59. This shrine's history and legends are described in detail in Depluvrez, *Notre-Dame de Tongre*.

60. During the High Middle Ages the Norman and Italian shrines dedicated to Saint Michael were linked by a highly developed route of penitential pilgrimage. See Tripputi, "Aspetti cultuali."

61. Turner and Turner, *Image and Pilgrimage*, pp. 154–55, summarize the implications of Mary as Theotokos in the context of the European pilgrimage tradition. As for the two images, Vinciotti, *I mille santuari*, illustrates only the dark image. A pamphlet, obtained at the shrine, mentioned that the dark image is thought to have once held a child figure, but, if so, it has been greatly modified. The current version has both hands raised, palms forward, in an ancient gesture of prayer. The pilgrimage is very popular throughout the month of May.

62. These stories are told in Vinciotti, *I mille santuari*, and repeated in booklets, pamphlets, and interviews collected at several of the shrines.

63. Christian, *Local Religion*, p. 91, suggests that the increasing emphasis on images was part of a process leading toward the Christianization of the landscape. Because of interruptions in the development of Christian pilgrimages resulting from greater or lesser periods of Moslem control, the passions generated by the events of the Reconquest, and a variety of other factors, generalization from Spanish data to European shrines in general is open to question. The Irish, for example, needed no images to Christianize their landscape.

64. An overview of the Belgian shrine is found in Dessay, *Basilica of Saint Hubert*. Works dealing with Einsiedeln and Walsingham have previously been cited. For an account of Saint Hemma's life, see Posch, *Hemma von Gurk*.

65. The 23 stories involving deaf-mute, or merely mute visionaries who subsequently begin to speak, are all from Italy. Fourteen of these visionaries were females, and all but one of these were described as girls. The other nine seers were males, most of them referred to as boys. At Cavallermaggiore, Italy, in 1452, Mary is said to have left a signed note with an adult male deaf-mute, saying she would care for the city in a time of plague and war. This seer seems to have remained deaf and unable to speak. In an Austrian case the seer's deaf-mute son was cured. Given the power of a sign involving a mute person who begins to speak, it seems curious that this type of shrine-formative account appears to be almost exclusively Italian.

66. Christian, *Religious Apparitions*, provides an appendix of documents related to the official investigations of several of the Spanish cases. There is no possibility of a later introduction of more modern elements into these fifteenth- and sixteenth-century apparition accounts. Interestingly, several of the Spanish versions have Mary

appearing as a child or a very young girl, a theme also found in Italy. The theme turns up fairly often in shrine literature but rarely in iconography.

67. The primary object of veneration at this mountain-top shrine is a dark image of the Madonna, but the seminarian who escorted us around the shrine complex showed us a curious stone about five feet high that looked rather like a woman's head and shoulders. He explained that this stone was the "image" discovered as a result of the Frenchman's visionary search. Details are contained in Espinel, *Peña de Francia*.

68. Servi di Maria, *Cenni storici*, gives details concerning the Vicenza apparitions and references to accounts in shrine archives. An account of the events, dated from 1430, still exists as an original.

69. According to Christian, *Religious Apparitions*, p. 230, the Caravággio shrine was important by at least 1470, although the earliest known written reference to the apparition story dates from the early seventeenth century. The story is clearly expressed in on-site shrine iconography and in a booklet by Bianchi, *La Madonna*. In addition to the prototypically modern-type apparitions of Renaissance Italy and Spain, there are numerous stories from the period that combine elements of the Turners' prototypically Medieval and Modern Marian visions in a variety of ways. Many of the sixteenth- through eighteenth-century American shrine stories are not classic Medieval shepherds' cycle tales, as suggested by the Turners. Most, including the cases described by the Turners to prove their point, contain elements that these authors view as essentially modern. The story of Mary's appearance to the Aztec Indian, Juan Diego, on the hill of Tepeyac in 1531 provides an example. As the Mexican Virgin of Guadalupe formation story has been told for centuries, Mary appeared alone. Her message, particularly her expression of concern for the Indian peoples of New Spain, obviously had political connotations. No cult image was found at the site as an immediate result of the vision. Instead, the seer reported his visions to the Spanish bishop who demanded proof. When Diego returned to the site for the third time, roses bloomed on the December hillside. He wrapped the flowers in his cloak and returned to the bishop. When the cloak was spread, the roses had been replaced with a painting of the Virgin as an Indian girl on the material of the garment. For various interpretations of the symbolism of this story see Demarest and Taylor, *The Dark Virgin*; Turner and Turner, *Image and Pilgrimage*, pp. 76–95; and Wolf, "The Virgin of Guadalupe."

70. Christian, *Religious Apparitions*.

71. The icon venerated at Montallegro shows Mary on her deathbed. A small figure representing her soul has left her body. A three-figured Christ as the Trinity stands at the bedside along with several saints. The ceiling painting above the shrine church altar shows Mary without the Christ Child addressing the visionary.

72. Although the Kevelaer story generally refers to the event as an apparition, the man apparently did not see the Virgin but merely heard her voice.

73. Danigo, *Sainte-Anne d'Auray*, tells the story of the Brittany shrine. When we were present at the July 26 pilgrimage Mass in 1980, the homily was about the

visionary who is being promoted for beatification. Music was provided by a choral group representing a subsidiary shrine to Saint Anne of Auray in a former French West African colony. For insights into the Canadian cultus at Sainte-Anne-de-Beaupré, see Lefebvre, *Saint Anne's Pilgrim People*. Several studies of French-Canadian pilgrimage traditions are found in Boglioni and Lacroix, *Les pèlerinages du Québec*. Saint Anne was popular in Brittany before the apparitions at Sainte-Anne-d'Auray. These particular visions, however, were promoted by Carmelites from 1628 onward and were probably the most influential manifestation of the Saint Anne cultus during the early seventeenth century. French settlement, much of it from Western France, began in Nova Scotia and up the Saint Lawrence in the first decade of the seventeenth century. The first chapel at Sainte-Anne-de-Beaupré was built in 1658, only 35 years after the Brittany apparition report.

74. Christian, *Religious Apparitions*, pp. 142–44, provides a detailed account of the records of the visions at Sant Aniol. A summary of records concerning the Vinay manifestations is found in Delarue, *Notre-Dame de l'Osier*. Turner and Turner mention the Le Laus story, but, in keeping with their preconceptions, state in a footnote that "the pilgrimage is a late instance of the 'shepherds' cycle' type, rather than a forerunner of the modern 'visionary' pilgrimage." The grounds for disclaiming this well-known seventeenth-century visionary shrine as "modern" seem to rest on the seer Benoîte Rencurel's versatility as a visionary. Although, during the 50-year period of her visions, she mostly saw Mary alone, she also saw the Madonna with Child at least once and conversed with Saint Maurice. A booklet available at the shrine, *Histoire du pèlerinage*, gives the currently promoted version of this story.

75. This version of the Heiligwasser story is based on Gugitz, *Österreichs Gnadenstätten*.

76. As is the case with most important epiphanies, the visions at Paray-le-Monial and the development of the cultus of the Sacred Heart of Christ have generated a substantial literature. For an introduction see Ladame, *Paray-le-Monial* and *Sainte Marguerite-Marie*. Harvey, "Monument and Myth," is useful for subsequent development of the cultus in France. Alvarez Gallego, *Santuario Nacional*, describes the later apparitions at Valladolid, Spain.

77. Beevers, *The Sun Her Mantle*, provides an introduction to these shrines and to that part of the extensive literature on modern, officially recognized Marian apparitional shrines published before the mid-1950s. Subsequent publications are numerous. The majority of these books and articles repeat the same things.

78. Scey, *Notre-Dame du Chêne*.

79. At the time of our visits to Collevalenza and San Vittorino in 1981, the religious founders were still alive. In both places, pilgrims told us much more than had occurred to us to ask about the cult-formative visions, the meaning of these visions, and the powers of the still-living seers. Shrine literature from both of these places provided subtle hints of visionary experiences but offered no details or proclamations of such happenings. Apparently, it becomes more appropriate to refer to a story of visions in

writing after the seer-founder is deceased. The visionary element in the story from Nossa Senhora do Sameiro at Braga is mentioned in shrine literature and the tomb of the founder, Martinho António Pereira da Silva, is visited by pilgrims to this shrine. For a detailed account of the origins and development of this cultus see Leite, *História do Sameiro*. Of the above-mentioned shrines, that at Schönstatt near Vallendar on the Rhine has become the most important for the development of secondary pilgrimage places in many parts of the world including the United States, Canada, Australia, South Africa, and several Latin American countries. An account of the Schönstatt movement is found in Monnerjahn, *Schönstatt*.

80. For references to some of the publications on these shrines see Chapter 4, n. 14.

81. Billet et al., *Vraies et fausses apparitions*, lists 199 apparitions in Europe and the USSR between 1929 and the mid-1970s. Christian, "Religious Apparitions and the Cold War," pp. 242–43, has supplemented this list with his own data from Spain and additional reports from Italy for a total of 220 visions, 44 percent of which occurred in Italy. Many twentieth-century apparitions outside of Europe have not become known beyond their native lands, even when they have given rise to pilgrimages. During a summer's investigation in western South America in 1984, we found four Ecuadorian shrines that had been established because of twentieth-century apparition accounts. Since 1980, apparitions of the Virgin Mary have been reported from such diverse places as Nicaragua, Venezuela, and Kenya. Nicaragua's Sandinista government, concerned about the political implications of the visions there, banned coverage of such events in the local presses. Nevertheless, large numbers of pilgrims visit Cuapa, Nicaragua, where a seer known as Bernardo reported in 1981 that the Virgin told him the Sandinistas were atheistic Communists. The local bishop, who was subsequently exiled, encouraged the development of this pilgrimage. The Venezuelan manifestations began in the Diocese of Los Teques on March 25, 1984, and are said to have been seen by 500 to 600 people. These reports were being investigated by the local bishop when he corresponded with us in 1985. The Kenyan events, according to a 1985 letter from the bishop of Eldoret, are stimulating a series of Marian pilgrimages and devotions to the rosary in that African country.

82. Christian, "Religious Apparitions and the Cold War."

Chapter Eight

1. Brown, *Cult of the Saints*, p. 88. Also see Delehaye, *Les origines*.

2. Several works by Brown deal with the theme of holy hermits. See especially "Rise and Function" and "Town, Village and Holy Man." For Celtic saints of the fifth through ninth centuries see Duckett, *The Wandering Saints*.

3. Several geographers have explored the idea of sacred places in a general way. Kickeler, "Fundamental Questions," stresses the importance of remoteness, loneliness, and inaccessibility as favoring sanctity of place in his discussion of linkages between

religion and landscape. Isaac, "God's Acre," p. 151, suggests that many places are "thought to possess, or be possessed by, the power of the holy," but also points out, p. 149, "that to elaborate on the theme of holiness is to intrude on a domain preempted by theology, and few ventures are as dangerous as the transgression of that sacred boundary." In "Religious Geography," Isaac explores the differences between sacred places that are taboo, and thus avoided, and those that attract, thus becoming pilgrimage centers. One of the most prolific writers on the meaning of places of various kinds is Tuan; see "Discrepancies," "Ambiguity in Attitudes," "Sign and Metaphor," and *Space and Place*. For a geographer's interpretation of changing European views of nature see Glacken, *Traces on the Rhodian Shore*.

4. Danigo, *Sainte-Anne d'Auray*, p. 25.

5. Data on town sizes and road classifications were drawn from a series of Esso road maps published during the 1970s. These maps were available at the same scale for all countries in the study area and used standardized symbols. Distances from the nearest city were measured using the kilometer figures given on these maps. Larger scale maps were used to estimate locational variables in the case of small communities and isolated shrines not appearing on the Esso maps. This procedure yielded a rough approximation that had the merit of consistency from one shrine to the next. The spatial relationship of the shrine to its community was recorded only in the 2,941 cases for which such information was provided in shrine literature, recorded in field notes, or apparent on large scale maps. Developing and recording this detailed locational information proved so time consuming that it was done only for those shrines inventoried before 1980, with a consequent emphasis on shrines in the areas where the largest amounts of information were collected early in the study—namely Austria, West Germany, France, Italy, and Ireland. The "convenience" sample is large enough to be considered meaningful in a general way, but does not allow for contrasts between all countries or areas in terms of shrine location. It was found that Irish shrines are, in general, considerably more "remote" by our definition than those on the Continent.

6. See especially L. White, "Historical Roots," and Moncrief, "Cultural Basis."

7. See Eliade, *Patterns*, *The Sacred and the Profane*, and *Images and Symbols*; Frazer, *The Golden Bough*; Graves, *The White Goddess*; James, *The Tree of Life*; Neumann, *Great Mother*. Also of interest are Weston, *From Ritual to Romance*, and Wilkins, *The Rose-Garden Game*.

8. For numerous examples of tree veneration in Germanic traditions see Grimm, *Teutonic Mythology*. On the average, accounts involving miraculous trees tend to be of more recent origin than those related to other types of site features and are strongly associated with the Virgin Mary.

9. Wieser and Dickermann, *Der Vierbergelauf*, illustrates this pilgrimage.

10. According to Fox, *Pagans and Christians*, pp. 206–7, in the pagan tradition, "Wherever there was water . . . there was a possible source of prophecy." Springs were part of the ritual at the major oracular shrines such as Delphi and Didyma, and people

tried to predict the future at numerous holy springs by throwing offerings into the water to see if they would sink or swim. Possibly, the connection between water and eyes extends beyond simple treatments for eye problems to reflect an ancient association between holy water and greater insight, or ability to "see" into the future.

11. A local priest told us that the romería to the saint's shrine upstream was a far more important event for the people of the town and the district than the pilgrimage and fiesta associated with Cuenca's Marian shrine.

12. For a discussion of literature related to oak veneration, see Taylor, "Tree Worship." This article argues for the theory of a connection between thunder, or sky gods, and the propensity of oaks to be struck by lightning more often than other trees. Ancient ideas about oaks as homes for female spirits and goddesses form another theme for the argument of a continuity in oak veneration, particularly as it relates to Marian cultus.

13. Geographer Clarissa Kimber (personal communication) has suggested that shrine offerings and plants collected at shrines be examined to determine what proportion have traditional uses as medicinal plants. Crosses made of twigs are found at a number of Austrian and Irish shrines.

14. Several of the places with stories about the Holy Family's flight from the Holy Land are old shrines, some of which appear to have been pre-Christian holy places. Other legends from Austria associate trace stones with the footprints or kneeprints of saints, as is common elsewhere. At least four Austrian trace stones are said to be the Devil's footprints.

15. A number of shrines with other types of sacred stones are also marked by cairns. Placing small stones at certain places along a pilgrim path or round is especially common in Ireland, but is also found in France, Italy, and Austria. A good discussion of the various ways in which Irish pilgrims behave toward sacred stones and other environmental features is found in Logan, *Holy Wells of Ireland*.

16. An important modern cultus, originally focused on what appeared to be an image of Mary in a broken rock, developed in southern Texas during the early 1940s. The rock was found by a Mexican-American woman near three water routing gates, or check valves, in an irrigation system and became revered in the local dialect as "La Virgen de los Tres Cheques." The local priest, who was of Basque origin, was concerned with the large numbers of people coming to the woman's home to venerate the rock. He placed an order with a carver in Guadalajara for a copy of an image of Mary revered as miraculous at San Juan de los Lagos in Jalisco, Mexico. After many adventures, including salvation from a serious car accident, the priest returned to San Juan, Texas, with the image and successfully preempted the growing folk cultus. The shrine of the Virgin of San Juan, Texas, is currently the most important pilgrimage center in the state and draws pilgrims from Mexican-American communities all over the United States. The irrigation canal rock seems to have disappeared.

17. Christian discusses the mystique that can develop around abandoned towns in *Local Religion*. Beresford and St. Joseph, *Medieval England*, p. 102, suggest that English

stories of images that insisted on walking to lonely sites may have been related to the parish churches abandoned when whole villages migrated or died in a plague.

18. Several West German shrines are particularly important for refugees from Eastern Europe. For southern Europe see Christian, "Religious Apparitions and the Cold War."

19. We are grateful to the late David Sopher for pointing out to us the especially strong connections between the locations of European pilgrimage shrines and places where special events occurred or are thought to have occurred. This was also mentioned in his paper on "The Message of Place." Also see Kickeler, "Fundamental Questions," p. 95.

20. The themes of pilgrimage as an enactment of mankind's position as a wayfarer and stranger in this world and of pilgrimage as a metaphor of the struggle of human existence are found in several articles in Kriss-Rettenbeck and Mohler, *Wallfahrt kennt keine Grenzen*. See especially Kriss-Rettenbeck, Kriss-Rettenbeck, and Illich, "Homo Viator," and Baumer, "Wallfahrt als Metapher." These modern writers accept the earthly act of pilgrimage to particular places as a viable way to deal with the stresses of the human condition.

21. See Graber, *Wilderness as Sacred Space*, and Erickson, "Ceremonial Landscapes."

Bibliography

ADAC. *Der grosse ADAC Generalatlas.* Stuttgart: Mairs Geographischer Verlag, 1980.
Adair, J. *The Pilgrim's Way: Shrines and Saints in Britain and Ireland.* Over Wallop, Hampshire: Thames & Hudson, 1978.
Albareda, Anselmo M. *Historia de Montserrat.* Montserrat, 1974.
Alders, Alfons. *Das Gnadenbild "an gen Trappenboom": 550 Jahre Wallfahrt nach Marienbaum.* Kleve: Boss-Druck und Verlag, 1980.
Almagro, Martin. *Guia de Mérida.* Valencia: Artes Graficas Solar, 1983.
Altgott, Christel. *Heroldsbach: Eine mütterliche Mahnung Mariens.* Monchengladbach, 1979.
Alvarez Gallego, Emilio. *Santuario Nacional de la Gran Promesa de Valladolid.* Madrid: Imprenta Avilista, 1953.
———. *Santuario Nacional de la Gran Promesa.* Valladolid: Imprenta Obra Social del Santuario Nacional, 1975.
Amodei, Tito. *Il Santuario di Nettuno: Nostra Signora delle Grazie e Santa Maria Goretti.* Rome: Editore Torre, 1978.
Angely, Jean. *Notre-Dame de Bon-Encontre.* Bon-Encontre, Lot-et-Garonne: Les Editions du Sanctuaire, 1949.
Angerhausen, Julius. *Die schwarze Muttergottes Legenden und die schmerzhafte Mutter von Telgte.* Warendorf, Westfalen: Verlag J. Schnellsche, 1961.
Anibarro Espeso, Emiliano. *Estampas del Cerro de los Ángeles, tabor, calvario y altar mayor de España.* Madrid: Obra Nacional del Cerro de los Ángeles, 1975.
Antier, Jean-Jacques. *Le pèlerinage retrouvé.* Paris: Le Centurion, 1979.
Aradi, Zsolt. *Shrines of Our Lady around the World.* New York: Farrar, Straus & Young, 1954.
Ashe, Geoffrey. *The Discovery of King Arthur.* Garden City, N.Y.: Anchor Press/Doubleday, 1985.
Attwater, Donald. *The Penguin Dictionary of Saints.* Harmondsworth, Middlesex: Penguin Books, 1965.
Auer, Max, et al. *Heilig Kreuz Donauwörth: 950 Jahre Kreuzpartikel.* Donauwörth: Druckerei Ludwig Auer, 1979.
Automobile Association of Great Britain. *AA Road Guide to France.* New York: Automobile Association of Great Britain, 1969.
Bagnaia, Sante. *Santuario Madonna della Quércia.* Viterbo: Archimede Quatrini e Figli, 1974.

———. *Museo della basilica di S. Maria della Quércia in Viterbo*. Viterbo: Tipolitografia Quatrini Archimede e Figli, 1979.

Baker, George W., and Chapman, Dwight W., eds. *Man and Society in Disaster*. New York: Basic Books, 1962.

Bardout, Michele. *La paille et le feu: Traditions vivantes d'Alsace*. Paris: Berger-Levrault, 1980.

Barruol, Jean. *Sainte-Anne d'Apt d'après une documentation nouvelle*. Apt: F. et M. Reboulin, 1964.

Barthes, Gilles. *La Sainte-Baume*. Toulon: Frère Gardien de la Sainte-Baume, 1970.

Bascher, Jacques de. *La Vierge noire de Paris: Notre-Dame de Bonne Délivrance*. Paris: Tequi, 1979.

Baumer, Iso. "Gestalt und Sinn der Wallfahrt heute." In *Wallfahrt heute*, edited by Iso Baumer and Walter Heim, pp. 11–38. Freiburg: Kanisius Verlag, 1978.

———. "Wallfahrt als Metapher." In *Wallfahrt kennt keine Grenzen*, edited by Lenz Kriss-Rettenbeck and Gerda Mohler, pp. 55–64. Munich and Zurich: Verlag Schnell & Steiner, 1984.

Beckwith, John. *The Art of Constantinople: An Introduction to Byzantine Art, 330–1453*. Greenwich, Conn.: Phaidon Publishers, 1961.

———. *Early Medieval Art*. New York: Frederick A. Praeger, 1964.

———. *Early Christian and Byzantine Art*. Harmondsworth, Middlesex: Penguin Books, 1970.

Beevers, John. *The Sun Her Mantle*. Westminster, Md.: The Newman Press, 1954.

Begg, Ean. *The Cult of the Black Virgin*. London and New York: Arkana—Routledge & Kegan Paul, 1985.

Beicht, Walter, ed. *200 Jahre Pfarr- und Wallfahrtskirche Maria Himmelfahrt Ludwigshafen-Oggersheim*. Ludwigshafen-Oggersheim: Nitsch, 1977.

Belgian National Tourist Office. *Belgium: Festivals and Folklore*. Liège: Tourist Office, 1976.

Beresford, M. W., and St. Joseph, J. K. S. *Medieval England: An Aerial Survey*. Cambridge: Cambridge University Press, 1979.

Bernhard, Frater. *Kirchwald: Wallfahrtskirche und Einsiedelei am Heuberg Pfarrei Nussdorf/Inn*. Rosenheim: Kunstverlag Alois Gartner, 1977.

Berthou, Marie. *Saint-Hervé: Patron des chanteurs et des musiciens*. Quimper: L'Imprimerie Cornouaillaise, 1973.

Bhardwaj, Surinder. *Hindu Places of Pilgrimage in India: A Study in Cultural Geography*. Berkeley, Los Angeles, and London: University of California Press, 1973.

Bianchi, Alberto. *La Madonna di Caravaggio*. Caravaggio: Merisio Editore, 1958.

Billet, Bernard, et al. *Vraies et fausses apparitions dans l'Église*. 2d ed. Paris: Editions P. Lethielleux, 1976.

Boglioni, Pierre, and Lacroix, Benoit, eds. *Les pèlerinages du Québec*. Actes du colloque du Centre d'Études des Religions Populaires, Trois-Rivieres, Oct. 2, 1976. Québec: Université Laval, 1981.

Boix, Maur M. *What Is Montserrat: A Mountain, a Sanctuary, a Monastery, a Spiritual Community.* Barcelona: Publicaciones de l'Abidia de Montserrat, 1974.

Bomhard, Peter. *Halfing/Oberbayern: Pfarr- und Wallfahrtskirche.* Munich and Zurich: Verlag Schnell & Steiner, 1975.

Brandicourt, Joseph. *Saint-Christophe et les pèlerinages automobiles à Saint-Christopher-le-Jajolet.* Abbeville: Somme, 1934.

Broekhuizen, S., ed. *Atlas of Cereal Growing Areas in Europe.* Vol. 2. New York: Elsevier Publishing, 1965.

Brown, Peter. *The Cult of the Saints: Its Rise and Function in Latin Christianity.* Chicago: University of Chicago Press, 1981.

———. "A Dark Age Crisis: Aspects of the Iconoclastic Controversy." In *Society and the Holy in Late Antiquity*, pp. 251–301. Berkeley and Los Angeles: University of California Press, 1982.

———. "Relics and Social Status in the Age of Gregory of Tours." In *Society and the Holy in Late Antiquity*, pp. 222–50. Berkeley and Los Angeles: University of California Press, 1982.

———. "The Rise and Function of the Holy Man in Late Antiquity." In *Society and the Holy in Late Antiquity*, pp. 103–52. Berkeley and Los Angeles: University of California Press, 1982.

———. "Town, Village and Holy Man: The Case of Syria." In *Society and the Holy in Late Antiquity*, pp. 153–65. Berkeley and Los Angeles: University of California Press, 1982.

Brückner, Wolfgang. *Die Wallfahrt Walldürn.* Walldürn: Verlag Augustinerkloster, 1977.

———. "Fusswallfahrt Heute." In *Wallfahrt kennt keine Grenzen*, edited by Lenz Kriss-Rettenbeck and Gerda Mohler, pp. 101–13. Munich and Zurich: Verlag Schnell & Steiner, 1984.

Burton, Ian; Kates, Robert W.; and White, Gilbert F. *The Environment as Hazard.* New York: Oxford University Press, 1978.

Caplan, Anita. "Pilgrims and Priests as Links between a Sacred Center and the Hindu Culture Region: Prayag's Magh Mela Pilgrimage." Ph.D. dissertation, University of Michigan, 1982.

Caraman, Philip. *Saint Cuthbert Mayne.* London: Catholic Truth Society, n.d.

Carrara, Athos. *Bocche parlanti: Gli ex voto di Montenero.* Montenero: Collana Marilux, 1969.

Carroll, Michael. "Visions of the Virgin Mary: The Effect of Family Structures on Marian Apparitions." *Journal for the Scientific Study of Religion* 22, no. 1 (1983): 205–22.

———. "The Virgin Mary at La Salette and Lourdes: Whom Did the Children See?" *Journal for the Scientific Study of Religion* 24, no. 1 (1985): 56–74.

"Carte qui donné les principaux sanctuaires marials d'Italie qui n'évoqué pas les saints." *Missi* 414 (1978): 237.

Cartwright, J. K. *The Catholic Shrines of Europe.* New York: McGraw-Hill, 1955.

Cazes, Albert, et al. *Ex-voto du Roussillon.* Villefranche de Conflent: Syndicat d'Initiative, 1976.

Cempanari, Atanasio, and Amodei, Tito. *Il Santuario di Nostra Signora delle Grazie e di Santa Maria Goretti.* Rome: P. P. Passionisti, 1964.

Cenni storici di Nostra Signora di Montallegro. Rapallo: S. G. Emiliani, 1962.

Charles-Edwards, T. *Saint Winefride and Her Well: The Historical Background.* London: The Catholic Truth Society, 1971.

Cheetam, Nicolas. *Keepers of the Keys: A History of the Popes from St. Peter to John Paul II.* New York: Charles Scribner's Sons, 1983.

Chelini, Jean, and Branthomme, Henry, eds. *Les chemins de Dieu: Histoire des pèlerinages chrétiens des origines à nos jours.* Paris, 1982.

Chorherr, Edith. "Bibliographie." In *Wallfahrt kennt keine Grenzen*, edited by Lenz Kriss-Rettenbeck and Gerda Mohler, pp. 543–68. Munich and Zurich: Verlag Schnell & Steiner, 1984.

Christian, William A., Jr. *Person and God in a Spanish Valley.* New York and London: Seminar Press, 1972.

―――. "Holy People in Peasant Europe." *Comparative Studies in Society and History* 15 (1973): 106–14.

―――. "De los santos a María: Panorama de las devociónes a santuarios españoles desde el principio de Edad Media hasta nuestros días." In *Temas de antropologia española*, edited by C. L. Tolosana, pp. 49–106. Madrid: Akal, 1976.

―――. *Local Religion in Sixteenth Century Spain.* Princeton: Princeton University Press, 1981.

―――. *Religious Apparitions in Late Medieval and Renaissance Spain.* Princeton: Princeton University Press, 1981.

―――. "Religious Apparitions and the Cold War in South Europe." In *Religion, Power and Protest in Local Communities: The Northern Shore of the Mediterranean*, edited by Eric R. Wolf, pp. 239–66. Berlin, New York, and Amsterdam: Mouton Publishers, 1984.

―――. "Devotion to Dark Images in Catalonia: The Case of the Virgin of Montserrat." Paper presented at the Conference on the Dark Madonna, University of California, Los Angeles, November 1985.

Ciarrochi, A., and Mori, E. *Le tavolette votive italiane.* Udine: Edizioni Doretti, 1960.

Clayton, M., and Kormoss, I. B. F., eds. *Oxford Regional Economic Atlas: Western Europe.* Oxford: Oxford University Press, 1971.

Cohen, Ester. "In the Name of God and Profit: The Pilgrimage Industry in Southern France in the Late Middle Ages." Ph.D. dissertation, Brown University, 1976.

Colangeli, Mario. *Le feste dell'anno.* Rome: Sugar Edizioni, 1977.

Collins, Roger. *Early Medieval Spain: Unity in Diversity, 400–1000.* New York: St. Martin's Press, 1983.

Connelly, Roland. *The Slipper Chapel*. Great Wakering, Essex: The Pilgrim Bureau, 1975.

———. *Walsingham Pilgrim Book: A Guide to the Shrine*. Great Wakering, Essex: The Pilgrim Bureau, 1975.

———. *Walsingham Is for Today: The Place of England's National Shrine in the Modern World*. London: The Catholic Truth Society, n.d.

Consejo Superior de Investigaciones Científicas, comp. "Santuarios." In *Diccionario de historia eclesiástica de España*, 4:2207–2381. Madrid: Instituto Enrique Florez, 1978.

Costa Clavell, Xavier, ed. "Romerías gallegas." In *Bandolerismo, romerías y jergas gallegas*. La Coruna: Biblioteca Gallega, 1980.

Cousin, Bernard. *Ex-voto de Provence: Images de la religion populaire et de la vie d'autrefois*. Paris: Desclee de Brouwer, 1981.

Couturier de Chefdubois, Isabelle. *Mille pèlerinages de Notre-Dame*. 3 vols. Paris: Éditions Spes, 1953.

Coxe, Antony D. Hippisley. *Haunted Britain: A Guide to the Supernatural in England, Scotland and Wales*. London: Pan Books, 1973.

Crumrine, N. Ross. "Three Coastal Peruvian Pilgrimages." *El Dorado* 2, no. 1 (1977): 76–89.

———. "The Peruvian Pilgrimage: A Ritual Drama." *Americas* 30, no. 8 (1978): 28–34.

———. and Morinis, E. Alan, eds. *La Peregrinación: The Pilgrimage in Latin America*. Westport, Conn.: Greenwood Press, forthcoming.

Cruz, Joan Carroll. *The Incorruptibles*. Rockford, Ill.: Tan Books Publishers, 1977.

———. *Relics*. Huntington, Ind.: Our Sunday Visitor, 1984.

Daniel, Glyn. "Megalithic Monuments." *Scientific American* 243, no. 1 (1980): 78–90.

Danigo, J. M. *Sainte-Anne d'Auray*. Translated by E. Robo. Lyon: Lescuyer et Fils, 1955.

David, Christopher. *St. Winefride's Well: A History and Guide*. Slough: Kenion Press, 1969.

Davidson, H. R. E. *Gods and Myths of Northern Europe*. Harmondsworth, Middlesex: Penguin Books, 1973.

Davis, Nancy. "The Role of the Russian Orthodox Church in Five Pacific Eskimo Villages as Revealed by the Earthquake." In *The Great Alaska Earthquake of 1964: Human Ecology*, National Research Council, pp. 125–46. Washington, D.C.: National Academy of Sciences, 1970.

Deffontaines, Pierre. *Géographie et religions*. Paris: Gallimard, 1948.

Delaney, John J. *Dictionary of Saints*. Garden City, N.Y.: Doubleday & Company, 1980.

Delarue, Louis. *Notre-Dame de l'Osier, les origines du pèlerinage d'après les manuscrits et imprimes du temps de 1649 à 1686*. Lyon: M. Lescuyer et Fils, 1966.

———. *Notre-Dame des Lumières*. Lyon: E.I.S.E., 1973.
Delaruelle, Etienne. *La piété populaire du moyen age*. Turin: Bottega d'Erasmo, 1975.
Delcourt, Marie. *Les Grands Sanctuaires de la Grèce*. Paris: Presses Universitaires de France, 1947.
Delehaye, Hippolyte. *Les origines du culte des martyres*. Brussels: Société des Bollandistes, 1933.
De Leon, Ángel. *Mendigo por Dios: Vida de Fray Leopoldo de Alpandeire*. Granada: Litografia Anel, 1974.
Demarest, Donald, and Taylor, Coley, eds. *The Dark Virgin: The Book of Our Lady of Guadalupe*. New York: Coley Taylor, 1956.
Dempsey, Thomas. *Richard Gwyn, Man of Maclor: Martyr or Traitor*. Farnworth: The Catholic Printing Company of Farnworth, 1970.
Demus, Otto. *Byzantine Art and the West*. New York: New York University Press, 1970.
Depluvrez, Jean-Marc, comp. *Notre-Dame de Tongre: Son culte, son patrimoine, 1081–1981*. Ath: Basilique de Nol, 1981.
Dessay, M. *The Basilica of Saint Hubert: History and Description*. Saint-Hubert: Editions Gofflot, 1959.
Diez, A. "Puig." In *Diccionario de historia eclesiástica de España*, compiled by Consejo Superior de Investigaciones Científicas, 4:2323. Madrid: Instituto Enrique Florez, 1978.
Di Flumeri, Gerardo, ed. *Padre Pio di Pietrelcina: Acts of the First Congress of Studies on Padre Pio's Spirituality*. San Giovanni Rotondo: Edizioni Padre Pio da Pietrelcina, 1972.
———. *The Mystery of the Cross of Padre Pio of Pietrelcina*. San Giovanni Rotondo: Edizioni Padre Pio da Pietrelcina, 1977.
Di Pietri, Michele. *Sulle orme di San Francesco nella terra reatina: Guida al santuari della Valle Santa*. Greccio, 1980.
Dorcy, Mary Jean. *Shrines of Our Lady*. New York: Sneed and Ward, 1956.
Dorn, Ludwig. *Die Wallfahrten des Bistums Augsburg*. Augsburg: Eos Verlag, 1975.
Dowse, Ivor. *The Pilgrim Shrines of England*. London: The Faith Press, 1963.
———. *The Pilgrim Shrines of Scotland*. London: The Faith Press, 1965.
Drochon, J. E. B. *Histoire illustrée des pèlerinages français de la très Sainte Vierge*. Paris: Plon, 1890.
Drunkenpolz, Engelbert. *Mariahilf ob Passau*. Munich and Zurich: Verlag Schnell & Steiner, 1974.
du Bourguet, Pierre. *Early Christian Painting*. Translated by Simon Watson Taylor. New York: The Viking Press, 1965.
Duckett, Eleanor. *The Wandering Saints*. London, 1959.
Dünninger, Hans. "Wahres Abbild: Bildwallfahrt und Gnadenbildkopie." In *Wallfahrt kennt keine Grenzen*, edited by Lenz Kriss-Rettenbeck and Gerda Mohler, pp. 274–83. Munich and Zurich: Verlag Schnell & Steiner, 1984.

Dunninger, J. "Fourteen Holy Helpers." In *New Catholic Encyclopedia*, 5:1045–46. New York: McGraw-Hill, 1968.

Dupront, Alphonse. *Du Sacré: Croisades et pèlerinages*. Paris: Gallimard, 1987.

Duret, Evelyne. *Fêtes de Haute Provence: Calendrier illustré et commenté*. Marseille: Editions Jeanne Laffitte, 1981.

Editorial Everest. *Mapa Everest de carreteras: España y Portugal*. 1:500,000. Leon-Madrid: Editorial Everest, 1980.

Effelborn, Karl. *Die Übertragung und Wunder des heiligen Marzellinus und Petrus von Einhard*. Darmstadt: Historischer Verein für Hessen, 1977.

Eliade, Mircea. *Birth and Rebirth: The Religious Meanings of Initiation in Human Culture*. Translated by William Trask. New York: Harper & Brothers, 1958.

———. *Patterns in Comparative Religion*. Translated by R. Sheed. London: Sheed and Ward, 1958.

———. *The Sacred and the Profane: The Nature of Religion*. New York: Harper Torchbooks, 1961.

———. *Images and Symbols: Studies in Religious Symbolism*. New York: Sheed and Ward, 1969.

Engelmeier, Paul. *Propsteikirche St. Clemens und Wallfahrtskapelle Telgte*. Telgte: Buchhandlung Joseph Hansen, 1973.

Engemann, Karl-Heinz. *Propsteikirche und Wallfahrtskapelle Telgte*. Munich and Zurich: Verlag Schnell & Steiner, 1978.

Epton, Nina. *Spanish Fiestas*. London: Cassell, 1968.

Erickson, Kenneth A. "Ceremonial Landscapes of the American West." *Landscape* 22, no. 1 (1977): 39–47.

Espinel, Jose Luis. *Peña de Francia: Historia, peregrinos, paisajes*. Salamanca: Imprenta Calatrava, n.d.

Evans, E. Estyn. *Irish Folk Ways*. London, Henley, and Boston: Routledge & Kegan Paul, 1957.

Fahrmann, Willi. *Führer durch den Dom von Xanten*. Xanten: Verlag Gesthuysen, 1979.

Fastner, Herbert. *"Oh, heilige Mutter Anna, hilf!" Eine vergessene Heilige in ihrer Verehrung und in der Volkskunst*. Grafenau: Morsak Verlag, 1986.

Ferrer, Joachim. *Notre-Dame de Font-Romeu et son sanctuaire*. Perpignan: Imprimeur Sinthe, 1976.

Finucane, Ronald C. *Miracles and Pilgrims: Popular Beliefs in Medieval England*. London: Dent, 1977.

Fischer, R., and Stoll, A. *Kleines Handbuch österreichischer Marien-Wallfahrtskirchen*. 3 vols. Vienna: Bergland Verlag, 1977–79.

Floc'h, Loeiz A. *Perros-Guirec: Notre-Dame de la Clarté*. Lyon: Lescuyer, n.d.

Fontenrose, Joseph. *Python: A Study in Delphic Myth and Its Origins*. New York, 1974.

Forsyth, Ilene H. *The Throne of Wisdom: Wood Sculptures of the Madonna in Romanesque France*. Princeton: Princeton University Press, 1972.

Fowler, W. Warde. *The Roman Festivals of the Period of the Republic: An Introduction to the Study of the Religion of the Romans*. 1899. Reprint. Port Washington, N.Y.: Kennikat Press, 1969.
Fox, Robin Lane. *Pagans and Christians*. New York: Alfred A. Knopf, 1987.
France. Institut Géographique National. "Pèlerinages et fêtes religieuses." On *Carte touristique 1:250,000*. 16 maps. 1974–76.
Franziskaner von Bornhofen. *Bornhofen-Pilger*. Kamp-Bornhofen am Rhein, 1978.
Frazer, J. *The Golden Bough*. London: Macmillan & Co., 1955.
Freiburg, Archdiocese. *Wallfahrten und Wallfahrtsbrauchtum in der Erzdiozese Freiburg*. Freiburg: Meisterdruck Verlag, 1977.
Freytag-Berndt. *Auto Atlas Österreich 1:200,000*. Vienna: Verlags- u. Vertriebsges, 1975–76.
Friedel, Josef. *Maria Eich—Geschichte einer kleinen Wallfahrt*. Aalen-Ebnat: Katholisches Pfarramt, 1979.
Fry, Carl. *Nossa Donna della Glisch Trun/Grischun*. Munich and Zurich: Verlag Schnell & Steiner, 1969.
Gabriel, Jean. *San Damiano, Ruge an die Welt*. Bulle: Parvis-Verlag, 1968.
Gabrielli, Aldo. *Saints and Shrines of Italy*. Rome: Holy Year 1950 Publishing Company, 1949.
García Rodríguez, Carmen. "El culto de los santos en la España Romana y Visigoda." In *Monográfias de historia eclesiástica*, vol. 1. Madrid: Consejo Superior de Investigaciones Científicas, 1966.
Geary, Patrick J. *Furta Sacra: Thefts of Relics in the Central Middle Ages*. Princeton: Princeton University Press, 1978.
―――. "The Ninth-Century Relic Trade: A Response to Popular Piety." In *Religion and the People, 800–1700*, edited by James Obelkevich. Chapel Hill: University of North Carolina Press, 1979.
―――. "The Saint and the Shrine: The Pilgrims' Goal in the Middle Ages." In *Wallfahrt kennt keine Grenzen*, edited by Lenz Kriss-Rettenbeck and Gerda Mohler, pp. 265–73. Munich and Zurich: Verlag Schnell & Steiner, 1984.
Gegenfurtner, Wilhelm von. *Die Wallfahrten zur Gottesmutter im Bistum Regensburg*. Regensburg, 1973.
Gerhard, H. P. *World of Icons*. New York: Harper & Row, 1971.
Gillett, Henry Martin. *The Story of the Relics of the Passion*. Oxford: Basil Blackwell, 1935.
―――. *Famous Shrines of Our Lady*. London: Samuel Walker, 1949.
―――. *Famous Shrines of Our Lady in England and Wales*. London: Samuel Walker, 1957.
―――. "Shrines." In *New Catholic Encyclopedia*, 13:181–87. New York: McGraw-Hill, 1968.
Glacken, Clarence H. *Traces on the Rhodian Shore: Nature and Culture in Western*

Thought from Ancient Times to the End of the Eighteenth Century. Berkeley: University of California Press, 1967.

Godin, Joseph. *Rocamadour.* Translated by P. Tate and A. E. Tate. Luzech: Imprimerie de Boissor, 1979.

Goebeler, Heinz, and Schulten, Walter. *Ex Voto Weihgaben und kirchliche Kostbarkeiten.* Telgte: Heimathaus Münsterland, 1974.

Gomez, M. C. "Virgen del Pilar." In *Diccionario de historia eclesiástica de España*, compiled by Consejo Superior de Investigaciones Científicas, 4:2316–17. Madrid: Instituto Enrique Florez, 1978.

Gomez-Menor, J. "Virgen del Sagrario." In *Diccionario de historia eclesiástica de España*, compiled by Consejo Superior de Investigaciones Científicas, 4:2337. Madrid: Instituto Enrique Florez, 1978.

Gonzales, Conchita, and Daley, Harry. *Miracle at Garabandal: The Story of Mysterious Apparitions in Spain and a Message for the Whole World.* Garden City, N.Y.: Doubleday and Co., 1983.

Grabar, Andre. *Christian Iconography: A Study of Its Origins.* Bollingen Series 35, no. 10. Princeton: Princeton University Press, 1968.

Graber, Linda H. *Wilderness as Sacred Space.* Washington, D.C.: Association of American Geographers, 1976.

Gramlich, August. *250 Jahre Wallfahrtskirche zum Heiligen Blut in Walldürn.* Walldürn: Walldürner Druckerei Odenwald, 1978.

Graves, Robert. *The White Goddess.* London: Fabor and Fabor, 1954.

Greeley, Andrew. *The Mary Myth: On the Femininity of God.* New York: Seabury Press, 1977.

Greenwood, Davydd. "Culture by the Pound: An Anthropological Perspective on Tourism as Cultural Commoditization." In *Hosts and Guests: The Anthropology of Tourism*, edited by Valene Smith, pp. 129–38. Philadelphia: University of Pennsylvania Press, 1977.

Grimaldi, Floriano. "La Madonna di Loreto patrona degli aeronauti." In *Wallfahrt kennt keine Grenzen*, edited by Lenz Kriss-Rettenbeck and Gerda Mohler, pp. 300–305. Munich and Zurich: Verlag Schnell & Steiner, 1984.

Grimm, Jacob. *Teutonic Mythology.* 4 vols. *Deutsche Mythologie*, 4th ed. (1883–88), translated by J. S. Stallybrass. New York: Dover Publications, 1966.

Gross, Daniel R. "Ritual and Conformity: A Religious Pilgrimage to Northeastern Brazil." *Ethnology* 10 (1971): 129–48.

Grosse Boymann, Guido, and Grosse Boymann, Olga Lope de. *The Basilica in Kevelaer.* Munich and Zurich: Verlag Schnell & Steiner, 1979.

Guardians of the Shrine of Our Lady of Walsingham. *Walsingham: England's Nazareth.* Walsingham: Guardians of the Shrine, 1969.

———. *The Meaning of Walsingham.* Walsingham: Guardians of the Shrine, n.d.

Gugitz, Gustav. *Österreichs Gnadenstätten in Kult und Brauch.* 5 vols. Vienna: Verlag

Bruder Hollinek, 1956–58.

Guías Afrodisio Aguado. "Calendario de las fiestas principales." In *España turística*, pp. 85–112. 5th ed. Madrid: Afrodisio Aguado, Editores Libreros, 1964.

Le Guide religieux et touristique d'Alsace et de Moselle. Paris: Les Nouvelles Éditions Touristiques et Artistiques, 1979.

Guilford, Everard Leaver. *Travellers and Travelling in the Middle Ages*. London: Sheldon Press, 1924.

Guillaume, Paul. "Notre-Dame des Miracles." In *Comment visiter Orléans*, edited by Société Archeologique et Historique de l'Orléanais, 15. Orléans: Syndicat d'Initiative d'Orléans, n.d.

Gurgel, Klaus D. "Travel Patterns of Canadian Visitors to the Mormon Culture Hearth." *Canadian Geographer* 20, no. 5 (1976): 405–17.

Haas, Eugene; Kates, Robert W.; and Bowden, Martin J., eds. *Reconstruction following Disaster*. Cambridge: MIT Press, 1977.

Hahn, Maria Anna. *Siedlungs- und wirtschaftsgeographische Untersuchung der Wallfahrtsstatten in den Bistumern Aachen, Essen, Köln, Limburg, Münster, Paderborn, Trier*. Düsseldorf: Rheinland-Verlag, 1969.

Hall, D. J. *English Medieval Pilgrimage*. London: Routledge & Kegan Paul, 1965.

Hanson, R. P. C. *Saint Patrick, His Origins and Career*. Oxford: Oxford University Press, 1968.

Hartinger, Walter. "Mariahilf ob Passau: Entstehung und Verbreitung einer volkstümlichen Wallfahrt und Andachtsform." In *Wallfahrt kennt keine Grenzen*, edited by Lenz Kriss-Rettenbeck and Gerda Mohler, pp. 284–99. Munich and Zurich: Verlag Schnell & Steiner, 1984.

Harvey, David. "Monument and Myth." *Annals of the Association of American Geographers* 69, no. 3 (1979): 362–81.

Heath, Sidney. *Pilgrim Life in the Middle Ages*. Boston and New York: Houghton Mifflin, 1912.

Hell, Vera, and Hell, H. *The Great Pilgrimage of the Middle Ages: The Road to St. James of Compostela*. New York: Clarkson N. Potter, 1964.

Heller, John H. *Report on the Shroud of Turin*. Boston: Houghton Mifflin, 1983.

Henggeler, P. R. *Helvetia Sancta: Heilige Statten des Schweizerlandes*. Einsiedeln: Buchdruckerei Franz Kalin, 1968.

Herwaarden, Jan van. "St. James in Spain up to the 12th Century." In *Wallfahrt kennt keine Grenzen*, edited by Lenz Kriss-Rettenbeck and Gerda Mohler, pp. 235–47. Munich and Zurich: Verlag Schnell & Steiner, 1984.

Histoire de Notre-Dame de Délivrance et de la ceinture de la Sainte-Vierge à Quintin (Cotes-du-Nord). Quintin, 1963.

Histoire du pèlerinage de Notre-Dame du Laus. Gap, 1977.

Hoedl, Franz Xaver. *Altötting*. Altötting: Drittordensverlag, 1962.

Hohmann, Karl-Heinz. *Xanten-Marienbaum*. Cologne: Deutzer Freiheit, 1978.

Hole, Christina. *English Shrines and Sanctuaries*. London: Batsford, 1954.

Holstein, Damien. *Notre-Dame de Dusenbach*. Ribeauville: Frères Capucins de Dusenbach, 1976.
Howard, Donald R. *Writers and Pilgrims: Medieval Pilgrimage, Narratives and Their Posterity*. Berkeley, Los Angeles, and London: University of California Press, 1980.
Hunt, E. D. *Holy Land Pilgrimage in the Later Roman Empire, A.D. 312–460*. Oxford: Oxford University Press, 1982.
Hurst, M. E. *Transportation Geography*. New York: McGraw-Hill, 1974.
Huynen, Jacques. *L'Énigme des Vierges noires*. Paris: Editions Robert Lafont, 1972.
Isaac, Erich. "God's Acre." *Landscape* 14, no. 2 (1964–65): 149–57.
———. "Religious Geography and the Geography of Religion." In *Man and the Earth*, University of Colorado Studies, Series in Earth Sciences no. 3, pp. 1–14. Boulder: University of Colorado Press, 1965.
Jacobs, Jay., ed. *The Horizon Book of Great Cathedrals*. New York: American Heritage Publishing Company, 1968.
James, E. O. *The Cult of the Mother Goddess*. London: Thames & Hudson, 1959.
———. *Seasonal Feasts and Festivals*. New York: Barnes and Noble, 1961.
———. *The Tree of Life*. Leiden: E. J. Brill, 1966.
Jean-Haffen, Yvonne. *Les fontaines bretonnes*. Rennes: Ouest France, 1979.
Jenkins, Claude. "Christian Pilgrimages, A.D. 500–800." In *Travel and Travelers of the Middle Ages*, edited by A. P. Newton, pp. 39–69. New York: Alfred A. Knopf, 1950.
Johnson, Francis. *Addict for Christ: The Story of Venerable Matt Talbot*. London: Incorporated Catholic Truth Society, n.d.
Jones, Charles W. *Saint Nicholas of Myra, Bari, and Manhattan*. Chicago and London: The University of Chicago Press, 1978.
Jones, Francis. *The Holy Wells of Wales*. Cardiff: University of Wales Press, 1954.
Jusserand, J. J. *English Wayfaring Life in the Middle Ages*. London: T. Fisher Unwin, 1888.
Keiser, Josef. *Der Kaltenbrunnen bei Ranschbach in der Pfalz*. Ranschbach, 1978.
———. *Wallfahrtsort "zu unserer Lieben Frau von Kaltenbrunn."* Ranschbach, 1981.
Kendall, Alan. *Medieval Pilgrims*. New York: G. P. Putnam's Sons, 1970.
Ketchum, Richard M., ed. *The Horizon Book of the Renaissance*. New York: American Heritage Publishing Company, 1961.
Kickeler, Paul. "Fundamental Questions in the Geography of Religions." In *Readings in Cultural Geography*, edited by P. Wagner and M. Mikesell, pp. 44–117. Chicago: University of Chicago Press, 1962.
King, Ursula. "England's Nazareth: Pilgrimage to Walsingham during the Middle Ages and Today." In *Wallfahrt kennt keine Grenzen*, edited by Lenz Kriss-Rettenbeck and Gerda Mohler, pp. 527–42. Munich and Zurich: Verlag Schnell & Steiner, 1984.
Kitzinger, Ernst. "The Cult of Images before Iconoclasm." *Dumbarton Oaks Papers* 8 (1954): 83–150.
Knittel, G. "Les pèlerinages du Bas-Rhin." In *Guide des offices des cultes*, pp. 193–201. Brumath: REMA, 1980.

Koerbling, Anton. *Father Rupert Mayer: A Modern Priest and Witness for Christ.* Munich: Verlag Schnell & Steiner, 1956.

Kolb, Karl. *Grosse Wallfahrten in Europa.* Würzburg: Echter Verlag, 1976.

_____. *Marien-Gnadenbilder, Marienverehrung heute.* Würzburg: Echter Verlag, 1976.

_____. *Vom Heiligen Blut: Eine Bilddokumentation der Wallfahrt und Verehrung.* Würzburg: Echter Verlag, 1980.

Konas, Josef. *Märterle.* Ragersdorf, 1912.

Konrad, Anton H. *Bihlafingen bei Laupheim: Pfarrkirche St. Theodul und Wallfahrt zum gegeisselten Heiland.* Weissenhorn: Anton H. Konrad Verlag, 1968.

Kotting, Bernhard. "Wallfahrten zu lebenden Personen im Altertum." In *Wallfahrt kennt keine Grenzen,* edited by Lenz Kriss-Rettenbeck and Gerda Mohler, pp. 226–34. Munich and Zurich: Verlag Schnell & Steiner, 1984.

Kriss, Rudolf, and Kriss-Heinrich, Hubert. *Peregrinatio Neohellenika: Wallfahrtswanderungen im heutigen Griechenland und in Unteritalien.* Vienna: J. M. Selbstverlag des Österreichischen Museums für Volkskunde, 1955.

Kriss-Rettenbeck, Lenz. *Bilder und Zeichen religiosen Volksglaubens.* Munich: Verlag Georg D. W. Callwey, 1963.

_____. *Ex-voto, Zeichen, Bild und Abbild im christlichen Votivbrauchtum.* Zurich: Atlantis-Verlag, 1973.

_____; Kriss-Rettenbeck, Ruth; and Illich, Ivan. "Homo Viator—Ideen und Wirklichkeiten." In *Wallfahrt kennt keine Grenzen,* edited by Lenz Kriss-Rettenbeck and Gerda Mohler, pp. 10–22. Munich and Zurich: Verlag Schnell & Steiner, 1984.

_____, and Mohler, Gerda, eds. *Wallfahrt kennt keine Grenzen.* Munich and Zurich: Verlag Schnell & Steiner, 1984.

Kselman, Thomas A. "Miracles and Prophecies: Popular Religion and the Church in Nineteenth-Century France." Ph.D. dissertation, University of Michigan, 1978.

Labanchi, Edoardo. *Holy Year Rome 1975: Pilgrimage to the Four Basilicas.* Narni-Terni: Plurigraf, 1975.

Labande, E. R. "Pilgrimages: Medieval and Modern." In *New Catholic Encyclopedia,* 11:365–72. New York: McGraw-Hill, 1967.

La Barthe, Herve, and Renoy, Georges. *Het grote feestenboek: Folklore in Belgie.* Zaventem: Elsevier Sequoia, 1981.

Ladame, Jean. *Paray-le-Monial et le culte du Sacré-Cœur.* Lyon: Lescuyer, 1965.

_____. *Sainte Marguerite-Marie et la visitation de Paray.* Lyon: Lescuyer, 1977.

_____. *Notre-Dame de toute la France.* Paris: Éditions France-Empire, 1980.

Läpple, Alfred. *Deutschland, deine Wallfahrtsorte.* Aschaffenburg: Paul Pattloch Verlag, 1983.

Lasko, Peter. *Ars Sacra: 800–1200.* Harmondsworth, Middlesex: Penguin Books, 1972.

Laurentin, Rene. "The Persistence of Popular Piety." In *The Persistence of Religion,* edited by Andrew Greeley and Gregory Baum, pp. 144–56. New York: Herder & Herder, 1973.

———. *Pèlerinages, sanctuaires, apparitions: Annee sainte, redecouvir la religion populaire*. Paris: Office d'Edition, 1983.

———, and Rupcic, Ljudevit. *Is the Virgin Mary Appearing at Medjugorje?* Translated by Francis Martin. Washington, D.C.: The World Among Us Press, 1984.

Layton, T. A. *The Way of Saint James, or the Pilgrim's Road to Santiago de Compostela*. London: Allen & Unwin, 1976.

Lazzarini, Pietro. *Il Volto Santo di Lucca: Origine, memorie e culto del taumaturgo Crocifisso*. Lucca: Eurograf Viale C. Castracani, 1980.

Lefebvre, Eugene. *Saint Anne's Pilgrim People*. Quebec: Charrier et Dugal, 1981.

Lefèuvre, André. "Religious Tourism and Pilgrimage." *On the Move* 10, no. 30 (1980): 80–81. Vatican City: Pontifical Commission on the Pastoral Care of Migrants and Tourists.

Leite, Fernando. *História do Sameiro*. 2d ed. Melhorada, Braga: Confaria de Nossa Senhora do Sameiro, 1964.

Leroy, Jacques. *La tradition vivante de Notre-Dame des Miracles, la Vierge noire d'Orléans*. Sainte-Maxime: Éditions C.I.F., 1984.

Ljubic, Marijan. *Erscheinungen der Gottesmutter in Medjugorje*. Jestetten: Miriam-Verlag, 1983.

Logan, Patrick. *The Holy Wells of Ireland*. Gerrards Cross: Colin Smythe, 1980.

Long, George. *The Folklore Calendar*. London: Philip Allan, 1930.

Lundberg, Donald E. *The Tourist Business*. 4th ed. Boston: CBI Publishing Co., 1980.

Lumiansky, R. M. *The Canterbury Tales of Geoffrey Chaucer*. New York: Simon & Schuster, 1948.

Lüstenberger, Othmar. *Wallfahrtsorte in der Schweiz*. Einsiedeln: Benediktinerkloster, 1978.

Lüthold-Minder, Ida. *Helvetia Mariana: Die marianischen Gnadenstätten der Schweiz*. Stein-am-Rhein: Christiana-Verlag, 1979.

McGahey, Stan. *Playboy's Guide to Good Times Europe*. New York: Playboy Paperbacks, 1981.

McGoldrick, T. A. *Saint Margaret Clitherow*. London: The Catholic Truth Society, 1971.

MacGowan, Kenneth. *An Illustrated History of the House of Loreto*. Loreto: Congregazione Universale Santa Casa, 1976.

McIver, M. E. "Visitation of Mary." In *New Catholic Encyclopedia*, 14:721. New York: McGraw-Hill, 1967.

McKenna, Stephen. *Paganism and Pagan Survivals in Spain up to the Fall of the Visigothic Kingdom*. Washington, D.C.: The Catholic University of America, 1938.

McNaspy, Clement J. *A Guide to Christian Europe*. New York: Hawthorn, 1963.

MacNeill, Marie. *The Festival of Laghnasa: A Study of the Celtic Festival of the Beginning of Harvest*. London: Oxford University Press, 1962.

Madden, Daniel M. *A Religious Guide to Europe*. New York: Collier Books, 1975.

Mäder, Franz. *Wallfahrten im Bistum Passau*. Munich and Zurich: Verlag Schnell & Steiner, 1984.

Maier, Emanuel. "Torah as Moveable Territory." *Annals of the Association of American Geographers* 65, no. 1 (1975): 18–23.

Mâle, Émile. *Religious Art in France: The Twelfth Century:. A Study of the Origins of Medieval Iconography*. Edited by Harry Gober, translated by Marthiel Mathews. Bollingen Series 90, no. 1. Princeton: Princeton University Press, 1978.

———. *Religious Art in France: The Thirteenth Century: A Study of Medieval Iconography and Its Sources*. Edited by Harry Gober, translated by Marthiel Mathews. Bollingen Series 90, no. 2. Princeton: Princeton University Press, 1984.

Manfredi, Domingo. *Santuarios de la Virgen Maria en España y America*. Madrid: Editorial Edisa, 1954.

Marnham, Patrick. *Lourdes: A Modern Pilgrimage*. New York: Coward, MacCann & Geoghegan, 1980.

Matteotti, C. *La santa sindone: Solenne ostensione nel IV centenario del trasferimento a Torino*. Turin: Comitato per l'Ostensione della Santa Sindone, 1978.

Minoritenkloster, Kaiserslautern. *50 Jahre Kloster- und Gelobniskirche Maria Schutz in Kaiserslautern*. Kaiserslautern: Minoritenkloster, 1979.

Mischitelli, Silvesto. *Remembering Padre Pio*. San Giovanni Rotondo: Edizioni Padre Pio da Pietrelcina, 1973.

Mockenhaubt, Hubert. "Pèlerinages des catholiques allemands." *Missi* 414 (1978): 235.

Moisan, Bertrand. *Basilique Notre-Dame du Roncier Josselin*. Lyon: Lescuyer, n.d.

Monaco, Gabriele. *Notizie storiche della basilica-santuario della Madonna di Trapani*. Trapani: Carmelitani, 1950.

Moncrief, Lewis W. "The Cultural Basis of Our Environmental Crisis." *Science* 170 (1970): 508–12.

Monnerjahn, E. *Schönstatt: Eine Einfuhrung*. Münster: Verlag Orbis, 1980.

Montaigu, Henri. *Rocamadour ou la pierre des siècles*. Paris: Éditions S.V.S., 1974.

Montes Bardo, Joaquin. *Iconografia de Nuesta Señora de Guadalupe, Extremadura*. Seville: San Antonio, 1978.

Moss, Leonard W., and Cappannari, Stephen C. "In Quest of the Black Virgin: She Is Black because She Is Black." In *Mother Worship: Theme and Variations*, edited by James J. Preston, pp. 53–74. Chapel Hill: University of North Carolina Press, 1982.

Muir, Richard. *Riddles in the British Landscape*. London: Thames & Hudson, 1981.

Mullins, Edwin. *The Pilgrimage to Santiago*. New York: Taplinger Publishing Co., 1974.

Munich, Archdiocese. "Wallfahrten in der Erzdiozese." *Münchner Katholische Kirchenzeitung*, 23, no. 4 (June 1974). Photocopy.

Murphy, Osward. *Blessed Richard Gwyn: Schoolmaster and Martyr*. Cardiff: The Catholic Truth Society, 1955.

Navatte, Jean-Paul. *Les saints guérisseurs bretons*. Rennes: Ouest France, 1977.

Neumann, Erich. *The Great Mother.* Translated by Ralph Manheim. Princeton: Princeton University Press, 1972.
Newton, Arthur Percival, ed. *Travel and Travelers of the Middle Ages.* New York: Alfred A. Knopf, 1950.
Nolan, Mary Lee. "The Mexican Pilgrimage Tradition." *Pioneer America* 5, no. 2 (1973): 13–27.
———. *Research on Disaster and Environmental Hazard as Viewed from the Perspective of Response to the Eruption of the Volcano Parícutin in Michoacán, Mexico.* Environmental Quality Note 14. College Station: Texas A&M University Environmental Quality Program, 1973.
———. "Spatial and Temporal Aspects of Contemporary Western European Pilgrimage: A Preliminary Report." Department of Geography, Oregon State University, 1980. Photocopy.
———. "Irish Pilgrimage: The Different Tradition." *Annals of the Association of American Geographers* 73, no. 3 (1983): 421–38.
———. "The European Roots of Latin American Pilgrimage." In *La Peregrinación: The Pilgrimage in Latin America*, edited by N. Ross Crumrine and E. Alan Morinis. Westport, Conn.: Greenwood Press, forthcoming.
———. "Regional Variations in Western European Pilgrimage Traditions." In *Sacred Places, Sacred Spaces: The Geography of Pilgrimages*, edited by Robert H. Stoddard and Alan Morinis. Manuscript.
Notre-Dame de Panetière. Aire-sur-la-Lys: Imprimerie J. Mordacq, 1954.
Notre-Dame de Sion, 1873–1973: Un centenaire. Turin: Rotocalco Caprotti, 1973.
Oakeshott, Walter. *Classical Inspiration in Medieval Art.* New York: Frederick A. Praeger, 1959.
Ogilvie, R. M. *The Romans and Their Gods in the Age of Augustus.* New York: W. W. Norton, 1969.
Oomen, Johannes. *Kevelaer: Origin and History of Pilgrimage and Sanctuaries.* Kevelaer: Wallfahrtsleitung Priesterhaus, 1976.
"Les pèlerinages du Haut-Rhin." In *Guide des offices des cultes.* Édition E, 203–6. Brumath: REMA, 1980.
Peña García, Manuel. *Agreda: Santa Maria de los milagros.* Soria: Union Grafica, 1979.
Perche, François. *Sur les routes des pèlerinages en France: 40 itinéraires sur les pas des pèlerins du moyen age.* Paris: Librairie Artheme-Fayard, 1980.
Perez Lopez, Julian. *The Cathedral of Burgos.* 4th ed. Translated by Inlingua School of Languages. Burgos: Artes Graficas Santiago Rodriguez, 1978.
Perluter, Lawrence C., and Monty, Richard A. "The Importance of Perceived Control: Fact or Fantasy?" *American Scientist* 65, no. 26 (1977): 759–65.
Perowne, Stewart. *Holy Places of Christendom.* New York: Oxford University Press, 1976.
Pinto, Pio V. *The Pilgrim's Guide to Rome.* New York: Harper & Row, 1975.

Plechl, Pia Maria. *Wallfahrtsstätten in Niederösterreich*. St. Polten: Niederösterreichisches Presshaus, 1978.

Plenker, Werner. *St. Maria in der Kupfergasse Köln*. Cologne: Hans Zimmermann, 1975.

Pochin-Mould, Daphne. *Irish Pilgrimage*. Dublin: H. M. Gill & Son, 1955.

Portugal. (Untitled list of events.) Lisbon: Direccion Geral de Tourism, Sector de Animacao, 1980–81. Mimeo.

Posch, Waldemar. *Hemma von Gurk*. Zell-am-See: Verlag der Domkustodie Gurk, 1974.

Pötzl, Walter. "Santa-Casa-Kult in Loreto und in Bayern." In *Wallfahrt kennt keine Grenzen*, edited by Lenz Kriss-Rettenbeck and Gerda Mohler, pp. 368–82. Munich and Zurich: Verlag Schnell & Steiner, 1984.

Quinn, James. *Cavalier of Christ: John Ogilvie, S.J. (1579–1615)*. Glasgow: John S. Burns & Sons, 1976.

Raeber, Ludwig. *The Abbey of Einsiedeln*. Einsiedeln: Benziger, 1975.

Recta-Foldex. *Carte index, avec repertoire au verso: 1:250,000*. 15 maps. France: Éditions Cartographiques et Touristiques, 1980.

Reume, Auguste de. *Les Vierges miraculeuses de la Belgique, histoire des sanctuaires ou elles sont vénérées; légendes, pèlerinages, confréries*. Paris: Librairie Internationale-Catholique, 1878.

Ripley, Francis J. *The Holy Hand*. Ashton-in-Makerfield: St. Oswald's, 1970.

———. *Saint Edmund Arrowsmith*. London: The Catholic Truth Society, n.d.

Rocacher, Jean. *Rocamadour et son pèlerinage*. Rocamadour: Association des Amis de Rocamadour, 1979.

Rodríguez Becerra, Salvador, and Vazquez Soto, José María. *Exvotos de Andalucía*. Seville: Editorial Argantonio, Ediciones Andaluzas, 1980.

Rogers, Edith C. *Discussion of Holidays in the Latter Middle Ages*. New York: Columbia University Press, 1940.

Rombi, Bruno. *I segreti della provincia di Genova*. Genoa: Cappelli Editore, 1972.

Rosenegger, Josef, and Bartl, Edith. *Wallfahrten im Bayerischen Oberland*. Munich: Pannonia-Verlag, 1977.

———. *Wallfahrten in und um München*. Munich: Pannonia-Verlag, 1980.

———, and Molodovsky, Nikolai. *Wallfahrten zwischen Inn und Salzach*. Munich: Pannonia-Verlag, 1976.

Rothkrug, Lionel. "Popular Religion and Holy Shrines: Their Influence on the Origins of the German Reformation and Their Role in German Cultural Development." In *Religion and the People, 800–1700*, edited by James Obelkevich, pp. 20–86. Chapel Hill: University of North Carolina Press, 1979.

———. "Religious Practices and Collective Perceptions: Hidden Homologies in the Renaissance and Reformation." *Historical Reflections*, 1980.

Rouillard, P. "Marian Feasts." *New Catholic Encyclopedia*, 9:211–12. New York: McGraw-Hill, 1967.

Rouse, William Henry. *Greek Votive Offerings.* New York: Arno Press, 1975.
Rudel, Yves-Marie. *Le Folgoët.* Rennes: Ouest France, 1977.
Ruelle, M. *Notre-Dame du Chêne.* Bar-sur-Seine, Aube, 1969.
Saillens, Emile. *Nos Vierges noires: Leurs origines.* Paris: Les Éditions Universelles, 1945.
Salvini, A. *Cento santuari Mariani d'Italia.* Catania: Edizioni Paoline, 1970.
Sánchez, María Ángeles. *Guía de fiestas populares de España.* Madrid: Editorial Tania, 1982.
Sanchis, Pierre. "The Portuguese 'romarías'," translated by Jane Hodgkin and Stephen Wilson. In *Saints and Their Cults: Studies in Religious Sociology, Folklore and History,* edited by Stephen Wilson, pp. 261–89. Cambridge: Cambridge University Press, 1983.
Satzger, Alfons. *Wies Church: A Place of Pilgrimage near Steingaden, Upper Bavaria.* Tübingen: Verlag Gebruder Metz, n.d.
Saxer, V. *Le culte de Marie-Madeleine en occident des origines à la fin du moyen age.* 2 vols. Auxerre and Paris: Clavreuil, 1959.
Scey, Cure de. *Notre-Dame du Chêne au diocese de Besançon.* Besançon, 1950.
Schaffer, Gottfried, and Peda, Gregor. *Wallfahrten im Passauerland.* Munich: Pannonia-Verlag, 1978.
Scharfe, Martin; Schenda, Rudolf; and Schwedt, Herbert. *Volksfrömmigkeit-Bildzeugnisse aus Vergangenheit und Gegenwart.* Stuttgart: Spectrum Verlag, 1967.
Schneider, Philippe. *Saint-Israël, Saint-Theobald, ostensions: Pieces remarquables de la collégiale Saint-Pierre du Dorat.* Saint-Die: Imprimeries Loos, 1980.
Schnell, Hugo. *Votiv- und Wallfahrtskirche St. Anton Partenkirchen.* Munich and Zurich: Verlag Schnell & Steiner, 1973.
Schreiber, Georg, et al. *Die vierzehn Nothelfer in Volksfrömmigkeit und Sakralkultur, Symbolkraft und Herrschaftsbereich der Wallfahrtskapelle, vorab in Franken und Tirol.* Innsbruck: Schlern-Schriften Veroffentlichungen zur Landeskunde von Sudtirol, 1959.
Scullard, H. H. *Festivals and Ceremonies of the Roman Republic.* Ithaca: Cornell University Press, 1981.
Selhofer, Eva. *Votivtafelkapelle Maria Kirchental/Salzburg.* Salzburg: Verlag St. Peter, 1978.
Selzer, Alois. *St. Wendelin: Leben und Verehrung eines alemannisch-frankischen Volksheiligen.* Modling-bei-Wien: St. Gabriel-Verlag, 1962.
Servi di Maria, Cura dei. *Cenni storici e preghiere.* Vicenza: Santuario di Monte Berico, n.d.
Shair, Issa. "Spatial Patterns of Muslim Pilgrimage Circulation." Ph.D. dissertation, University of Kentucky, 1978.
Sharbrough, Stephen. "The Cult of the Mother in Europe: The Transformation of the Symbolism of Woman." Ph.D. dissertation, University of California, Los Angeles, 1977.

Sigal, Pierre André. "Les différents types de pèlerinage au moyen age." In *Wallfahrt kennt keine Grenzen*, edited by Lenz Kriss-Rettenbeck and Gerda Mohler, pp. 76–86. Munich and Zurich: Verlag Schnell & Steiner, 1984.

Silva Barros, Carlos Vitorino da. *Four Altars to the Virgin: Fátima, Batalha, Alcobaca, Nazare*. Lisbon: C. V. da Silva Barros, 1978.

Siostr Niepokalanek. *Z Dawna Polski Tys Krolowa Przewodnik po Sanktuariach Maryjnych Koronowane wizerunki Matki Bozej 1717–1983*. Szymanow: Siostry Niepokalanki, 1984.

Smith, Stephen. *Recreation Geography*. London and New York: Longmans, 1983.

Sopher, David E. *Geography of Religions*. Englewood Cliffs, N.J.: Prentice-Hall, 1967.

———. "Pilgrimage Circulation in Gujarat." *Geographical Review* 58 (1968): 392–427.

———. "The Message of Place: Addendum to a Geography of Indian Pilgrimage." Paper presented at the seminar on "Pilgrimage as Communication," Southern Asia Institute, Columbia University, New York, 1980.

Spain. Ministerio de Obras Publicas y Urbanismo. *España: Mapa oficial de carreteras*, 1:400,000. Madrid, 1980.

———. Ministerio de Transportes, Turismo y Comunicaciones. *Feasts and Festivals: Spain*. Madrid, 1980.

———. Ministerio de Transportes, Turismo y Comunicaciones. *Fiestas y festivales: España*. Madrid, 1982.

Speckbacher, Franz. *Garabandal . . . Donnerstag 20.30 Uhr*. Vienna: Mediatrix-Verlag, 1979.

Speyer, Diocese. "Wallfahrten." In *Handbuch des Bistums Speyer*, 493–520. Speyer: Herausgeber und Verlag Bischofliches Ordinariat, 1961.

Spicer, Dorothy Gladys. *Festivals of Western Europe*. New York: H. W. Wilson, 1958.

Stadelmaier, Rupert. *Wallfahrtskirche auf dem Hohenrechberg: Schwabische Alb*. Tübingen: Verlag Gebruder Metz, 1979.

Staehlin, Carlos María. *Apariciones*. Madrid: Razon y Fe, 1954.

Staercke, A. E. de. *Notre-Dame des Belges: Traditions et folklore du culte Marial en Belgique*. Brussels, 1954.

Stephenson, Colin. *Walsingham Way*. London: Longman & Todd, 1970.

Stoddard, Robert H. "Hindu Holy Sites in India." Ph.D. dissertation, State University of Iowa, 1966.

———. and Morinis, Alan. *Sacred Places, Sacred Spaces: The Geography of Pilgrimages*. Manuscript.

Strappazzon, Valentin. "Pèlerinages en pays D'Aude." *Foy* 40–41 (1980): 26–30.

Sullivan, Kay. *Journey of Love: A Pilgrimage to Pope John's Birthplace*. New York: Appleton-Century, 1966.

Sumption, Jonathan. *Pilgrimage: An Image of Medieval Religion*. Totowa, N.J.: Rowman and Littlefield, 1975.

Taaffe, Edward J., and Gauthier, Howard L. *Geography of Transportation*. Englewood Cliffs, N.J.: Prentice-Hall, 1973.

Tabanelli, Mario. *Gli Ex-voto poliviscerali Etruschi et Romani*. Florence, 1962.

Tanaka, Hiroshi. "Pilgrim Places: A Study of the Eighty-eight Sacred Precincts of the Shikoku Pilgrimage, Japan." Ph.D. dissertation, Simon Fraser University, 1975.

Taylor, John Walter. "Tree Worship." *The Mankind Quarterly* 20, no. 182 (1979): 79–141.

Telfer, W. *The Treasure of São Roque*. London: Society for Promoting Christian Knowledge, 1932.

Tempera, Antonio. *Gli ex-voto: Linguaggio di pieta Mariana: Testimonianze romane*. Vatican: Edizioni Orizzonte Medico, 1977.

Tentori, Tullio. "An Italian Religious Feast: The Fugjeti Rites of the Madonna dell'Arco, Naples." In *Mother Worship: Theme and Variation*, edited by James J. Preston, pp. 95–122. Chapel Hill: University of North Carolina Press, 1982.

Testini, Pasquale. *The Christian Catacombs in Rome*. Rome: Entre Provinciale per il Turismo di Roma, 1970.

Thomas, Denis. *The Face of Christ*. London: Hamlyn, 1979.

Thomson, Gladys Scott. *Medieval Pilgrimages*. London: Longmans, 1962.

Thurston, Herbert, and Attwater, Donald, eds. *Butler's Lives of the Saints*. 4 vols. New York: P. J. Kenedy & Sons, 1963.

Toor, Francis. *Festivals and Folkways of Italy*. New York: Crown Publishers, 1953.

Toschi, Paolo. *Bibliografia degli ex-voto italiani*. Florence: Editions Leo Olschki, 1970.

———, and Pennia, Renato. *Le tavolette votive della Madonna dell'Arco*. Cava dei Tipreni: Di Mauro Editore, 1971.

Trier Diocese. "Wallfahrtsorte des Bistums." In *Handbuch des Bistums Trier*, p. 984. Trier, 1952.

Tripputi, Anna Maria. "Aspetti cultuali e culturali dei pellegrinaggi pugliese." In *Wallfahrt kennt keine Grenzen*, edited by Lenz Kriss-Rettenbeck and Gerda Mohler, pp. 383–96. Munich and Zurich: Verlag Schnell & Steiner, 1984.

Trompetto, Mario. *Storia del santuario di Oropa*. Biella: Libreria Vittorio Giovannacci, 1979.

Tuan, Yi-Fu. "Discrepancies between Environmental Attitude and Behavior: Examples of Europe and China." *The Canadian Geographer* 12, no. 3 (1968): 176–91.

———. "Ambiguity in Attitudes toward Environment." *Annals of the Association of American Geographers* 63, no. 4 (1973): 411–23.

———. *Space and Place: The Perspective of Experience*. Minneapolis: University of Minnesota Press, 1977.

———. "Sign and Metaphor." *Annals of the Association of American Geographers* 68, no. 3 (1978): 363–72.

Turner, Victor. "The Center Out There: Pilgrim's Goal," *History of Religions* 21, no. 3 (1973): 191–230.

———. *Dramas, Fields and Metaphors: Symbolic Action in Human Society.* Ithaca: Cornell University Press, 1974.

———, and Turner, Edith. *Image and Pilgrimage in Christian Culture: Anthropological Perspectives.* New York: Columbia University Press, 1978.

Tyburn Convent. *They Died at Tyburn.* London, 1961.

Unglert, H. P. *Neun-Tage-Gebet zur Gnadenmutter von Bergatreute "Maria vom Blut."* Bergatreute, n.d.

U.S. Board on Geographic Names. *Gazetteer.* Washington, D.C.: Department of the Interior or Defense Mapping Agency (publishers and dates vary by countries).

Utz, Hans J. *Wallfahrten im Bistum Regensburg.* Munich and Zurich: Verlag Schnell & Steiner, 1981.

Van Doren, R. "Liturgical Year in the Roman Rite." In *New Catholic Encyclopedia*, 8:915–19. New York: McGraw-Hill, 1967.

Vatican. *Annuario pontificio per l'anno 1978.* Vatican City: Libreria Editrice Vaticana, 1978.

Villaviciosa, Sebastian de. *El siervo de Dios fray Leopoldo de Alpandeire: Hermano Capuchino, 1864–1956.* Granada, 1965.

Villefranche de Conflent, Syndicat d'Initiative. *Reliquaries du Roussillon.* Villefranche de Conflent: Pacques-Toussaint, 1978.

Villette, Jean. "Que savons-nous de la Vierge druidique de Chartres?" In *Notre-Dame de Chartres* 5, no. 21 (1974): 10–15.

Vinciotti, Alessandro. *I mille santuari mariani d'Italia illustrati.* Rome: Associazione Santuari Mariani, 1960.

Von Bruckner, Wolfgang. *Wallfahrt und Kirche Walldürn.* Walldürn: Verlag Augustinerkloster, 1977.

Vrancken, M. "Les pèlerinages en Belgique." *Missi* 414 (1978): 230.

Wagner, Margit. "Tradition der Askese bei Wallfahrten in Irland." In *Wallfahrt kennt keine Grenzen,* edited by Lenz Kriss-Rettenbeck and Gerda Mohler, pp. 45–54. Munich and Zurich: Verlag Schnell & Steiner, 1984.

Walsh, James. *Forty Martyrs of England and Wales Canonized by His Holiness Pope Paul IV on 25 October 1970.* London: Catholic Truth Society, 1972.

Walsh, William J., comp. *The Apparitions and Shrines of Heaven's Bright Queen in Legend, Poetry and History from the Earliest Ages to the Present Time.* New York and New Orleans: Carey-Stafford, 1904.

Walther, Elisabeth. "Wallfahrten im Westen Irlands." In *Wallfahrt kennt keine Grenzen,* edited by Lenz Kriss-Rettenbeck and Gerda Mohler, pp. 396–406. Munich and Zurich: Verlag Schnell & Steiner, 1984.

Ward, Benedicta. *Miracles and the Medieval Mind: Theory, Record and Event, 1000–1215.* Philadelphia: University of Pennsylvania Press, 1982.

Warner, Marina. *Alone of All Her Sex: The Myth and the Cult of the Virgin Mary.* New York: Wallaby Pocket Books, 1976.

Weitzmann, Kurt. *The Icon: Holy Images—Sixth to Fourteenth Century*. New York: George Braziller, 1978.

———. "Introduction: The Origins and Significance of Icons." In *The Icon*, pp. 3–10. New York: Alfred A. Knopf, 1982.

Wellnhofer, S. *Ettal*. Ettal: Buch-Kunstverlag, n.d.

Weston, Jesse L. *From Ritual to Romance*. Garden City, N.Y.: Doubleday, 1957.

White, Gilbert F., ed. *Natural Hazards: Local, National, Global*. New York: Oxford University Press, 1974.

White, Lynn, Jr. "The Historical Roots of Our Ecological Crisis." *Science* 155 (1967): 1203–7.

Whitfield, J. L. *Saint John Southworth*. London: Catholic Truth Society, 1977.

Wiebel-Fanderl, Oliva. "Die Verehrung der Altöttinger Muttergottes." In *Wallfahrt kennt keine Grenzen*, edited by Lenz Kriss-Rettenbeck and Gerda Mohler, pp. 499–512. Munich and Zurich: Verlag Schnell & Steiner, 1984.

Wierermüller, Maria Anna Augustina. *Heilige Walburga, Leben und Wirken*. Eichstätt: Abtei St. Walburg, 1979.

Wieser, Anton, and Dickermann, Fred. *Der Vierbergelauf-ein Karntner Brauch*. Klagenfurt: Karntner Druck- und Verlagsgesellschaft, 1981.

Wilkins, Eithne. *The Rose-Garden Game: The Symbolic Background to the European Prayer Beads*. London: Gollanez, 1969.

Williamson, Ronald. "Medieval English Pilgrims and Pilgrimages." In *Wallfahrt kennt keine Grenzen*, edited by Lenz Kriss-Rettenbeck and Gerda Mohler, pp. 114–26. Munich and Zurich: Verlag Schnell & Steiner, 1984.

Wilson, Stephen. "Annotated Bibliography." In *Saints and Their Cults*, edited by Stephen Wilson, pp. 309–417.

———. "Cults of Saints in the Churches of Central Paris." In *Saints and Their Cults*, edited by Stephen Wilson, pp. 233–60.

———. "Introduction." In *Saints and Their Cults*, edited by Stephen Wilson, pp. 1–53.

———, ed. *Saints and Their Cults: Studies in Religious Sociology, Folklore and History*. Cambridge: Cambridge University Press, 1983.

Wimet, Pierre-Andre. *Notre-Dame of Boulogne-sur-Mer, Pas-de-Calais*. Translated by Stan and Rita Morton. Colmar-Ingersheim: Imprimerie S.A.E.P., 1977.

Wolf, Eric R. "The Virgin of Guadalupe: A Mexican National Symbol." *Journal of American Folklore* 71 (1958): 34–39.

Het zwarte Christusbeeld in de Sint Maartenskerk te Vijk-Maastricht. Maastricht: Broederscap van het H. Kruis, 1959.

Index

Aachen, 94
Abruzzi-Molise, 124
Achatius, Saint, 149–50
Acts of Peter, 275
Afra, Saint, 149
Agreda, 192
Aire-sur-la-Lys, 233
Alba de Tormes, 132
Albania, 160, 255
Albocacer, 130
Alise-Sainte-Reine, 222–23
Alpandeire, Leopoldo de, 103
Alsace, 106, 108, 120, 198, 212
Altötting, 23, 99, 108, 202–3, 205, 207
Altura, 217
Amalfi, 129, 174
Ambrose of Milan, Saint, 275
Andalucía, 13
Andorra, 6, 22
Andrew, Saint, 129–30, 174
Angely, 214
Angers, 152
Anglican church: and pilgrimage activity, 8, 35, 109, 110, 114, 355 (n. 23)
Angosta, 278
Annaberg, 135, 172–73
Anne, Saint, 117, 134–35, 158–59, 172–73, 187, 283, 284, 376 (n. 73)
Annecy, 130
Anthony Abbot, Saint, 151
Anthony of Padua, Saint, 96, 108, 150, 151, 158–59, 172, 187, 236
Apleches, 6, 13

Apollonia, Saint, 141
Apparitions, 1, 60, 64, 104, 266
—of Christ, and shrine origin stories, 150, 195, 220, 226, 267, 275, 278, 284–85, 287
—of Mary: "postindustrial" type of, 98–99, 102–3, 112, 272–74; and shrine origin stories, 98–99, 102–3, 183–84, 195, 199, 201, 216, 217, 220, 238–39, 258–59, 266, 267, 275–87 passim, 306–8, 325, 372 (n. 48), 373 (n. 57); issue of church recognition of, 102, 285–87, 308–10, 372 (n. 50); "shepherds' cycle" type of, 259, 269–70, 272
—of saints, and shrine origin stories, 130, 135, 139, 150, 220, 267, 275–76, 278, 283, 284
Apt, 135, 172–73
Apulia, 67
Aragon, 142
Arcoa, 283
Arles-sur-Tech, 174–75
Arroyo de San Servan, 214
Ars-sur-Formans, 223–25
Aschaffenburg, 329
Ascoli Satriano, 93
Assisi, 21, 30, 39, 150, 164, 173
Augsburg, 92, 149
Augustinians, 151, 371 (n. 42)
Austria, 22; in South German region, 6; shrine distribution in, 30, 33, 35; religious vs. secular celebrations in, 48,

49, 50; saints' shrines in, 62, 122, 130, 135, 142, 143, 145–47, 148; minor shrines in, 64; pilgrims' offerings at shrines in, 68, 352 (n. 34); shrine formation periods in, 83, 92, 104–5, 108, 113; Marian shrines in, 96, 108, 119, 120; Christ-centered shrines in, 126, 128–29; venerated images and relics in, 184, 198, 202, 213; shrine origin stories in, 231, 236, 244, 245, 249, 255–56, 257, 284, 286, 287; shrine location in, 293, 302, 336; natural site features at shrines in, 310, 320, 321, 323, 324, 328, 329, 330, 379 (nn. 14, 15). *See also* Germanic regions; South German region

Auvergne, 182
Avenum, 169
Ávila, 132, 278
Aylesford, 103

Baden, 198
Baden-Württemberg, 6, 124
Bad Tölz, 147
Balearic Islands, 120
Bamberg, 150, 286
Banneux, 68, 285
Banz, 92
Barbara, Saint, 149
Bari, 95, 144, 174, 254
Bar-le-Duc, 244
Bartholomew, Saint, 351 (n. 26)
Basilicata, 126
Batalha, 233
Baud, 170
Bavaria, 51, 127, 231, 363 (n. 25); in South German region, 6; shrine distribution in, 35, 64,; pilgrims' offerings at shrines in, 72; shrine formation periods in, 107; Christ-centered shrines in, 126; saints' shrines in, 254, 264; shrine location in, 293. *See also* Germanic regions; South German region

Beauraing, 273, 285
Belgium: in French and North German regions, 6; shrine distribution in, 33, 34; religious vs. secular celebrations in, 49, 50; pilgrims' offerings at shrines in, 73–75; shrine formation periods in, 83, 92, 102, 113; Marian shrines in, 96, 119, 120; Christ-centered shrines in, 126; saints' shrines in, 144; shrine origin stories in, 236, 248, 249, 256, 280, 287

Belleville, 235
Benedictines, 90, 95, 142, 145, 251, 262
Benedict of Nursia, Saint (São Bento), 45–46, 90, 145, 187, 253–54, 351 (n. 26)
Benoîte-Vaux, 214
Bergatreute, 244
Bernadette Soubirous, Saint, 132, 199, 277, 285
Bernard, Saint(s), 150
Bernard of Clairvaux, Saint, 97, 206
Bernrain, 246
Bertinoro, 22
Bihlafingen, 365 (n. 44)
Bingen, 55
Blaise, Saint, 141, 149
Boario Terme, 234
Bóbbio, 90
Bologna, 168, 183
Bolsena, 179
Bolte, Father Anton, 231
Bom Jesu do Monte, 146
Bornhofen, 96
Boulogne, 202
Bourgillon, 246
Braga, 164, 238, 286
Brandea, 168
Bridget, Saint, 35, 145
British region: defined, 6; natural site

features at shrines in, 12, 162, 310, 323, 335; shrine distribution in, 30, 34–35; religious vs. secular celebrations in, 49–50; pilgrimage cycle in, 61; shrine formation periods in, 83, 87, 90, 92, 95, 100–101, 105, 109, 113, 114; Marian shrines in, 120; saints' shrines in, 154, 156; venerated images and relics in, 162; shrine origin stories in, 219, 225, 263
Brittany, 6, 13, 51–52, 106, 128, 134, 135, 292–93, 321, 331
Bruges, 177
Bulhoes, Ferdinand de, 151. *See also* Anthony of Padua, Saint
Burgos, 15–19
Burgundy, 122
Burresi, Brother Gino, 133, 239, 370 (n. 24)
Byzantine Empire: iconcolasm in, 93, 168, 277, 353–54 (n. 9)

Caimi, Father Bernardino, 237–38
Camáldoli, 95, 328
Cambrai, 168
Canada, 101, 124–26, 132, 135, 136, 139, 173, 283
Candida, Saint, 109
Canevale, 201
Canóscio, 201
Canterbury, 95, 110, 150
Capáccio, 277
Capuchins, 100
Caravággio, 98, 199, 282
Carmelites, 95, 376 (n. 73)
Casarano, 90
Cáscia, 99
Cathaldus, Saint, 90
Catherine of Alexandria, Saint, 141, 149–50
Cavallermaggiore, 374 (n. 65)
Cebrero, 179

Celles, 325
Celtic Christianity, 90, 92, 164, 222, 290, 311; saints, 90–92, 95, 111, 144–45, 162, 222, 225
Cerro de los Ángeles, 103, 154, 190, 211
Cesena, 75
Charlemagne, 94, 105, 251
Charles Borromeo, Saint, 100, 238
Charles of Salerno, 141
Chartres, 44, 92, 170, 190, 202
Château-Quinipily, 170
Chiávari, 161, 253
Chipiona, 202, 259, 371 (n. 44)
Christ, 20, 162, 255; miracles associated with images and relics of, 17, 42, 168, 169, 177–78, 190–91, 217, 244; as Christ Child, 115, 135, 187, 190–91, 192–96, 210, 211–12, 244, 246, 254, 277, 279, 280, 285, 286, 287, 323; as part of Trinity, 116, 126; and male aspects of divinity, 117; and Mary, 135, 165, 187, 191, 192–99, 202, 211–12, 246, 254, 259, 274, 275, 277, 279, 280, 286, 323, 330; and Saint John the Baptist, 136–37; and Saint Mary Magdalene, 140; and Saint Michael the Archangel, 140; and Saint Christopher, 144, 187; and Saint Anthony of Padua, 151, 187; and Saint Joseph, 187, 194–95; and Saint Peter, 275
—shrines dedicated to, 115, 117–19, 128, 157, 237, 354 (n. 13); in inventory used for this study, 9; pilgrimage cycle at, 62; distribution of, 62, 119, 122, 124–26, 127–28, 152–56, 158, 356 (n. 3); formation periods of, 93, 100, 103, 152–56, 158; primary and secondary subjects of devotion at, 116–17, 119; apparitional shrines, 150, 195, 220, 226, 267, 275, 278, 284–85, 287; and Marian shrines,

154; size and drawing power of, 157; significant site shrines, 219; devotional shrines, 219–20; found object shrines, 220, 221, 261, 264, 293–94; acquired object shrines, 220, 249; spontaneous miracle shrines, 249; location of, 299–300; natural site features at, 315–16
—veneration of images and relics of, 17, 42, 124, 165–66, 168, 171, 176, 177–79, 186, 211–12, 220, 221, 261, 264, 293–94, 299–300, 363 (n. 25), 365 (n. 44); Holy Blood, 94, 95, 155, 171, 176–77, 251, 252, 363–64 (n. 32); True Cross, 124, 126, 155, 165, 171, 176, 179, 251, 252; and lack of mortal remains, 175; Holy Shroud, 176, 190; and iconography, 187, 188–91, 192–99, 202, 209
Christ of Burgos, 17, 19
Christ of Lucca, 93, 202, 205, 209
Christopher, Saint, 141, 143–44, 149–50, 187
Cistercians, 110–11, 152
Città di Castello, 201
Clare, Saint, 164
Clavijo, battle of, 276
Clemente, Saint, 164
Clovis I (Frankish king), 147
Cluniac reforms, 95
Cluny, 149
Cochem, 322
Cocullo, 95
Collevalenza, 102, 191, 286, 287, 322
Cologne, 44, 96, 130, 149, 251, 294
Conques, 27
Conrad of Parzham, Saint, 225
Constantinople, 96, 194, 251, 254
Convento San Matteo, 352 (n. 34)
Conversano, 90
Copenhagen, 202
Corpillos, 17

Corsica, 120
Cortona, 164
Council of Basel, 62
Council of Ephesus, 90, 277
Council of Nicaea, Second, 163, 164
Council of Trent, 100
Covadonga, 334
Cranach, Lukas, 186
Crea, 90
Cristo del Pano, 186
Croagh Patrick, 50, 275, 301, 320
Crucifix, 188
Crusades, 96; First, 95, 97; Second, 251
Cubas, 282
Cuenca, 323
Curé d'Ars (Saint Jean Baptiste Marie Vianney), 132, 223–25
Cyriac, Saint, 149–50
Czechoslovakia, 108
Częstochowa, 168, 207

Dax, 225
Deggendorf, 189
Denis of Paris, Saint, 149, 170
Denmark, 115. *See also* Scandinavia
Discalced Carmelites, 100
Disentis, 248
Dolina, 286
Doménico Abate, Saint, 124, 173
Dominicans, 95, 150, 198
"Domini Quo Vadis" church, 275
Domrémy-la-Pucelle, 131
Donauwörth, 251
Donegal, 323
Downpatrick, 144
Drogheda, 160
Dublin, 103, 111

Eberweis, 235
Edelschrott, 128
Edmund Arrowsmith, Saint, 355 (n. 22)
Edward the Confessor, Saint, 27

Egg, 231
Eichstätt, 174
Einsiedeln, 108, 149, 160, 202–3, 205, 207, 278
Elizabeth of Hungary, Saint, 252
El Miracle, 282
El Torn, 282
England, 99–100, 102, 142; in British region, 6; shrine revitalization in, 109–10, 114; Christ-centered shrines in, 126; saints' shrines in, 145; venerated images and relics in, 202, 213; shrine origin stories in, 226, 256, 257, 258, 267. *See also* British region
Epiphanius of Salamis, 166
Erasmus, Saint, 149
Erding, 177, 352 (n. 34)
Eric, Saint, 35
Ermelo, 46
Escalona, 282
Espinheiro, 191
Esplay-Le Puy, 136
Ettal, 15, 44, 364 (n. 34)
Ettenheim, 223
Eulalia, Saint, 353 (n. 7)
Euphemia, Saint, 141
Eustace, Saint, 149–50
Evesham Abbey, 275
Évron, 175
Externstein, 188
Extremadura, 124, 214

"Faith and Light" pilgrimage (Walsingham), 68
Fátima: as international pilgrimage center, 1, 23; secondary shrines of, 20, 133, 239, 285; "Fátima Day" pilgrimages, 59, 285; pilgrimage cycle at, 63–64; pilgrims' offerings at, 71; Marian apparitions and origin story of, 102, 273, 285; Marian image at, 182, 199
Faverney, 179

Feast days: and pilgrimage cycle, 56–57, 58, 59, 62
Fécamp, 177
Ferrer, Fray Bonifacio, 217
Festas, 13, 49
Finland, 33, 35, 120–22. *See also* Scandinavia
Flanders, 106
Florence, 201, 280
Font-Romeu, 202, 203
Forno Canavese, 201
Four Mountain pilgrimage, 320
Fourteen Holy Helpers, 115, 149–50
Foy, Saint, 27, 166
Fraine, 277
France, 3, 24; in French region, 6; *pardons* and *apleches* in, 6; shrine distribution in, 30, 33, 34; religious vs. secular celebrations in, 48, 49, 50, 51–52; Marian shrines in, 62, 92, 96, 119–20, 154, 156; foot pilgrimage in, 64; pilgrims' offerings at shrines in, 72–73, 352 (n. 34); shrine formation periods in, 83, 87, 92, 95, 97, 100, 102, 104–5, 113; Christ-centered shrines in, 126, 128–29; saints' shrines in, 128, 130, 131, 132, 135, 136, 139, 140–41, 145, 154; venerated images and relics in, 166, 169–70, 171, 182, 184–86, 194, 198, 201, 202, 207, 209–10, 213, 361 (n. 11); shrine origin stories in, 225, 226, 236, 245, 263, 273, 277, 280, 285–86, 287, 289; shrine location in, 302; natural site features at shrines in, 310, 311, 328, 329, 330, 331, 379 (n. 15)
Franche-Comté, 122
Franciscans, 62, 95–96, 100, 150, 151, 184, 253, 355 (n. 22)
Francis de Sales, Saint, 100, 130
Francis of Assisi, Saint, 30, 39, 95–96, 105, 150–51, 173, 279–80

Francis Xavier, Saint, 152
Franco, Francisco, 137
French region: defined, 6; terminology for shrines and pilgrimages in, 13; pilgrimage cycle in, 60; shrine formation periods in, 97, 99, 105–6, 113; Marian shrines in, 158; shrine origin stories in, 219, 267, 287; shrine location in, 302; natural site features at shrines in, 328
French Revolution: and shrine formation, 103–4; concealment of cult objects during, 128, 232, 256, 263; destruction of cult objects during, 135, 207, 211, 214, 234
Fribourg, 246

Gabriel (the Angel), Saint, 139
Galicia, 64, 120, 145, 302
Gall, Saint, 275
Gap, 285
Garabandal. *See* San Sebastián de Garabandal
Gargano Peninsula, 87, 139, 276
Geiersberg, 147
Genazzano, 98, 160, 206, 255
Genoa, 98, 142, 201, 209
George, Saint, 115, 141, 142, 150
Gerard (Gerardus) Majella, Saint, 103, 132, 152, 174
Germanic regions, 102, 142, 163; terminology for shrines and pilgrimages in, 14, 31; drawing power of shrines in, 23; shrine distribution in, 30–33, 35; religious vs. secular celebrations in, 50–51; pilgrimage cycle in, 61, 62, 349–50 (n. 20); minor shrines in, 65; pilgrims' offerings at shrines in, 71–72, 78; shrine formation periods in, 86, 92, 93–94, 96, 97, 112–13; Christ-centered shrines in, 100, 124, 126, 155, 156, 158, 179, 188–89, 363 (n. 25); saints' shrines in, 143, 145, 149–50, 152, 154; Marian shrines in, 152, 155, 156; venerated images and relics in, 171, 179, 181, 184–86, 187, 188–89, 198, 207, 363 (n. 25); shrine origin stories in, 219, 226, 235, 239, 245, 249, 254, 256, 257, 258, 263, 266, 267, 272, 280, 281, 283, 284; shrine location in, 297, 301–2; natural site features at shrines in, 311, 312, 324, 325–26, 328, 329, 331
Gernsheim, 367 (n. 68)
Getafe, 103
Gheel, 92
Giles, Saint, 149–50
Glastonbury, 110
Globasnitz, 128
Gobnait, Saint, 145
God the Father, 116, 126, 190, 199
Goult, 211
Gräbern, 129
Granada, 102
Gréccio, 328
Gregory of Tours, 169
Gregory the Great (pope), 90, 169
Gregory II (pope), 93
Guadalupe, 96, 202, 204–5
Guimarães, 320
Guipúzcoa, 131
Gurk, 129, 278

Halfing, 365 (n. 51)
Halle, 202, 251, 256
Hardenberg, 184
Hart im Zillertal, 323
Hauenstein, 41
Hazelwood Castle, 355 (n. 22)
Heiligengrab, 189
Heiligenkreuz, 44–45, 351 (n. 25)
Heiligkreuz, 248
Heiligwasser, 284

Helena, Saint, 249
Hemma, Saint, 128–29, 278
Hemmaberg, 128
Henrik, Saint, 35
Henry II (duke of Brabant), 251
Henry II (Holy Roman Emperor), 147
Henry VIII (king of England), 99–100
Heroldsbach, 102, 286
Hervé, Saint, 128
Hildesheim, 124
History of Joseph, 135
Hodegetria, 194
Hohenpeißenberg Madonna, 191–92
Holbein, Hans, the Elder, 264
Holy Cross Abbey, 111
Holy Cross Church, 251
Holy day processions: and pilgrimages, 14–15, 17
Holy Family, 115, 135, 194–95, 330
Holy House, 107, 255
Holy Island, 109
Holy Shroud, 176, 190, 217
Holy Shroud chapel, 100, 217
Holy Spirit, 116, 126, 199, 356 (n. 3)
Holywell, 109, 221, 222
Holy wells: distribution of, 12, 35, 109, 128, 162; as only object of cultus at some shrines, 12, 90, 162; pilgrimage cycle at, 54; pilgrims' offerings at, 68, 69–70, 71; shrine formation at, 90, 222–23, 225; baptized by Saint Patrick, 291; and "wishing wells," 345 (n. 15). *See also* Shrines—natural site features at: water
Holy Year pilgrimages, 20, 95
Hötting, 235–36
Hubert, Saint, 144, 278
Huelva, 66
Hungary, 336

Iberian region, 102; defined, 6; *romerías* in, 6, 13, 19, 37; terminology for shrines and pilgrimages in, 13, 37; shrine distribution in, 33; pilgrims' offerings at shrines in, 71, 352 (n. 34); shrine formation periods in, 83, 92, 93, 95, 97, 99, 105, 106–7, 113; Marian shrines in, 92, 156; Christ-centered shrines in, 100, 124, 156, 158; saints' shrines in, 122, 137–39, 145; venerated images and relics in, 170–71, 181, 184–86, 187, 188, 189, 202, 213; shrine origin stories in, 219, 245–46, 266, 267, 272, 277–78, 279; shrine location in, 302; natural site features at shrines in, 310, 329, 330, 331, 333
Iconoclasts, 259. *See also* Byzantine Empire; French Revolution; Moslems; Protestants and Protestantism; Spanish Civil War
Ildephonsus, Saint, 171, 275, 353 (n. 7), 373 (n. 57)
Ignatius Loyola, Saint, 131–32
Images. *See* Christ—veneration of images and relics of; Mary, Saint—veneration of images and relics of; Saints—veneration of images and relics of
Immense, 231
Incoronata, 54, 202, 276–77, 352 (n. 34)
Industrial Revolution: effect of on pilgrimage activity, 112, 113, 273, 289
Innocent III (pope), 177
Innsbruck, 235–36
Inquisition, 282, 284
Interamna (now Terni), 142
Iona, 90, 109
Ireland: in Irish region, 6; natural site features at shrines in, 11, 12, 22, 90, 109, 110, 160, 162, 310, 311, 315, 321, 323, 324, 325, 330, 331, 333, 335, 379 (n. 15); shrine distribution in, 35; religious vs. secular celebra-

tions in, 49, 50; pilgrimage cycle in, 54, 61; pilgrims' offerings at shrines in, 68, 69, 71; shrine formation periods in, 87, 90, 91, 95, 100–101; Celtic Christianity in, 90, 91, 144–45; British efforts to suppress pilgrimage activity in, 111, 112, 119, 162; Marian shrines in, 119, 120–22; saints' shrines in, 122, 144–45, 154, 156, 157, 158, 315; Christ-centered shrines in, 126; venerated images and relics in, 162, 175, 188; shrine origin stories in, 219, 225, 226, 236, 248, 263, 267; shrine location in, 299, 301, 302

Irish region, 110–11, 113; defined, 6

Isabel (Holy Queen Isabel; queen of Aragon), 126

Isis, 129, 170, 197, 198, 208

Italian region: defined, 6; terminology for shrines and pilgrimages in, 13; shrine formation periods in, 97, 99, 105, 113; Marian shrines in, 99; Catholic missionaries from, 102, 105; shrine origin stories in, 257; natural site features at shrines in, 310

Italy, 22; in Italian region, 6; drawing power of shrines in, 24; shrine distribution in, 30, 33, 34; religious vs. secular celebrations in, 49, 50; penitential processions in, 58; pilgrimage cycle in, 60; Marian shrines in, 62, 90, 93, 96, 98–99, 119–20, 154, 156, 358 (n. 29); minor shrines in, 66, 67; pilgrims' offerings at shrines in, 71, 72, 75; shrine formation periods in, 83, 87–100 passim, 112, 113; Christ-centered shrines in, 126; saints' shrines in, 129–30, 132, 136, 139, 145, 150, 154; venerated images and relics in, 161, 164, 167, 182–83, 184–86, 187, 189, 194, 195, 199, 201, 202, 213, 353 (n. 9); shrine origin stories in, 219, 225, 226, 230–31, 236, 239, 245, 246, 248, 249, 255, 256, 257, 263–89 passim, 374 (n. 60); shrine location in, 302; natural site features at shrines in, 310, 323, 328, 329, 330–31, 333, 379 (n. 15)

Itri, 93

James the Greater, Saint (Santiago), 92, 93, 137–39, 187, 257, 275, 276
Januarius, Saint, 175
Jesi, 195
Jesuits, 100, 109, 132
Jesus. *See* Christ
Joachim, Saint, 134
Joan of Arc, Saint, 131
John XV (pope), 94, 149
John XXIII (pope), 103, 132
John Paul II (pope), 287, 309
John the Baptist, Saint, 134, 136–37, 232
Joseph, Saint, 115, 134, 135–36, 187, 255
Josselin, 214
Jude (Judas Thaddeus), Saint, 137
Julian, Saint, 323

Kaiserslautern, 233
Kaltenbrunn Chapel, 225
Karnabrunn, 231
Kärnten, 128
Kaufmann, Johann Anton, 236
Kaulbach, 237
Kemble, John, 355 (n. 22)
Kempten, 248
Kentenich, Father Joseph, 23
Kerizinen, 102
Kevelaer, 23, 100, 183
Kirchberg, 236
Kirchwald, 253

Klausen, 198
Klein-Körtzenburg, 329
Kloster Andechs, 72
Kloster Arnsburg, 336
Kloster Arnstein, 190, 367 (n. 68)
Kloster Schönstatt, 23–24, 286
Knock, 102, 111, 285, 297–98
Koblenz, 23, 296
Konrad II (Holy Roman Emperor), 251
Koylio, 35
Kreimbach-Kaulbach, 237
Kundl, 147

La Bruna, 168, 202
Lac-Sainte-Anne, 173
Lady Chapel, 355 (n. 22)
Lahn River, 190
Lanciano, 177
Landolin, Saint, 223
Langhein, 150
Languedoc, 6, 13
Lanhouarneau, 128
La Sainte Tombe, 174–75
La Salette, 113, 273, 285, 287, 320
Las Fruguas, 278, 331
Las Huelgas, 17–19
Latin America, 112, 257, 272; pilgrims from at Western European shrines, 23, 24; pilgrimage cycle in, 60, 348 (n. 17); pilgrims' offerings at shrines in, 78; Catholic missionaries and pilgrimage traditions in, 86, 101–2, 124, 354 (n. 13), 372–73 (n. 52); Christ-centered shrines in, 124, 191, 209, 354 (n. 13); saints' shrines in, 139; venerated relics and images in, 182, 191, 209; shrine origin stories in, 254, 261, 371 (n. 40); natural site features at shrines in, 333
Lautrec, Marshal, 243–44
Le Délivrade, 202
Le Dorat, 124

Le Folgoët, 202, 205
Le Laus, 284
Le Mont-Saint-Michel, 87, 139, 276
Leo III (Byzantine emperor), 93
Leonard (Leonhard), Saint, 145–47, 150
Leopold, Saint, 115
L'Épine, 99
Le Puy, 92, 202, 207, 208, 211
Léon, 124, 258–59
Leschtal, 199
Lich, 336
Liège, 247
Liesse, 214
Lieu de pèlerinage, 13
Limoges, 120, 122–24, 147
Limpias, 217
Linares de Río Frío, 201
Lipari Islands, 183
Lisbon, 151
Lisieux, 103, 132
"Little Rocks of the Virgin," 330
Liturgical year: and pilgrimage cycle, 58–60
Locherboden, 318
Lokerem, 234
London, 27
Longpont-sur-Orge, 170
Loreto, 20, 96, 107, 202, 204, 207, 255
Loreto Aprutino, 254–55, 256
Lorraine, 120, 262
Lough Derg, 20, 323
Lourdes, 39, 106, 132, 282; as international pilgrimage center, 1, 11, 20, 21, 23, 285, 297–98; secondary shrines of, 20, 60, 65, 225, 285, 333; as curative shrine, 21, 68, 323; pilgrimage cycle at, 55, 60; pilgrims' offerings at, 68; Marian apparitions and origin story of, 102, 104, 216, 217, 273, 277, 285, 287; formation period of, 113, 285; Marian image at, 199; Grotto at, 199, 301, 333

Lucca, 164, 209
Lucy, Saint, 141, 143, 187, 351 (n. 26)
Lugares de peregrinación, 13
Luke, Saint, 168
Lutheran church: and pilgrimage activity, 8, 35
Lutzel, 296
Luxembourg, 6, 33
Lyon, 92, 223, 300

Maastricht, 124
Madonna del Buon Consiglio, 255
Madonna della Clemenza, 167
Madonna del Lago, 22
Madonna della Grazie, 253
Madonna della Guárdia, 98, 209
Madonna della Misericordia, 201
Madonna della Orto, 161
Madonna della Quércia, 75, 162, 352 (n. 34)
Madonna dell'Arco, 244, 352 (n. 34)
Madonna del Terzito, 183
Madonna di Alpine, 234
Madonna di Novi Velia, 90
Madonna di San Luca, 168, 182–83
Madrid, 24, 30, 103, 154, 186, 190, 211
Mais, 142–43,
Malta, 195–96
Mama Rosa, 306–8, 309
Manriquez de Lara, María, 191
Mantua, 94, 95
Margaret, Saint, 149, 164
Marguerite-Marie, Saint, 190
Maria Birnbaum, 329
Maria Brunnlein, 322
Maria Dreieichen, 198
Maria Egg, 335
Maria Eich, 247
Maria Elend, 128–29
Maria Goretti, Saint, 103, 132, 154
Maria Herzelied, 41–42

Mariahilf, 107–8, 186, 296, 364 (n. 38)
Maria im Stein, 235
Maria Kirchental, 352 (n. 34)
Maria Lavant, 352 (n. 34)
Maria Licht, 248
Maria Luggau, 199
Maria Martental, 322
Mariaort, 254
Maria Plain, 352 (n. 34)
Mariastein, 280
Maria Taferl, 100
Maria Thann, 275
Mariazell, 22, 96, 206
Marienbaum, 202–3, 281
Mark, Saint, 129
Marseilles, 92, 300
Martele, 231
Martin of Tours, Saint, 144
Mary, Saint, 162, 237, 255; miracles associated with images and relics of, 42, 116, 169, 170–71, 183–84, 208, 211–12, 234, 235, 244–45, 246, 247, 249, 281, 282, 283, 329; feast days associated with, 56, 62, 93, 348 (n. 19); as Mother of God (*Theotokos*), 90, 277, 283; and Immaculate Conception, 104, 277; and female aspects of divinity, 117; and ancient mother goddesses, 126, 154, 170, 171, 196–98, 206, 208, 302, 358–59 (n. 29); and Saint Anne, 134–35, 187; and Christ, 135, 165, 187, 191, 192–99, 202, 211–12, 246, 254, 259, 274, 275, 277, 279, 280, 286, 323, 330; and Saint Joseph, 135, 194–95; and Saint James the Greater, 139, 275; and Saint Michael the Archangel, 140
—cult of: Protestant attitude toward, 8, 99, 119, 168, 349–50 (n. 20); Eastern origins of, 90, 93; Bernard of Clairvaux and, 97, 152, 206; landscape of

European pilgrimage changed by, 152, 358–59 (n. 29); stages in development of, 272–74
—shrines dedicated to, 115, 128, 157; in inventory used for this study, 9; size and drawing power of, 23, 156–58; pilgrimage cycle at, 62; distribution of, 62, 119–22, 152–56, 158, 356 (n. 3); formation periods of, 90, 92, 93, 95, 96, 102–3, 152–56, 158; transformation of saints' shrines into, 96, 153–55, 219–20, 226; apparitional shrines, 98–99, 102–3, 183–84, 195, 199, 201, 216, 217, 220, 238–39, 258–59, 266, 267, 275–87 passim, 306–8, 325, 372 (n. 48), 373 (n. 57); issue of church recognition of, 102, 285–87; as predominant kind of shrine in Europe, 116, 117–19, 122, 133, 153; primary and secondary subjects of devotion at, 116–17, 119; and Christ-centered shrines, 126, 154; significant site shrines, 219; devotional shrines, 219–20, 241; acquired object shrines, 220, 249, 253, 254, 257; found object shrines, 220, 257–58, 259, 261, 262, 263, 269–70, 277–78; votive shrines, 233, 234, 235, 236; spontaneous miracle shrines, 244–45, 246, 247, 248, 249, 281, 282, 283, 329; location of, 299–300; natural site features at, 315–16
—veneration of images and relics of, 27, 42, 116, 124, 165–66, 167, 168, 169–71, 182, 183–84, 186, 210–12, 213, 214, 217, 238, 249, 253, 254, 257–58, 261, 262, 299–300, 308, 335, 353 (n. 7), 365–66 (n. 51), 375 (n. 71); milk, 165, 175, 249, 300; and lack of mortal remains, 175; hair, 175, 249, 300; clothing, 175–76, 249, 300; and iconography, 187, 188–91, 192–99, 202, 209

Mary Magdalene, Saint, 139, 140–41
Marzellinus, Saint, 251
Massabielle Grotto, 301
Mass Rocks, 111, 333
Materdómini, 132, 133
Materdómini di Nocera, 277
Matthew, Saint, 96
Maurilius, Saint, 275
Maximinus, Saint, 140
Mayer, Rupert, 102
Medjugorje, 266, 289, 372 (n. 48)
Mérida, 92, 353 (n. 7)
Meritxell, 22
Mettenbach, 286
Michael the Archangel, Saint, 87, 139–40, 267, 276, 278, 374 (n. 60)
Midi-Pyrénées, 106
Milan, 103, 141
Milk Grotto, 175
Miracles: modern concept of, 12–13; shrine origins in thank offerings for, 98; proof of required for canonization, 132; Eucharistic, 177–79, 243, 249, 363–64 (n. 32); definitions of, 360 (n. 2). *See also* Christ: miracles associated with images and relics of; Mary, Saint: miracles associated with images and relics of; Saints: miracles associated with; Saints: miracles associated with images and relics of; Shrines: and miracles; Shrines—origin stories of: spontaneous miracle shrines
Mittelzell, 251
Mittendorf, 235
Moclin, 186, 189
Moll Valley, 231
Montallegro, 100, 201, 282–83, 297, 375 (n. 71)
Mont Bruilly, 235

Monte Bérico, 201, 282
Montecassino, 44–45, 90, 145, 253
Montenero, 96, 352 (n. 34)
Monte Oliveto Maggiore, 201
Monte Sacro, 90
Monte Sant'Angelo, 68, 87, 139, 276, 278, 301, 318, 334
Montfort, Saint-Louis Marie Grignion de, 238
Montpellier, 150, 151, 152
Montserrat, 93, 168, 202, 206, 207, 208, 217, 218, 258
Moslems, 170–71, 262–63, 276, 278
Motta di Livenza, 282
Munich, 51, 72, 103, 124, 177
Münster, 120, 124, 127, 233
Murcia, 124
Myans, 202
Myra, 254

Nantes Cathedral, 128
Naples, 30, 168, 175, 244
Narbonne, 169
Navarre, 335
Navas de Tolosa, battle of, 17
Nebor, Saint, 262
Netherlands: in North German region, 6; shrine distribution in, 30, 33, 34–35; religious vs. secular celebrations in, 49–50; shrine formation periods in, 83, 108, 113; Marian shrines in, 120; saints' shrines in, 132–33; venerated images and relics in, 209; shrine origin stories in, 226, 236, 257
Nettuno, 103, 132, 154, 160, 253
Neukirchen bei Heiligenblut, 72
Nevers, 132
Neviges, 184
Nicholas, Saint, 95, 144, 150, 254
Nicholas of Flue, Saint, 225
Nicolazic, Yvon, 135

Niederösterreich, 120
Nieva, 258
Nievenheim, 190
Northern Ireland, 6, 34. *See also* Irish region
North German region: defined, 6; shrine distribution in, 33; shrine formation periods in, 99, 108–9, 113; shrine origin stories in, 236, 239. *See also* Germanic regions
Norway, 33, 35, 120–22. *See also* Scandinavia
Nossa Senhora do Sameiro, 238
Notre-Dame, Basilica of (Évron, France), 175
Notre-Dame de Altbronn, 335
Notre-Dame de Clarté, 235
Notre-Dame de Dusenbach, 212–13
Notre-Dame de Font Sainte, 182
Notre-Dame de Grace, 168
Notre-Dame de Lumières, 211–12
Notre-Dame de Panetière, 233
Notre-Dame de Paris, 44, 294
Notre-Dame des Miracles, 169
Notre-Dame de Theirenbach, 352 (n. 34)
Notre-Dame de Vie, 191
Notre-Dame du Bischenberg, 198
Notre-Dame du Chêne, 247
Nuestra Señora de Atocha, 24
Nuestra Señora de Codes, 335
Nuestra Señora de Indejo, 331
Nuestra Señora de la Cabeza, 202, 204–5
Nuestra Señora de la Cueva Santa, 217–19
Nuria, 202, 297, 320
Nursia (Nórica), 145

Oberammergau Passion play, 15
Odilia, Saint, 144

Olaf, Saint, 35
Oliver Plunket, Saint, 160
Orans, 286
Orléans, 92, 169–70, 204
Oropa, 90, 202, 320
Orvieto, 179
Ostensions, 122–24
Ostrach Valley, 264
Oswald, Saint, 150
Ottobeuren, 281
Our Lady of Consolation of the Afflicted (Kevelaer), 183–84
Our Lady of Mercy, 201
Our Lady of Oudenberg, 75
Oviedo, 353 (n. 7)

Padre Pio, 103, 132, 133, 308
Padua, 96, 108, 151, 172
Pantaleon, Saint, 149–50
Paray-le-Monial, 103, 126, 284–85
Pardo, 189
Pardons, 6, 13, 51–52, 128
Paris, 30, 103, 170, 285, 294
Partenkirchen, 217, 233
Pascual Bailón, Saint, 174
Passau, 107–8, 225, 364 (n. 38)
Passion: relics of. *See* Christ—veneration of images and relics of
Patrick, Saint, 90, 144–45, 222, 275, 291
Paul, Saint, 130, 137, 266
Peiting, 335
Pelayo (king of Asturias), 334
Pellevoisin, 286
Peña de Francia, 99, 202, 281, 318
Penne, 254–55
Peregrinación/peregrinação, 13
Pereira da Silva, Martinho Antonio, 238
Perros-Guirec, 235
Peter, Saint, 137, 275
Petrus von Einhard, Saint, 251

Pfaffenhofen, 102, 286
Piacenza, 102, 152, 286, 306
Pietàs. *See* Mary, Saint: and Christ
Pietralba, 100, 352 (n. 34)
Pilgerfahrt, 14
Pinos, 282
Playa de Lanzada, 323
Plombariola, 145
Pompeii, 103, 270
Pontchâteau, 238
Pontifical Commission on the Pastoral Care of Migrants and Tourists, 4–5, 42–43
Pontmain, 285
Poor Clares, 201
Portugal, 142; in Iberian region, 6; *romerías* in, 6, 46, 49, 50; drawing power of shrines in, 24; shrine distribution in, 30, 33, 34, 35; venerated images and relics in, 45–46, 145, 162, 164, 186; religious vs. secular celebrations in, 49, 50; pilgrimage cycle in, 61; saints' shrines in, 62, 119, 120, 139, 145; minor shrines in, 64, 66, 67; pilgrims' offerings at shrines in, 67, 71, 351 (n. 26); shrine formation periods in, 83, 107, 113; Marian shrines in, 119–20; Christ-centered shrines in, 119, 126; shrine origin stories in, 236, 248; shrine location in, 302. *See also* Iberian region
Prague, 191
Prato, 175–76
Protestants and Protestantism, 44, 50, 234, 248; suppression of shrines and pilgrimages by, 8, 63, 84, 95, 99, 103, 108, 112, 113, 162, 225, 337, 349–50 (n. 20); attitude toward Mary and her cult, 8, 99, 119, 168, 283, 349–50 (n. 20); attitude toward veneration of relics and images, 8, 168, 212, 246,

262–63, 283; and distribution of Catholic shrines, 30, 34–35, 158, 336
Provence, 140
Puig, 210–11

Quintela da Lapa, 191

"Rag wells," 69–70, 109, 351 (n. 28)
Ramiro I (king of Léon), 276
Rangersdorf, 231
Ranschbach, 225
Rapallo, 100, 201, 282–83, 297
Raphael (the Angel), Saint, 139
Re, 244
Redemptorists, 132–33
Reformation, Catholic, 102, 135, 213, 256, 280; and shrine formation, 100, 107, 112, 124, 273, 281, 282–85; saints associated with, 131–32, 152; and Christ cultus, 156, 188, 189, 191, 354 (n. 13); and missionaries in Latin America, 354 (n. 13), 372–73 (n. 52)
Reformation, Protestant: and shrine formation, 86, 99; suppression of pilgrimage activity as result of, 92, 95, 108–9, 111–12, 113, 130, 162, 225, 256, 272, 282, 336
Regensburg, 124, 149, 150, 254
Reichenau Island, 251
Relics. *See* Christ—veneration of images and relics of; Mary, Saint—veneration of images and relics of; Saints—veneration of images and relics of
Religious tourism. *See* Shrines: and tourism
Rencurel, Benoîte, 376 (n. 74)
Reus River, 323
Rheinland-Pfalz, 255–56
Rhineland, 188
Ribeaupierre, Maximin II de, 212
Ribeauville, 212

Ribordone Canavese, 283
Ried, 147
Rieti, 30
Rita of Cáscia, Saint, 99, 132, 133, 150, 234
Rocamadour, 96, 202, 203
Roccaporena, 99
Roch, Saint, 55, 97, 150, 151–52,.253
Rocio, 13
Roman Catholic church: and recognition of pilgrimage sites, 1, 8; and liturgical year, 58, 93; and recognition of apparitions, 102, 285–87, 308–10, 372 (n. 50); "feminization" of, 288–89
Roman Catholics, 234, 256; and Rome, 20; and shrine distribution, 30, 33–35; and missionaries to Americas, 86, 101–2; in Protestant areas of Germany, 108–9, 237, 239–41; in Britain, 109–10, 113, 355 (n. 22)
Roman Empire: beginnings of shrine formation and pilgrimage activity in, 3, 37, 86–87, 141, 163–64
Rome, 45, 90, 145, 149, 151, 167, 217, 239, 266, 275, 278, 286; as international pilgrimage center, 1, 20, 21, 137, 257; shrines in and around, 30, 92, 141–42, 221; relics taken to other sites from, 251, 253, 254, 256
Romerías, 6, 13, 19, 37, 49–50, 67, 351 (n. 26)
Romeros/romeiros, 13
Ronchamp, 96
Rosental, 128–29
Rue-de-Bac, 285
Ruhr, 108, 184
Rülzheim, 92

Saarland, 262
Sacré Cœur de Montmartre, 103
Sacred Heart of Christ, 103, 124–26, 190, 211, 285

Sacred Savior shrine, 333
Sacred stones, 12, 35, 162, 223. *See also* Mass Rocks; Shrines—natural site features at: stones
Sacro Monte, 237–38
Saint Andrew's, 130
Saint Anthony chapel (Partenkirchen), 217, 233
Saint-Avold, 262
Saint-Bauzille-de-la-Sylve, 286
Saint-Benîot-sur-Loire (formerly Abbey of Saint-Pierre-de-Fleury), 145, 253–54
Saint Blaise, church of, 150
Saint Columban's, 90
"Saint Cuthbert's beads," 331
Sainte-Anne-d'Auray, 51, 100, 135, 172–73, 269, 293
Sainte-Anne-de-Beaupré, 173, 283, 376 (n. 73)
Sainte-Anne-de-la-Rochelle, 173
Sainte-Anne-de-Micmacs, 173
Saintes-Maries-de-la-Mer, 324
Saint-Florent-le-Vieil, 275
Saint Francis, Church of, 179
Saint Germain, Church of, 170
Saint-Hippolyte, 182
Saint-Hubert, 144, 278
Saint John's Basilica, 92
Saint-Léonard-de-Noblat, 147
Saint Mark's Cathedral, 129
St. Mawgan, 355 (n. 22)
Saint-Maximin-la-Sainte-Baume, 140–41, 301, 328, 334
Saint-Michel-de-Frigolet, 139
Saint Patrick's Purgatory, 20
Saint Paul's Outside the Walls, 92, 130
Saint Peter's (Bologna), 183
Saint Peter's Basilica, 92, 137, 216–17
Saints: canonization of, 94, 132, 149, 164; and pre-Christian deities, 126, 129, 147, 149, 222; miracles associated with, 132, 142, 147, 151; miracles associated with images and relics of, 160–61, 163–64, 167, 173–75, 249; visions of as part of shrine origin stories, 269, 272, 275, 278
—shrines dedicated to, 115, 128–52, 153–54, 157; in inventory used for this study, 9; pilgrimage cycle at, 62; distribution of, 62, 119, 122–24, 127–28, 158, 356 (n. 3); formation periods of, 92, 94, 97, 103, 110, 152–56, 158; transformation of into Marian shrines, 96, 153–55, 219–20, 226; and shrines to uncanonized folk saints, 103, 115, 128, 132, 133; primary and secondary subjects of devotion at, 116–17, 154; males vs. females as subjects of devotion at, 117–19, 126–28; apparitional shrines, 130, 135, 139, 150, 220, 267, 275–76, 278, 283, 284; found object shrines, 136, 221, 257, 261; size and drawing power of, 156–57; significant site shrines, 219, 221–25, 226, 267; acquired object shrines, 220, 221, 249, 252; spontaneous miracle shrines, 249; location of, 299–300; natural site features at, 315–16
—veneration of images and relics of, 122, 160–61, 171–72, 179, 252, 299–30; historical origins and development of, 3, 163–68; Protestant attitude toward, 8, 162; at particular shrines, 126, 129, 130, 135, 136, 140–41, 142, 145, 161, 172–75; and iconography, 187–88, 195, 201
Saints' day celebrations: and pilgrimages, 7, 14, 157
Saint Séverin church, 247
Salus Populi Romani, 168
Salzburg, 148, 149, 236
San Damiano, 102, 286, 287, 306

San Giovanni Rotondo, 103, 133, 308
Sankt Antonius church, 236
Sankt Gallen, 90, 92, 149
Sankt Georgenberg, 142
Sankt Kanzian, 293–94
Sankt Trudpert, 275
Sankt Wendel, 92, 148
Sankt Wolfgang am See, 149
Sannazzaro d'Burgondi, 235
San Sebastián de Garabandal, 1, 102, 201, 286, 287, 326
San Sebastiano, catacombs of, 142
San Severo, 202
Santa Maria de Ara Coeli, Basilica of, 190
Santa Maria degli Angeli, 150
Santa Maria del Monte, 352 (n. 34)
Santa Maria in Trastevere, 167
Santa Maria Maggiore (Saint Mary Major; Saint Mary of the Snows), Basilica of, 92, 168, 275
Sant 'Aniol, 283
Santiago. *See* James the Greater, Saint
Santiago de Compostela, 93, 95, 137–39, 147, 257, 281
Santuario/sanctuaire, 13
Santuario di Monte Vérgine, 202
San Vittorino, 133, 286, 370 (n. 24)
São Bento de Porto Aberto, 46
São Torcato, 276
Sardinia, 120, 124
Sarnen, 191
Saronno, 282
Savona, 283
Scandinavia: in North German region, 6; shrine distribution in, 30, 35; religious vs. secular celebrations in, 49–50; shrine formation periods in, 83, 103, 108; Marian shrines in, 120; shrine origin stories in, 226, 236
Scherenheuval, 96
Scholastica, Saint, 145, 254

Schönstatt Apostolic Movement, 23
Schwäbisch-Gmünd, 333
Schwaz, 142
Scotland, 6, 35, 69, 109–11, 114, 323. *See also* British region
Sebastian, Saint, 141–42, 150, 187, 253
Seligenstadt, 251
Serenus of Marseilles, 169
Serra San Bruno, 95
Servites, 201, 280
Seville, 15
Sexias, 46
Shrines: and tourism, 1–2, 8, 14–19, 25–27, 42–46, 292; inventory and analysis of used in this study, 4–10; macro-regional traditions of, 5–6; active vs. dormant, 6, 8, 83; drawing power of, 7, 21–25; church recognition of, 8; and miracles, 8, 12–13, 17, 45, 98, 116, 142, 160–61, 225, 237, 238, 239–41, 284, 307–10, 324–26 (*see also* Christ: miracles associated with images and relics of; Mary: miracles associated with images and relics of; Saints: miracles associated with images and relics of; Shrines—origin stories of: spontaneous miracle shrines); nature and purpose of, 11–13; terminology for, 13–14; varying importance of, 19–28; distribution of, 28–35; individual vs. communal pilgrimage to, 36–42; and pagan holy places, 37, 71, 75, 82–83, 90, 109, 111, 126, 128, 129, 139, 170, 182, 188, 208, 222, 223, 225, 259, 276, 291–92, 300, 301–3, 306, 317, 335; sacred and secular behavior at, 46–53; and pilgrimage cycle, 53–64, 349–50 (n. 20); minor, continued vitality of, 64–67; pilgrims' offerings at, 67–68, 98, 351 (n. 25); location of, 291–303, 336–38

—formation of, 80, 111–14; dating of, 82–83; cycle of, 84–86; in Early Christian period (first century–699), 86–92; in Early Medieval period (700–1099), 93–95; in High Medieval period (1100–1399), 95–97; in Renaissance period (1400–1529), 97–99; in Post-Reformation period (1530–1779), 99–102; in Modern period (1780–1980), 102–5; regional variations in, 105–11

—natural site features at, 12, 95, 109, 139, 160, 164, 226, 259, 291–94, 303–10; heights, 139, 140, 144, 223, 259, 291, 300–321 passim; caves and grottoes, 139, 140, 223, 259, 291, 303–20 passim, 333–35; trees and groves, 223, 259, 303–17 passim, 324–29; water, 259, 291, 303–24 passim (*see also* Holy wells); stones, 259, 303, 306, 311, 312, 314, 315, 316, 317, 320, 330–33 (*see also* Sacred stones); abandoned villages and churches, 335–36

—objects of veneration at, 160–63; images, 160–62, 166–72, 179–87, 242–43; relics, 160–66, 171–72, 173–79; origins and development of veneration of, 163–71; and iconography, 187–209; and image modification and replacement, 209–15. *See also* Christ—veneration of images and relics of; Mary, Saint—veneration of images and relics of; Saints—veneration of images and relics of

—origin stories of, 216–20, 368–69 (n. 3); votive shrines, 97–98, 217, 219, 226–37, 300; spontaneous miracle shrines, 100, 116, 208, 211–12, 217, 219, 229, 241–49, 300; found object shrines, 136, 217, 219, 220, 221, 257–66, 269–89 passim, 293, 300; apparitional shrines, 144, 219, 227, 238–39, 258, 259, 266–69 (*see also* Apparitions); significant site shrines, 216–26 passim, 267, 300; acquired object shrines, 217, 219, 220, 221, 249–57, 300; devotional shrines, 217, 221, 137–41, 300; vision-related stories, 269–89; and continued shrine establishment, 289–90

—subjects of devotion at: primary vs. secondary, 115, 116–17; male vs. female, 117–19, 126–28; in relation to shrine formation periods, 152–56; in relation to shrine size and drawing power, 156–57. *See also* Christ—shrines dedicated to; Mary, Saint—shrines dedicated to; Saints—shrines dedicated to

Sicily, 120, 143
Silvester, Saint (pope), 144
Sideon, 190
Sielenbach, 329
Siena, 179
Silo (king of Asturias), 353 (n. 7)
Sion, 25, 93, 318
Siracusa, 143, 244
Sixtus, Saint, 150
Slipper Chapel, 67, 355 (n. 23)
Sollheim, 236
Sonntagberg, 126
Sonsoles, 278
Sophie (princess of Hungary), 251
Sotto il Monte, 103
South German region: defined, 6; shrine distribution in, 33; shrine formation periods in, 94, 95, 97, 99, 100, 105, 107–8, 113; Christ-centered shrines in, 126; saints' shrines in, 145–47, 149–50; venerated images and relics in, 184–86. *See also* Germanic regions
Spain, 127; in Iberian region, 6; *romerías* in, 6; drawing power of shrines in, 24;

shrine distribution in, 30, 33, 34; religious vs. secular celebrations in, 49, 50; penitential processions in, 58; pilgrimage cycle in, 60–61; Marian shrines in, 62, 96, 98, 119–20, 358 (n. 29); minor shrines in, 66; pilgrims' offerings at shrines in, 71; shrine formation periods in, 83, 97, 98, 105, 107, 112, 113; Christ-centered shrines in, 124, 152; saints' shrines in, 129–30, 131–32, 137–39, 145; venerated images and relics in, 161, 162, 170–71, 181, 182, 184–86, 192, 194, 201, 202, 204–5, 209, 213, 214, 362–63 (n. 24); shrine origin stories in, 248, 256, 257, 258, 259, 264, 266, 270, 272, 273, 277–78, 280, 282, 285, 289; natural site features at shrines in, 328. *See also* Iberian region

Spanish Civil War: destruction of cult objects during, 210, 211, 214, 234, 353–54 (n. 9); concealment of cult objects during, 211, 263

Speyer, 41–42

Spoleto, 99

Stams, 318

Station Island, 20

Stations of the Cross, 188

Stephen, Saint(s), 150

Stiklestad, 35

Styria, 128

Subiaco, 45, 46, 90, 145

Sudetenland, 336

Superga, 233

Swabia, 198

Sweden, 35. *See also* Scandinavia

Switzerland: in French, Italian, and South German regions, 6; shrine distribution in, 30, 33, 35; religious vs. secular celebrations in, 49, 50; minor shrines in, 64; pilgrims' offerings at shrines in, 71, 352 (n. 34); shrine formation periods in, 83, 92, 104–5, 108, 113; Marian shrines in, 108, 119, 120; Christ-centered shrines in, 119; saints' shrines in, 119, 122, 135, 148; venerated images and relics in, 162, 202–3; shrine origin stories in, 231, 236, 245, 248, 255–56, 283; natural site features at shrines in, 312. *See also* French region; Germanic regions; Italian region; North German region; South German region

Tagliacozzo, 93
Talbot, Matt, 103, 110
Táranto Cathedral, 90
Telgte, 181, 202–3, 367 (n. 70)
Teresa of Ávila, Saint, 132
Théodulf of Orléans, 170
Theresa of Lisieux, Saint (The Little Flower), 103, 132
Thirty Years' War, 198, 283; and shrine formation, 86, 107, 233, 234
Tholey, 147
Thomas (the Apostle), Saint, 130
Thomas Becket, Saint, 94, 110, 150
Three Kings, shrine of, 96, 130, 294
Tipperary, 111
Tirol: Italian, 108; Austrian, 147
Todi, 201
Toledo, 92, 275, 353 (n. 7)
Tongre, 191, 275
Torcato, Saint, 275–76
Tortosa, 175–76
Tosters, 324
Toulouse, 92
Tours, 92
Trani, 280
Trápani, 253
Tre Fontane, 286
Trentino-Alto Adige, 124, 126, 198
Treviglio, 243–44
Trier, 96, 147, 198

Trieste, 103
Trinity, 116, 117, 126, 190, 199
Trois-Épis, 99
Trondheim, 35
Tropea, 93
Truce of God movement, 95
Trudpert, Saint, 275
Truns, 248
Tulle, 232
Turin, 100, 190, 217, 233, 251
Tuscany, 67

Ulrich (Ulric), Saint, 94, 149
United Kingdom. *See* British region
United States, 34, 283; pilgrims from at Western European shrines, 23, 24; saints' shrines in, 132, 135, 136, 139, 173
Uppsala, 35

Vadstena, 34
Valencia, 127, 210
Valentine, Saint, 141, 142–43
Valladolid, 285
Vallendar, 23
Vallombrosa, 95
Valverde, 279
Varallo, 237
Varese, 90, 275
Vatican Library and Archives, 4
Vatican II, 144, 287
Venice, 129, 142
Vézelay, 140–41
Via Flamínia, 142
Vicenza, 98, 201, 281–82
Victor, Saint, 249
Vienna, 172–73
Vierzehnheiligen, 150
Viggiano, 90
Villefranche de Conflent, 191
Vinay, 283–84
Vincent de Paul, Saint, 225

Vincent Ferrer, Saint, 217
Vion, 247
Virgen de Almudena, 186
Virgen de Atocha, 24
Virgen de la Cabeza, 13, 367 (n. 70)
Virgen del Sagrario, 353 (n. 7)
Virgin Mary. *See* Mary, Saint
Virgin of Częstochowa, 168
Visions. *See* Apparitions
Viterbo, 75, 162
Vitus, Saint, 149–50
Volto Santo. *See* Christ of Lucca
Vosges Mountains, 144

Waitsbach, 147
Walburga, Saint, 174
Walcourt, 246
Wales, 6, 35, 109–10, 114, 127. *See also* British region
Wallfahrt, 14
Wallfahrtkapelle, 14, 41–42
Wallfahrtskirche, 14
Wallfahrtsorte, 14, 31
Walldürn, 99, 177–79, 251
Walsingham, 35, 67, 68, 103, 110, 210, 278, 355 (n. 23), 369 (n. 9)
Weingarten, 177
Wemding, 322
Wendel, Saint, 108, 147–48
Weng, 225
Western Schism, 97
West Germany, 22, 127; in South German and North German regions, 6; drawing power of shrines in, 23–24, shrine distribution in, 30, 34; religious vs. secular celebrations in, 48, 49, 50–51; pilgrimage cycle in, 61; saints' shrines in, 62, 122, 145–47, 148, 149; district pilgrimages in, 64; shrine formation periods in, 83, 92, 108, 109, 113; Marian shrines in, 96, 108, 119, 120; Christ-centered

shrines in, 124; venerated images and relics in, 181, 183–84, 188, 194, 202–3, 213; shrine origin stories in, 226, 236, 244, 248, 249, 255–56, 257, 264, 286, 289; natural site features at shrines in, 310, 328, 329, 330; pilgrims' offerings at shrines in, 352 (n. 34). *See also* Germanic regions; North German region; South German region
Westminster Abbey, 27
Wetten, 202
Whitchurch Canonisorm, 109
Wies church, 188–89
Wilhelm von Freisach, Saint, 128, 129, 278
Winefride, Saint, 109, 221
Wittem, 103, 133
Wolfgang, Saint, 149, 150
Wolfstein, 237

Xanten, 249–51

Zafferena Etnea, 235
Zaragoza, 92, 275
Zell, 149
Zermatt, 235
Zita, Saint, 164
Ziteil, 283
Zopito, Saint, 254–55, 256
Zuccone, Giovanni, 244
Zugspitze, 319